# THE MARY LINCOLN ENIGMA

# THE MARY LINCOLN ENIGMA

## HISTORIANS ON AMERICA'S MOST CONTROVERSIAL FIRST LADY

EDITED BY
FRANK J. WILLIAMS AND MICHAEL BURKHIMER

WITH AN EPILOGUE BY
CATHERINE CLINTON

SOUTHERN ILLINOIS UNIVERSITY PRESS
CARBONDALE AND EDWARDSVILLE

Library of Congress Cataloging-in-Publication Data
The Mary Lincoln enigma : historians on America's most controversial
First Lady / edited by Frank J. Williams and Michael Burkhimer.
    p. cm.
Includes bibliographical references and index.
    ISBN-13: 978-0-8093-3124-6 (cloth : alk. paper)
    ISBN-10: 0-8093-3124-1 (cloth : alk. paper)
    ISBN-13: 978-0-8093-3125-3 (ebook)
    ISBN-10: 0-8093-3125-X (ebook)
 1. Lincoln, Mary Todd, 1818–1882. 2. Lincoln, Abraham, 1809–1865—
    Family. 3. Presidents' spouses—United States—Biography.
    I. Williams, Frank J. II. Burkhimer, Michael, 1973–
E457.25.L55M37 2012
973.7092—dc23
[B]                                                    2011037896

Frontispiece: Francis B. Carpenter, [Mary Lincoln]. Oil
on canvas, Washington, c. 1864. Courtesy Lilly Library,
Indiana University, Bloomington, Indiana

Printed on recycled paper. ♻

The paper used in this publication meets the minimum
requirements of American National Standard for
Information Sciences—Permanence of Paper for
Printed Library Materials, ANSI Z39.48-1992. ∞

*For a pioneer scholar of Mary Lincoln,*
*"Little Sister" Emilie Todd Helm (1836–1930)*

# Contents

# CONTENTS

# Illustrations

# Acknowledgments

For us, the editors, as well as for the contributors, this book presented many challenges in our attempt to find the real Mary Lincoln. She has been persistently misunderstood for over 150 years, and the contributors—Stephen Berry, Dr. James S. Brust, Catherine Clinton, Brian R. Dirck, Jason Emerson, Richard W. Etulain, Harold Holzer, Donna D. McCreary, Richard Lawrence Miller, Wayne C. Temple, Douglas L. Wilson, and Kenneth J. Winkle—make valiant and successful efforts to define Mary. For that they deserve our praise and gratitude. We could not have completed this work without the unending support of our editor, Sylvia Frank Rodrigue, whose advice was cogent and always relevant. Nicole Dulude Benjamin, Esq., and Professor William D. Pederson weighed in with great insight and editorial support. A special thanks to Jason Emerson, who prepared the index—a large and tedious feat. Finally, our wives, Virginia Williams and Beth Burkhimer, proved to be the best "First Ladies" with their love, patience, and support.

# THE MARY LINCOLN ENIGMA

## INTRODUCTION

*Frank J. Williams*

Few historical figures have created such a wide disparity in interpretation as Mary Lincoln. In the most extreme viewpoints, she has been portrayed as an almost demonic figure: a violent and corrupt shrew that made Abraham Lincoln's life a living hell. At the same time, others have portrayed her as a loving and affectionate wife and mother and a brilliant political partner for her husband. Some say her posthumous reputation has suffered due to the sexism and bias of male historians. Others say her own behavior is the cause of her poor historical reputation, adding that blaming historians is, at best, misguided. With all the recent work and increased attention on Abraham Lincoln, the passage of time, and the insights that advance in the study of women's history and psychohistory, we can now move beyond simplistic interpretations of one of the most famous First Ladies. "Who was the real Mary Lincoln?" is still very much an open question, which today's historians should at least attempt to resolve. Mary Lincoln deserves a more nuanced picture than the caricatures given by both apologists and critics heretofore.

This volume explores this enigma by gathering a number of scholars who approach Mary Lincoln from different perspectives. Each focuses on one controversial aspect of her life, including her relationship with her siblings and parents; her often tempestuous courtship and marriage with Abraham Lincoln; her political opinions and her influence on her husband's political career; her relationship with her son, Robert Lincoln; her relationship with slaves and slavery; and her insanity trial, among other topics. These essays provide readers new ways to examine her life and memory and will help solve the mysteries that continue to surround her. For better or worse, Mary Lincoln was a very influential figure during the Civil War. An undertaking that seeks to understand her as a real person acting in an actual time period provides an additional key in understanding mid-nineteenth-century America and its greatest leader, her husband, Abraham Lincoln.

With the rare exception of persons like Eleanor Roosevelt and Jacqueline Kennedy, First Ladies have for the most part remained invisible to the public and to historians, relegated to the private inner sphere of domesticity and the family circle. Mary Lincoln, a bright, well-educated, and ambitious young woman, was born and reared in the first half of the nineteenth century, when women were expected to be pious, pure, submissive, and confined to the home. Beginning in early childhood, Mary failed to conform completely to the roles expected of her. She loved parties and elaborate clothing, and she thoroughly enjoyed exercising her wit, especially in the forbidden realm of politics, and when she married Abraham Lincoln, she determined to be an active part of his political career. As a result, harsh criticism followed her throughout her life, persisting even into contemporary times. Tragedy followed her as well, leaving her vulnerable to the seduction of the spiritualist movement and to the maneuverings of her eldest son, who had her committed to an insane asylum. History's portrait of Mary Lincoln is rarely flattering, yet behind it lies the intelligent and resourceful woman, often foolish, sometimes courageous, unquestionably devoted, who recognized the potential in an uncultured backwoods lawyer. Her refusal to live her life on any but her own terms seems very modern; for that alone, her life deserves our attention.

## Lonely Daughter

Mary Ann Todd was born in 1818, into the aristocratic ranks of the Todds and Parkers, two of the leading families of Lexington, Kentucky. At the age of six, she suffered her first loss when her mother died of a fever contracted during childbirth. With the arrival of Betsey Todd, an unsympathetic stepmother, and eventually her stepsiblings, Mary lost the attention she needed from her father. She responded to these losses with mischievous behavior at home and by spending an unusual number of years in school, first at the Shelby Female Academy, and later at Madam Mentelle's Boarding School. It was from this haven, less than two miles from her home, that Mary first entered the social world of Lexington and began to learn the manners of a Southern lady. However, her extra education, sharp mind, and even sharper tongue, along with her interest in politics, set her apart from the other young women of Lexington's upper class. Descriptions portray most Lexington girls of Mary's age as interested primarily in genteel sociability and high fashion and as using "more eye shadow and rouge than any group outside Paris."[1] Part of Mary's interest in politics stemmed from her attempts to attract the attention of her father, a leading Whig of the day. But her father became too absorbed with squabbles between his new wife and the children of his first marriage. Those of his contemporaries who read Mary's letters on political affairs considered her political acumen to be extraordinary.

In "There's Something about Mary: Mary Lincoln and Her Siblings," Stephen Berry sees Mary in light of the neglect that characterized her childhood and adult relationships with her brothers and sisters. According to a cousin, the Todds "were a large family of boys and girls who jested much and seized on the slightest pretext to tease each other unmercifully."[2] In the Todd family, no quarter was given or sought. No wonder, then, that Mary's tongue cut like a "Damascus blade." Volatility and lashing wits were part of a common bond. In comparing Mary to her siblings, one gains a better vantage not only on her unique attributes and faults, but also on those traits that were common to her family, her region, and her times. Mary's siblings benefitted from her and suffered by her and with her; they were there at the beginning and there at the end in ways that no one—not even her husband—could be.

Her exposure to the Lexington slave auctions and her Southern family's antislavery activities only increased her avid interest in the political issues of her day. While historians have closely examined Abraham Lincoln's views on slavery and race, comparatively few have looked at Mary's perspective—and her possible influence on her husband—concerning these issues. In "Mary Lincoln, Race and Slavery," Brian Dirck discusses Mary's encounters with slavery as a young woman in Kentucky, in particular her relationship with "Mammy Sally," an African American slave in the Todd household who provided Mary with crucial emotional support and influenced Mary's lifelong negative views about slavery. She was remarkably comfortable around African Americans, both as a child and an adult, and she was an early advocate of emancipation during the Civil War.

When Mary finished her education at Madam Mentelle's, she left Lexington to live with her older sister, Elizabeth, who had recently married Ninian Edwards and settled in Springfield, Illinois. From this home, she entered into the social life of Springfield, all the while maintaining her keen interest in politics. It was also from here that she courted and later married the rustic young Illinois lawyer, Abraham Lincoln. Despite their rocky courtship, which was interrupted by a painful breakup at the end of 1840, and despite as well as the disapproval of the Edwardses, who felt Lincoln was not a suitable match for her, she married the only man who ever filled her lonely heart, Abraham Lincoln.

## Insecure Mother

After they married, what was the life they lived at home like? Richard Lawrence Miller has used correspondence files, contemporary newspaper articles, retrospective interviews and recollections in memoirs in "Life at Eighth and Jackson" to show that the Springfield years for Abraham and Mary were warm and affectionate. He recalls playful interactions among husband, wife, and children as well as with neighbors demonstrating an intimate parlor life with relatives and friends. Reports of an unhappy and tumultuous marriage during the Springfield years are questioned.

Marriage and motherhood were, for Mary Lincoln, quite different experiences from those of her mother, grandmother, stepmother, and sisters. Lincoln's long absences as a circuit-riding lawyer during the early years of their marriage often left Mary at home alone with two small children. Her desire to pinch pennies led her to manage her own household and to nurse and rear her children without the accustomed help of domestic servants. Much of Mary's own upbringing had been in the hands of family slaves, and all of her female relatives still relied on this form of labor. Although she did at times hire help, her exacting standards and parsimonious nature meant that none of these women ever stayed for long.

Along with her first two sons, Robert (b. 1843) and Edward (b. 1846), she accompanied Lincoln to Washington during his one term in the House of Representatives. This decision to take a wife and children to the capital was unconventional, and the noisy toddler and screaming baby were not popular at the Lincolns' boarding house. But Mary refused to be separated from either her husband, whom she earnestly believed needed her for advice, or her children, whom she loved in a manner bordering on the obsessive.

Lincoln returned to Springfield in March 1849 at the end of his term, and Mary's cycle of loss began again. Her father, with whom she had never completely reconciled, died in 1849, and then in 1850, her maternal grandmother, Eliza Parker, the only woman to have singled her out for affection and attention during her childhood, died, leaving Mary without the mature and warm counsel she desired. Later that year, the Lincolns lost their second son, Eddie, to tuberculosis. Within one month of his death, the Lincolns conceived their third son, William, born at the end of 1850. Thomas (Tad) followed in 1853, and the Lincoln family settled down to a life of domesticity on Mary's part and fluctuating political fortunes on her husband's.

Contemporary accounts of the children's wildness and lack of discipline point to a motherly fondness and desire for emotional closeness perhaps missing from her own childhood. Mary had learned early that beloved family members could desert her, and so she clung to her husband and sons. In the end she would lose them all: Eddie, Willie, and Tad to disease; her husband to assassination; and Robert, allegedly, to greed.

In "'An Unladylike Profession': Mary Lincoln's Preparation for Greatness," Kenneth J. Winkle discusses Mary Lincoln as a woman of extremes. Her reputation ran the gamut from the love of Abraham Lincoln's life, his greatest supporter and confidante, and an elegant hostess and gracious matriarch, to a shrewish and headstrong wife and mother, a profligate spendthrift of both private and public funds, and a secret sympathizer with slavery and even an abettor of the Confederate cause. Historical depictions of Mary Lincoln tend toward either extreme, as well, and both biographers and the general public hold more disparate opinions of her influence on her husband than on possibly any other subject within the scope of Lincoln scholarship. Biographical depictions of Mary Lincoln frequently reflect current conceptions of gender roles and family life. This essay reconsiders Mary Lincoln during the quarter century she spent as woman, wife, and mother in Springfield, Illinois, within the context of both Victorian society and culture in general and, more specifically, in comparison with the other women who lived in this western community in the three decades before the Civil War. The result is a more objective portrait of Mary Lincoln's life before her husband's presidency.

In "William H. Herndon and Mary Todd Lincoln," Douglas L. Wilson examines the basis for two related and widely held beliefs: (a) that William H. Herndon, Lincoln's law partner and biographer, "hated" his partner's wife, Mary Lincoln, and (b) that because of his personal antagonism, Herndon offered a colored or falsified the picture of her in his biographical writings. The first belief, especially when represented as a lifelong antagonism going back to their first meeting, is shown to have a very questionable basis and to lack corroboration in contemporary evidence. The second belief is the more consequential because of the position Herndon occupies, not only as the joint author of what has been called the most influential biography of Abraham Lincoln, but as the compiler of by far the most extensive archive of personal information about Lincoln on record. Thus, Wilson has a different take than Winkle on how biased this evidence collected about Mary was. It also puts him at odds with Miller on the happiness of Lincoln's home life. According to Wilson, the evidence indicates the outbreak and development of an open and genuine conflict between Herndon and Mary Lincoln the year after Lincoln's assassination, with justifiable reasons for hostility on both sides. Both of these pervasive beliefs now seem questionable to Wilson, such that the whole issue of the relationship between William H. Herndon and Mary Lincoln and its consequences are reconsidered here.

## Unconventional First Lady

Mary Lincoln's active participation in her husband's career was both unusual and controversial. Throughout her life, she refused to confine herself to what was then assumed to be the proper sphere of women, the home. Nowhere is this more evident than in her conduct during the years leading up to and including Lincoln's presidency. The political entertaining and letter-writing campaigns of their years in Springfield merely whetted Mary's political appetite. Once in the White House, this president's wife refused to play the submissive wife. Instead, her many critics confirm that Mary fulfilled her desire to "loom large" in the political affairs of the nation's Executive Mansion.

Finding the White House a threadbare wreck upon her arrival in Washington, Mary quickly outspent the four-year $20,000 budget allotted for repairs in a whirlwind of redecoration and refurbishment, both inside and out. After insulting the local merchants by making her purchases in New York, Boston, and Philadelphia, she then embarked on a course of duplicity to hide the enormous bills from her husband and Congress. With the help of several men, including the commissioner of public buildings and her gardener, Mary quickly learned how to pad bills and shift accounts to accomplish her goals. She generated even more criticism with her love of high fashion and dress styles copied from European royalty.

Although her extravagant taste might require as much as twenty-five yards of silk for one gown, she believed this was only fitting for the wife of a US president. Moreover, her appetite for consumer goods and her reputation for extravagant spending, both of which gained momentum during the White House years, would continue to haunt her to the end of her life.

In addition to consumer goods, Mary also spent money on travel. Unlike many of her generation, Mary Lincoln was fond of sojourns. Wayne C. Temple's "I Am So Fond of *Sightseeing*: Mary Lincoln's Travels up to 1865" explores Mary's break with tradition and explores what her interest in travelling says about her vision of her role as First Lady. We see here that Mary was ahead of her time in many ways and foreshadowed later First Ladies who did and do travel the world. Mary's life was congruent with the widespread use of the steamboat, and Temple takes the reader on a journey with Mary around the country. The contrast of other essays' stressing Mary Lincoln as a homebody against Temple's view of her as a lover of travel shows once again how enigmatic Mary is.

Mary also loved to entertain, particularly when she was, as so often happened, one of the only women present in a social gathering. However, her lavish White House parties were at odds with the mood of the country, which was consumed by the Civil War. Her Southern accent and mannerisms and her Confederate family members led to accusations of Confederate sympathies. Criticized as unrefined because of her upbringing in the West, she often chose colors and styles not considered appropriate for her age and figure, and she continually refused to retire into the background as had so many other presidential wives. Donna McCreary examines Mary's wardrobe and discusses whether her dress was innovative or disastrous in "Fashion Plate or Fashion Trendsetter."

Perhaps Mary's greatest alleged transgression against the standards of the time was her determination to remain an active political force in her husband's life. She was more outspoken and much more knowledgeable about politics than a delicately nurtured female should have been. Mary was also widely criticized for her traffic in political favors. Like much else that she did, Mary did not confine her exchange of favors on behalf of the men in her family, but she dared to mine the political waters to repay her own debts and gain other advantages for herself. Since the 1990s, it has become axiomatic in Lincoln literature to assert one of the most important aspects of the Lincolns' relationship—the political partnership between the spouses. This has appeared time and time again in both popular and scholarly works. But what exactly does the term "political partnership" mean? Did the Lincolns share an ambition for his advancement? Did Lincoln's marriage further his political career? Did the Lincolns agree on politics? Most importantly, did Lincoln follow Mary's political advice? "The Reports of the Lincolns' Political Partnership Have Been Greatly Exaggerated," by Michael Burkhimer, attempts to clarify this important political aspect of the Mary Lincoln enigma. He reaches differing conclusions about Mary's importance in Lincoln's political success than Winkle's essay, which suggests the debates about this subject are not going to die anytime soon.

## Eccentric Widow

The greatest loss of Mary Lincoln's life occurred on April 14, 1865, when an assassin's bullet fatally wounded her husband, seated at her side at Ford's Theatre. Although she continually visited the room where he lay dying, kissing him and begging him to awaken, she was not present at the moment of his death. Prostrated with grief, which she had never known how to handle, she took to her bed for more than a month, refusing to vacate the White House for Lincoln's successor. When she finally did arise, she donned the heavy Victorian black mourning that she would wear for the rest of her life.

The shock of the assassination perhaps ultimately led to one of the most controversial aspects of Mary's life, her insanity trial and confinement to a sanatorium. In "A Psychiatrist Looks at Mary Lincoln," Dr. James S. Brust focuses on the psychiatric and medical aspects of Mrs. Lincoln. Dr. Brust reviews the existing literature on Mrs. Lincoln written by physicians and presents a psychiatric diagnosis for her. Brust provides a robust defense of psychiatry and its uses in history. He rightfully admits that without Mary present to examine, all conclusions are tentative, but he does come to the conclusion that Mary probably did indeed suffer from a mental illness.

The years following Lincoln's death were difficult for Mary and not just because of her confinement. The executor of the estate procrastinated, and she found herself forced to exist on a very small allowance. Her attempts to raise more funds were criticized and belittled; no one seemed interested in helping create or donate to a fund for the widow of America's hero. In an act of true desperation and self-sacrifice, she discreetly tried to sell her wardrobe, one of her only remaining assets, but for this she reaped only scorn, ridicule, and a bill for the services of the would-be sellers. During this time, she continued to turn to the increasingly popular practice of spiritualism to help assuage her grief. For many years, she dabbled with séances and mediums, even training herself to fall into a kind of trance in which her dear departed sons and husband would come to her. Although these beliefs and practices were consoling for Mary, they were a sore point for her son, Robert, and with others who viewed them as ungodly.

Upon receiving her portion of Lincoln's estate, she took her son Tad to Germany for two years, an action unprecedented and unapproved for a woman, widowed or not. Her return to America only worsened her lot. In 1871, Tad died, her estrangement from Robert increased, and she was unable to find a suitable home. In addition, her deteriorating physical state led her to use certain drugs that may have accentuated her peculiarities, such as her excessive mourning and her use of shopping as a therapy for loneliness and grief.

As mentioned above, the ultimate indignity visited upon her occurred when Robert decided that his mother's irritating behavior must have been caused by insanity. With the help of a few obliging male doctors and lawyers, he took his mother to court and had her committed to a genteel asylum, Bellevue Place. He also gained control of her assets, which, despite her continual sense of poverty, were quite extensive for a woman. Within three months, and with the help of one of America's first female lawyers, Myra Bradwell, Mary left Bellevue to live with her sister Elizabeth in Springfield. This experience, however, caused irreparable damage to her relationship with Robert.

Jason Emerson examines the relationship between Mary Lincoln and her oldest son, Robert, from his birth in 1843 until her death in 1882 in "'I Miss Bob, So Much': Mary Lincoln's Relationship with Her Oldest Son." This relationship was one of the most important in all of Mary's life and the author studies the misunderstandings, misrepresentations, and documentation employed by previous historians and biographers. Emerson stresses the often very positive relationship that the two had over conventional views that focus primarily on the negative way the insanity trial affected their relationship.

Since Mary's death, her life has become a subject that novelists have looked to for the basis of a good story. Richard W. Etulain, in "Mary Lincoln among the Novelists: Fictional Interpretations of the First Lady," examines how fiction writers have treated Mary Lincoln in literature. The author also seeks to see if there have been any discernible interpretive trends from the early novels about Mrs. Lincoln—Honoré Willsie Morrow's *Mary Todd Lincoln* (1928) and Bernie Babcock, *Lincoln's Mary and the Babies* (1929)—and the more recent works: Barbara Hambly, *The Emancipator's Wife* (2005), Janis Cooke Newman, *Mary* (2006), and Ann Rinaldi, *An Unlikely Friendship: A Novel of Mary Todd Lincoln and Elizabeth Keckley* (2008). The portraits of Mary in these novels are also compared to those that deal with both Abraham and Mary: Irving Stone, *Love Is Eternal* (1954); William Safire, *Freedom* (1995); and Gore Vidal, *Lincoln* (2000). Continuing with how Mary has been viewed, in "'I Look Too Stern': Mary Lincoln and Her Image in the Graphic Arts," Harold Holzer examines the visual accompaniment to the Mary Lincoln literature: the iconography of Mary Lincoln and how her image has been reflected in popular culture and memory. Many stories have been written about Lincoln's portraiture, but few about his wife. In fact, Mary was a frequent subject for artists of her time, but this chapter shows less than her alleged vanity would have suggested.

Catherine Clinton's epilogue, "The Compelling Mrs. Lincoln," reflects on the larger questions, incorporating some of the materials from the other authors. It is a meditation on what draws scholars to this topic and causes such wildly fluctuating interpretations of Mary Lincoln. Clinton, a Mary Lincoln biographer herself, is well aware of these differing interpretations and has had to come down on one side or the other on many of these issues. She attempts to evaluate the sometimes dramatic differences among the essays in this volume; thus explaining, with the other contributors, the Mary Lincoln enigma.

## Notes

1. Jean H. Baker, *Mary Todd Lincoln: A Biography* (New York: W. W. Norton, 1987), 61.

2. Elizabeth L. Norris to Emily Todd Helm, September 28, 1895, William H. Townsend Papers, Abraham Lincoln Presidential Library.

## Sources and Suggested Reading

Baker, Jean H. *Mary Todd Lincoln: A Biography* (New York: W. W. Norton, 1987).

Berry, Stephen. *House of Abraham: Lincoln and the Todds, a Family Divided by War* (Boston: Houghton-Mifflin, 2007).

Clinton, Catherine. *Mrs. Lincoln: A Life* (New York: Harper Collins, 2009).

Emerson, Jason. *The Madness of Mary Lincoln* (Carbondale: Southern Illinois University Press, 2007).

Epstein, Daniel Mark. *The Lincolns: Portrait of a Marriage* (New York: Random House, 2008).

Evans, W. A. *Mrs. Abraham Lincoln* (New York: Alfred A. Knopf, 1932).

Fleischner, Jennifer. *Mrs. Lincoln and Mrs. Keckly: The Remarkable Story of a Friendship between a First Lady and a Former Slave* (New York: Broadway, 2003).

Helm, Katherine. *The True Story of Mary, Wife of Lincoln* (New York: Harper, 1928).

Keckley, Elizabeth. *Behind the Scenes; or, Thirty Years a Slave, and Four Years in the White House* (New York: Oxford University Press, 1989).

Lorant, Stefan. *Lincoln: A Picture Story of His Life* (New York: W. W. Norton, 1969).

Neely, Mark E., Jr., and R. Gerald McMurtry. *The Insanity File: The Case of Mary Todd Lincoln* (Carbondale: Southern Illinois University Press, 1986).

Ostendorf, Lloyd, and Walter Olesky, eds. *Lincoln's Unknown Private Life: An Oral History by His Black Housekeeper Mariah Vance, 1850–1860* (Mamaroneck, NY: Hastings House, 1995).

Randall, Ruth Painter. *Mary Lincoln: Biography of a Marriage* (New York: Little Brown, 1953).

Sandburg, Carl, and Paul M. Angle. *Mary Lincoln: Wife and Widow* (New York: Harcourt Brace, 1932).

Shreiner, Samuel A., Jr., *The Trials of Mrs. Lincoln: The Harrowing, Never-Before-Told Story of Mary Todd Lincoln's Last and Finest Years* (New York: Donald I. Fine, 1987).

Turner, Justin G., and Linda Levitt Turner. *Mary Todd Lincoln: Her Life and Letters* (New York: Alfred A. Knopf, 1972).

## There's Something about Mary
### Mary Lincoln and Her Siblings

*Stephen Berry*

L arge families have different dynamics than small ones. The webs of affection and intrigue are more complicated. The parents are more splintered and exhausted. Full of crying babies and slamming doors, stomping feet and petty disputes, their home is a bedlam of colliding minidramas. There is always an infant to be changed, rocked to sleep, or buried; there is always a child to be scolded, congratulated, or married. Everyone is always getting ready—for school, for church, for bed—and rarely at rest. Peace is fleeting; privacy is nonexistent; emotional turbulence is constant. The house is not a home but a hive.

This was certainly true for the Todds. Mary compared it to living in a boarding house. She and her siblings, she implied, were but guests in a common building, always on their way out, preoccupied by their own lives, own friends, own destinies. But she made this uncharitable assessment later in life, while bitter and looking back. In truth, the Todds were like any big family. They loved and hated each other at the same time. They hugged or they throttled each other, depending on the emotional needs of the moment. They were, remembered one observer, "a large family of boys and girls who jested much and seized on the slightest pretext to tease each other unmercifully." In the Todd family, there was no quarter given or sought. No one cried "uncle." Everyone gave as good as they got, and if they didn't, they licked their wounds and plotted their revenge. Sharp tongues and quick tempers were not resented; they were required. Volatility and lashing wits were part of a common bond. Thus, whatever they might later say, the Todds were, always and inevitably, a family. They shared a common parent, common experiences, common memories. They knew the same people, went to the same schools, told the same stories. And, most important, they formed genuine attachments, as children always do with the playmates of their youth. However they ended their lives, the Todds did not begin them as a bitter or a divided family. They were simply a big one, teeming and tempestuous.[1]

Robert S. and Eliza Parker Todd had six children who survived infancy: Elizabeth (1813), Frances (1815), Levi (1817), Mary (1818), Ann (1824), and George (1825). After George was born, Eliza developed what was probably childbed fever. Robert rounded up all available doctors, including the leading authorities from the nearby medical school at Transylvania University. The physicians consulted and conferred. Most likely, Eliza was cupped, bled, and liberally dosed with emetics and laudanum. If so, she spent her last hours deliriously vomiting and, at the age of thirty-one, joined the millions of women who had left the world the same way.

Her children had been spared such scenes. They were sent across the street to their grandmother's at the first sign of trouble. There they sat on her porch and stared at their mother's drawn curtains. At ages eleven and nine, Elizabeth and Frances had some sense of what was going on. At seven and six, Levi and Mary had only that odd combination of unspecified dread and hyperspecific images: doctors pulling up in hurried gigs; slaves raising little dust devils as they ran to and from the drugstore; pained expressions on the faces of adults who, until then, had seemed to know everything. On July 6, 1825, the first iteration of Todd children returned to their home, put on their best clothes, and sat as still as possible while the reverend prayed for their mother's soul. Then they followed her body to the churchyard and began their motherless lives.[2]

Robert's wifeless life did not last long. Within weeks, he began secretly courting Elizabeth "Betsey" Humphreys. The Humphreys were a socially prominent Frankfort family. Two of Betsey's uncles were professors at Transylvania, and two were US senators—one from Kentucky and the other from Louisiana. As Robert figured it, an alliance with the Humphreys would be, if anything, more advantageous than his alliance with the Parkers had been. But the timing of his suit was scandalous. Custom required that when a relatively young man lost a wife in childbirth, he should give his community time enough to pity his situation and eulogize the self-sacrificing mother who had gone so gracefully to God's Kingdom. By pursuing Betsey so early, Robert had breached a public trust.[3]

He had breached a private trust, too. His children needed him. They needed to know that he had loved their mother and loved them still. But he had laid his grief aside. He was already pursuing a second family. He had not even told them of his new romance. They learned of it second-hand—from a friend of first-born Elizabeth's who lived in Frankfort. They were left to whisper among themselves as he got on with his life. Their mother was dead; their father was cold comfort and keeping secrets.

Betsey gave birth nine times in the next fifteen years. Her pregnancies took their toll on her body and her mood. Each time her belly grew bigger, she grew more irritable and her husband more distant—but always he came back long enough to impregnate her again. Their first baby was a boy. Optimistically, Robert again named the child after himself. He was commemorating his new wife, his new family, his new start. Again the baby died, this time after just a few days. Robert had tried twice to pass on his name, and he would never try again—a small sign, perhaps, of his declining interest in his swelling family. In rough two-year increments, baby piled upon baby: Margaret, born 1828, was followed by Samuel (1830), David (1832), Martha (1833), Emilie (1836), Alexander (1839), Elodie (1840), and Catherine (1841). After that, Betsey slipped mercifully into menopause. The number of Todd children would be frozen at fourteen: six from the first marriage and eight from the second.

In day-to-day control of this Todd tempest was "Mammy Sally," the Todds' slave nurse. Certainly, she was the most constant presence in the children's early lives. With most patriarchs of the period, Robert Todd believed childrearing, like childbearing, was natural only to women. What he wanted from his progeny was pleasant, episodic contact. They should be presentable in public, peaceable in private, and a delightfully rare diversion from civic affairs. Betsey, too, was a distracted parent. She had inherited six children—and one cantankerous "mother-in-law"—from her predecessor, and she was for all her fertile life beset by babies, at her breast or in her belly. Three years, one miscarriage, and one pregnancy into her marriage, she was already looking "very thin & badly," according to a cousin. Eleven years and eight babies later, she was simply a husk. No one knew exactly when, but at some point the children had o'erstormed her mental ramparts. Betsey had withdrawn irritably into a shadow-world of vague maladies her family referred to simply as her "frailty." Whether physiological or psychological in origin, her partial retreat left her little engaged in the moral development of her children, even the ones who were fully hers.[4]

By default, then, Mammy Sally was the children's day to day "authority" figure. In their collective memory, "Sally was a jewel of a black mammy. She alternately spoiled and scolded [us,] . . . but [we] loved her and never rebelled against her." Undoubtedly they did love her, and she probably loved them back. But the idea that they never crossed her is ridiculous. Stories abound of the Todd children testing Sally's patience. Indeed, she seems to have been the butt of every joke they didn't play on each other. Tellingly, the children's claim that they "never rebelled" was made after the Civil War, when many Southern families were writing happy fictions about the softer side of slavery. The Todd children knew that Mammy Sally was a slave. This may not have affected their love for her, but it certainly affected their obedience to her. They were numerous and white. She was singular and black—and she was the only thing standing in their way. Of course they rebelled—and not occasionally but daily.[5]

This combination of an absent father, frail mother, enslaved nurse, and large family meant that the Todd children grew up just a little wild. They never fully learned a child's most important lesson: self-restraint. The authorities in their lives were all too remote: Father was someone to aspire to; Mother was someone to appeal to; Sally was someone to laugh at. But it fell to their wider society to teach them what proper men and women should do and be.[6]

The town of Lexington is nestled in a soft and undulating valley. The land around it rises and falls like a gentle green ocean, frozen in time. While the Todds lived there, the town's pretenses were at their zenith. Lexington was the self-declared "Athens of the West," an "oasis of civilization" over the Alleghenies. Like most overblown claims, this one had some basis in fact. The town itself was gorgeous. The roads were wide and well-kept; the sidewalks were accommodating; the brick homes that lined them were ample and well-appointed. The appearance of sophistication, which is in some measure sophistication itself, was nurtured at every turn. The town had the requisite number of churches (three) and newspapers (three) to show that it supported a diversity of views without encouraging eccentrics or extremists. There was a theater and a waxwork museum. There was a candy shop and a public library. While most of the West was listening to campfire songs, tom-toms, or crickets, Lexingtonians gathered by the hundreds to listen to Beethoven and Mozart. On July 14, 1819, an Italian harpist gave a concert in Lexington. For the first time west of the Alleghenies, the sweet strains of the angels' instrument wafted out over the frozen ocean of green. Some intimation of the town's refinement may be gleaned from the fact that it was renowned for its hats. Any town that offers a living at something so fashionable, and yet so expendable, as haberdashery must be civilized—and must be doing all right for itself.[7]

The town had substance as well as sophistication. The local university, Transylvania, had a law school and a prestigious medical school. The sons of governors, senators, and congressmen were among its students. Then too Lexington was the seat of Western Whiggery, being the home of

Henry Clay, three-time presidential candidate (if a three-time loser). Clay was a great favorite with the Todds. He was often a guest in their home. Robert campaigned for him, threw receptions for him, and never stopped believing that he would one day be president. Clay's vision for the West was different from that of his main Democratic rival, Andrew Jackson. Jackson spoke for the common man, the rifle-happy dirt farmers who dreamed of fat women, fat vegetables, and taking potshots at the census man. Clay spoke for the common man on the make, the progress-happy hat merchants who gushed over new postal routes and macadamized roads. Clay's popularity in Lexington, while in no way universal, made the town more respectable. His bids for the presidency put the town on the political map. And most important, his speeches on internal improvements fed the dreams of men like Robert Todd, who believed that with positive press, positive thinking, and a plank road or two their town might rival Philadelphia or Boston.

But Lexington's veneer of respectability was as thin as muslin. The local piano merchant was also an undertaker. The local bookstore sold violins and pistols on the same shelf. The town's various boosters and boards could buff out its rough edges, but Lexington remained rough somewhere near its heart. Whatever its pretensions, the city was essentially western. From the age of fourteen, many of its males carried concealed weapons, pocket pistols, dirks, knives, or cane swords. Like their watch fobs, these discrete death-dealers were essential accoutrements for the discriminating gentleman. Unfortunately, they were not mere fashion accessories. Lexington's homicide rate was approximately four times that of the eastern cities it sought to emulate. "If you go into the Northern states," remarked Kentucky lawyer Ben Hardin, "it is a rare thing if you can find a man in ten thousand with a deadly weapon on his person. . . . In these [Southern] states you may arm yourself to the teeth, and track your steps in blood with impunity." The town's leaders lamented the problem, but they were at a loss to explain it. Had their Scottish forbears left a "homicidal humor" in their blood? Had the Indian wars brutalized their impulses?[8]

The answers are more prosaic, less flattering. For starters, they drank too much. Alcohol flowed like a river through the town. The bourbon that would one day make Kentucky famous then made it infamous. Kentucky was, and remains, ideal bourbon country. The salt in the soil insures that the corn and the water have very low concentrations of iron, which tend to blacken and sour the mash. Then too the Bluegrass's hot summers and cold winters are ideal for distilling. Following the dictates of their land, then, nine-tenths of Lexington's antebellum farmers operated stills. Four taverns and 139 local distilleries served Lexington itself. The purest whiskey was ten dollars a barrel, and it was so good, slobbered a witness, that "[a] Man might Get Drunk on [it] Evry Day in the year for a Life time & never have the Delerium Tremens nor Sick Stomack or nerverous Head achake." Virtually every male drank to occasional excess, and if he didn't, he made a spectacle of himself. No home, with the possible exception of the reverend's, hosted a dry party without risking its reputation, and no public man could make it in politics if he couldn't hold his liquor. "Them days the Bank officers and welthy men woold Come down and Fish, up the Creek a week at a time" remembered one local, and they "Came prepaird to Engoy the Sport. They Brot the Best provisions and always The Best of old Burbon . . . to Make one Feel Renewed after the toils of Fishing." Lexington's men didn't just drink after the "toils" of fishing, however. Then, as now, alcohol served as a social lubricant, making cotillions more convivial and conversations more interesting. But, then as now, alcohol served as a social irritant too. Coupled with the concealed arsenals, bar brawls became murder scenes, and misunderstandings ended at the morgue. In 1824, the governor's own son killed the man he had been drinking with, and no one, including him, could remember exactly why.[9]

Lexington's "refinement" aggravated the problem. The town's shallow sophistication gave its sons more pride than humility. What they best understood about manhood was that cowardice was its opposite; they dreamed of opportunities to prove their courage, not their decency. They were what observers called "bowie-knife gentry"—toughs in tailored suits spoiling for a fight. "I think I never saw a place more strongly tinged with presumptuous, self-confident vulgarity," noted one visitor. Like most Southerners, Lexingtonians subscribed to the code duello. Honor was a man's most prized possession, and he defended it with his life. But dueling in Kentucky had little of the esprit de corps that marked affairs of honor elsewhere. Antagonists chose deadlier weapons at closer ranges, and they were rarely "satisfied" until their opponent was bleeding. The code was supposed to contain violence, but in Kentucky it merely justified it. In 1829, the Todds' cousin Charles Wickliffe shot the editor of Lexington's local paper because he had published a letter "uncomplimentary" to his father. The editor was unarmed, fleeing the building, and shot in the back, but the jury deliberated for only seven minutes before concluding that the boy had done right. His family's honor had been insulted, and an insult was something "no man in Kentucky could submit to without loss of character." Inevitably, such violence fed upon itself. Shortly after his acquittal, Wickliffe was called out by one of the editor's friends, who shot him through the heart at the ridiculously close dueling range of eight paces. This editorial avenger was then himself hounded into a sanitarium by the relentless persecution of Wickliffe partisans. In Lexington, the traditions of the duel were commingled with the traditions of the feud. Violence was bloody, clannish, and committed in a self-justifying cycle.[10]

Slavery too played a role in desensitizing Lexington's residents to violence. In keeping with its self-image, the town strove to appear moderate on the issue. Colonization schemes were soberly discussed. Antislavery proponents were heard out. Lexington even had its own homegrown abolitionist, Cassius Clay, who printed and posted his broadsides with relative impunity. The town's essential moderation was captured by a local paper that claimed that no family should hold more than ten slaves. At higher numbers, the author reasoned, slavery lost its personal touch. Masters were forced to hire abusive overseers, and slaves became faceless drones in far-off fields rather than integral members in a closely knit household. This was the happy fiction many elite Lexington families loved to believe, that slaves were simply domestic servants who worked for room and board and the ultimate job security—a hereditary position.

But it was the personal touch that made the institution so foul. Behind the lace curtains adorning Lexington's prettiest homes, slavery could be just as brutal as it was in the malarial rice fields a world away. Robert's friend, Fielding Turner, for example, appeared to be a model master. He was a retired judge and a leading citizen of the town. His wife, Caroline, was a Boston-born daughter of a wealthy and well-placed family. Their house was the finest in the city; their bank account was ample, and their servants numerous. But Caroline Turner had a dark cast of mind. Large and muscular, she discovered something at the heart of slavery that she loved and perhaps became addicted to—an outlet for her sadistic urges. Her neighbors whispered about what went on: She beat her slaves too often, too viciously, too happily. But they only whispered and did nothing. Then in the spring of 1837, Caroline threw a young slave boy out a second-story window. He landed awkwardly on the Turner's prim flagstone courtyard, breaking his arm and leg, injuring his spine, and crippling him for life. In the wake of the incident, Fielding revealed what the town must already have guessed. Caroline had a psychotic temper that fell most savagely on her slaves. "She has been the immediate [cause of the] death of six of my servants by her severities," Fielding admitted sadly, and the only way to protect the ones who remained was to have her committed. Robert was one of a handful of men called in to review the case, but, despite Fielding's revelations, nothing could be done. Caroline might be vindictive and cruel, but she was perfectly sane. And so she went back to beating her slaves behind lacy curtains. A few years later, Fielding Turner died, but he tried one last time to quiet his wife's rages. "None of [my slaves] are to go to . . . Caroline," he noted in his will, "for it would . . . doom them to misery in life & a speedy death." Somehow Caroline again thwarted her husband. She contested the will, retained possession of some of the slaves, and even bought some more. On August 22, 1844, her reign of terror came to an end. She chained a young slave to a wall and had begun flogging him when he broke free. In a frenzied instant, he grabbed her by the throat and broke her neck.[11]

Caroline Turner was an unusually cruel mistress. Most Lexingtonians didn't beat their slaves—they sent them down to the slave jail to be beaten (sometimes publicly) by a professional. But this is a distinction without a difference. The institution of slavery rested on a kind of violence that brutalized the tastes and impulses of the entire town. When word of an insurrection in Tennessee reached them, Bluegrass masters set to torturing the truth out of their servants with an abandon that shocked even a longtime resident. The insurrection proved nothing but a wild rumor, but that didn't stop whites from indulging in "unwarrantable cruelties to the negroes, reviving in many instances the exploded tortures of the Middle Ages and of the Inquisition." And just down the street from the Todd's front door lay Lewis Robards's infamous slave pens. The center of a shadowy kidnapping ring, Robards's operatives swooped down on Ohio's free black families and snatched as many children as they could find. Some were broken in Robards's dungeon and sold to points further South. Others joined his "select stock" of "yellow girls" who lived in a sumptuous upstairs apartment where their favors could be bought for a night or a lifetime. Even in the most radical households, families discussed eventual manumission over a dinner cooked and served by slaves. Growing up amid their enslaved servants, white children gained an inflated estimate of their own power. Thomas Jefferson knew this aspect of slavery intimately: "The parent storms [while] the child looks on, catches the lineaments of wrath, puts on the same airs in the circle of smaller slaves, *gives loose to his worst passions*; and, thus, *nursed, educated, and daily exercised in tyranny,* cannot but be stamped by it with odious peculiarities."[12]

The town's final problem was that it was dying, and the Todds were partly to blame. Together with the rest of Lexington's founders, John and Levi Todd had located their "Athens of the West" fifteen miles from the nearest navigable stream. Henry Clay could say all he wanted about plank roads, but waterways provided the biggest economic boost in the years before railroads. As the steamboat revolutionized transportation, Louisville and Cincinnati became bustling centers of commerce while Lexington's significance shrank to the point where it was *only* making hats. Businesses drifted away, as did Transylvania's medical school, as did many new migrants. "I don't like the idea of living in a finished or decaying place," noted one, "[nor] of raising our children where they cannot find employment." And so, ultimately, the town was left in the care of those founding families whose pedigree made them too stubborn to leave. They spent their lives polishing their ancestors and bickering about the past, never admitting that the future had passed them by.[13]

What did the Todd children learn growing up in a dying town amid slavery, arms, honor, and alcohol? First, it should be noted that there is no evidence that Robert Todd was an alcoholic or anything like it. In an era when even the bank president kept a jug cooling in the local creek, Robert was unusually snobbish about his refreshments. He shipped his spirits, like his best furniture, upriver from New Orleans. His supply of wine was ample but also select; his mint juleps were legendary but always served in cut crystal. Robert's watchword was moderation. He kept his liquor cabinet well-provisioned because it was expected of a successful host. His guests may have swayed a little when they rose from his table, but they never fell down. In short, Robert drank like he walked or practiced politics—decorously—ever mindful of the ladies, his reputation, and his name.

Three of his sons proved less discriminating. As they grew up, Levi, George, and David all developed a dependence on alcohol. For them, the availability of booze, coupled with the town's declining fortunes, created a problem. There was no work to do that slaves weren't already doing. There was no profession that appealed to them more than that of a gentleman, which they understood to include gambling, drinking, and puffing one's chest. This should not be held against them. Henry Clay's sons fared little better in Lexington. Clay was the "Star of the West," the leading light of his political party and a genius rightly acclaimed for his decency. And yet his sons were, according to a sympathetic witness, "all a disgrace to his name." The first was driven to a lunatic asylum by "the violence of his passions," the second was a "sot," the third was "so jealous & irritable in his temper that there is no living with him," and the last two gave "no great promise of steadiness" either. The temptations held out by Lexington were legion; opportunities were scant. Lexington's sons were left to indulge themselves with bright dreams of their coming greatness while they availed themselves of the town's cheap liquor and cheaper women. Of the Todd boys, only the youngest, Aleck, escaped the cycle fully, and he had an unusual advantage. By the time he was born, Betsey was so exhausted from childrearing that she hired an extra nurse from New Orleans. To get back at a system that enslaved her, the nurse made a habit of holding Aleck's infant body upside down against a wall until his face turned almost black. His parents suspected that he was being abused, but they never found a mark on him, so the practice continued unabated for a year. Perversely, it may have been one of the reasons that he developed such an unusually clingy disposition.[14]

The Todd girls had problems living in Lexington too. As one member of the household noted, we "had few privileges & led very dull lives. We had no amusements to vary the monotony, no parties to bring us in contact with girls beyond our homes, and worse than all no books with charming little stories to excite noble impulses and stimulate us to acts of kindness and courtesy." Instead, the girls dreamed mostly of joining the world they could see beyond their windows: a town bustling with women so preoccupied with not looking western that they tended to overachieve. As one visitor from Boston noted: "The ladies of Lexington pay their respects properly and promptly according to the town's social custom of forenoon [but I] was astonished to see callers arrive in satin and silk as if they were going to an evening function. No Boston lady would ever be so conspicuous. 'How is Dr. Holley,' they would ask and would adjust their flounces, scarcely touching their backs to the parlor chair lest they form a wrinkle or disturb a hair." Given their environment, it was quite natural for the Todd girls to mistake raiment for refinement. With no one to tell them otherwise, they came to understand that if they could only display themselves properly, the world would embrace them. Certainly this is what prompted Mary at the age of twelve to stay up all night sewing willow branches into her hemline. So far as she knew looking like a lady was the most important part of being one.[15]

Another story from Mary's childhood offers similar insights. The most authoritative version begins: "A small white pony galloped down the shady street, on his back a slender thirteen-year-old girl." The particulars of the story are straightforward. Robert, the indulgent father, buys Mary a small white pony from an itinerant theater troupe. Seizing the opportunity for display, Mary rides the pony over to Ashland, the home of the revered statesman Henry Clay. Galloping up to the door, she is informed by a servant that "Mr. Clay is entertaining five or six fine gentlemens." (The servant's grammar, we must understand, was part of the story's "charm.") Mary, being a "vivid, little person," will not be put off. Her business is every bit as urgent as any gentlemens.' "I've come all the way out to Ashland to show Mr. Clay my new pony," she says peevishly. "You go right back and tell him that *Mary Todd* would like him to step out here for a moment." Amused by the message, Clay emerges with his guests. "My father says you are the best judge of horse-flesh in Fayette County," Mary informs him. "What do you think about this pony?" Happy to be complimented in front of guests, Clay responds that the horse "is as spirited as [its] jockey" and, whisking Mary from the saddle, escorts her in to dinner. There, amid a lull in the adult conversation, Mary blurts out, "Mr. Clay, my father says you will be the next President of the United States. I wish I could go to Washington and live in the White House. I begged my father to be President but he only laughed and said he would rather see you there than to be President himself. He must like you more than he does himself. My father is a very, very peculiar man, Mr. Clay. I don't think he really wants to be President." Charmed in equal parts by her verve and her artlessness, Clay responds, "Well, if I am ever President I shall expect Mary Todd to be one of my first guests. Will you come?" Overwhelmed by his offer, Mary's crush on the great man bursts its bounds. "If you were not already married," she offers demurely, "I would wait for you." At this, the room erupts with laughter. Mary can feel that some of the amusement comes at her expense, but she's unsure how much. "I've been gone a long time," she says, slipping off her chair, "Mammy will be wild! When I put salt in her coffee this morning she called me a limb of Satan and said I was loping down the broad road . . . to destruction." Mary curtsies grandly. She mounts her little pony and off she rides, all ribbons and curls bouncing on the breeze.[16]

In this story, the Todds saw their sister and their sister saw herself; this was the Mary they all knew: bold, bright, and, by whatever twist of fortune, headed for the White House. But the story captures other features the family was blind to, possibly because they shared them. Mary could not imagine a man who both loved himself and didn't want to be president—not because the president could do the most good but because he lived in the nicest house and was the most distinguished, the most prominent, the most envied man in the country. Only someone "very, very peculiar" would want less than that for themselves. Mary, like the rest of the Todd children, prayed for prominence, not contentment. She craved the world's envy more than its love. Any other way of thinking was as odd to her as a man who didn't want to be president.

This air of entitlement, coupled with a lack of self-reflection and restraint, ensured that as they grew to adulthood, the Todds would move from temper tantrums (that broke and passed like summer storms) to periods of true dysfunction that could last for decades. Even before the Civil War split them in half, the siblings sued and slandered each other and, in various combinations, were often not on speaking terms. During one such cold snap, Mary Lincoln described her sister Ann as malicious, miserable, false, wrathful, and vindictive. Glancing over the list, Ann recognized the traits instantly: "Mary was writing about herself," she responded coolly. Sister Elodie was more self-aware, though no less critical. Above all, she warned her fiancé, "I am a *Todd*, and some of these days you may be unfortunate enough to find out what they are." Of course, with his gift for language, it was Lincoln himself who most pithily lampooned the pretensions of his wife's family. "One 'd' was good enough for God," he drolled, "but not for the Todds."[17]

None of this is to deny that Mary Lincoln grew from a tart-tongued Todd into a seriously accomplished, usually misunderstood, and often unjustly savaged woman who possessed a shrewd political mind and many tender impulses. But as the girl is the mother of the woman, it is worth teasing out some continuities of character, rooted in their common childhood, that she shared with her siblings.

Mary's clearest mental preoccupation, for instance, was a desire to be properly *valued*. Yes, she was all the time in the garret or the cellar, and depression (or bipolarity) was an important part of her mental make-up. But the greater key to her personality lies in her temper: When did she get angry, and why? In most cases Mary lashed out when she felt she wasn't getting her proper due, her required attention, her just desserts. How tragic, then, that in marrying her version of Henry Clay (whom Lincoln was said to resemble) she married a man who didn't want to stay home to pet and husband his resources. Instead she married a slightly feral giraffe who could never be properly domesticated. In a veiled reference to marriage, Lincoln had told Joshua Speed what his father had always told him, "if you make a bad bargain, hug it the tighter." But Lincoln would not, perhaps could not, hug Mary tight enough. Instead, for the whole of his marriage, he absented himself in every way possible. He hid in Springfield's drug store, with the men around the pot-bellied stove; he hid in his law office among his books or his cronies; he hid on the circuit, at the hustings, among the people. If his Shakespeare was handy, Lincoln could hide in full view of Mary. Staring into a fire or out of a window, he could achieve a trancelike state of absentia that was actually alarming. Maybe you don't wake such a man by hitting him in the head with a block of wood. But such distractedness ruffled Mary's feathers where they had always been thinnest. She called Lincoln "father" after all, and his failure to pay attention made her life an endless recrudescence of early childhood demands to be noticed.[18]

Obviously *all* children crave love, attention, and the recognition of their unique qualities. But only some children, not getting (and never reconciling themselves to not getting) these things, erect on the ruin of their childhood expectations an ersatz self that can demand and take them, often heedless of the consequences to others. Lost in a large household, not getting her due strokes from her dead mother, absent father, and preoccupied stepmother, Mary sometimes invented a new reality to live in, one in which she was uniquely insightful and deserving. Her own feelings and opinions became magnified in importance and expression. The feelings and opinions of others grew distant and disposable. Thus, her reaction to another's advancement was often, "Why should *she* benefit?" And her reaction to another's misfortune was often, "Why *shouldn't* he suffer?" Lincoln was not entirely exempt from this trend in her thinking. Certainly, as the hot coffee dripped down her husband's scalded face, Mary felt no immediate pang of conscience for throwing it there. But when he accepted such treatment with a sad understanding, she was inclined, occasionally, to allow him to comfort the wounded child in her who was, at base, the malevolent architect of such things.

And then of course Lincoln was taken from her too. For weeks after the assassination, Mary lolled inconsolably in a White House bedroom while servants and interlopers supposedly "looted" the downstairs, and Andrew Johnson, the new president, worked out of a tiny office at the Treasury. When finally she did pack up and leave, the city and the nation seemed glad to be rid of her. In truth, they had never liked her, and, not even for Lincoln's sake, were they going to start now. Though she had been holding her husband's hand when he was shot in the head, she would remain to a merciless nation a pathetic, but not a pitiable, figure.[19]

Why? Her sister Elizabeth said it best: "Mary has had much to bear though she don't bear it well; She has acted foolishly—unwisely and made the world hate her." No biography of Mary Lincoln has ever explained it better. She did have much to bear. All that might have made her content with herself—her mother, her father, her boys, her husband, her "advancement"—were systematically stripped from her. She ascended to the White House only to have a son die and a husband murdered; Lincoln became a martyr to the Civil War while she became a scapegoat. Nor was her "baptism of sorrow" complete in 1865. In 1871, at the age of eighteen, Tad came down with pleurisy and wheezed his way out of the world strapped upright for a month in a sleeping chair. In 1875, Mary's only remaining son, Robert, betrayed her so completely she would refer to him as a "monster of mankind." The entirety of her life had unfolded like the final scene of a Shakespearean tragedy. Mother dead early, father dead early, extended family shattered, nuclear family eradicated, she was left alone on the stage, alone on the planet.[20]

Given her disappointments, it is sad that Mary's contemporaries expected her to "bear it well." But they did. However heartbroken, a widow was supposed to mourn with decorum and could only be pitied to the extent that she refused to pity herself and stoically accepted God's plan. Mary did none of these things. Her suffering, she claimed, was not merely inconsolable but incomparable. "No *such sorrow* was ever visited upon a people or a family," she said, as if it were a contest. And to make sure that people knew she was winning the contest, she *always* wore black, *always* wrote on black-bordered stationery. And self-pity dripped from her as she wrote. "Marked out by fate for sorrow," hers was a "daily crucifixion" that would end only at the grave. Her contemporaries, however, refused to see a woman who might be redeemed by suffering; they saw instead a diva of grief whose histrionic performances seemed an unwelcome encore to a life of indulgence and aggrandizement.[21]

Some, then and now, think she was just plain crazy, but Mary's had always been a disordered but not a deranged mind. Her spiritualism, coupled with her medications, made her see strange things and say strange things, but her hovering dead did no one any harm and were one of her few remaining consolations in a world where God kept taking things from her. "I would not care to live a day," she wrote a friend, without "the beautiful & consoling belief that our beloved ones, whose home is in Heaven can, unseen by us, enter into our midst, witness the anguish we suffer [and] console us by their invisible presence."[22]

More problematic than her ghosts was her monomania on the subject of money—another exaggeration of features rooted in childhood preoccupations with class and dress. In her later years, Mary became a sort of financial bulimic. The control of money, not food, alternately stabilized and destabilized her psyche. She horded and spent, instead of binged and purged, in an endless cycle of indulgence and regret. Having refigured her personal vulnerability and personal insecurity as financial vulnerability and financial insecurity, she stitched bonds into her dress, haggled with clerks, became paranoid that people were out to steal from her, tackily sold off her dresses, petitioned Congress for cash, and complained of penury—all in the face of the irrefutable fact that Lincoln's estate had left her relatively well off. She did not want the money for itself, however; money had come to represent love, and justice—and no one can have enough of those. When the Grants were given a house, when the widow Garfield was given a larger pension, when the public failed to pay enough for her dresses—Mary took it personally because she was not being properly *valued.* In revenge, she revalued herself in occasional binges of purchasing: curtains she'd never need or gloves in numbers she could never use—the items themselves didn't matter. Shopping made her feel important and pampered; pretty things distracted her from ugly realities. None of this made her crazy but it did make her embarrassing—especially to Robert—who finally convinced himself that confining his mother was the only way to control her.[23]

Ultimately, it was sister Elizabeth who helped to rescue Mary from Bellevue. The two had been estranged since the war, but when her doctor (and jailor) asked Mary if she had any option to confinement, she did not hesitate. "It is the most natural thing in the world to live with my sister," she told him. "She raised me and I regard her as a sort of mother." Elizabeth agreed and gently reconciled Robert to the idea of restoring Mary's freedom to embarrass him. He groused a little about his "Aunt Lizzie's interference with my painful duty," but Robert eventually acceded and Mary was returned to the Edwards's. There, on the top floor, her cataracts having all but claimed her eyesight, she turned ever tighter circles, surrounded by her "swag," until the lights went out on July 16, 1882.[24]

In tracing Mary back to the childhood she shared with her siblings, one gains a better vantage not only on her unique attributes and faults, but also on those traits common to her family, her region, and her times. In valuing display, in demanding recognition at the point of a knife, or a tongue, Mary was a lot like her siblings. The Todds were the matrix in which Mary was formed and lived her life; more than anyone else, they benefitted from her, suffered by her and beside her; they were there at the beginning and there at the end in ways that no one—not even her husband—could be.

And if we grant that the Todds knew Mary best, it seems only logical that those seeking to understand her should consult them first. Elizabeth's one-sentence biography of her sister—that she "had much to bear though she don't bear it well"—should hereafter be every historian's point of departure on Mary. Certainly if all of her biographers had been so even-handed, we might not now have to scrape away layers of controversy to get at the human complexities that make America's first First Lady (and first First Widow) so sadly compelling.

### Notes

1. "[A] large family of boys and girls": Elizabeth L. Norris to Emily Todd Helm, September 28, 1895, William H. Townsend Papers, Abraham Lincoln Presidential Library (hereafter ALPL).

2. Jean H. Baker, *Mary Todd Lincoln: A Biography* (New York: Norton, 1987), 19–24.

3. See Catherine Clinton, *Mrs. Lincoln: A Life* (New York: Harper Collins, 2009), 9–47.

4. "[V]ery thin & badly": Henrietta M. Brown to Louisa V. Rucks, September 27, 1829, Joseph Adger Stuart Papers, Filson Historical Society.

5. "Sally was a jewel": quoted in Katherine Helm, *Mary, Wife of Lincoln* (New York: Harper, 1928), 23. See also William H. Townsend, *Lincoln and the Bluegrass: Slavery and Civil War in Kentucky* (Lexington: University of Kentucky Press, 1955), 72–73.

6. In treating Lexington itself as an important "character" in Mary's childhood, I follow the particular lead of Baker, *Mary Todd Lincoln*, 53–73

7. On early music in Lexington, see Joy Carden, *Music in Lexington before 1840* (Cincinnati: C. J. Krehbiel, 1980), 50. On Lexington as "the Great Hat Market," see Frances L. S. Dugan and Jacqueline P. Bull, eds., *Bluegrass Craftsman: Being the Reminiscences of Ebenezer Hiram Stedman, Papermaker, 1808–1885* (Lexington: University of Kentucky Press, 1959), 61.

8. "If you go into the Northern states": Robert M. Ireland, "Homicide in Nineteenth-Century Kentucky," *Register of the Kentucky Historical Society*, 134–53. Quotation, 136–37.

9. "A Man might Get Drunk"; "Them days the Bank officers": Dugan and Bull, *Bluegrass Craftsman*, 23; 181. On the 1824 murder, see Hal Morris, ed., "Murder, Banking, and Kentucky Politics, 1824," *Jacksonian Miscellanies* 39 (November 1997).

10. On the 1829 Wickliffe shooting, see Ireland, "Homicide in Nineteenth-Century Kentucky," 152–53; quotation, "no man in Kentucky," 147.

11. On Caroline Turner, see Townsend, *Lincoln and the Bluegrass*, 74–75; Randolph Paul Runyon, *Delia Webster and the Underground Railroad* (Lexington: University Press of Kentucky, 1999), 26–27.

12. "[U]nwarrantable cruelties": Orlando Brown to Orlando Brown Jr., December 24, 1856, Orlando Brown Papers, Filson Historical Society. For more on Lewis Robards's infamous slave pens, see Townsend, *Lincoln and the Bluegrass*, 185–87.

13. On Lexington's declining fortunes in the period, see J. Winston Coleman Jr., *Lexington: Athens of the West* (Lexington: Winburn, 1981), 21. "I don't like the idea": Eliza Kinkead to Ellen S. Bodley, December 10, 1850, Bodley Family Papers, Filson Historical Society.

14. "[A]ll a disgrace": John Spalding Gatton, "'Mr. Clay & I got stung': Harriet Martineau in Lexington," *Kentucky Review* 1, no. 1 (Autumn 1979): 52. See also S. J. Yandell to mother, Sarah Wendell, October 13, 1831 in Yandell Family Papers, Filson Historical Society. For more on the slave nurse who held Alex upside down, see Elizabeth L. Norris to Emilie Todd Helm, July 18, 1895, Elizabeth L. Norris Collection, hereafter Norris Collection, ALPL.

15. "[H]ad few privileges": Elizabeth L. Norris to Emilie Todd Helm, September 28, 1895, Norris Collection, ALPL. "The ladies of Lexington": quoted in Baker, *Mary Todd Lincoln*, 61. On Mary sewing willow branches into her hemline, see Elizabeth L. Norris to Emilie Todd Helm, September 28, 1895, Norris Collection, ALPL.

16. "A small white pony" and other quotations in paragraph: Helm, *Mary, Wife of Lincoln*, 1–5.

17. "[M]alicious, miserable": Mary Lincoln to Elizabeth Todd Grimsley, September 29, 1861, Justin G. Turner and Linda Levitt Turner, eds., *Mary Todd Lincoln: Her Life and Letters* (New York: Knopf, 1972), 105; "Mary was writing about herself": W. A. Evans, *Mrs. Abraham Lincoln: A Study of Her Personality and Her Influence on Lincoln* (New York: Knopf, 1932), 47. Laudably, Jason Emerson has brought this odd, important book back into print (Carbondale: Southern Illinois University Press, 2009); "I am a Todd": Elodie Todd to Nathaniel Dawson, May 23, 1861, Nathaniel Henry Rhodes Dawson Papers, Southern Historical Collection, University of North Carolina at Chapel Hill; "One 'd' was good enough for God": Like most of his gags, Lincoln used this one in various forms, making an authoritative version impossible. According to one source, Lincoln acquired the gag from the politician David Tod, governor of Ohio during the Civil War: "One evening when Tod was in town Lincoln invited him over to the White House. They had a long chat together, when Lincoln finally said: Look here, Tod, how is it that you spell your name with only one d?' . . . Old Tod looked at Lincoln for a moment . . . then replied: 'Mr. President, God spells his name with only one d, and what is good enough for God is good enough for me.' Lincoln used to repeat this story to some of his more intimate friends, and every time he did so he would laugh until the tears ran down over that furrowed but grand face." According to another "family tradition," relayed by a Todd relative, Lincoln used a variation of the line on his father-in-law in the 1840s: "After Lincoln had been married for some time, and had written several letters to his wife's folks, the old man Todd, Mrs. Lincoln's father, came for a visit. After the customary greetings had taken place between father-in-law and son-in-law, Mr. Todd said 'Abe, you are always bragging on your abilities as a speller; how does it come that you always address me with the surname spelled with a single "d," T-o-d?' Abe's reply came quick and to the point; 'Well, dad, ever since I can remember God has been spelling his name with a single "d," and he is certainly of a family equally as prominent as any of the Todds.'" Both "origin" stories have their problems (the idea of Lincoln calling his father-in-law "dad" for instance), and they cannot both be right. The truth is probably this: the gag has existed for as long as there have been Todds and Tods. Given his appetite for such things, and his panache for working them into conversation, Lincoln undoubtedly picked the gag up and made it his own in a variety of contexts and phrasings. See "Why Mr. Tod Scorned the Double D," *Boston Traveler*, August 6, 1886; and "The Byes and Todds," *Knoxville (IA) Journal*, February 12, 1909.

18. Different biographers have called this quality by different names. Catherine Clinton describes it as a "penchant for melodrama" with a source in an understandable chafing at "the restraints that fenced women" of the period in (see Clinton, *Mary Lincoln*, 17). Jean Baker's conception is more clinical: narcissistic personality disorder (see Baker, *Mary Todd Lincoln*, 330–32.) The best case for bipolarity is made in Jason Emerson, *The Madness of Mary Lincoln* (Carbondale: Southern Illinois University Press, 2007). On Henry Clay as husbandman, see Wade Hall, "Henry

Clay: Livestock Breeder; An Unpublished Letter," *Filson Club History Quarterly* 59, no. 2 (1985): 251–57.

19. In *Mary Todd Lincoln*, Jean Baker partly shields Mary from the charge that she looted the White House herself, pointing to instances in which objects belonging to the house later showed up elsewhere. Nevertheless, it seems more than probable that Mary took her share: See Michael Burlingame, ed., *At Lincoln's Side: John Hay's Civil War Correspondence and Selected Writings* (Carbondale: Southern Illinois University Press, 2000), 200–201.

20. "Mary has had much to bear": Douglas L. Wilson and Rodney O. Davis, *Herndon's Informants: Letters, Interviews, and Statements about Abraham Lincoln* (Urbana: University of Illinois Press, 1998), 444; "monster of mankind": quoted in Baker, *Mary Todd Lincoln*, 349.

21. "No *such sorrow*" and "daily crucifixion": quoted in Baker, *Mary Todd Lincoln*, 256, 257.

22. "I would not care": Mary Lincoln to Mrs. White, December 14, 1866, Gilder Lehrman Collection, New York Historical Society. On Mary Lincoln's trial and confinement, see Emerson, *The Madness of Mary Lincoln*; Baker, *Mary Todd Lincoln*, 315–50; and Mark E. Neely Jr. and R. Gerald McMurtry, *The Insanity File: The Case of Mary Todd Lincoln* (Carbondale: Southern Illinois University Press, 1986).

23. On the pension struggle, specifically, see Thomas Schwartz and Anne V. Shaughnessy, "Unpublished Mary Lincoln Letters," *Journal of the Abraham Lincoln Association*, January 1990, 35–49.

24. "It is the most natural thing" and "Aunt Lizzie's interference": quoted in Baker, *Mary Todd Lincoln*, 340.

## MARY LINCOLN, RACE, AND SLAVERY

*Brian Dirck*

Mary Lincoln always seemed to walk Abraham Lincoln's walk. Before she even knew him, she left her birthplace in Lexington, Kentucky, and travelled to his town of Springfield, Illinois. After they married, she moved first to the Globe Tavern in Springfield—where Abraham felt right at home, but Mary was shocked by the crude atmosphere—and then to their middling-class house at Eighth and Jackson, which bore little resemblance to the genteel Southern mansions of her youth. When he went to Congress in 1846, she accompanied him to a rough-and-ready, masculine Washington, DC, boarding house; and fifteen years later when he was elected president, she again followed him to the White House. Whither Abraham went, Mary followed—not always happily, but followed nevertheless.

On one occasion, however, Abraham stood on Mary's turf. Following his election to Congress, Abraham, Mary, and their sons Robert and Edward stopped for an extended three-week visit in Lexington: relatively unfamiliar territory for Abraham, but home for his wife. Unlike Abraham, who left Kentucky as a child, Mary had lived in the Bluegrass State until she was twenty-one. She absorbed more of the South's culture and way of life than her husband ever could.

This included slavery. Growing up in Lexington, Mary saw the peculiar institution every day, and often in the worst possible light. Her hometown, dubbed the "Athens of the West," was famous for its bourbon, thoroughbred horses, fine homes—and slave auctions.[1] Lexington was "one of the largest slave markets in the United States, and is the great place from which the South is supplied," according to one European visitor, who added that "these pens give one a much more revolting idea of the institution than seeing slaves in regular service." The Lexington mansion in which the Lincolns lodged belonged to Mary's grandmother Elizabeth Parker and was located only a few yards away from the slave-trading firm owned by William Pullum. Pullum's holding pens were directly adjacent to the Parker property, facing Mechanic's Alley. The sight would have been nearly impossible for anyone in the Parker home to avoid—seven foot high walls surrounding the slave "coops," with iron riveted and barred windows, and cold brick flooring.[2]

Mary was accustomed to seeing the slave system's machinery for buying and selling human beings. Slave coffles were a common sight in the streets of the town. "Slaves! Slaves! Slaves! Fresh Arrivals Weekly!" read local newspaper advertisements; or "Negroes! Negroes! Negroes!" along with assurances that local planters could dispose of black people "rendered unfit for labor by Yaws, Scrofula, Chronic Diarrhea, Negro Consumption, Rheumatism" and the like.[3] There was no mistaking the wrack of a system that chewed up blacks and spit them out—not in the streets of Lexington, not across Mechanic's Alley.

But white Southerners did their best to paper over these awful realities with a thick slathering of genteel—and entirely unrealistic—paternal romanticism. When the Lincolns arrived at the Todd family home, they found a warm greeting worthy of a scene from Margaret Mitchell's imagination. "The whole family stood near the front door with welcoming arms," recalled Mary's niece. Behind the Todd clan stood several African Americans. "In true patriarchal style, the colored contingent filled the rear of the hall to shake hands with the long absent one [Mary] and 'make a miration' over the babies," as her niece put it. "To my mind [Mary] was lovely," added her sister Emilie, with "clear, sparkling, blue eyes, [and] lovely smooth white skin with a fresh, faint wild-rose color in her cheeks."[4]

Quite the image, this white Southern woman of perfect Scarlett O'Hara–
type Southern manners (at least in Emilie's recollections) stepping back
into the bosom of her slaveholding Southern family, with the so-called
"colored contingent" loyally gathered—appropriately in the background, as
befitted Southerners' slaveholding mores—to express their joy at the home-
coming. It could have passed for the perfect set-piece image of antebellum
Southern life, at least according to the white slaveholding gentry, with each
figure well-crafted to maintain the Moonlight-and-Magnolias mythos.

But of course antebellum slave life was never so simple; and neither was
Mary Todd Lincoln. As with so much else involving Mary, contradictions
and unexpected realities cut across the grain of what we would otherwise
expect in her perceptions of slavery and African Americans. She was far
more than the white Southern belle she appeared to be, because of her
unique circumstances growing up in a difficult Todd household, and
because of her own unique psychology. Her attitudes concerning race
and slavery were jumbled, contradictory, and not quite what anyone who
merely looked at the surface of her life would expect.

She grew up in a household that idolized Henry Clay, more so even
than most others in Lexington. Mary's mother, Eliza, was a good friend
of Henry and his wife, Lucretia, and the Todd family's politics generally
reflected Clay's Whiggery. Mary herself knew Clay from an early age and
developed a fierce admiration for both the man and his political party.
"Mary when fourteen years of age was a violent little Whig," noted another
Todd family member, who also remembered Mary observing that "Mr.
Henry Clay is the handsomest man in town and has the best manners of
anybody—except my father."[5]

Influence is hard to measure, and we should be careful in not drawing
too direct a line between Clay and Mary. Still, Mary's attitude concerning
slavery looked quite a bit like Clay's. Clay owned slaves—a lot of them,
in fact—but he habitually denounced the institution as a moral blight on
Kentucky and the South, and he was a leading proponent of gradual, com-
pensated emancipation (albeit accompanied by a firm belief in African

Americans' innate inferiority, and the need for their immediate removal to Africa). "Few, if any, of the citizens of the United States, would be found to favor [the introduction of slavery]" if it did not already exist, he claimed, and "No man in [the United States] would oppose ... [slavery's] admission with more determined resolution and conscientious repugnance than I should."[6]

Clay both benefited from and squirmed uncomfortably in the presence of slavery. So did Mary. The context was much different, of course. Clay was a nationally prominent politician and leader, a man who in a man's world formulated policies, made decisions, and pulled the levers of power. Mary was a woman—intelligent, politically astute, and outspoken—but a woman nonetheless. Her attitudes concerning African Americans and slavery were formed in the context of an early-nineteenth-century America that would not tolerate much in the way of a female openly expressing opinions about such matters. We can take the measure of a man like Henry Clay by reading what he wrote and said; where Mary is concerned, we can only draw inferences from her surroundings, and descriptions of her behavior from her friends and family.

We do know that she kept the company of people whose feelings concerning slavery were that same mixture of self-interest, moral guilt, and white supremacy that animated Henry Clay. Mary Brown Humphreys, for example, was Mary's stepgrandmother, with whom Mary spent a good deal of time while growing up. Mrs. Humphreys was one of Lexington's leading ladies—a "highly educated old lady who, naughtily for her day and generation, read Voltaire in French." She was something of a freethinker on other matters as well. She manumitted her slaves in her will. According to Mary's cousin, Humphreys was "an emancipationist [who] had great influence in forming Mary [Todd's] views on that subject."[7]

More generally, Mary's community was not uniformly proslavery. Lexington's slave-trading status was offset at least a bit by the fact that it also hosted critics of the institution, most famously Cassius Clay. Clay, whose Garrisonian abolitionism inspired slavery's detractors (and outraged the institution's defenders) was educated at Lexington's Transylvania

University (which Mary also attended) and published his abolitionist newspaper, *The True American*, from a downtown Lexington office.[8] Kentucky itself was often divided in its sentiments towards the peculiar institution. A border state with smaller farms holding fewer slaves than one might find in, say, South Carolina, the state never lacked for doubters concerning the efficacy and morality of slavery. Henry Clay and Cassius Clay were only the most visible examples of a Kentucky antislavery tradition with deep roots; not deep enough to persuade most of the state's white denizens to seriously pursue emancipation, to be sure, but a significant presence nevertheless. As a well-educated young white woman, Mary would surely have been exposed in some fashion to the antislavery writings of Kentucky emancipationists like "Father" David Price—a determined Presbyterian minister from Danville who wrote a well-known pamphlet entitled "Slavery Inconsistent with Justice and Good Policy"—or at least heard rumors of the activities of Kentuckians like Calvin Fairbank, who claimed to have helped nearly fifty fugitive slaves escape to freedom.[9]

Mary's education at Transylvania University may also have stimulated critical thinking about slavery. While not so readily identified with antislavery principles as some other nearby institutions—Berea College, for example, which was founded in 1855 by an abolitionist—Transylvania nevertheless possessed its share of divergent viewpoints on the issue. Mary would not likely have been exposed to the more extreme strands of abolitionist thought while at Transylvania, but she quite likely overheard (and participated in) conversations that questioned the efficacy, morality, and long-term future of the institution. In April 1835, for example, the president of Transylvania University, John C. Young, delivered an address embracing the idea of gradual emancipation as the best way to eradicate what he believed was a blight on Kentucky and the South. "The difference, then, between the gradual emancipator and the abolitionist is not a difference as to the criminal nature of slavery," Young declared, for "they agree in considering it an enormous evil—but it is a difference as to the best mode of getting rid of this evil."[10]

Clearly Mary Todd was not surrounded by uniformly proslavery people in her Southern upbringing—her landscape contained conflicting images, from the darkest heart of slavery's auction blocks to the denunciations—both outspoken and muted—of the institution she surely heard or read. She profited from the daily toil of enslaved African Americans, but she also felt crosscurrents of other kinds: doubts, misgivings, and a degree of sympathy for the enslaved.

Even as she lived within sight and sound of Pullum's and other such establishments, Mary recoiled at slavery's violent aspects, probably because she was herself an emotionally sensitive person who seems to have been entirely averse to real brutality or cruel behavior. There were rumors in Springfield that she was sometimes physically violent with Abraham during their marriage—gossip had her chasing him with a knife during a quarrel, for example—but these were rumors only, and if they did happen, seem to have been marks of sudden, brief outbursts, rather than a pattern of violent behavior.[11]

A cousin recalled that Mary was "horrified" when she read newspaper accounts of slave brutality and whippings. One particularly gruesome story that made national headlines—concerning a group of "unfortunate slaves" who were found chained in the attic of a New Orleans home—caused Mary to "shiver with horror." "We were horrified and talked of nothing else for days," remembered Mary's stepgrandmother; "if one such case could happen, it damned the whole institution."[12]

Part of Mary's shocked reaction was rooted in her particular psychological makeup. Even as a child, family members recalled that Mary was an emotional sort. "She was very highly strung, nervous, impulsive, [and] excitable," recalled a family friend, "having an emotional temperament much like an April day, sunning all over with laughter one moment, the next crying as though her heart would break." It was a characteristic that followed her into adulthood and old age.[13]

Gendered stereotypes of her time held that women were fragile and overwrought, indulging in the most facile emotional reactions to any difficulty, so the testimony of people who described Mary as "flighty" or easily upset must be treated with caution. Nevertheless, throughout her life, Mary does seem to have been a remarkably sensitive person, evincing highly charged responses to any situation that seemed intense or difficult: a child's willful disobedience, a house servant's defiance, one of her husband's numerous lapses in manners and etiquette, or even something much more commonplace. "She was usually timid and nervous during a thunderstorm," remembered a friend, "and whenever one threatened, her husband made it a point to leave whatever he was engaged in, if it was a possible thing, and go home, to stay with her until it passed over."[14]

Mary's critics over the years put the most disagreeable spin on such behavior, as evidence of her ungovernable disposition. "She had a very extreme temper," went a typical indictment, "and made things at home more or less disagreeable [for Abraham]."[15] However much this may (or may not) have been so, it is equally possible to place a different emphasis on her emotional sensitivity—as a source of unusual empathy and emotional connectivity.

Another reason for Mary's underlying empathy lay in the influence of "Mammy Sally," the Todd family's quintessential maid, wet nurse, and unofficial head of the Todd household slaves. She was described by a family member as "a jewel of a black mammy [who] alternately spoiled and scolded the children, but they loved her and never rebelled against her authority."[16]

"Never rebelled" was likely an exaggeration, for by all accounts young Mary could be quite a handful. Still, she seems to have been genuinely fond of Sally. Her fondness went to the extraordinary length of looking the other way, and sometimes actively participating, when Sally undertook a dangerous pastime—aiding fugitive slaves. This was a serious matter in Lexington, where local and state laws provided severe punishments for anyone caught doing so.[17]

Nevertheless, Sally surreptitiously participated in what seems to have been a Lexington underground railroad. She left a "mark" on the fence in front of the Todd mansion as a sign that aid was available there for runaways. "All of 'em knows the sign, I have fed many a one," Sally told Mary. At first, Mary's response was shock; "Mammy, it is against the law to help run-a-way slaves." But then, thinking better of it, she announced her intention to go help the fugitives herself by bringing them food. Sally restrained her. The runaway "would hide from you like a scared rabbit, nothing but a black hand reaching out to him can give that nigger corn-bread and bacon." Mary relented, and she said nothing to anyone about Sally's secret aid.[18]

Taken together, the combined influences of Clay, her family members, and "Mammy Sally" gave Mary a well of antislavery sentiment upon which to draw. But there were definite limits to Mary's perceptions. She encountered Sally via a master/servant relationship. Mary's "model was the dynamic between mistress and family slave," historian Jennifer Fleischner has observed. "Sally, our faithful old black mammy," as one of Mary's sisters described her, functioned within the complex role of the Southern black mammy, and surely was compelled to feign subservience—towards Mary and the rest of the Todd family—which was expected by the whites of the day. Sally's submission was far from complete, as her aid to fugitive slaves indicates.[19]

"Faithful old black mammy" was the border that bracketed Mary's vision of color, and that border was (at least outwardly) benign. Elizabeth Humphreys (Mary's cousin) recalled a conversation with Mary in which the two girls speculated about whether or not Sally actually wanted to be free. "We concluded she did not," Elizabeth wrote; "how could we do without Mammy, and how could she exist without us?" Leaving aside the obviously self-serving content of such an observation, it lays bare both the inescapably lopsided relationship between Sally and her white owners, and a basic lack of understanding concerning Sally's lot in life as a form of human "property." Growing up in Lexington, Mary Todd probably never encountered a black person on a basis of equal power, and this was as true in the gilded cage that was the Todd family mansion as it was in the dark cells of Pullum's auction house. No matter how often she heard the moral hand-wringing of a Henry Clay, or the "emancipationist" exhortations of her stepgrandmother, or read the headlines concerning this or that outrage perpetrated against Southern blacks, Mary failed to grasp the essential, basic injustice of the relationship between master and slave—or if she did, she never recorded the sentiment.

Moreover, *slavery* is not *race*. Whatever doubts she may have felt concerning the treatment of black people as property, she harbored the same nagging prejudices and attitudes about people of color that bedeviled nearly every white American of the era. For all the care and reverence she felt for Mammy Sally, Mary played endless pranks on her (salting Sally's coffee, for example), and she would sometimes poke fun at Sally's speech: "Ole Man Satan's done got the latch pulled," Mary imitated Sally within hearing of her sister one evening (and Abraham, who "was highly amused and laughed heartily over [Mary's] impression"). She attended minstrel and blackface shows and was not averse to using the term "darkey" in describing black people, though she avoided the word "nigger," her stepmother having admonished her that this was "'a mode of speaking of the negro at once scornful and inelegant.'"[20]

When Mary moved to Springfield in 1839 to live with her sister Elizabeth (who had married Ninian Edwards, a prominent Springfield politician and lawyer), she ostensibly relocated from slave to free territory. But the difference was not nearly so stark as might be expected. Illinois was arguably the most repressive Northern state in the Union towards African Americans. The state's "black laws," adopted in 1819 severely restricted emigration of African Americans by requiring any who entered the state to produce paperwork proving their freedom; if they could not do so, they could be sold into indentured servitude. In an attempt to prevent Southern slaveholders from dumping "old and decrepit and broken down Negroes" in the state (as Stephen Douglas pungently put it), the law required an owner to post a one–thousand-dollar bond for each freed slave brought across Illinois's borders. Black Illinoisans were also subjected to ongoing ostracism, discrimination, and even outright violence from their white neighbors.[21]

Antiblack prejudice was so pervasive in Illinois that its white citizens sometimes looked the other way when Southern emigrants brought slaves with them into the state and continued to hold their slaves in bondage despite its illegality. Mary witnessed an example of this in her own sister's home. Elizabeth and Ninian brought several African American slave servants with them when they settled in Springfield, and they remained in the Edwardses' home, ensconced somewhere between servitude and slavery.[22]

Neither Mary nor Abraham ever owned slaves, but they did employ numerous women of color as servants when they moved into their home on Eighth and Jackson, along with Anglo and Irish girls, and even some girls who resided in an expatriate Portuguese community near Springfield. Like many other middle-class white women of her day, Mary experienced difficulty finding and keeping good help. In this she did not discriminate: She found the going rough, regardless of whether the servant in question was Anglo, Irish, or African American.[23]

Mary's loudest complaints about servants came in relation to Irish servant girls. Here she exhibited a form of ethnic bigotry directed at the Irish, which in Mary and in many of her contemporaries could contain as much vitriol as that of anything directed at African Americans. This was a fairly common attitude among white Americans of the day, many of whom saw "Paddy" as a racial epithet, and believed the Irish were a degenerate breed—even to the point of founding a political party, the "Know-Nothings," that had anti-Irish sentiment in its foundation. "If some of you Kentuckians, had to deal with the 'wild Irish,' as we housekeepers are sometimes called upon to do, the south would certainly elect Mr. Fillmore next time," she groused to her sister, referencing Millard Fillmore's 1856 candidacy for the nativist Know-Nothing Party.[24]

According to one account, Mary found dealing with free servants a more exasperating and frustrating experience than her dealings with slaves at the Todd mansion years previous. John Bradford, a friend and political ally of Lincoln from his days in Springfield, related that he drove to the Lincoln home to show off a new carriage he had acquired, and invited Mary to accompany him and his family for a ride. "When [Mary] came down the front steps to join us in the carriage, she appeared to be very nervous and wrought up," Bradford remembered; "we suspected that there had been a collision or disagreement of some kind with her servant, for, just as she settled back in her seat, she exclaimed with a sigh, 'Well, one thing is certain; if Mr. Lincoln should happen to die, his spirit will never find me living outside the boundaries of a slave state.'"[25] Whatever the exact circumstances of this little incident, it does reinforce the point: Mary's interaction with the various Irish and African American women who came and went in her Springfield domestic world occurred, as in Lexington, within the context of a master/servant relationship.

It is impossible to know what she shared with her husband in terms of their respective perceptions of African Americans and slavery. Lincoln's hatred of slavery long predated his association with Mary. Perhaps she fed that hatred with stories of Lexington's slave pens and the like from her youth; or perhaps not. There is no reliable record of any conversations concerning the peculiar institution that may have passed between them.

Despite his lifelong hatred of slavery as an institution, Abraham—at least at this stage in his life—appears to have been fairly conventional in his attitude towards African Americans for a white person of his time. He occasionally used the term "nigger" (more so, apparently, than Mary), sometimes told racial jokes, and when pressed on the political circuit denied that he in any way supported racial equality. "Anything that argues me into his idea of perfect social and political equality with the negro, is but a specious and fantastic arrangement of words, by which a man can prove a horse chestnut to be a chestnut horse," he famously declared during his first debate with Stephen Douglas; "I have no purpose to introduce political and social equality between the white and the black races. There is a physical difference between the two, which in my judgment will probably forever forbid their living together upon the footing of perfect equality, and inasmuch as it becomes a necessity that there must be a difference, I, as well as Judge Douglas, am in favor of the race to which I belong, having the superior position."[26]

These sentiments were probably echoed by his wife. The qualifier "probably" is necessary because Mary actually said and wrote little about the political environment in which her husband was so heavily embroiled. She did have political opinions—more so perhaps than what was considered seemly by the conventions of her day. Even Mary knew this. "This fall I became quite a *politician*," she confessed to a friend in 1840—referring to her intense interest in the presidential election, which resulted in a rare Whig victory by William Henry Harrison—adding sheepishly that it was "rather an unladylike profession."[27]

Her husband tried during the 1850s to steer a moderate antislavery course, arguing for the limitation and eventual end of slavery while studiously avoiding any association with abolitionism. Mary seems to have approved of this course and felt likewise in her own political sentiments. Her husband's perspective was in large measure modeled on Henry Clay's ideas, which would have entirely met with Mary's approval.

But again, there were definite limitations to Mary's embrace of an antislavery standard; and she would likely have had no sympathies with the more extreme forms of antislavery activism, or anything that smacked of racial equality. Moreover, she worried about the impression she and Abraham made on her Kentucky relatives. She hastened to reassure them that her husband was no extremist, even after he joined the fledgling Republican Party in 1854. "Although Mr. L[incoln] is, or was a *Frèmont* man [John C. Frèmont, the Republican candidate for the presidency in 1856], you must not include him with so many of those, who belong to *that party*, an *Abolitionist*," she wrote her sister; "all he desires is, that slavery, shall not be extended, let it remain, where it is." During his Senate race in 1858, she dismissed the notion that Lincoln, merely because of his antislavery politics, might ever "countenance social equality with a race so far inferior to [his] own."[28]

Lincoln sometimes struggled to both embrace antislavery principles and avoid association with a politically disastrous pursuit of racial equality: People wondered whether he was at heart a conservative—when he spoke of Southerners' constitutional right to own slaves and denied any intention of interfering with the institution where it already existed—or an extremist, following his assertion that a "house divided against itself cannot stand." In truth, Lincoln was a bit of both. He was uncompromising in his hatred of the peculiar institution, but he had a healthy respect for the power of white supremacy in America. He wanted to find a way that would end slavery without unduly offending white sensibilities—an exceedingly difficult matter.[29]

Mary walked this walk, as well. Her attempt to steer a difficult middle course between her Todd family's slaveholding sensibilities and her husband's antislavery politics produced its own sort of confusion; not so much concerning her politics—as a woman, she was not really supposed to have a "politics"—but rather her cultural affinity. She seemed on one level to be so very Southern, in her manners, fashion, and lineage. Yet she simultaneously supported her husband as he ascended the ranks of the antislavery Republican Party. After the war, some speculated that she "belonged to the proslavery crowd" during the 1850s, but there is no firm evidence of this, and the suggestion that Mary approved of the institution seems to have been an assumption attached to her Southern roots, and little else.[30]

Her Southern background was in some antislavery circles a political liability for Abraham, because it was assumed that she had unthinkingly imbibed the prejudices and proslavery attitudes of her region, and passed these attitudes on to her husband. Or perhaps he had chosen Mary for a wife precisely because of those attitudes, and in doing so revealed his own proslavery heart. Many abolitionists were inclined to dismiss Lincoln anyway, for his Kentucky roots and his supposedly soft antislavery principles. Having Mary at his side only made matters worse. "His wife, you, know, is a Todd, of a pro-slavery family, and so are all his kin," sniffed one newspaper editor, by way of castigating Lincoln's own antislavery credentials.[31]

When the Lincolns entered the White House in 1860, Mary's social and political ambivalence was thrown into the much harsher glare of the national press, and Washington, DC, society; and among the many rumors about Mary that swirled in Washington concerned her supposed pro-Southern, proslavery influence on the president. This was an entirely superficial judgment, based upon surface appearances. Indeed, an opposite reaction took place in Mary's thinking. Whereas before the war she carried a mixture of contradictory sentiments and ideas about slavery, the war served to quietly harden her into a staunch advocate of emancipation. Far from acting the part of a Southern apologist, Mary wanted her husband to adopt some sort of emancipation policy; she "urged him to Emancipation, as a matter of right, long before he saw it as a matter of necessity," remarked Jane Grey Swisshelm, an abolitionist who became acquainted with Mary during the war. There is also no reliable extant record of any disparaging comments made by Mary concerning African Americans along the lines of their being a "far inferior" race.[32]

Lost among the many sensationalized stories and rumors concerning Mary's time in the White House—her borderline insanity over the death of the Lincolns' son Willie, her profligate spending habits, her sometimes embarrassing public temper tantrums—is the fact that she wrought a little revolution in the way black people were treated at the White House. While Abraham granted unprecedented access to African American leaders like Sojourner Truth and Frederick Douglass, Mary did much the same— quietly, and with far less fanfare. She once invited an African American teacher for an afternoon tea at the White House—a rare enough event in itself—and when Mary discovered that the teacher had been shown the servant's entrance by the White House doorman, she was both enraged at the doorman and particularly kind to the teacher, to the extent that she made it a point to shake the woman's hand as she was leaving. It seems a small thing, this handshake, but it earned her the scorn of Kate Chase (daughter of treasury secretary Salmon Chase) who having witnessed the affair, later remarked disdainfully at a cabinet dinner that the First Lady was "making too much of the Negro."[33]

This was far from the behavior one would expect of a typical Southern white woman, acting the part of a mistress in her own home. More astute observers than Kate Chase saw that Mary Lincoln had become more than merely the sum of her Southern parts. "It was often charged that her sympathies were with the South," noted Mary's African American seamstress (and close friend) Elizabeth Keckly, but "those who made the charge were never more widely mistaken."[34]

Why did the war have this effect upon Mary? Perhaps part of the reason lay, again, in her psychology. Her personality was such that she tended to divide the world along stark black-and-white lines, defined by her own intense likes and dislikes. People who found themselves on Mary's bad side discovered that they tended to remain there permanently, and that her disdain was absolute. Those who were predisposed to dislike Mary interpreted this facet of her personality as an angry streak of vengefulness: "greedy, spiteful, and vindictive," as one observer put it.[35] But it would be more fair to suggest that Mary was simply given to emotionally charged judgments: concerning those whom she loved, and also those whom she felt had wronged her in some fashion. After 1861, this last category included the slaveholding Confederate South. "I never failed to urge my husband to be an extreme Republican," Mary heatedly declared after the war. She was incensed at the suggestion her Todd family roots had somehow compromised her loyalties. I "left Kentucky at an early age [and my] sympathies were entirely Republican," she insisted.[36]

Keckly recalled a revealing incident in this regard. In August 1862, word reached Washington that one of Mary's brothers, Alexander Todd, was killed while fighting for the Confederacy in Louisiana. Keckly heard the rumors but hesitated to mention it to Mary, "judging that it would be painful news to her." Much to the seamstress's surprise, Mary herself mentioned, in an oddly casual way, Alexander's death. When Keckly voiced her reluctance about broaching such a painful subject, Mary dismissed her concerns. "You need not hesitate," she said; "[Alexander] made his choice long ago. He decided against my husband, and through him against me. He has been fighting against us; and since he chose to be our deadly enemy, I see no special reason why I should bitterly mourn his death." Keckly discovered in subsequent conversations with Mary that she "had no sympathy for the South." Mary saw the conflict in starkly personal terms. "Are they not against me?" she said of the Rebels. "They would hang my husband tomorrow if it was in their power, and perhaps gibbet me with him. How then can I sympathize with a people at war with me and mine?" [37]

Mary's utter rejection of "a people," down to even the pro-Confederate members of her own family, suggests a blanket rejection of the entire value system that the Confederacy represented—a value system with the institution of human slavery at its very core. On the very day he took office, her husband stated his belief that slavery was the root cause of the conflict between North and South. Given how closely Mary's politics mirrored Abraham's, there is no reason to believe she disagreed with this assessment. In turning her back on the pro-Confederate Todds and the Confederacy itself, Mary was turning her back on slavery, as well. It was a package deal.[38]

Mary was also influenced by the company she kept. Again, the more highly sensationalized stories of her acquaintance with rather shady characters—Henry Wikoff, for example, a roguish gossip and influence peddler who wormed his way into Mary's confidence—underplayed more wholesome connections she made in Washington. Chief among these was her close friendship with Massachusetts senator Charles Sumner, perhaps the most famous antislavery Republican in America, and a leader of the party's radical wing.

Well-educated, polished, and courteous, Sumner was the very sort of sophisticated and intelligent gentleman to whom Mary was drawn. For his part, Sumner seems to have cultivated friendship with the First

Lady for a mixture of reasons; having her ear could certainly do him no harm politically, but he also seems to have held Mary in genuine high regard personally. Personal affinity aside—and there was unfounded gossip in Washington during the war that Sumner and the First Lady were romantically involved—their relationship was saturated with politics. Mary penned letters full of political advice to the senator, pausing only briefly to acknowledge "perhaps, you will consider it unbecoming in *me* to write you thus," before plunging ahead anyway. Sumner seems to have tolerated Mary's importunities with more patience than might have been expected from many other men in that time, which no doubt encouraged Mary in her friendship with the senator.[39]

Sumner's politics were fundamentally antislavery in nature, and Mary well understood this. As the war progressed she became an active participant in that cause. "I take the liberty of introducing to your distinguished notice, these two colored persons," Mary wrote in a formal letter of introduction to Sumner in April 1864. The two African Americans, a Mr. Hamilton and Mrs. Johnson, traveled from Philadelphia to Washington, DC, to see Sumner, apparently as representatives of Philadelphia's free black community. Johnson in particular was known to Mary as someone who had spent the war working with wounded soldiers; and they approached the First Lady as a means of gaining introduction to the senator. Mary happily obliged. "They promised some of our prominent Philadelphia friends they would call to see you, whom all the oppressed colored race, have so much cause, to honor" Mary wrote.[40]

Mary's closest association with African Americans during the war came through her friendship with her African American seamstress, Elizabeth Keckly. Keckly was a middle-aged former slave who had purchased her own freedom (and that of her son) from an abusive former owner, and then used her business acumen and sewing skills to build a fairly comfortable life for herself and her family in Washington, DC. She came highly recommended to Mary when the Lincolns arrived in Washington (Keckly had previously worked for Jefferson Davis's wife, Varina), and Mary soon came to depend upon her as a seamstress, fashion advisor, and eventually close confidant. Mary referred to Elizabeth as her "colored Mantuamaker . . . a very remarkable woman."[41]

Mary's relationship with Keckly on one level resembled her relationships with other African Americans through the years: that of an employer/mistress dealing with an employee/servant. She could be imperious and sometimes abrasive with Keckly. "You have disappointed me—deceived me," Mary once berated Keckly over a mishap concerning last-minute delivery of a dress prior to an important social function; "you are not in time . . . you have bitterly disappointed me."[42] Mary also retained an unfortunate residue of racial bigotry even in her feelings towards the seamstress, sometimes seeing her as a rare hard worker among a people otherwise given to laziness. Writing to recommend Keckly for government employment in March 1863, Mary described Keckly as "most estimable" and "although colored, is very industrious."[43]

But if Mary often treated Keckly like a servant, she also developed a genuine personal regard for her. Their friendship would not survive the postwar years, not after Keckly chose to write a memoir of her White House years that Mary considered a betrayal of her trust. But during the war and for some time afterwards, Mary exhibited an emotional dependency on Keckly that rivaled or even exceeded what she had felt for Mammy Sally. Keckly consoled Mary in the difficult wake of her son Willie's death in 1862; and in the hours following Abraham's assassination, when Mary became unhinged from grief, she sought out her seamstress for comfort. "'Is there no one, Mrs. Lincoln, that you desire to have with you in this terrible affliction?'" asked the wife of secretary of the navy Gideon Welles. "'Yes, send for Elizabeth Keckly, I want her just as soon as she can be brought here.'"[44]

Keckly also faithfully kept Mary's confidence and her secrets, particularly regarding the First Lady's extravagant spending habits, which by 1864 had proven to be a major source of stress for Mary. "Mrs. Lincoln sometimes feared that the politicians would get hold of the particulars of her debts,"

Keckly recalled, "and use them in the Presidential campaign against her husband." Lacking close friends among the more sophisticated white ladies of Washington society, Mary unburdened herself to Keckly. "If [Abraham] is re-elected, I can keep him in ignorance of my affairs," she exclaimed one afternoon, after she had anxiously asked Keckly what she thought were Lincoln's chances for victory, "but if he is defeated, then the bills will be sent in, and he will know all." At this point, according to Keckly, Mary let out "something like an hysterical sob," as the seamstress tried to calm her.[45]

While Keckly proved to be a source of emotional support for Mary, the First Lady in turn supported Keckly's efforts to raise money for the assistance of the many African American freedmen who had been made destitute by the dislocations of the war. Appealing to her church for help, Keckly organized the Contraband Relief Association, and Mary became one of her first supporters, contributing the not insignificant sum of two hundred dollars, and making regular contributions thereafter. Keckly "says the immense number of Contrabands in W[ashington] are suffering intensely," Mary informed Abraham in November 1862; "many without bed covering and having to use any bits of carpeting to cover themselves [and] many dying of want. . . . I have given her the privilege of investing $200 here[e] in bed covering . . . I am sure, you will not object to being used in this way—The cause of humanity requires it."[46]

The First Lady had perhaps begun to see African Americans as more than mere servants of one sort or another. While it probably would be too great a stretch to suggest that she actually viewed black people on a level plane with herself and other whites, Mary does seem by 1865 to have evolved to a point far removed from her privileged Southern youth. Her attitude towards slavery and African Americans still carried its share of blind spots and contradictions—Elizabeth Keckly's status as a good worker, "although colored," for example—but by the war's end she certainly stood firmly in the camp of those who viewed slavery as an unmitigated evil, emancipation as a welcome wartime measure, and the freedmen as worthy of sympathy and aid.

Just how much influence she worked on her husband in this (or any other regard) is impossible to say. Lincoln came to the place he did during the war—Great Emancipator and, towards the end, an advocate of at least some measure of legal, political, and economic equality for African Americans—from a variety of pressures and influences, of which Mary's constituted only one. He was a notoriously private man, who rarely revealed his internal thought processes to anyone. And Mary's ability to influence any aspect of her husband's presidency was further hampered by the fact that she was forced to endure long absences away from him. "I consider myself fortunate, if at eleven o'clock, I once more find myself, in my pleasant room and very especially, if my tired and weary husband, is there, resting in the lounge to receive me—to chat over the occurrences of the day," she sighed.[47]

We do know they shared a common high regard for the most prominent African American in the nation, Frederick Douglass. Lincoln developed a rapport with Douglass, despite their occasional policy disagreements, and met with him at the White House on three separate occasions. Lincoln famously admitted Douglass to the White House reception following his second inauguration, after White House guards refused to admit him because he was a black man. Insisting upon Douglass's admittance, the president pointedly shook Douglass's hand in front of the lily-white crowd and warmly greeted him. Mary's response to this episode was a profound sense of disappointment—disappointment that she had been unable to shake Douglass's hand as well. "Why was not Mr. Douglass introduced to me?" she asked Lincoln. "I do not know," Lincoln replied; "I thought he was presented. . . . I am sorry you did not meet him."[48]

Mary tried to rectify that oversight, at least a bit, following Abraham's death. She was often preoccupied with the accumulation of things (a source of her compulsive shopping), and one way she coped with death was to rid herself of the things that reminded her of the deceased. Following Willie's death, she had emptied the White House of the child's toys and other belongings ("any trifling memento that recalled him would motivate her to tears," Keckly remembered), and following her husband's assassination, she rid herself of any mementoes that reminded her of him, and of her loss.[49]

Among those items she gave away was Abraham's favorite walking stick, which she bestowed upon Frederick Douglass. It was a kingly gift, considering how desperately many rich and well-heeled white men were scrambling to snap up any Lincoln-related souvenirs. It was a fitting little statement about Mary Lincoln, as well: a quiet, behind-the-scenes gesture of respect and consideration for a black man who, in her Kentucky youth, would hardly have merited a passing glance from the aristocratic Mary Todd of Lexington.

### Notes

1. *(KY) Reporter*, October 30, 1820; Marion Brunson Lucas, *A History of Blacks in Kentucky: From Slavery to Segregation, 1760–1891* (Louisville: Kentucky Historical Society, 2003), 89–90.

2. J. Winston Coleman Jr., "Lexington's Slave Dealers and Their Southern Trade," *Filson Club History Quarterly* 12 (January 1938), 11; Isabella Strange Trotter, *First Impressions of the New World on Two Travellers* (London: Longman, Brown, Green, Longmans, and Roberts, 1859), 252.

3. Coleman, "Lexington's Slave Dealers," 17.

4. Katherine Helm, *The True Story of Mary, Wife of Lincoln* (1928; reprinted 3rd. ed. New York: Academy, 2001), 99–100.

5. On the friendship between Eliza Todd and the Clays, see Jean H. Baker, *Mary Todd Lincoln: A Biography* (New York: W. W. Norton, 1987), 19; Helm, *Mary, Life of Lincoln*, 41, 43.

6. Daniel Mallory, ed., *The Life and Speeches of the Honorable Henry Clay* (New York: Robert P. Bixby, 1843), 2:367; on Clay's racial attitudes, see Robert V. Remini, *Henry Clay: Statesman for the Union* (New York: W. W. Norton, 1993), 314–15, 484fn.

7. Helm, *Mary, The True Story of Mary*, 35.

8. Lucas, *A History of Blacks in Kentucky*, 32.

9. See, e.g., Lowell H. Harrison, *The Antislavery Movement in Kentucky* (Lexington: University Press of Kentucky, 1978), 19, 61–62, 80–85 and *passim*.

10. Young's address reprinted in Daniel Reaves Goodloe, *Inquiry into the Causes Which Have Retarded the Accumulation of Wealth and Increase of Population in the Southern States* (Washington, DC: W. Blanchard, 1846), 68; see also John D. Wright Jr., *Transylvania: Tutor to the West* (Lexington: University Press of Kentucky, 1978), 163–67.

11. These rumors were based almost entirely on neighborhood stories gathered by Lincoln's law partner William H. Herndon, whom Mary had grown to detest (and vice versa) by the time Herndon gathered such stories; while scholars differ greatly on this matter, I tend to be very skeptical of Herndon-related evidence as a source for Mary's behavior. See, e.g., Stephen Whitehurst, interview with William H. Herndon, c. 1885–1889, in Douglas L. Wilson and Rodney O. Davis, eds., *Herndon's Informants: Letters, Interviews, and Statements about Abraham Lincoln* (Urbana: University of Illinois Press, 2007), 722.

12. Helm, *The True Story of Mary*, 38–39; on the Todd family's antislavery leanings, see Stephen Berry, *House of Abraham* (Boston: Houghton Mifflin, 2007), 40–41.

13. Passage from a letter written by Margaret Stuart Woodrow, copied in Helm, *The True Story of Mary*, 32.

14. Gibson William Harris, "My Recollections of Abraham Lincoln," in William Haig Miller et al., *The Leisure Hour* 4 (1903–4), 450.

15. Milton Hay, interview with Jesse W. Weik, c. 1883–1888, in Wilson and Davis, *Herndon's Informants*, 729.

16. Helm, *The True Story of Mary*, 23; on Mary's relationship with Sally, see Baker, *Mary Todd Lincoln*, 65–68; Fleischner; *Mrs. Lincoln and Mrs. Keckly: The Remarkable Story of the Friendship between a First Lady and a Former Slave* (New York: Random House, 2003), 5, 20, 50 and *passim*.

17. Catherine Clinton, *Mrs. Lincoln: A Life* (New York: HarperCollins, 2009), 20, makes a compelling argument for Mary's emotional closeness to Sally stemming from the death of her mother at an early age.

18. Helm, *The True Story of Mary*, 40.

19. Helm, *The True Story of Mary*, 175; 103. For a general examination of the complex relationships between white and black Southern women under the slave system, see generally Elizabeth Fox-Genovese, *Within the Plantation Household: Black and White Women of the Old South* (Chapel Hill: University of North Carolina Press, 1988).

20. Helm, *The True Story of Mary*, 19, 51, 111–12, 140–41; Epstein, 175–76. Fleischner, *Mrs. Lincoln and Mrs. Keckly*, 50, interprets the practical jokes Mary played on Sally differently than I do here, suggesting that these actions were a ritual "meant to restage and prove" Sally's emotional bonds with Mary; while a plausible interpretation, I would still suggest that such jokes also reinforced a racial differentiation between the two women.

21. Stephen Middleton, *The Black Laws of the Old Northwest: A Documentary History* (Westport: Greenwood, 1993), 272–73.

22. On the Edwardses' slaves, see Baker, *Mary Todd Lincoln*, 105–6.

23. Baker, *Mary Todd Lincoln*, 106; see also Elizabeth Todd Edwards, interview with William H. Herndon, c. 1865–1866, Wilson and Davis, *Herndon's Informants*, 445.

24. Mary Todd Lincoln to Emilie Todd Helm, November 23, 1856, in Justin G. Turner and Linda Levitt Turner, eds., *Mary Todd Lincoln: Her Life and Letters* (New York: Alfred A. Knopf, 1972), 46; see also Baker, *Mary Todd Lincoln*, 106–8.

25. John S. Bradford, interview with Jesse W. Weik, c. 1883–89, Wilson and Davis, *Herndon's Informants*, 729.

26. Lincoln, first debate with Stephen Douglas, August 21, 1858, in Roy P. Basler, Marion Dolores Pratt, and Lloyd A. Dunlap, eds., *The Collected Works of Abraham Lincoln* (New Brunswick: Rutgers University Press, 1953), 3:16; on Lincoln's antebellum attitude towards African Americans, the best recent studies are George M. Frederickson, *Big Enough to be Inconsistent: Abraham Lincoln Confronts Slavery and Race* (Cambridge: Harvard University Press, 2008); and Eric Foner, *The Fiery Trial: Abraham Lincoln and American Slavery* (New York: W. W. Norton, 2010).

27. Mary Todd Lincoln to Mercy Ann Levering, December 15, 1840, Turner and Turner, *Mary Todd Lincoln*, 21 (emphasis in original).

28. Mary Todd Lincoln to Emilie Todd Helm, November 23, 1856, Turner and Turner, *Mary Todd Lincoln*, 46 (emphasis in original).

29. See generally Foner, *The Fiery Trial*, esp. chaps. 2–3.

30. See, e.g., Henry Whitney to William H. Herndon, August 27, 1887, Wilson and Davis, *Herndon's Informants*, 631.

31. Quoted in Foner, *The Fiery Trial*, 75.

32. On Mary's urging that Lincoln adopt emancipation, see Clinton, *Mrs. Lincoln*, 182; Swisshelm's comments in Turner and Turner, *Mary Todd Lincoln*, 145.

33. Description of this affair in Ishbel Ross, *Proud Kate: Portrait of an Ambitious Woman* (New York: Harper and Row, 1953), 90; Clinton, *Mrs. Lincoln*, 171, makes the point that Kate Chase spread this tale as a way of scoring political points for her father.

34. Elizabeth Keckly, *Behind the Scenes in the Lincoln White House: Memoirs of an African-American Seamstress* (1868; Mineola: Dover, 2006), 57; throughout this article I have used the spelling "Keckly," rather than the "Keckley" that appears in many earlier works; Fleischner, *Mrs. Lincoln and Mrs. Keckly*, 7, makes a compelling case for the former spelling.

35. Quote is from Gilbert A. Tracy to Jesse W. Weik, March 14, 1914, in Jesse W. Weik, *The Real Lincoln: A Portrait* (1922; Lincoln: University of Nebraska Press, 2002), 377.

36. Mary Lincoln to Elizabeth Keckly, October 29, 1867, Turner and Turner, *Mary Todd Lincoln*, 447.

37. Keckly, *Behind the Scenes*, 57.

38. For a good general discussion of Mary's complex wartime relationship with the Todd family, see Stephen Berry's astute study *House of Abraham: Lincoln and the Todds; A Family Divided by War* (Boston: Houghton Mifflin, 2007).

39. Mary Lincoln to Charles Sumner, November 20, 1864, Turner and Turner, *Mary Todd Lincoln*, 192 (emphasis in original).

40. Mary Lincoln to Charles Sumner, April 5, 1864, Turner and Turner, *Mary Todd Lincoln*, 174.

41. Mary Lincoln to Elizabeth Todd Grimsley, September 29, 1861, Turner and Turner, *Mary Todd Lincoln*, 106.

42. Keckly, *Behind the Scenes*, 34–35.

43. Mary Lincoln to George Harrington, March 20, 1863, in Turner and Turner, *Mary Todd Lincoln*, 149.

44. Keckly, *Behind the Scenes*, 80.

45. Keckly, *Behind the Scenes*, 63–64.

46. Keckly, *Behind the Scenes*, 48–49; Mary Lincoln to Abraham Lincoln, November 3, 1862, Turner and Turner, *Mary Todd Lincoln*, 141.

47. Mary Lincoln to Mercy Levering Conkling, November 19, 1864, Turner and Turner, *Mary Todd Lincoln*, 187.

48. Keckly, *Behind the Scenes*, 68.

49. Keckly, *Behind the Scenes*, 49.

## LIFE AT EIGHTH AND JACKSON

*Richard Lawrence Miller*

Abraham Lincoln's home life has been described as horrific. Actually, however, family life for him was a diversion from cares, not a cause of them. Activity at Eighth and Jackson was sometimes chaotic but generally happy.

Normally Abraham would rouse himself at seven or eight o'clock in the morning, perhaps prompted by Mary yelling at him to split wood for the breakfast stove. If need be, however, he would get up earlier and go to the baker or butcher. "Of a winter's morning he might be seen stalking and stilting it toward the market house," his law partner Billy Herndon said, "basket on his arm, his old gray shawl, rope-like, wrapped around his neck, his little Willie or Tad running along at his father's heels."[1] He would bring back his selections and have breakfast. "Mr. Lincoln was what I call a hearty eater and enjoyed a good meal of victuals as much as anyone I ever knew," said his niece Harriet Hanks, a longtime household member in the 1840s. "I have often heard him say that he could eat corn cakes as fast as two women could make them."[2] When done with breakfast, Lincoln walked a few blocks to his office. After first going through newspapers, he would begin his work. At midday he would lunch at home. Typically, at some point he would stop by the drugstore run by his brother-in-law Dr. William Wallace and visit the mercantile and banking business of Jacob Bunn. In late afternoon, Lincoln called at various lawyers' offices to learn what was going on. William Walker reminisced, "I well remember his coming in the office of Col. Baker, where I studied and read law, almost every afternoon." Lincoln "always made the hour he spent with us interesting and instructive. . . . After the hour so spent, he could go to a back yard, used by the students, and join them in a game of [hand] ball, with as much zest as any of us. But, when his watch told him the hour was out, he would at once quit the game, and bid us good-evening."[3]

He was expected home for supper at around six o'clock. Mary would see him coming, and welcome him in the front yard. They would walk the few steps to the house holding hands while engaged in amusing banter. A visitor found the home atmosphere agreeable: "I was met at the door by a servant, who ushered me into the parlor. . . . The house was neatly without being extravagantly furnished. An air of quiet refinement pervaded. . . . There were flowers upon the table, there were pictures upon the walls. . . . The hand of the domestic artist was everywhere visible."[4] A guest found it to be "the residence of an American gentleman in easy circumstances, and is furnished in like manner. . . . It is a comfortable, cozy home, in which it would seem that a man could enjoy life, surrounded by his family."[5]

Normally suppertime included only the parents and children. Billy Herndon never shared a meal with them, and Mary's first cousin John Stuart commented, "I have been at Lincoln's house a hundred times and never was asked to dine. . . . [Lincoln] never asked [David] Davis to dine with him."[6] Davis was, however, invited to visit after supper. He thought the reluctance to have dinner guests implied trouble in the Lincoln marriage. More probably Abraham and Mary wanted to spare visitors from having meals with rambunctious undisciplined youngsters. Perhaps Mary also thought her food offerings were too simple for visitors and that she lacked enough money to afford proper hospitality. The "table at home was usually set very sparingly," Harriet Hanks said. "Mrs. Lincoln was very economical."[7] There was also the question of Abraham's table manners. Schuyler Colfax, who served as Speaker of the US House of Representatives during the Civil War, depicted the kind of problem Mary faced, with a husband who had learned to eat "in log-cabin style—not a piece of iron or steel on the table. The chickens, beef, pork, and bread were cut up before the guests were called, and every man used the fingers and jack-knife."[8] I suspect Abraham's table etiquette constantly concerned Mary, who understood the importance of having him perceived as a gentleman, in order to be better accepted by the state and national political elites.

Proper attire was another issue. Harriet Hanks recorded that Abraham "often went to the table in his shirt sleeves, which practice annoyed his wife very much."[9] She also frowned on his receiving callers unannounced at the door, like a pioneer instead of a gentleman. A relative suggested to her that such concern was misplaced: "Mary, if I had a husband with a mind such as yours has, I would not care what he did." Mary respected that perspective and responded, "It is foolish; a very small thing to complain of."[10] Harriet observed that Abraham "seldom ever wore his coat when in the house."[11] He even used casual clothes in public, which must have vexed Mary. Next-door neighbor James Gourley remarked, "He used to come to our house, his feet in a pair of loose slippers, and wearing an old, faded pair of trousers fastened with one suspender."[12] Harriet Hanks sniffed that Mary "loved to put on *style*."[13] To a "down home, corn fed" farm girl like Harriet, Mary's concern about appearances may have seemed like gaudy—even conceited—frivolousness. Mary's efforts, however, were at least partly powered by a desire to help Springfield's elite accept Lincoln as one of them. She understood the importance of "presentation." At least one aristocrat was pleased with what he saw, both on the surface and deeper; Mary's father, Robert, wrote: "I feel more than grateful that my daughters all have married gentlemen whom I respect and esteem."[14]

After supper, Abraham and Mary would go to the parlor. A guest recalled playing checkers with little Bob as sundown eased into night. While chitchatting, Mary did embroidery, and Abraham simply gazed at the stove's flames. Gradually his participation in conversation stopped, prompting Mary to grasp his hand and remark temperately, "Your silence is remarkably soothing, Mr. Lincoln, but we are not quite ready for sleep just yet." Abraham then returned to his surroundings, telling a funny story, "which broke up the game of checkers and left us all speechless with laughter."[15] Abraham's trances spooked his fellow lawyers, but apparently the family circle found ways to integrate those states into pleasant family life. Another nighttime leisure activity was reading. Mary Lincoln's sister Frances reminisced, "I used to go over and see my sister, and Lincoln . . . would read generally aloud."[16] Mary selected books for his evening relaxation. Husband and wife had some similar literary interests, and occasionally Mary would give Abraham detailed reports on volumes she perused. Like her husband, she, too, would read aloud, from the *Lexington Observer and Reporter*. In addition to providing news about her old hometown, the newspaper supplied a Southern Whig perspective on events. On a typical night, Abraham might also do his own reading and go to bed around eleven.

Evening visitors were common. Some were just making social rounds and stayed for a short while, but some passed the evening at Eighth and Jackson. Mary charmed her husband's law student Gibson Harris. "As a frequent visitor I was made welcome at the Lincoln home. . . . I always found her most pleasant-mannered. She was a bright, witty and accomplished young woman, naturally fond of fun and frolic. . . . I was impressed with her brilliant conversational powers, and the superior education she constantly evinced."[17]

Such were ordinary nights, but occasionally the Lincolns threw parties. Abraham handled invitations to politicians and wives; Mary notified lady friends, their husbands, and marriageable daughters. Participants in smaller gatherings arrived toward seven o'clock and conversed until a meal was served at nine. State legislator Isaac Arnold recalled that the Lincolns bestowed "a cordial, hearty, Western welcome, which put every guest perfectly at ease. Her table was famed for the excellence of its rare Kentucky dishes, and in season was loaded with venison, wild turkeys, prairie chickens, quails, and other game, which in those early days was abundant. Yet it was the genial manner and ever kind welcome of the hostess, and the wit and humor, anecdote, and unrivaled conversation of the host, which formed the chief attraction."[18] State representative Franklin Blades remembered that "guests were received in an informal and friendly manner by Mrs. Lincoln. On being ushered upstairs I found Mr. Lincoln and the Democratic State Auditor . . . sitting on a high post bed [in a bedroom that doubled as home office], chatting with each other, Mr. Lincoln particularly greeting all who came into the room."[19] The reputation of such gatherings assured good turnouts even if rain poured down on mud streets. In February 1857, Orville Browning told his diary, "Raining and very foggy. . . . At night attended large and pleasant party at Lincoln's."[20] *Illinois State Journal* coeditor William Bailhache said of the same event, "Last night the weather was a trifle worse if possible, and yet I found a perfect *jam* at Ab. Lincoln's party."[21] And Mary reported,[22] "I am recovering from the slight fatigue of a very large and I really believe a very handsome and agreeable entertainment, as least our friends flatter us by saying so. About 500 were invited; yet owing to an unlucky rain 300 only favored us by their presence." Such a big event was unusual, but guests' enjoyment was typical. And even though children didn't attend, a young neighbor mentioned years later that they were "very happy when the Lincolns entertained, as always the next morning the Lincolns' colored servant would come over to the house carrying a large tray filled with delicious things."[23]

On some other nights Abraham and Mary paid calls on friends. A young lady wrote, "We went to a euchre party at Mrs. [O. M.] Sheldon's a few days since. I[t] was very pleasant. I played at the same table that Mr. Lincoln did. He is the most amusing man I ever saw almost. He kept us laughing all the time."[24] If Abraham declined a party invitation he would tell Mary to feel free to attend, an advanced outlook in an upper-middle-class marriage. When Abraham was on his own at night, he sometimes visited merchant and banker Robert Irwin, noted as "a merry wag of a man who liked a good game of chess before the fire."[25] On some evenings Abraham attended a concert, a reading, or lecture. Mary probably came with him; presumably the boys stayed home or with friends. Other nights (perhaps Mary's sewing circle Thursdays, for example) Abraham walked downtown to the statehouse, where he "held court" and traded stories with lawyers. Billy Herndon said, "These gatherings rarely adjourned before midnight. . . . Lincoln and I would leave for our homes at the same time walking to a certain spot where our paths diverged. I recall one occasion. It was much past midnight and Lincoln was still jolly and bubbling over with the merriment and amusing incidents of the evening. . . . I believe I never saw him in happier spirits."[26]

On weekends, Abraham didn't flee the house. To the contrary. "I used to come to their house Saturdays and Sundays almost every week," the son of Ninian Wirt Edwards said. "I never saw a more loving couple. I never heard a harsh word or anything out the way. . . . She was devoted to him. Mr. Lincoln was a home man. On Sundays he was to be found here. He would go downtown for his mail, stop in at the drug store for a few minutes, and then come home to stay."[27]

Gibson Harris had routine opportunity to observe Mr. and Mrs. Lincoln. "If there was no love between them, as the world has been so persistently exhorted to believe, I must say they had a strange way of showing it, a way that hoodwinked me completely."[28] According to a Civil War telegraph operator, the president "at all times showed a most tender regard for Mrs. Lincoln."[29] "Lincoln thoroughly loved his wife," said law circuit colleague Henry Whitney. "I had many reasons to know this in my intimacy with him, and she therefore wrought a great influence over him."[30] In 1851, circuit judge David Davis reported that "Lincoln speaks very affectionately of his wife and children. He is a very warm-hearted man."[31] Mary's sister Emilie said Mary "was full of coquetry, and often patted his arm and slipped her lovely little white hand into his."[32] Abraham "petted and idolized" her, Mary herself declared.[33] During an 1855 visit to Springfield, Emilie observed "complete harmony and loving kindness between Mary and her husband, consideration for each other's wishes and . . . they seemed congenial in all things."[34] Someone who was a neighbor boy in the late 1850s declared subsequently, "Mr. Lincoln's home life was all happiness and content as far as I could ever know. He seemed to idolize his wife and boys and they one and all loved him."[35] A repeated guest at the Springfield home said, "I never saw a frown upon his brow or heard him utter a harsh or unkind word to his lady"; Abraham "seemed overflowing with geniality, good humor, and kindness."[36] Gibson Harris observed, "Mr. Lincoln showed great consideration for his wife. . . . She was unusually timid and nervous during a thunder-storm, and whenever one threatened, her husband made it a point to leave whatever he was engaged upon, if it was a possible thing, and go home, to stay with her until it passed over."[37] "So indulgent a husband—every want anticipated," Mary said.[38] Two days before the fatal evening at Ford's Theatre he sent her a note, "a few lines, playfully and tenderly worded," just one in a stack of similar correspondence.[39] A War Department telegrapher spoke of "many telegrams written by Mr. Lincoln . . . which indicated that between husband and wife there was deep affection and close confidence."[40]

Money occasionally stirred conflict, but contrary to popular opinion, in the Springfield years, Abraham encouraged spending, and Mary was the flinty one. "Stingy," said Abraham's niece Harriet Chapman.[41] "Of very saving habits," agreed Stephen Logan's son-in-law Milton Hay.[42] James Matheny, too, described Mary as no spendthrift.[43] A female relative called her "not only economical, but close."[44] A neighbor said that in the late 1840s, Mary "was very plain in her ways, and I remember that she used to go to church wearing a cheap calico dress and a sun bonnet. She didn't have silk or satin dresses."[45] By the mid-1850s, however, she wore finer apparel and slowly acquired first-rate household furnishings, but only as her husband's income grew. A biographer wrote, "Those of her associates living in Springfield in the late nineties with whom I talked, all spoke of her economies."[46] For example, she locked away the sugar bowl and made a substantial part of the family's clothes. She and a neighbor even exchanged dresses. Tradesmen had mixed experience with Mary. Sometimes she would pay an asking price immediately; other times she haggled over penny items. Mary would hire neighbor boys for little jobs but was sometimes slow to pay. Joseph Kent recalled:

> One hot summer afternoon in '58 or '59, Link Dubois and I were standing on the sidewalk in front of my father's house trying to devise some way to obtain money with which to buy watermelons or ice cream. Link (who was always resourceful) suddenly exclaimed: "Did Mrs. Lincoln ever pay you that money? . . . There comes Old Abe now, you dun him; he'll pay you." On looking up, I discovered Mr. Lincoln coming east on Market Street, going home. I remember that it required an extra prod from Link. Then I started forward and met Mr. Lincoln at Eighth and Capitol Avenue. I at once proceeded to lay my case before him. He immediately shoved his hand into his trousers pocket and produced a handful of silver coin. Handing me a twenty-five cent piece saying, "Here is a quarter for the Myers errand." Then another quarter saying, "Here is for the horse you took to Dr. Wallace," and then another quarter, saying, "This is for the interest on your money, seventy-five cents in all." Becoming suddenly rich again we were likewise happy.[47]

Occasionally Abraham's view that Mary was too frugal caused wrangling. For example, Mary once refused a servant's request for a raise. Abraham thereupon sought to overturn Mary's veto, proposing a side deal where he would fund the raise himself. Mary, however, discovered the negotiation and suddenly materialized: "What are you doing? I heard some conversation. Couldn't understand it. I'm not going to be deceived. Miss, you can leave. And as for you, Mr. Lincoln, I'd be ashamed of myself."[48] Here Abraham was interfering with Mary's household management, a realm where an upper-middle-class wife had full authority. Mary reported that Abraham "said to me always, when I asked for anything, 'You know what you want, go and get it.' He never asked me if it was necessary."[49] In context, what Abraham had attempted to do about the servant's raise was no different than if Mary somehow interjected a courtroom comment challenging a case being made by Abraham. The incident is an excellent example of how Abraham could provoke a domestic argument.

Of all the aspects to Abraham and Mary's life, children were the joy, their own youngsters and others. Even in New Salem and earlier, Abraham's acquaintances noted children's ability to beguile him. As he strolled home from his Springfield office, kids would come from every direction. A participant later said they would "gambol by his side, and as many as could get hold of him, would swing from his hands. He had a kind word and a smile for all."[50] Boys invited Abraham into their play, such as marble shooting, and pulled pranks on him, knowing that his reaction would be good natured. He enjoyed giving small presents; Freddie Dubois remembered Abraham leading a group of boys downtown to buy them candy and nuts. He would seek out particular children; a parent remembered, "Mr. Lincoln took my little Fanny on his knee, put one arm around Corwin and told them stories for half an hour. That was his way of resting."[51] Even the very youngest received Abraham's affectionate attention. A neighbor recalled, "Often he would say 'Mrs. Miner, where's the baby' and my mother would bring me to him in my long white clothes. He would take me in his arms and would hold me in such a comfortable way I would soon drop to sleep."[52] A Springfield parent said simply, "His fondness for children and their love for him were always in evidence. I think he never passed a child without a smile and a touch."[53]

Both Lincolns enjoyed having neighborhood youngsters in the house. One said of Mary, "I never knew her to be impatient with us boys, and we were at their house a great deal and no doubt deserved many scoldings. Instead of being harsh with us when we were too boisterous in her house or in her yard she would give us 'cookies' and other good things to eat and in other ways was motherly and kindly, and always had the regard of the boys."[54] Mary would read to her own children, join in their play, and set up parties. One party guest reported that "all the young people were assured a good time. Mrs. Lincoln was a charming hostess, the boys full of fun, and Mr. Lincoln the prince of entertainers."[55] Billy

Herndon remembered that when important company came to the home Mary would show off the boys, "get them to monkey around, talk, dance, speak, quote poetry, etc., etc. Then she would become enthusiastic and eloquent over the children."[56] Billy saw the same pride in Abraham, who "worshiped his children and what they worshiped; he loved what they loved and hated what they hated."[57] Mary got upset if people failed to appreciate her sons. Harriet Hanks talked of how "Lincoln took Bob, a baby, around town. When he returned he told his wife he had met [Stephen] Douglas on the street. Mrs. Lincoln asked if Douglas thought Bob was pretty, and when Mr. Lincoln said he failed to notice or ask about Bob she became very indignant."[58]

The law circuit and political travels took Abraham away from Springfield for weeks at a time, putting Mary's mothering abilities to the test. When in town, however, Abraham helped care for their children. The daughter of a state senator noted that Mary "would have him put their latest baby in its wagon and wheel it on the street until he had to go to his office. A neighbor called to him one morning: 'That is pretty business for a lawyer.' Mr. Lincoln's quiet reply was: 'I promised to give him the air; he was so tired and heated.'"[59] Neighbor girl Anna Eastman reminisced, "I can see him now, walking slowly past the house pushing a baby carriage with one hand, while in the other he held an open book which he was reading studiously!"[60]

Corporal punishment of the boys seems rare. Mary occasionally resorted to it, although she said "a gentle loving word was all sufficient with them. And if *I* have erred, it has been in being too indulgent."[61] A neighbor girl saw Abraham snap a switch off a tree or bush when irked but never saw him use it. Abraham's style of discipline was verbal, conversing with the boy about what had happened, explaining the problem and getting his son's viewpoint before taking action. Mary declared that in parenting, Abraham "was very, very indulgent to his children—chided or praised for it he always said, 'It is my pleasure that my children are free—happy and unrestrained by paternal tyranny. Love is the chain whereby to lock a child to its parent.'"[62]

To outsiders, the boys appeared uncontrolled. Someone who met Abraham at the house to discuss politics reported, "He sat with one leg thrown over the other, . . . and all the while two little boys, his sons, clambered over those legs, patted his cheeks, pulled his nose, and poked their fingers in his eyes, without causing reprimand or even notice."[63] He enjoyed his boys' rambunctiousness; a railway passenger became peeved as Abraham encouraged Robert and Eddie in shenanigans that vexed other coach travelers. In Springfield, when Abraham beckoned Mary to examine a portrait of him, she came with Tad. The artist reported, "Tad was everywhere at once, being repeatedly recaptured by his mother, and waiting but for a favorable diversion to be off again. I noticed with what interested pride [Abraham] Lincoln's eyes followed him about the room."[64]

Abraham and Mary didn't "spare the rod" to escape child-rearing responsibilities, however. Their boys had to perform chores, such as cleaning the family carriage and stabling the horse after an excursion. Mary instructed in manners; Bob learned to assist his Aunt Emilie in entering and leaving a carriage. Abraham taught honesty. A Springfield merchant's grandson said his grandfather "saw Mr. Lincoln coming along the flagstones escorting (I think) Tad, who was lugging a length of stovepipe. Mr. Lincoln was making his son return what he had 'lifted' without permission." The boy was "complaining bitterly at the heat of the way on his bare feet," and Abraham responded "firmly that the heat was nothing to what he would suffer if he went on taking what did not belong to him."[65] Abraham also taught ethics. As a political colleague watched, Abraham confronted his son Bob who had exploited younger brother Tad in a trade of candy for Tad's knife. Wilting under his father's questioning, Bob acknowledged unfairness in the transaction and returned the knife. Then, with injustice corrected and lesson learned, Abraham sent both boys off with money to buy themselves treats.

Abraham and Mary twice went through the death of a small child. Many couples break up after one such experience. That Abraham and Mary stayed together after two such tragedies indicates solid strength in their relationship.

Probably the hardest strain on their marriage was Abraham's repeated and lengthy trips around the law circuit and on political campaigning. He was gone

> 175 days in 1850
> 152 days in 1851
> 156 days in 1852
> 129 days in 1853
> 126 days in 1854
> 125 days in 1855.

Abraham noted in May 1858, "I am from home perhaps more than half my time,"[66] and that observation preceded the Lincoln-Douglas Senate election campaign. The couple's frequent separation depressed Mary. In 1859 she said to a friend, "What would I not give for a few hours' conversation with you this evening. I hope you may never feel as lonely as I sometimes do, surrounded by much that renders life desirable."[67] And, "I am generally very lonely. Miss Cochran made a little stay of two months with us." Mary hoped Cochran's presence would "render my evenings less lonely. . . . Robert leaves the first of September, and I fear I shall grow cowardly again."[68] Here we see another element of Mary's anxiety about Abraham's absence. Politician John Weber witnessed an example. "One day I heard the scream 'Murder'—'Murder'—'Murder.' Turned round, saw Mrs. Lincoln up on the fence, hands up, screaming. Went to her. She said a big ferocious man had entered her house. [I] saw an umbrella man come out. I suppose he had entered to ask for old umbrellas to mend."[69] Neighbor James Gourley thought some of her dreads were caused by imagination, but some were plausible: "When Lincoln was away from home Mrs. Lincoln had a bad [servant] girl living with her. The boys and men used to come to her house in Lincoln's absence and scare her. She [Mary] was crying and wailing one night."[70]

Significantly, when Mary wrote the 1859 letters quoted in the previous paragraph, Abraham was in town, yet she was forlorn and wanted to spend evenings with someone. As the 1850s progressed, maybe

Abraham sacrificed home life to make time for politics. Perhaps his departures seemed like the abandonment associated with her father's lengthy absences. Mary seemed to think that she was to blame if the men she loved went away, so to get them back she had to demonstrate more love for them. James Gourley reported, "She always said that if her husband had stayed at home as he ought to, that she could love him better."[71] Here I think she expressed no displeasure with Abraham; instead I see Mary wanting to improve her displays of affection for him. "Mary fairly worshiped him," her sister Frances proclaimed.[72] Sister Emilie agreed: "Oh, how she did love this man!"[73]

The couple's quarrels became notorious; but I believe the arguments' frequency and intensity are exaggerated. For example, as the Lincolns got ready for a party that Abraham desired to avoid, Mary's dress was laid out on a chair. A visitor appeared, and Abraham facetiously suggested that the visitor sit on the dress and wrinkle it so Mary would want to stay home. I suspect that in other instances such playful ideas were consummated in pranks on Mary, sometimes with help from the boys. When goaded she responded strongly but within reason. Flare-ups were brief and didn't seem to disturb Abraham. James Gourley remembered, "At first he would apparently pay no attention to her. Frequently he would laugh at her, which is a risky thing to do in the face of an infuriated wife."[74] A story tells of Abraham fleeing the house as Mary hurled potatoes at him. Springfield residents said she could become so tempestuous that Abraham would grab one of the boys, and the two would go away until the storm blew itself off. A casual Washington acquaintance noted, "The clouds would not last long with her, and she would soon be laughing as heartily as ever."[75] A Springfield visitor told of typical horseplay, an election night incident in November 1860: "Mr. Lincoln was in fine spirits. He told us he thought he had a good joke on his wife. Pointing to Mrs. Lincoln he said, 'She locked me out.' Mrs. Lincoln said to him: 'Don't ever tell that again.' But Mr. Lincoln laughed and went on with the story. He said Mrs. Lincoln had said when he went downtown in the evening to hear the returns that if he wasn't at home by 10 o'clock she would lock him out. And she did so. But, Mr. Lincoln said that when she heard the music coming to serenade them she turned the key in a hurry."[76]

Two unlikely stories portray Mary as making life-threatening attacks on her husband. Margaret Ryan claimed to have been a live-in servant and asserted that Mary got angry once when Abraham didn't freshen the south parlor fire fast enough to suit her, and Mary struck him on the face with firewood, cutting his nose. Only a psychopath would club someone on such trivial grounds. Margaret Ryan asserted she witnessed the incident, but didn't explain why the muscular Abraham sat meekly instead of snatching the club away.

Margaret appears to have been an imposter. Census records and family correspondence fail to confirm her presence in the Lincoln household. Jesse Weik, who had much to do with spreading her story, also wrote about the Lincoln household's servant wages, based on testimony from Ryan. In print, however, Weik indicated that his material about wages came from Mary Johnson and Mariah Vance, domestic workers whose presence in the Lincoln household is unquestioned. Such adjustment of sources suggests that Weik knew that Ryan's credibility was shaky. And in *The Real Lincoln*, Weik stated Ryan "claimed in her girlhood days to have lived as a servant in the Lincoln household,"[77] the word "claimed" indicating doubt about her testimony. Ryan also told of meeting President Lincoln on April 14, 1865. In Weik's words, "He was glad to see her, gave her a basket of fruit, and directed her to call the next day and obtain a pass through the lines and money to buy clothes for herself and children."[78] The nearly minute-by-minute chronology of Lincoln's last hours gives no support to Ryan's implausible White House tale.

Another well-known story about Mary Lincoln's making a life-threatening attack on Abraham says he fled from her in the backyard as she followed, brandishing a butcher knife.[79] Herndon explicitly told Weik that Mary had "a butcher knife in her hand." But Herndon's memorandum of his interview with Stephen Whitehurst, an eyewitness who originated the story, says "a table knife or a butcher knife." Two aspects indicate Mary brandished the less ominous object. First, Whitehurst states that another witness thought the Lincolns were engaged in "sport or fun." Second, Whitehurst saw Abraham nab Mary, whap her buttocks, and rush her back inside the house while admonishing her to behave. Nothing was said about disarming her, a silence implying she was carrying nothing dangerous. Herndon's dislike of Mary could have motivated the negative slant in his report to Weik, but Whitehurst's motive for embarrassing Abraham is lesser known.

Whitehurst edited the *Springfield Conservative* during the 1856 Buchanan–Frémont–Fillmore presidential election. Supposedly, the proslavery newspaper was a Fillmore organ, but actually it was run by Buchanan backers, allowing them to hit Frémont and the Republicans with arguments that Democrats couldn't use openly. Herndon, in language shaped by ghostwriter Weik, revealed Lincoln's counterattack. "One day I read in the *Richmond Enquirer* an article endorsing slavery, and arguing that from principle the enslavement of either whites or blacks was justifiable and right. I showed it to Lincoln, who remarked that it was 'rather rank doctrine for Northern Democrats to endorse. I should like to see,' he said, with emphasis, 'some of these Illinois [Democratic] newspapers champion that.'" Such an improbable occurrence would hand a golden issue to the Republicans. Herndon suggested that he give the *Enquirer* piece to Whitehurst, who might well print it as a slavery defense without noticing that it provided an opening for enslaving whites. Lincoln

> laughed and said, "Go in." I cut the slip out and succeeded in getting it in the paper named [Whitehurst's]. Of course it was a trick, but it acted admirably. Its appearance in the new organ [*Springfield Conservative*], although without comment, almost ruined that valuable journal, and my good-natured friend the editor was nearly overcome by the denunciation of those who were responsible for the organ's existence. My connection, and Lincoln's too, . . . was eventually discovered. . . . The antislavery people quoted the article as having been endorsed by a Democratic newspaper

in Springfield, and Lincoln himself used it with telling effect. He joined in the popular denunciation, expressing great astonishment that such a sentiment could find lodgment in any paper in Illinois, although he knew full well how the whole thing had been carried through.

Privately, Herndon was blunter.

> Lincoln told me that John T. Stuart, [James] Matheny, and the leading Fillmore men in this section were bribed by the Buchanan corruption fund, said that he believed that the Fillmore party, i.e., leaders of it through the state, were bought and sold like hogs are sold in the market. That induced me to kill the *Conservative* published here. I had two ideas in getting in the *Richmond Enquirer* article: first, I wanted it published in the *Conservative* so as to show the rank and file of the Fillmore boys the course they were expected to move, vote, and act, and in the end shout for slavery; and, in the second place, I wanted to kill the *Conservative* out and out. It did soon die, possibly for want of funds or because of the *Richmond Enquirer* piece.[80]

A final twist is that Whitehurst and James Matheny were brothers-in-law, and Matheny was one of the two persons (the other being Herndon) who urged Weik to interview Margaret Ryan.

Two other accounts of hostile physical contact between the Lincolns in the Springfield years are too credible to dismiss. Billy Herndon reported that he arrived for work one Monday morning and found a sorrowful Abraham already in the office, having left home at daybreak. When Mary had been badgering him the previous morning; he lost patience and shoved her toward the door with the declaration, "You make the house intolerable, damn you, get out of it!" He had never touched Mary in anger before. Abraham was shocked at his loss of self-control and by the possibility that his performance had been observed by persons on the sidewalk.[81] His remorse was understandable, but the incident may have been unique. In the other incident, Abraham's friend and political ally Jesse Dubois said that he crossed paths with Abraham as Lincoln was taking a purchase of meat home. Together the two proceeded to Lincoln's house where Abraham delivered the food. According to notes of Jesse Weik's interview with Dubois, "Upon opening the paper of meat she became enraged at the kind Lincoln had bought. She abused Lincoln outrageously, and finally was so mad she struck him in the face," drawing blood. After Abraham cleaned his face, the two men departed the house.[82] Such a performance by Mary in front of a third party raises questions about possible worse conduct in private.

I cannot disbelieve that these two incidents occurred, but surely they were rare exceptions to the predominant evidence describing pleasant home life. I am especially impressed by unanimous testimony from neighborhood youngsters, describing the Lincoln home as having a warm and welcoming atmosphere with so much fun that children enjoyed hanging around there. Kids don't seek out a place exuding strife and *angst*. If life at Eighth and Jackson had been as unpleasant as some adults assumed it to be, neighborhood children would have avoided the place. Instead they thronged to it.

The closer someone resided to the Lincoln home, the more agreeable it seemed. Reverend Noyes Miner described Abraham as "a delightful neighbor. Always kind, obliging, affable."[83] "I lived next-door neighbor to Lincoln nineteen years," James Gourley said. "I don't think that Mrs. Lincoln was as bad a woman as she is represented."[84] Looking backward years later, neighbor Julia Sprigg suspected that female gossip on the topic was motivated by jealousy. An occasional storm may occur in the fairest climate, but reports of a glowering atmosphere at Eighth and Jackson originate mostly, and perhaps entirely, in hearsay (rather than firsthand observations) from gossipers possessing grudges against Abraham or Mary or both. After April 1865, attacking the martyred leader of the Union was impossible; but he could be assaulted through his wife, who had already received much unfavorable publicity during the White House years and was an open target. Many contemporaries who portrayed the Springfield home life as a hell were using a rhetorical trick, as in "I shall not mention my opponent's criminal record." On the surface, their portrayal of a saint as vexed by a demon was inspirational, but the saint's decision to live with a tormenting demon raised subliminal questions about his judgment. That is why stories of a troubled home were welcomed and publicized. And after that gossiping generation passed from the scene, their reports remained behind, were easily accessible, and seemed to come from reliable authorities whose inaccurate claims sounded plausible.

Incorrect assertions of continual misery at Eighth and Jackson have persisted. Correcting those errors is a task still underway but is already producing a pleasing portrait of the Springfield life enjoyed by Abraham and Mary Lincoln.

### Notes

Quotations from nineteenth-century sources are silently modernized in spelling and punctuation.

1. William H. Herndon (hereafter WHH), "Analysis of the Character of Abraham Lincoln," *Abraham Lincoln Quarterly* 1 (September 1941): 359–60.

2. Harriet Chapman, December 10, 1866, Douglas L. Wilson and Rodney O. Davis, eds., *Herndon's Informants: Letters, Interviews, and Statements about Abraham Lincoln* (Urbana: University of Illinois Press, 1998) 512. See also Chapman interview with J. Weik, c. 1886, 646.

3. WHH to I. Arnold, October 24, 1883, printed in WHH, *A Letter from Wm. H. Herndon to Isaac N. Arnold Relating to Abraham Lincoln, His Wife, and Their Life in Springfield* (privately printed 1937; reprinted Chicago and Springfield: R. R. Donnelley and Sons, and Frye, n.d.), n.p.; Jesse W. Weik, *The Real Lincoln: A Portrait* (Boston: Houghton Mifflin, 1922), 206–9; *Illinois State Register*, June 14, 1849; William Walker in Osborn Hamiline Oldroyd, *The Lincoln Memorial: Album of Immortelles*, nonsubscription ed. (New York: G. W. Carleton, 1882), 213.

4. *Utica (NY) Morning Herald*, June 27, 1860, clipped in *New York Semi-Weekly Tribune*, July 6, 1860, Louis A. Warren, "An Evening with Lincoln," *Lincoln Lore*, no. 845 (June 18, 1945); Kenneth Scott, "Lincoln's Home in 1860," *Journal of the Illinois State Historical Society* 46 (1953): 10; Rufus Rockwell Wilson, "An Editor Measures Candidate Lincoln," *Lincoln Herald* 46 (February 1944), 26–27.

5. Scott, "Lincoln's," 10.

6. WHH, "Lincoln's Domestic Life" (including Stuart's remarks), Douglas L. Wilson, "William H. Herndon and Mary Todd Lincoln," *Journal of the Abraham Lincoln Association* 22 (2001): 6. See also Stuart, July 21, 1865, Wilson and Davis, *Herndon's Informants*, 77.

7. Harriet Chapman, December 10, 1866, Wilson and Davis, *Herndon's Informants*, 512. See also Chapman interview with J. Weik, c. 1886, Wilson and Davis, *Herndon's Informants*, 646.

8. O. J. Hollister, *Life of Schuyler Colfax* (New York: Funk and Wagnalls, 1887), 27.

9. Chapman to WHH, December 10, 1866, Wilson and Davis, *Herndon's Informants*, 512.

10. Quotations in Katherine Helm, *The True Story of Mary, Wife of Lincoln* (New York: Harper and Brothers 1928), 116. See also 479 and W. A. Evans, *Mrs. Abraham Lincoln: A Study of Her Personality and Her Influence on Lincoln* (New York: Alfred A. Knopf, 1932), 152.

11. Harriet Chapman, December 10, 1866, Wilson and Davis, *Herndon's Informants*, 512. See also Chapman interview with J. Weik, c. 1886, Wilson and Davis, *Herndon's Informants*, 646.

12. Weik, *Real*, 120. See also Gourley in Henry Clay Whitney, *Life on the Circuit with Lincoln* (Boston, 1892; reprinted Caldwell, ID: Caxton, 1940), 48.

13. Harriet Chapman, December 10, 1866, Wilson and Davis, *Herndon's Informants*, 512. See also Chapman interview with J. Weik, c. 1886, Wilson and Davis, *Herndon's Informants*, 646.

14. Todd to Ninian Wirt Edwards, December 1844, Walter Barlow Stevens, *A Reporter's Lincoln* (St. Louis: Missouri Historical Society, 1916), 79.

15. Emilie Todd Helm, Helm, *True*, 110.

16. Frances Todd Wallace, c. 1865, *Herndon's Informants*, 485–86.

17. Gibson William Harris, "My Recollections of Abraham Lincoln," *Farm and Fireside* December 1, 1904, 23.

18. Isaac N. Arnold, *The Life of Abraham Lincoln* (Chicago: A. C. McClurg, 1884; reprinted 4th ed. Lincoln: University of Nebraska Press: Bison, 1994), 82–83. See also Isaac N. Arnold, *Reminiscences of the Illinois Bar Forty Years Ago: Lincoln and Douglas as Orators and Lawyers*, Fergus Historical Series no. 14. (Chicago: Fergus, 1881), 137–38.

19. Blades, "Recollections," in Paul M. Angle, *Abraham Lincoln by Some Men Who Knew Him* (Freeport, NY: Books for Libraries, 1969. Essay Index Reprint Series), 79.

20. Browning diary, February 5, 1857, "Lincoln before a New York Audience," *Journal of the Illinois State Historical Society* 49 (1956): 215n3.

21. W. Bailhache to J. Bailhache, February 6, 1857, "Lincoln before a New," 215n3.

22. February 16, 1857.

23. Memoirs, 1, Mary Miner Hill Papers, Small Collection 1985, Abraham Lincoln Presidential Library (hereafter ALPL).

24. Mary Hedges Hubbard to E. Hubbard, August 28, 1859, "Lincoln Played Euchre," *Journal of the Illinois State Historical Society* 48 (1955): 202.

25. Octavia Roberts, *Lincoln in Illinois* (Boston: Houghton Mifflin, 1918), 47.

26. WHH, Weik, *Real*, 207–8. P. Enos (c. 1865, Wilson and Davis, *Herndon's Informants*, 449) tells of an instance when Lincoln stayed out all night.

27. Albert Stevenson Edwards, Stevens, *Reporter's*, 79.

28. Harris, "My Recollections," December 1, 1904, 23.

29. David Homer Bates, *Lincoln in the Telegraph Office: Recollections of the United States Military Telegraph Corps during the Civil War* (New York: Century, 1907), 208.

30. Whitney, *Life*, 111.

31. D. Davis to Sarah Davis, November 3, 1851, Davis Papers.

32. Emilie Todd Helm, Helm, *True*, 109.

33. Mary Todd Lincoln to E. Keckley, November 15, 1867, Justin G. Turner and Linda Levitt Turner, eds., *Mary Todd Lincoln: Her Life and Letters* (New York: Knopf, 1972).

34. Emilie Todd Helm, Helm, *True*, 113. See also 479 and E. Helm, Evans, *Mrs.*, 151–52.

35. J. Kent, Rufus Rockwell Wilson, ed., *Intimate Memories of Lincoln* (Elmira: Primavera, 1945), 138.

36. Smith to WHH, January 24, 1867, Wilson and Davis, *Herndon's Informants*, 549.

37. Harris, "My Recollections," December 1, 1904, 23. See also G. Harris as given in Edward J. Kempf, *Abraham Lincoln's Philosophy of Common Sense: An Analytical Biography of a Great Mind*, Special Publications of the New York Academy of Sciences (New York: Academy, 1965), 6:400.

38. Mary Todd Lincoln to J. Forney, June 27, 1868, Turner and Turner, *Mary*.

39. Mary Todd Lincoln to M. Welles, July 11, 1865, Turner and Turner, *Mary*.

40. Bates, *Lincoln*, 208.

41. Chapman to WHH, December 10, 1866, Wilson and Davis, *Herndon's Informants*, 512.

42. Weik, *Real*, 91; Wilson and Davis, *Herndon's Informants*, 729.

43. Weik, *Real*, 91; Wilson and Davis, *Herndon's Informants*, 729.

44. Weik, *Real*, 94.

45. *Illinois State Journal*, February 12, 1895; John E. Washington, *They Knew Lincoln* (New York: E. P. Dutton, 1942), 243.

46. Ida M. Tarbell, *In the Footsteps of the Lincolns* (New York: Harper and Brothers, 1924), 254–55.

47. Joseph Kent, *Illinois State Journal*, January 9, 1909; Wilson, *Intimate*, 137–38; variant in Weik, *Real*, 123–24.

48. Elizabeth Todd Edwards, c. 1866, Williams and Davis, *Herndon's Informants*, 445.

49. "Lincoln. What Mrs. Lincoln Said to Mr. Herndon," in WHH to *St. Louis Democrat*, January 12, 1874, printed in clipping, *Abraham Lincoln Scrapbook*, 63 (ALPL). This is a polished version from WHH's interview with Mary Lincoln c. September 1866 in Wilson and Davis, *Herndon's Informants*, 357, 359.

50. Charles B. Strozier, *Lincoln's Quest Union: Public and Private Meanings* (New York: Basic, 1982), 124.

51. Jane Martin Johns, *Personal Recollections of Early Decatur, Abraham Lincoln, Richard J. Oglesby, and the Civil War*, Howard C. Schaub, ed. (Decatur: Decatur Chapter Daughters of the American Revolution, 1912), 67.

52. Memoirs, 1–2, Mary Miner Hill Papers SC 1985, ALPL.

53. Johns, *Personal*, 67.

54. Fred T. Dubois, "Another Boy's Memories of the Lincolns," *New York Tribune*, February 12, 1927, reprinted in Rufus Rockwell Wilson, ed., *Lincoln among His Friends: A Sheaf of Intimate Memories* (Caldwell, ID: Caxton, 1942), 99. See also comment about Willie Arthur in "Lincoln and the Children," *Lincoln Lore*, no. 22 (September 9, 1929).

55. T. Vredenburgh to J. Van Cleave, July 7, 1908, Lincoln Centennial Association Papers (ALPL).

56. WHH to J. Weik, January 8, 1886, Emanuel Hertz, ed., *The Hidden Lincoln: From the Letters and Papers of William H. Herndon* (Viking, 1938; reprinted New York: Blue Ribbon, 1940), 128.

57. WHH to J. Weik, January 8, 1886, February 18, 1887, Hertz, *Hidden*, 128–29, 177.

58. Harriet Chapman interview with J. Weik, October 16, 1914, Jesse W. Weik Papers, ALPL.

59. Elizabeth Allen Bradner, Wilson, *Intimate*, 122. See also Strozier, *Lincoln's*, 125; Stevens, *Reporter's*, 60.

60. A. Longfellow Fiske interview of Anna Eastman Johnson, Wilson, *Intimate*, 134. See also Josiah G. Holland, *The Life of Abraham Lincoln* (Springfield, MA: Gurdon Bill, 1866), 125.

61. Mary Todd Lincoln to Alexander Williamson, June 15, 1865, Turner and Turner, *Mary*, 250–51.

62. September 1866, Wilson and Davis, *Herndon's Informants*, 357. See also 359.

63. Donn Piatt, *Memories of the Men Who Saved the Union* (New York: Belford, Clark, 1887), 29.

64. Alban Jasper Conant, "A Portrait Painter's Reminiscences of Lincoln," *McClure's* 32 (1909): 515. See also R. Gerald McMurtry, "Alban Jasper Conant's 'Smiling Lincoln,'" *Lincoln Lore*, no. 1472 (October 1960).

65. H. Boynton letter, February 20, 1948, Milton H. Shutes, *Lincoln's Emotional Life* (Philadelphia: Dorrance, 1957), 102.

66. Lincoln to S. Caldwell, May 27, 1858, *Collected Works*, 11:14–15.

67. Mary Todd Lincoln to H. Shearer, June 26, 1859, Turner and Turner, *Mary*, 56–57.

68. Mary Todd Lincoln to H. Shearer, July 10, 1859, Thomas F. Schwartz and Kim M. Bauer, "Unpublished Mary Todd Lincoln," *Journal of the Abraham Lincoln Association* 17 (Summer 1996): 2.

69. C. November. 1, 1866, Wilson and Davis, *Herndon's Informants*, 389–90.

70. C. 1865, Wilson and Davis, *Herndon's Informants*, 452. See also Gourley in Weik, *Real*, 121.

71. C. 1865, Wilson and Davis, *Herndon's Informants*, 453. Variant in Weik, *Real*, 122.

72. Quoted in Helm, *True*, 113.

73. Emilie Todd Helm, Helm, *True*, 111.

74. Quoted in Weik, *Real*, 121. Variant in interview with WHH, c. 1865, Wilson and Davis, *Herndon's Informants*, 453.

75. Howard Glyndon [pseud. for Laura Catherine Searing], "The Truth about Mrs. Lincoln," *The Independent*, August. 10, 1882.

76. Mrs. Bradner, Stevens, *Reporter's*, 60.

77. Weik, *Real*, 100.

78. William H. Herndon and Jesse W. Weik, *Herndon's Life of Lincoln* (1942; reprinted New York: Da Capo, 1983), 346. See also Margaret Ryan interview with Weik, October 27, 1886, Wilson and Davis, *Herndon's Informants*, 597.

79. Stephen Whitehurst, c. 1885, Wilson and Davis, *Herndon's Informants*, 722–23; WHH to J. Weik, January 23, 1886, Hertz, *Hidden*, 140–41.

80. Herndon and Weik, *Herndon's*, 297–98; WHH to Weik, January 11, 23, 1889, February 21, 1891, Hertz, *Hidden*, 235, 239, 264.

81. William E. Barton, *The Women Lincoln Loved* (Indianapolis: Bobbs-Merrill, 1927), 290–91; Carl Sandburg and Paul M. Angle, *Mary Lincoln: Wife and Widow* (1932; reprinted New York: Harcourt, Brace and World, 1960), 70–71.

82. Dubois, c. 1883, Wilson and Davis, *Herndon's Informants*, 692.

83. N. W. Miner, "Personal Recollections of Abraham Lincoln," 9–10, N. W. Miner Papers, Small Collection 1052, ALPL.

84. C. 1865, Wilson and Davis, *Herndon's Informants*, 452–53.

## "An Unladylike Profession"
### Mary Lincoln's Preparation for Greatness

*Kenneth J. Winkle*

One of the essential and most compelling themes in Abraham Lincoln biography is his slow but steady rise in life from unpromising beginnings to surprising success as a lawyer and politician and unexcelled greatness as president. Biographers and historians have written hundreds of books and articles exploring a kaleidoscopic assortment of facets in Lincoln's character and early life that either facilitated or threatened his rise from obscurity as a youth to eminence as a statesman. Factors that have received scrutiny and credit for his improbable rise include his conspicuous native intelligence, his dedicated determination to improve himself through diligent self-education, his lifelong immersion in reading and writing that culminated in his renowned rhetorical eloquence, his judicious engagement with slavery and cogent articulation of a workable yet principled approach to ending it, his choice of a marriage partner and consequent in-laws, and even the very adversities that he had to overcome, such as his legendary melancholy and even his obsession with death.[1]

Among the most constructive contributions, Paul Simon's *Lincoln's Preparation for Greatness* is exemplary in its focus on a specific learning and character-shaping experience in Lincoln's early development that would not have distinguished him had it ended there but provided an immense boost on his journey toward national prominence. "Lincoln's contribution to state government was not particularly significant," Simon concluded. But "what he received from the Illinois House of Representatives was right for the times and right for the man. The experience was his first step toward the Presidency; it was a big step and a long step." Despite his unexceptional legislative career, Lincoln learned a lot, learned the right lessons, and grew significantly, as he did from every personal, professional, and political opportunity or setback during his lifetime.[2]

Lincoln biographers have traditionally portrayed Mary Lincoln as an appurtenance to her husband's personal life and professional career and have therefore approached her as primarily an asset or a liability to his development and success, based primarily on her positive or negative impact on his "preparation for greatness." This almost pervasive biographical perspective recognizes, quite appropriately, the all-too-real and deep-seated Victorian insistence on a "separate sphere" for women that was ancillary to the public careers and private activities of men, as well as their commonly conceived "domestic duty" to rear children and keep house while satisfying their own ambitions through the achievements of their husbands and sons.[3] But this biographical convention also flows imperceptibly from the debate that raged during Mary Lincoln's lifetime over her character, if not competence, as a wife and mother in the Lincoln home, her controversial role as First Lady during her husband's presidency, and her comportment and indeed sanity during her decade and a half of widowhood. Many of Abraham Lincoln's earliest biographers knew the couple, betrayed their biases, and literally took sides, typically to Mary Lincoln's lasting detriment. All too often, both Abraham Lincoln and Mary Lincoln biographers have been taking sides ever since.

The portrayal of Mary Lincoln as a negative influence in her husband's life began with his former law partner, William Herndon. In the wake of the apotheosis that followed Lincoln's assassination, Herndon delivered a series of lectures in Springfield in 1865 and 1866 presenting what he considered "a good understanding of Mr. Lincoln's life." While praising Lincoln's public character, conduct, and accomplishments, Herndon nevertheless portrayed him as gloomy, pessimistic, and—through a life-long religious skepticism—fatalistic in his private moments. Herndon's fourth, final, and by far most famous lecture identified Lincoln's relationship with Ann Rutledge as an important source of his purported melancholy. Arguing that "Abraham Lincoln loved Ann Rutledge with all his soul, mind and strength," Herndon concluded that after her death he never truly loved another woman, including his wife. Overall, he portrayed the couple's marriage as stormy, dysfunctional, and, on Abraham Lincoln's part, loveless. Herndon's influence on this resilient negative image of Mary Lincoln drew its subsequent force and longevity not only from his personal knowledge of the couple but more so through his decades-long effort to compile supporting evidence. After Lincoln's death, Herndon implemented a remarkable plan to interview and correspond with others who knew the Lincolns in Kentucky, Indiana, Illinois, and Washington, DC, what he termed "the memories of men, women and children all over this broad land." In the process, he devised what can best be characterized as one of the first oral history projects ever undertaken in American history.[4]

Within a mere eighteen months, the number of his respondents who wrote letters or sat for interviews reached more than four hundred. Their reminiscences, most of which Herndon recorded personally in his idiosyncratic shorthand, still represent the single most important source of knowledge we have about the Lincolns' personal relationship. Not only did Herndon disparage Mary Lincoln's influence in both his lectures and his subsequent biography, but he also compiled a cache of evidence that is indispensable to any meticulous biographer yet is mostly negative in tone. In short, much of what we know about the Lincolns' personal lives, particularly during the period preceding the presidency, originates with Herndon and his collection of letters and interviews. Many scholars suspect that Herndon, who was an experienced trial attorney, biased the tone of the reminiscences by consciously or unconsciously eliciting negative recollections or recording those more fully than the positive ones. After reading Herndon's fourth lecture, Mary Lincoln herself characterized

Herndon as her husband's "crazy drinking law partner," a "renowned scamp & humbug," and even a "dirty dog." Herndon retaliated by labeling Lincoln's widow a "she-wolf," a "wild cat," and a "liar."[5]

At any rate, many other reminiscences, both published and unpublished, contain evidence enough to support both favorable and unfavorable portraits of Mary Lincoln. Biographers can cherry-pick anecdotes and reflections aplenty to justify their opinions, which all too often come preconceived. As biographer Jean Baker so aptly put it, "we have too many historians deciding that they don't like Mary Lincoln and with extraordinary vehemence extrapolating their personal judgments onto the marriage."[6] On the other hand, there are now more than enough reminiscences to go around, and sympathetic biographers can just as readily privilege the good over the bad, if so inclined. Any conscientious biographer, of course, will sift, weigh, and corroborate evidence from both sides of the story before rendering an informed judgment. At the risk of oversimplification, however, even a fair-minded biographer who depends too heavily on reminiscence will tend to evaluate Mary Lincoln's life as the sum total of her positive contributions minus her negative influences, as viewed within the context of her husband's life, both public and private, and especially his political career. An apt example is the oft-repeated charge that she consistently overstepped her bounds by meddling in the political affairs of her husband and, as First Lady, the nation. A mere sampling of reminiscences regarding her political instincts and endeavors turns up the observations that she possessed a "natural want of tact," a "deficiency in the sense of the fitness of things," a "blundering outspokenness," and an "impolitic disregard of diplomatic considerations." In his biography, Herndon himself wrote, "She not only had a quick intellect but an intuitive judgment of men and their motives." But "when offended or antagonized, her agreeable qualities disappeared beneath a wave of stinging satire and sarcastic bitterness." A Union general concluded that during his presidency, Lincoln's wife caused him "incredible embarrassments in the discharge of his public duties." In the White House, she clashed with her husband's private secretaries, who took to labeling her "the hellcat," "the enemy," and even "Her Satanic Majesty."[7]

Even her biographers have never thoroughly explored the sources of the political interest, acumen, and admittedly brazen outspokenness that contrasted so starkly with contemporary conventions and the comportment of her peers. The "he said, she said" of dueling reminiscences is a diverting but ultimately fruitless exercise that inhibits a thoroughgoing historical comprehension of this couple's marriage and the society and culture that they inhabited. Further, we need to contextualize not only Mary Lincoln's character and demeanor but her specific actions during specific periods of her life if we are to understand the motivations that underlay the outward behavior of this enigmatic woman. The biography that almost single-handedly revolutionized our modern conception of Mary Lincoln through its insistence on documentary rigor, scholarly circumspection, and historical contextualization was Ruth Painter Randall's *Mary Lincoln: Biography of a Marriage*.[8] Yet, even its title, with its emphasis on evaluating its subject as one-half of a marriage, constricts our focus to begin with and thereby limits our likely conclusions. The rigid gender roles that circumscribed middle-class women's lives during the mid-nineteenth century, above all their fundamental emphasis upon marriage and family, make it difficult to imagine approaching Mary Lincoln's life (as well as those of most of her contemporaries) from any other perspective. In an effort to understand her renowned and rare political ambition and outspokenness, however, we can try imagining that Mary Lincoln underwent a "preparation for greatness" of her own, and of her own making, which was lifelong, preceded her marriage, and succeeded it, as well.

Our first question might ask whether a woman in Mary Lincoln's social and cultural situation would even dream of "preparing for greatness" within the realm of politics, during an age when women could not vote or aspire to office and were even discouraged from forming political opinions. Antebellum social and cultural strictures, particularly within the South, strongly discouraged any notion of political involvement among women. Their political role was meant at most to be indirect, exerted through their salutary civic influence as wives and mothers on their husbands and sons.[9] Despite the restrictive gender boundaries that hindered most women from engaging in or even commenting on public affairs and especially partisan politics, the young Mary Todd received a thorough socialization into the maelstrom of discussion and discourse that lay at the heart of the principles and organization that was developing into the Whig Party. In fact, her father, Robert Todd, encouraged his daughter to pursue an active and outspoken interest in politics. Simply put, with her father's blessing she imbibed his passion for politics and developed an avid, informed, and outspoken partisan enthusiasm all her own. This lifelong personal engagement in politics was one of the most important legacies of the childhood that she spent in this otherwise dysfunctional family, which she labeled "desolate" upon later self-reflection.[10]

The Todds were a prominent, wealthy, slave-owning family, who helped to found Lexington, Kentucky. Through political and military leadership, land speculation, slave-owning, and community service, the Todds prospered, and an extended family of forty Todds eventually dominated the social and political life of the Bluegrass Country. Lexington's leading families valued education and founded Transylvania University, the first university west of the Alleghenies, along with a law school, a medical school, and a host of girls' and boys' academies. As Kentucky's largest town and its cultural capital, Lexington earned its reputation as the "Athens of the West." Mary Lincoln's father was born into Lexington's second generation and attended Transylvania University, which his own family had helped to establish (they donated over $5,000) near their home in the center of the town. He studied law and was admitted to the bar but, as practical pursuits, preferred banking, commerce, and land speculation. More important in shaping his daughter's development, he devoted himself to politics and became a prominent Whig. Robert Todd enjoyed a long and successful career in the state legislature, serving successively as clerk of the House of Representatives, assemblyman in the House for three terms, and then state senator for another three. In Lexington, he was councilman, magistrate, and sheriff. He felt at ease in the headiest political, financial, and legal circles in Kentucky, associating with the likes of Henry Clay, John Crittenden, and distant relative John Breckenridge, eventually key figures in the sectional crisis and the Civil War.[11]

Establishing a tradition of dynastic marriages that his descendants would pursue in both Lexington, Kentucky, and Springfield, Illinois, Robert Todd married a second cousin, Eliza Parker, daughter of another of Lexington's original founding families. Between 1812 and 1825, Eliza Parker Todd bore seven children, including Mary Todd. When Eliza Todd died in 1825, Robert Todd remarried within a year and a half. His new wife, Elizabeth Humphreys, went on to bear nine children in the succeeding fifteen years. In all, Robert Todd fathered sixteen children, emerging in the process as the patriarch of one of the most distinguished, and certainly extensive, families in Kentucky. The Parker family, however, never forgave Todd for his overhasty remarriage, and a breach developed between Eliza Todd's and Betsey Todd's children. Biographers' focus on this estrangement, which later abetted a division in the family between the Union and the Confederacy, has obscured an essential element in Mary Todd's upbringing that held implications of equal import.[12]

We can never know Robert Todd's motives in transgressing prohibitions on feminine political involvement, beyond his undoubted interest in raising a daughter who might make a favorable dynastic match, socially, economically, and politically. Still, historians have begun arguing that women played a unique and perhaps essential role within the Whig Party in the early years of its formation. Focusing on the Upper South, specifically Virginia, historian Elizabeth Varon has compared early Whigs' and Democrats' attitudes not only toward women but families more generally. "Although the Democrats sought to maintain a strict boundary between the private and public spheres and resented attempts to politicize domestic life," she concludes, "the Whigs invested the family—and women in particular—with the distinct political function of forming the stable American character on which national well-being depended." These early Whigs' investment of family life with political resonance and the corresponding politicization of female virtue began with the election of 1828, during which John Quincy Adams's supporters pushed the morality of Democratic candidate Andrew Jackson's complex relationship with his wife, Rachel, to the fore as a campaign issue. In short, the attacks on Jackson blurred the distinction between public and private, opening not only the candidate's public character but his private virtue—and that of his family, as well—to political scrutiny. In modern parlance, after 1828, a presidential candidate's (and a president's) private life would increasingly become "fair game." (Mary Lincoln would ironically suffer more from this new merging of public and private identities than any other First Lady in American history.) As their party coalesced, Whigs developed what Varon labels a doctrine of "female civic duty," under which female purity served political purposes by ensuring, or at least symbolizing, the integrity of specific male candidates as well as party principles in general. "Over the course of the antebellum period," she argues, "the doctrine of separate spheres came to coexist with a countervailing conception of female civic duty."[13]

Beginning in the late 1820s and persisting until the rise of the Republican Party, Whig Party doctrine encouraged the idea of "Whig womanhood" as a counterweight to the "separate spheres" ideology that proscribed women from the political arena. While not yet even dreaming of the right to vote or hold office, "Whig women" could play an important symbolic role in political contests by testifying to the virtue of their party's candidates and their programs. Achieving even limited visibility in a relatively minor public political role—literally "parading" their virtue during election campaigns—represented a considerable step forward for women who had spent the postrevolutionary generation supporting their husbands in private while mothering their sons from infancy into future political actors. Ten years old in 1828, Mary Todd's apprenticeship into politics at the feet of her father would have coincided with the first articulation of the new doctrine of Whig womanhood.[14]

Whig women's new visibility on the public political stage built on a tradition of involvement in benevolent reform movements that stretched their private realms of home and family into the public sphere, and this was also true of the Todds. Historians have understated the extent of the Todd family's involvement in the postrevolutionary antislavery reform movement, and particularly the Todd women's contributions. Before the sectional crisis stifled public dissent on the subject, the Todds were surprisingly thoughtful and persistent critics of slavery. In 1777, while serving in the Virginia legislature, Mary Todd's uncle John advocated the elimination of slavery in Kentucky County. Later, when Kentucky entered the Union, members of her stepmother's family proposed prohibiting slavery in the new state. Mary Todd's two maternal grandmothers set a considerable example by freeing their own slaves upon their deaths, in 1836 and 1850. Lexington also boasted the Kentucky Colonization Society, which Robert Todd supported, and in 1833, the state banned the importation of any additional slaves, legislation that received his vote and his daughter's vocal support. When he ran for the Kentucky Senate in 1840, Democrats labeled him the "Emancipation Candidate." He admitted that he was "ever in favor of the Act of 1833, prohibiting the importation of slaves into the Commonwealth," but denied supporting emancipation itself. Sounding quite like the Great Compromiser Henry Clay and even his son-in-law, Abraham Lincoln, Todd labeled emancipation "an impracticable question and particularly so, in the absence of an unanimity which is indispensable to its success." The Todds as a whole were so involved in Kentucky's ephemeral antislavery movement that historian Jean Baker has labeled them "a mostly antislavery family in a slave state."[15]

In short, Mary Todd hailed from about as extreme a reform tradition as we might expect to find in antebellum Kentucky. As biographer Jennifer Fleischner has observed, "All of the Todd children grew up listening to their father and his dinner guests exchanging news and opinions about the vexing questions of the day." In addition to all that she learned at home, Mary Todd obtained a first-rate education at the finest schools in

Lexington, which intentionally or otherwise provided her the intellectual skills to engage in political discourse and, of course, to marry into politics, if she so chose. At age nine, she began attending Shelby Female Academy, directed by an Episcopalian minister, the Reverend John Ward, and his wife, Sarah. Ward's academy offered a thoroughly liberal education for the daughters of Lexington's elite—reading, writing, arithmetic, geography, history, and science—everything that a young woman who aspired to be a mother might need to know to provide a basic education to her own children. Ward's "complete system of female education" also included the *beaux arts* "accomplishments"—music, painting, and sewing—that might help a woman acquire a husband in the first place. The Todds paid extra for her lessons in French, considered a social asset, in which she grew proficient. Mary threw herself into her schoolwork, excelled, and could be seen running the three blocks to school to start the day. At age fourteen, most girls had completed their education, but after six years at Ward's academy, Mary Todd graduated up to Madame Mentelle's Boarding School. For the next four years, she spent the five weekdays a mile and a half away at Madame Mentelle's, returning home only on weekends. Overall, she received nearly ten years of schooling, an exceptional education during the nineteenth century, even for a daughter of the slave-owning elite.[16]

As Jennifer Fleischner has observed, "Mary's earliest political ambitions were tied to her father's success before they were tied to her husband's." Early on, she urged her father to aspire to the presidency and resolved that, one way or another, she would someday live in the White House. In the meantime, she supported Lexington's favorite son, Henry Clay, when he ran against President Jackson in 1832. According to family tradition, the young Mary rode her pony out to Clay's estate, Ashland, at the edge of town and announced, "Mr. Clay, my father says you will be the next President of the United States. I wish I could go to Washington and live in the White House." Clay responded: "Well, if I am ever President, I shall expect Mary Todd to be one of my first guests." As she grew older, she began to dream instead of marrying a man who would become president and never hesitated to pursue such jointly personal and political ambitions openly. As her eldest sister, Elizabeth Todd Edwards, later recounted to William Herndon, "She was an Extremely Ambitious woman and in Ky often & often Contended that She was destined to be the wife of some future President—Said it in my presence in Springfield and Said it in Earnest." According to Fleischner, "For Mary, politics was already an all-consuming affair of the heart."[17]

As Mary Todd approached adulthood, however, Lexington began slipping into decline, economically and politically, eclipsed by the region's growing river towns—Louisville, St. Louis, and Memphis—as the focus of trade and agricultural production increasingly shifted to the southwest. Between 1830 and 1860, Lexington's population stagnated and then declined. Once a major producer of hemp for baling cotton, the Bluegrass Country now became an exporter of slaves for the more economically vibrant southwestern frontier centered on New Orleans and Natchez. Flatboats carried them by the score down the Ohio and Mississippi Rivers bound for New Orleans, as Abraham Lincoln later attested personally, when he called up the visceral image of slaves "strung together precisely like so many fish upon a trot-line." Indeed, when Robert Todd died in 1849, Mary's brothers auctioned off the family's longtime household slaves to repay debts and liquidate the estate. As Lexington slowly declined, Robert Todd realized that despite all his efforts to the contrary, he could never hope to keep his children from moving westward in the typical fashion of the common yeomanry.[18]

Like so many other Southern families, both yeomen and aristocrats, the Todds hived off westward when their fortunes began to decline, along with the city of Lexington. In 1827, the Todds began a classic "chain migration" to Springfield, and eventually only one of Robert Todd's sixteen children remained in the Bluegrass. The first family member to settle in Springfield was John Todd, Robert Todd's brother and Mary Todd's uncle, who became one of the town's foremost physicians. Above all, his arrival

initiated a steady migration stream that eventually made him the patriarch of an emergent Todd dynasty in Springfield. A year later, John Todd
Stuart, Mary Todd's cousin and Abraham Lincoln's future law partner,
joined his uncle John, eventually becoming one of Springfield's foremost
attorneys, a longtime legislator, and a US representative. Serving with
Lincoln in the Black Hawk War of 1832 and later in the legislature, he was
the perfect role model for the young Lincoln. He shrewdly recognized
the seeds of success in his untutored but promising colleague, urged him
to study law, and then took him on as his law partner in Springfield.[19]

With two of its men ensconced securely in Springfield, the Todd family began a five-year process of sending its daughters, one by one, to
join them. This generation of Todd women understood that their greatest contribution to their family's future was marrying well in Illinois,
not only economically and socially but also politically. In 1832, Robert
Todd's oldest daughter, Elizabeth, made a crucial dynastic contribution
to the family by marrying Ninian W. Edwards a lawyer and member of
another distinguished Kentucky family that resettled in Illinois. Like the
Todds, a dedicated Whig, Edwards fell in easily with John Todd and John
Todd Stuart. By 1835, the core of the Springfield Todd family was complete—three Todd men, two lawyers and a physician, heading what was
generally known in Springfield as the "Todd-Stuart-Edwards family" or,
more derisively, *the aristocracy.*" The final link in the patriarchal family
chain that stretched from Lexington to Springfield was cousin Stephen T.
Logan. After leaving his law partnership with John Todd Stuart, Lincoln
served as junior partner with Logan for three years, between 1841 and
1844. Lincoln's first two law partners were Todds.[20]

The Edwards home in Springfield became the new center of the Todd
family circle and gained renown as the focus of the young town's bur-
geoning social and cultural life. Maintaining a busy social schedule,
Elizabeth Edwards next introduced her sister Frances to Springfield society, especially to the eligible young professionals who were now gathering in the town. Frances soon met and married a young physician from

Pennsylvania, William Wallace. The couple moved into a Springfield boarding house, the Globe Tavern, opening a place in the Edwards home for the next Todd daughter, Mary, who was losing her sisters successively to Springfield and undoubtedly felt the center of gravity of her own family steadily shifting westward.[21]

Conducting an elaborate chain migration, the Todds had established a secure family outpost in Springfield and then painstakingly settled sons and daughters there one-by-one in a calculated process that lasted well over a decade. In 1839, twenty-one-year-old Mary Todd left Lexington and moved in with the Edwardses to grace Springfield's social scene and to look for a husband of her own. The Edwardses' location, both geographical and social, was perfect for this transplanted Lexingtonian. Their brick home on "quality hill" attracted the wealthiest and most powerful Springfielders, particularly the town's rising Whig elite of young professionals, who provided a surplus of marriageable merchants, physicians, and lawyers. Every legislative session welcomed more eligible men from across Illinois to the new state capital. The Edwardses cultivated their "Coterie" of dependable social partners with overlapping family, professional, and increasingly political connections and enough lively wit and spending money to keep the town's most eligible ladies constantly entertained. Robert Todd gave Mary an annual allowance of $120, which went toward a suitable wardrobe and all the accoutrements she would need to attract and enamor a worthy husband, a judicious investment indeed in the Todd family's future if she, like her sisters, managed to marry well. Mary Todd understood, if only through her relatives' example, the imperative to make the right kind of connections—social, professional, and political.[22]

She arrived in Springfield just in time for the 1840 presidential campaign season. In electing their first president, the Whigs, according to Elizabeth Varon, "initiated a revolution in campaign tactics by encouraging women to attend Whig rallies and other party events." Around the country, Whigs not only invited but welcomed and even cajoled women to join their husbands in the campaign, not just in sentiment but in person by participating, for the first time in their lives, in the rallies, parades, and tableaus that would become vital ingredients of nineteenth-century politics. By their very physical presence in campaigns, women had the opportunity and the duty to "symbolize virtue and beauty" within the otherwise ruggedly male political landscape. "What was new about Whig womanhood was its equation of female patriotism with partisanship and its assumption that women had the duty to bring their moral beneficence into the public sphere," according to Varon. "No longer was patriotism a matter of teaching sons to love the Republic." Now, in tune with the national party, Springfield's Whigs embraced the notion of "Whig womanhood," calling on women to enter the partisan fray not just as an opportunity to contribute but as a patriotic duty.[23]

To broaden support for Harrison, Springfield's Whigs launched a "Log Cabin Campaign," which invited women to enter the contest as visible, if not vocal, participants. Emulating party leaders across the country, they encouraged Whig women to help their husbands and sons campaign by writing letters and poems for the local newspaper, attending rallies and pole raisings, watching (but not marching in) parades, and sewing banners. This unwonted opportunity to participate politically required an educational campaign of sorts to teach women how, and indeed why, they might help elect Harrison. Prompted by Springfield's *Sangamon Journal*, the town's Whig women underwent a crash course in the novel feminine endeavor of political campaigning. Anyone following the weekly columns of the *Journal* could not miss the message. In May, for example, a "female reader" reported that some of Springfield's "ladies" were planning to prepare banners for local campaign events. "Would it not be doing a service to our country, (by assisting in this way, the cause of Harrison and Tyler,) for the ladies generally to get up a number of such banners with appropriate mottos, and have our husbands and brothers carry them in the procession?" she asked. "We are not called on to vote, but can we not do something in this way to contribute to the success of whig principles? We feel as much interested in the success of Harrison and Tyler, as do those who are near and dear to us." In June, the newspaper reported the presence of seven "carriages with ladies" near the front of a procession through Springfield, which was accompanied by "the waving of handkerchiefs by the ladies." In August, Whigs praised women for "inspiring their fathers, brothers and sons, with renewed energy to prosecute the great work of reforming our government." Women, who were rapidly turning into the most important consumers, could boost the Whigs in more tangible ways, as well. In September, the *Journal* reported: "Last Saturday Mrs. Dillon went into the grocery of a rabid loco foco in Springfield, to buy some groceries. In conversation the store keeper said to another present, that he did not want whig's money; and immediately turned to Mrs. Dillon and asked her what she wished to purchase. 'Oh,' the reply was, 'you don't want whig money—I had some to lay out with you—but I must go somewhere else.'" Reporting a log cabin raising in November, three days before the election, the *Journal* emphasized that "60 ladies were present." Overall, the message rang out that women were now partisans, too, and morally responsible for raising and keeping a "truly whig family."[24]

Mary Todd arrived in Springfield in the glow of this mounting campaign to recruit women into Whig electoral politics. She met Abraham Lincoln at a political event, a cotillion at the new American House hotel held in December 1839 to celebrate the convening of the first legislative session in the new state capital. As one of the assembly's Whig leaders, Abraham Lincoln was named a "manager" of the event, which likely vexed him but undoubtedly impressed her. Although shrouded in some mystery and a great deal of historical controversy, their courtship likely began during the first three months of 1840 but was forced to subside, with Lincoln campaigning for William Henry Harrison (and serving as one of his electors, which imposed extensive campaign duties); with his riding the Eighth Circuit (which he did regularly for up to ten weeks at a time); and on top of it all, his serving in the legislature. Historians have fiercely debated the circumstances of Mary Todd's courtship of Abraham Lincoln, as well as the couple's engagement and marriage, but the election cycle of 1840–44 provided the crucial context. In short, Mary Todd conducted a courtship that was not only personal and social in character but also political.[25]

She was twenty-one during the election of 1840, the age at which a man would have acquired the franchise and cast his first vote for president. Not surprisingly, she proved an avid reader of the *Journal* and its associated Whig campaign literature. When she traveled to Missouri in the midst of the campaign, for example, she wrote her close friend, Mercy Levering: "Every week since I left Springfield, have had the felicity of receiving various numbers of their interesting papers, Old Soldiers, Journals & even the *Hickory Club*," the last of which she hinted Abraham Lincoln had sent to her. (She probably knew that Lincoln himself had written a good portion of this campaign literature.) Although prohibited from voting, she may well have felt empowered and certainly emboldened by the novel Whig emphasis on women's political value and responsibilities. Paul Simon wrote of Abraham Lincoln that "what he received from the Illinois House of Representatives was right for the times and right for the man." The Log Cabin Campaign in Springfield was the right time and place for the woman, Mary Todd, to come of age politically. In a new and ultimately fleeting partisan setting that imperceptibly melded the social with the political, she boldly jumped into the fray. "This fall I became quite a *politician*, rather an unladylike profession," she confided to Mercy Levering, "yet at such a *crisis*, whose heart could remain untouched while the energies of all were called into question?"[26]

For his part, Lincoln was clearly attracted to the political side of Mary Lincoln's disposition. "He was charmed with Mary's wit and fascinated with her quick sagacity—her will—her nature—and Culture," her sister Elizabeth Edwards explained. Lincoln, however, "Could not hold a lengthy Conversation with a lady—was not sufficiently Educated and intelligent in the female line to so." Yet he was fascinated with the lovely young woman who poured out her heart to him. "I have happened in the room where they were sitting often & often Mary led the Conversation," her sister remembered. "Lincoln would listen & gaze on her as if drawn by some Superior power, irresistably So: he listened—never Scarcely Said a word." As many observers have since remarked, Mary was clearly looking for a good listener. Lincoln surely welcomed a woman who was fluent in his favorite subject, politics. She never hesitated to offer her political advice, assuring William Herndon a quarter century later: "My husband placed great Confidence in my knowledge in human nature: he had not much knowledge of men." Above all, this was the man who had, unexpectedly, endorsed female suffrage during his campaign for reelection to the legislature in 1836. In his eight-sentence statement of principles, which ran in the *Sangamon Journal*, Lincoln devoted two of the sentences to an unprompted declaration of support for the political rights of women: "I go for all sharing the priveleges of the government, who assist in bearing its burthens. Consequently I go for admitting all whites to the right of suffrage, who pay taxes or bear arms, (by no means excluding females)." Historians have never fully understood this innovative declaration, which foreshadowed the appearance of the "Whig woman," nor its implications for Lincoln's future. In his otherwise detailed analysis of Lincoln's legislative career, a clearly puzzled Paul Simon mustered a single sentence in response to Lincoln's parenthetical pledge: "One of the more unusual items in that letter is that the young bachelor candidate advocated women's suffrage, at that time a somewhat radical position to take."[27]

Like most of the eligible women in town, Mary Todd entertained—and assiduously appraised—multiple suitors, all of them rising young politicians, whom she playfully labeled "the new recruits." She seemed most serious about three young lawyers and legislators—Lincoln; Edwin Webb, another Whig; and Stephen Douglas, one of the state's Democratic stars and Lincoln's longtime political rival and adversary. Webb, she wrote just after the election of 1840, "is our principal lion, dances attendance very frequently, we expect a very gay winter." Douglas, she wrote, "is talented

& agreeable & sometimes *countenances* me." Elizabeth Edwards attested to Douglas's genuine romantic interest, telling Herndon twenty-five years later that "Mr Douglas used to come to see Mary—probably: it is quite likely that his intentions were true & Sincere. Mary was asked one day by some of her friends which She intended to have— 'Him who has the best prospects of being President[,'] Said Miss Todd." Elizabeth Edwards herself preferred Lincoln, whom she considered "a great man long years Since—Knew he was a rising Man and nothing Else modifying this, desired Mary at first to Marry L." Mary Todd later claimed that Douglas actually proposed to her and that she turned him down. Herndon himself wrote that "Miss Todd used Douglas as a mere tool—refused his hand." Biographers suspect that she engrossed both Douglas and Webb merely to maneuver Lincoln into making a commitment. Indeed, it is hard to imagine her marrying a Democrat, even one as promising as Douglas. It is not difficult at all, however, to imagine her having her pick of two of the leading personalities in Illinois's 1840 presidential campaign (who later became two of the presidential nominees in 1860). During the campaign, the *Sangamon Journal* described one of their typical stare-downs: "At the close of Lincoln's speech, which was responded to by three hearty cheers, the 'little giant' ascended the rostrum, but it was no go. The Big Giant had effectually used his candidate up." The same could have been have said of the personal rivalry that the two were conducting in private. Mary Todd, of course, preferred the Big Giant.[28]

Sometime during 1840, in great secrecy, Abraham Lincoln and Mary Todd discreetly made plans to marry. Despite Lincoln's genuine fascination with her and his remarkable endorsement of women's place in politics, however, the couple had a falling out of some kind in early 1841. After Lincoln's death, William Herndon concocted a compelling but dubious story in which his law partner left his fiancée standing at the altar on January 1. In later years, the Edwardses claimed that they changed their minds about Lincoln and discouraged the match. More likely, both members of the couple felt unready to marry, and the parting was a mutual if not amicable decision. Biographers have suggested that Lincoln's genuine interest in another woman (Matilda Edwards, Ninian Edwards's cousin) and Mary Todd's feigned attentions to another man (Edwin Webb or even Stephen Douglas) strained the relationship and led to the breach.[29]

For a year and a half, from early 1841 until late 1842, Lincoln and Mary Todd maintained a cordial distance. Mary wrote to her friend Mercy Levering that Lincoln "deems me unworthy of notice, as I have not met *him* in the gay world for months." Wistfully, she admitted, "I would that the case were different, that he would once more resume his Station in Society." Lincoln confided in Mary's cousin, John Todd Stuart, "I am now the most miserable man living. If what I feel were equally distributed to the whole human family, there would not be one cheerful face on the earth. Whether I shall ever be better I can not tell; I awfully forebode I shall not." Hinting at suicide, Lincoln concluded: "To remain as I am is impossible; I must die or be better, it appears to me." Feeling the sting of his sister-in-law's unhappiness, perhaps, Ninian Edwards described Lincoln as "crazy as a *Loon*." He neglected his duties in the legislature, was described as ill, and uncharacteristically missed an entire week at his post.[30]

Lincoln's reconciliation with Mary Todd occurred unexpectedly yet characteristically within a political setting. Encouraged by the wife of Simeon Francis, editor of the *Sangamon Journal*, the couple began meeting at the Francises' home, away from the by now disapproving eyes of the Edwards family. During the summer of 1842, they hatched a plot to carry their mutual political interests into the public pages of the *Journal*. After the collapse of the State Bank of Illinois in February, the state auditor, James Shields, issued a circular refusing its bank notes as payment for taxes. Whigs pilloried Shields, a rising young Democrat, and now Lincoln and Mary Todd joined in. Together with Mary's best friend and later bridesmaid, Julia Jayne (later the wife of Senator Lyman Trumbull), the couple published a series of letters in the *Journal* that lampooned Shields. Known as the "Rebecca Letters," after their pseudonymous author, they caricatured Shields with a wit that only Abraham Lincoln and Mary Todd could have summoned. The letters made a sensation and held the town in thrall for weeks. When Shields demanded the true identity of the author, Lincoln gallantly took sole credit for the insults to preserve the women's honor. Shields promptly demanded that Lincoln defend his own honor and challenged him to a duel.[31]

The impending duel with Shields was a real threat to both men's lives. Lincoln selected broadswords and seems to have had every intention of defending himself. "I did not intend to hurt Shields unless I did so clearly in self-defense," he later confided to Herndon. "If it had been necessary I could have split him from the crown of his head to the end of his backbone." To maintain his "reverence for the law," however, the lawyerly Lincoln agreed to cross the Mississippi River to Missouri, where dueling was legal, to face off against Shields at the appropriately named Bloody Island. At the last moment, John J. Hardin, a fellow Whig leader and another of Mary Todd's relatives, convinced Shields to withdraw the challenge as a compromise that allowed both men to save face. But the "duelling business," as Lincoln termed it, was infectious. Shields soon challenged William Butler, one of Lincoln's seconds, to what Lincoln labeled "duel No. 2." A third duel loomed when one of Shields's seconds challenged another of Lincoln's friends. Like duel No. 1, however, the succeeding affairs ended peaceably.[32]

Often viewed as a comedy of errors that simply got out of hand, in fact the Shields affair was instrumental in bringing the quarreling couple together again. Writing the "Rebecca Letters" resembled the kind of close collaboration that would draw the Lincolns together and preoccupy them during their married life—advancing Lincoln's political career. Their publication—under a feminine pseudonym—empowered Mary Todd by granting her a political voice that she had never enjoyed before, and never would again. Finally, the duel allowed Lincoln to demonstrate his emotional commitment to Mary Todd by defending her honor in a conspicuously partisan arena. The couple married in November 1842 in the parlor of the Edwardses' house on Aristocrat's Hill. The new Mrs. Lincoln must have imagined that her political career and influence were just beginning, indeed that they were on the rise.

Whigs continued their paeans to female virtue into the 1844 campaign, in which Mary Lincoln's childhood patron and her husband's "beau ideal of a statesman," Henry Clay, headed the ticket. Local Democrats had by this time co-opted the tactic for their own benefit, as when the Democratic Ladies of Springfield provided a flag to fly atop the hundred-foot-high "Young Hickory Pole," named for their candidate, James K. Polk. The local Democratic newspaper mimicked the Whigs in observing, "The zeal and patriotism of the ladies is fairly awakened," effectively neutralizing—and even trivializing—the statement's rhetorical value. During the same campaign, the Whig *Journal* reprinted the "Clay Girl's Song," urging Whig women to marry only devoted Clay men:

> If e'er I consent to be married,
> (And I am not quite sure that I may.)
> The lad that I give my fair hand to
> Must stand by the Patriot, Clay.

Challenging this poetic empowerment of women, however, Democrats sneered in response, "beware young men, how you allow yourselves to be influenced by the dictation of some masculine fair one; and we now tell you, that a fair damsel, who will offer herself in marriage only on condition that her sweetheart, will vote as she directs him will not fail, after marriage, to try to wear the breeches." Reaffirming traditional gender roles, they concluded, "The young man who succumbs to such an influence will deserve to be, what he shurely will be—a henpecked husband." In fact, after the election of 1844, women's political role, even within Whig campaigns, began to decline.[33]

For the rest of the century, as historian Paula Baker has reiterated, two parallel political cultures functioned side-by-side, the formal male culture of electoral politics, which grew grittier than ever, and the informal and primarily nonpartisan reform efforts of women. By 1847, even

Simeon Francis's *Journal* had conducted a seemingly thorough retreat. In an effort to acknowledge that not all Democrats were dunderheaded, Francis conceded, "If ninnies should happen to vote for democrats, it wouldn't follow that the democrats are all ninnies. If the ignorant and uninformed should happen to vote for them, it wouldn't follow that they are all ignorant and uninformed. Nay, if the women should vote for them, it wouldn't follow that all democrats are women." Comparing women with ignorant and uninformed "ninnies" surely signaled the demise of the short-lived career of the "Whig woman" in Springfield, which Francis had himself encouraged in Mary Todd. As Elizabeth Varon has observed, "For all its homages to female influence, Whig womanhood still ultimately rested on women's power in male proxies." A fitting example was one of Lincoln's debates with Douglas, in 1854, when "women waved their white handkerchiefs in token of woman's silent but heartfelt assent." In a single sentence, "women" became the monolithic "woman," a mere platitude, all over again. The use of the word "token," if not studied, was surely apt. All too soon, the *Journal* was repeating the familiar strictures of republican motherhood, under which the "child at the mother's knee imbibes those principles which strengthen in after life and grow to fixed sentiments of the soul," all in the name of the "firmness and purity of our political institutions for the future; the beauty, virtue and elevation of our government, and the spread of our vital religious truths." Women no longer had a public voice in Whig politics, certainly no visible partisan role to play. Indeed, the next time Simeon Francis published anything written by Mary Lincoln in his Springfield *Journal* was in 1850, when she submitted an anonymous poem on the death of her four-year-old son Eddie, a purely domestic production from a grieving wife and mother.[34]

She, however, was determined to remain decidedly visible. During her husband's single term in Congress, for example, she broke with tradition and joined him in Washington, along with their two sons, making two trips of about three months each. On hearing of this decision, Lincoln's legal colleague David Davis wrote to his wife, "Mrs. L., I am told, accompanies her husband to Washington city next winter. She wishes to loom largely." This unusual arrangement made her the only congressional wife at Mrs. Sprigg's boardinghouse, a traditional Whig preserve across the street from the Capitol, among the seven representatives who boarded there. She took the even more unusual step of attending her husband's speeches, sitting in the gallery of the House of Representatives—more than a decade before the establishment of the separate "ladies" section—to hear him challenge President Polk's motives for pursuing the war with Mexico through his famous "Spot" resolutions. Still, she found the decidedly masculine atmosphere and the lack of female company—even Lincoln complained of being "surrounded by men and noise"—disquieting and left after three months to spend the rest of the first session with her family in Lexington.[35]

Tellingly, however, Lincoln soon missed her and confided, "In this troublesome world, we are never quite satisfied. When you were here, I thought you hindered me some in attending to business; but now, having nothing but business—no variety—it has grown exceedingly tasteless to me." Two months later he wrote to implore her to "come along, and that as soon as possible. Having got the idea in my head, I shall be impatient till I see you." In the meantime, he sent Mary copies of speeches and newspapers to keep her current on political events in the capital, where she and the boys soon joined him for another three months at the end of the first session. Mary considered her time in the national capital a valuable political asset and referred nearly a decade later to the "*advantages* of some winter's[*sic*] in Washington." Observing the House debates and attending a presidential reception at the White House undoubtedly helped her prepare for her eventual role as First Lady.[36]

Above all, after returning from Washington, she devoted herself to helping her husband attain a national office that would take him back there. Lincoln campaigned for Zachary Taylor during the presidential election of 1848 and in the wake of that Whig victory felt entitled to a position in the new administration. He actively pursued the lucrative and influential Commissioner of the Public Land Office and traveled to Washington to lobby for it. Back in Springfield, Mary Lincoln helped by writing out letters soliciting support, to which she signed her husband's name. Instead, President Taylor offered to appoint him governor of Oregon Territory, a position that—short of a diplomatic posting—could not have taken him farther away from Washington. Lincoln was tempted by the offer but, according to Herndon, "his wife put her foot squarely down on it with a firm and emphatic No. That always ended it with Lincoln." Throughout the 1850s, Mary Lincoln continued to work assiduously to advance her husband's political career. According to her sister Elizabeth Edwards, Lincoln read his speeches to her with the injunction: "Mary, now listen to this," to which she would respond, "saying so-and-so would sound better." As in Washington, Mary attended some of Lincoln's most important speeches, including his last debate with Douglas in Alton during the senatorial campaign of 1858.[37]

Still, as a "political wife"—some called them "political widows"—Mary Lincoln's public responsibilities were fundamentally social in nature. Abraham Lincoln's profession and his career ambitions demanded endless rounds of entertaining, which under Victorian strictures fell disproportionately, perhaps exclusively, on his wife. When the couple received an invitation to a "large entertainment" at the governor's house, she reported that "Mr L—— *gives me* permission to go, but declines, the honor himself." In tune with their improving social situation, the Lincolns competed to entertain within the city's loftiest social circles. In 1857, Mary Lincoln described the disappointing turnout at one of her parties. "About 500 hundred were invited," she wrote to her half sister Emilie Todd Helm, "yet owing to an *unlucky* rain, 300 only favored us by their presence, and the same evening in Jacksonville Col Warren, gave a bridal party to his son." The swirling social scene was exhausting, however, especially for the hostess, and Mary reported with undoubted understatement a "slight fatigue." One summer she wrote a friend, "For the last two weeks, we have had a continual round of strawberry parties, this last week I have spent five evenings out—and you may suppose, that this day of rest, I am happy to enjoy." Her most recent "strawberry company" had included seventy guests. Looking forward to the social demands of New Year's Day, 1860, she wrote wearily to a friend that "it is quite late in the evening & tomorrow I must rise early, as it is *receiving* day." At these social gatherings, she was of course always at the ready to promote her husband's political career. In 1847, more than a decade before his election, for example, Mary Lincoln told a guest in their home, "He is to be President of the United States some day; if I had not thought so I never would have married him, for you can see he is not pretty. But look at him! Doesn't he look as if he would make a magnificent President?"[38]

Simply put, when Mary Todd had thrown herself into politics during the Harrison and Clay campaigns, she was only doing what she had been socialized to do by her family in Kentucky, indoctrinated to do by the Whig Party in Springfield and the local press (including the editor of the *Journal* and his wife), and abetted in doing by her future husband. Now, as first and foremost a wife and mother, Mary Lincoln found herself relegated to the fate of similarly situated "Whig women," expected to fulfill her own ambitions, or pursue her "unladylike profession," as she termed it, through a male proxy, her husband. Her good fortune, or more properly her good foresight, lay in her choice of that proxy. But it also proved her husband's good fortune. She now had three essential roles to fulfill, first, turning their home into an island of tranquility amid the stormy sea of Springfield's professional and political life, second, supporting and spurring Lincoln's ambitions, and, third, acting as gracious hostess in the service of his political career. The house at Eighth and Jackson was tailormade to serve just such a purpose. "Mary Todd came into Lincoln's life at one of its most important and critical periods," one of Lincoln's legal colleagues observed. "He needed far more than most men a refined and well-appointed home." Even more so, as Elizabeth Edwards emphasized, "Mrs. Lincoln was an ambitious woman—the most ambitious woman I ever saw—spurred up Mr. Lincoln, pushed him along and upward—made him struggle and seize his opportunities." As her nemesis Herndon put it more negatively, she was "like a toothache, keeping her husband awake to politics day and night."[39]

Indeed, before attaining her status of First Lady in the national capital, Mary Lincoln spent nearly two decades building her reputation as one of the most accomplished political hostesses in the Illinois capital. "In her modest and simple home, everything orderly and refined, there was always, on the part of both host and hostess, a cordial and hearty Western welcome," one frequent guest noted. "Mrs. Lincoln's table was famed for the excellence of many rare Kentucky dishes, and in season, it was loaded with venison, wild turkeys, prairie chickens, quail and other game." Yet nine-year-old Willie's birthday "gala" at the beginning of the 1860 presidential election season, which attracted "50 or 60 boys & girls" into the Lincoln home, led Mary to the forthright conclusion that such purely social occasions "are nonsensical affairs." Perhaps her greatest fault was her open dissatisfaction with the domestic side of politics and her spirited proclivity toward outspokenness. After Lincoln's nomination for president, Mary's cousin Annie Dickson, herself the wife of a lawyer and judge, wrote to congratulate her. "You are an ambitious little woman," she observed and then added, "I have a little ambition myself in a *quiet way*." Bred for something more than a merely ornamental role in politics, Mary Lincoln once asked wearily, "What would my poor father say if he found me doing this kind of work."[40]

## Notes

1. A representative sampling of studies that exemplify this theme in Lincoln scholarship and explore these and other factors in an attempt to probe his "rise" to "greatness" might include William E. Baringer, *Lincoln's Rise to Power* (Boston: Little, Brown, 1937); Don E. Fehrenbacher, *Prelude to Greatness: Lincoln in the 1950's* (Stanford: Stanford University Press, 1962); Paul Simon, *Lincoln's Preparation for Greatness: The Illinois Legislative Years* (Norman: University of Oklahoma Press, 1965); George B. Forgie, *Patricide in the House Divided: A Psychological Interpretation of Lincoln and His Age* (New York: W. W. Norton, 1979); Kenneth J. Winkle, *The Young Eagle: The Rise of Abraham Lincoln* (Dallas: Taylor Trade, 2001);

Ronald C. White Jr., *The Eloquent President: A Portrait of Lincoln through His Words* (New York: Random House, 2005); Joshua Wolf Shenk, *Lincoln's Melancholy: How Depression Challenged a President and Fueled His Greatness* (New York: Mariner, 2006); William C. Harris, *Lincoln's Rise to the Presidency* (Lawrence: University Press of Kansas, 2007); Stephen Berry, *House of Abraham: Lincoln and the Todds; A Family Divided by War* (New York: Houghton Mifflin, 2007).

2. Simon, *Lincoln's Preparation for Greatness*, 293.

3. Important studies of Victorian gender roles in middle-class American families include Nancy F. Cott, *The Bonds of Womanhood: 'Woman's Sphere' in New England, 1780–1835* (New Haven, CT: Yale University Press, 1977); Carl N. Degler, *At Odds: Women and the Family in America from the Revolution to the Present* (New York: Oxford University Press, 1980); Steven Mintz and Susan Kellogg, *Domestic Revolutions: A Social History of American Family Life* (New York: Free, 1988), 43–65; Glenna Matthews, *"Just a Housewife": The Rise and Fall of Domesticity in America* (New York: Oxford University Press, 1987); Jeanne Boydston, *Home and Work: Housework, Wages, and the Ideology of Labor in the Early Republic* (New York: Oxford University Press, 1990); Stuart M. Blumin, *The Emergence of the Middle Class: Social Experience in the American City, 1760–1900* (New York: Cambridge University Press, 1989); and Mary P. Ryan, *Cradle of the Middle Class: The Family in Oneida County, New York, 1790–1865* (New York: Cambridge University Press, 1981).

4. William H. Herndon, *Abraham Lincoln, Miss Ann Rutledge, New Salem, Pioneering and the Poem: A Lecture Delivered in the Old Sangamon County Court House, November, 1866* (Springfield: Collector's Edition, 1910), 4, 7, 54. Herndon's collection of interviews and letters has been available for decades in manuscript at the Library of Congress and on microfilm and has recently appeared in a carefully edited and annotated edition, Douglas L. Wilson and Rodney O. Davis, eds., *Herndon's Informants: Letters, Interviews, and Statements about Abraham Lincoln* (Urbana: University of Illinois Press, 1998), and is available in searchable format online at <http://durer.press.illinois.edu/wilson/html/737.html>. David Donald, *Lincoln's Herndon* (New York: Alfred A. Knopf, 1948), 167–241, explores in detail Herndon's efforts to solicit and record what he labeled his "Lincoln Record," as well as his initial series of lectures.

5. Justin G. Turner and Linda Levitt Turner, *Mary Todd Lincoln: Her Life and Letters* (New York: Fromm International, 1987), 414, 416, 464, 568. Herndon ultimately coauthored his biographical account, which he published in 1889. The biography has recently been annotated and republished as William H. Herndon and Jesse W. Weik, *Herndon's Lincoln*, ed. Douglas L. Wilson and Rodney O. Davis (Urbana: University of Illinois Press, 2006).

6. Jean H. Baker, "Mary and Abraham: A Marriage," in Gabor Boritt, ed., *The Lincoln Enigma: The Changing Faces of an American Icon* (New York: Oxford University Press, 2001), 37. Beyond Wilson and Davis, eds., *Herndon's Informants*, the

fullest published collections of Lincoln-related reminiscences appears in Michael Burlingame's exhaustive *Abraham Lincoln: A Life*. Baltimore: Johns Hopkins University Press, 2 vols., 2008. A lengthier, unpublished version of Burlingame's biography that includes additional primary observations about their marriage is available online at <http://www.knox.edu/Academics/Distinctive-Programs/Lincoln-Studies-Center /Burlingame-Abraham-Lincoln-A-Life.html>.

7. Burlingame, *Abraham Lincoln: A Life*, 1:178–79, 212; Herndon and Weik, *Herndon's Lincoln*, 234; Ronald D. Rietveld, "The Lincoln White House Community," *Journal of the Abraham Lincoln Association* 20 (Summer 1999): 17–48; Daniel Mark Epstein, *Lincoln's Men: The President and His Private Secretaries* (New York: Collins, 2009), 76.

8. Ruth Painter Randall, *Mary Lincoln: Biography of a Marriage* (Boston: Little, Brown, 1953).

9. Linda Kerber, "The Republican Mother: Women and the Enlightenment—An American Perspective," *American Quarterly* 28 (Summer 1976): 187–205; Ruth M. Bloch, "American Feminine Ideals in Transition: The Rise of the Moral Mother, 1785–1815," *Feminist Studies* 4 (June 1978): 101–26; Jan Lewis, "The Republican Wife: Virtue and Seduction in the Early Republic," *William and Mary Quarterly* 44 (October 1987): 689–721; Anne Firor Scott, *The Southern Lady: From Pedestal to Politics, 1830–1930* (Chicago: University of Chicago Press, 1970); Glenna Matthews, *The Rise of Public Woman: Woman's Power and Woman's Place in the United States, 1630–1970* (New York: Oxford University Press, 1992), 52–71.

10. Jean H. Baker, *Mary Todd Lincoln: A Biography* (New York: W. W. Norton, 1987), 60–61; Berry, *House of Abraham*, 6–12; Burlingame, *Abraham Lincoln: A Life*, 1:177; Jennifer Fleischner, *Mrs. Lincoln and Mrs. Keckly* (New York: Broadway, 2003), 57–58.

11. Baker, *Mary Todd Lincoln*, 6–7, 12–13, 19, 28; Fleischner, *Mrs. Lincoln and Mrs. Keckly*, 9, 11, 16–17, 19.

12. Baker, *Mary Todd Lincoln*, 16, 17–24, 30–31; Fleischner, *Mrs. Lincoln and Mrs. Keckly*, 26–27, 45–46.

13. Elizabeth R. Varon, *We Mean to Be Counted: White Women and Politics in Antebellum Virginia* (Chapel Hill: University of North Carolina Press, 1998), 2, 82; Norma Basch, "Marriage, Morals, and Politics in the Election of 1828," *Journal of American History* 80 (December 1993): 890–918.

14. Varon, *We Mean to Be Counted*, 80; Paula Baker, "The Domestication of Politics: Women and American Political Society, 1780–1920," *American Historical Review* 89 (June 1984): 620–47; Michael McGerr, "Political Style and Women's Power, 1830–1930," *Journal of American History* 77 (December 1990): 864–85.

15. Lori D. Ginzberg, *Women and the Work of Benevolence: Morality, Politics, and Class in the Nineteenth-Century United States* (New Haven: Yale University Press, 1990); Baker, *Mary Todd Lincoln*, 66; Fleischner, *Mrs. Lincoln and Mrs. Keckly*, 54–56; William H. Townsend, *Lincoln and the Bluegrass: Slavery and Civil War in Kentucky* (Lexington: University of Kentucky Press, 1955), 165–66; Berry, *House of Abraham*, 15.

16. Fleischner, *Mrs. Lincoln and Mrs. Keckly*, 57–62; Baker, *Mary Todd Lincoln*, 34–41.

17. Fleischner, *Mrs. Lincoln and Mrs. Keckly*, 57–58; Catherine Clinton, *Mrs. Lincoln: A Life* (New York: Harper, 2009), 17; Wilson and Davis, *Herndon's Informants*, 443.

18. Roy P. Basler, Marion Dolores Pratt, and Lloyd A. Dunlap, eds., *The Collected Works of Abraham Lincoln* (New Brunswick: Rutgers University Press, 1953), 1:260; Baker, *Mary Todd Lincoln*, 54–55, 57, 66–67; Fleischner, *Mrs. Lincoln and Mrs. Keckly*, 19, 24.

19. John Carroll Power, *History of the Early Settlers of Sangamon County, Illinois* (Springfield: Edwin A. Wilson, 1876), 696–97, 715–17; Joseph Wallace, *Past and Present of the City of Springfield and Sangamon County, Illinois* (Chicago: S. J. Clarke, 1904), 43, 44–45; Winkle, *Young Eagle*, 161–62.

20. Baker, *Mary Todd Lincoln*, 40, 48, 74, 78, 79; Power, *Early Settlers*, 46, 278–79, 466; Wallace, *Past and Present*, 49; Wilson and Davis, *Herndon's Informants*, 252, 432; J. Duane Squires, "Lincoln's Todd In-Laws," *Lincoln Herald* 61 (Fall 1967): 121–28; Basler et al., *Collected Works*, 2:313; John J. Duff, *Abraham Lincoln: Prairie Lawyer* (New York: Bramwell House, 1960), 78–96; Winkle, *Young Eagle*, 163.

21. Baker, *Mary Todd Lincoln*, 74, 78, 79; Power, *Early Settlers*, 748; William Townsend, *Lincoln and His Wife's Home Town* (Indianapolis: Bobbs-Merrill, 1929), 69, 75; Squires, "Lincoln's Todd In-Laws"; Winkle, *Young Eagle*, 163.

22. Baker, *Mary Todd Lincoln*, 77–78; Clinton, *Mrs. Lincoln*, 47; Fleischner, *Mrs. Lincoln and Mrs. Keckly*, 98–99.

23. Varon, *We Mean to Be Counted*, 3, 77, 80; McGerr, "Political Style and Women's Power," 867. According to Varon, 73, "Historians agree that the Whigs' 1840 campaign marks the first time a political party systematically included women in its public rituals. All around the country women turned out at Whig rallies; on occasion they even made speeches, conducted political meetings, and wrote pamphlets on behalf of the Whigs."

24. *(Springfield) Sangamon Journal*, May 15, June 5, August 2, September 18, November 6, 1840; Varon, *We Mean to Be Counted*, 74, 76; McGerr, "Political Style and Women's Power," 867; Robert Gray Gunderson, *The Log-Cabin Campaign* (Lexington: University of Kentucky Press, 1957).

25. Fleischner, *Mrs. Lincoln and Mrs. Keckly*, 96–97, 105–7.

26. Turner and Turner, *Mary Todd Lincoln: Her Life and Letters*, 16, 20; Simon, *Lincoln's Preparation for Greatness*, 29.

27. Wilson and Davis, *Herndon's Informants*, 358, 443; *(Springfield) Sangamon Journal*, June 18, 1836; Simon, *Lincoln's Preparation for Greatness*, 43.

28. Turner and Turner, *Mary Todd Lincoln: Her Life and Letters*, 20, 21, 27; Wilson and Davis, *Herndon's Informants*, 443, 444, 623, 646; *(Springfield) Sangamon Journal*, May 15, 1840; Baker, *Mary Todd Lincoln*, 84–85.

29. Wilson and Davis, *Herndon's Informants*, 443; Baker, *Mary Todd Lincoln*, 85–86.

30. Basler et al., *Collected Works*, 1:268, 269; Turner and Turner, *Mary Todd Lincoln: Her Life and Letters*, 27; Wilson and Davis, *Herndon's Informants*, 133; Douglas L. Wilson, "Abraham Lincoln and 'That Fatal First of January,'" *Civil War History* 38 (June 1992): 101–30; Winkle, *Young Eagle*, 208–10.

31. Roy P. Basler, "The Authorship of the 'Rebecca' Letters," *Abraham Lincoln Quarterly* 2 (March 1942): 80–90; David Herbert Donald, *Lincoln* (New York: Simon and Schuster, 1995), 90–93; Winkle, *Young Eagle*, 210.

32. Basler et al., *Collected Works*, 1:302–3; Donald, *Lincoln*, 91–92; Baker, *Mary Todd Lincoln*, 96–97; Winkle, *Young Eagle*, 211–12. James E. Myers, *The Astonishing Saber Duel of Abraham Lincoln* (Springfield: Lincoln-Herndon Building, 1968), provides the fullest narrative of the duel.

33. *(Springfield) Illinois State Register*, March 15, July 12, 1844; *(Springfield) Illinois Journal* February 29, 1844; Basler et al., *Collected Works*, 3:29.

34. *(Springfield) Illinois Journal* September 16, 1847, January 19, 1849, February 7, 1850, October 10, 1854; Baker, "Domestication of Politics," 647; Varon, *We Mean to Be Counted*, 93.

35. Baker, *Mary Todd Lincoln*, 136, 138; Fleischner, *Mrs. Lincoln and Mrs. Keckly*, 163; Basler et al., *Collected Works*, 1:474; Donald W. Riddle, *Congressman Abraham Lincoln* (Urbana: University of Illinois Press, 1957), 173; Kate Masur, *An Example for All the Land: Emancipation and the Struggle over Equality in Washington, D.C.* (Chapel Hill: University of North Carolina Press, 2010), 93.

36. Basler et al., *Collected Works*, 1:465, 477; Fleischner, *Mrs. Lincoln and Mrs. Keckly*, 167, 171; Turner and Turner, *Mary Todd Lincoln: Her Life and Letters*, 47.

37. Herndon and Weik, *Herndon's Lincoln*, 192–93; Fleischner, *Mrs. Lincoln and Mrs. Keckly*, 168, 169; Baker, *Mary Todd Lincoln: A Biography*, 154.

38. Turner and Turner, *Mary Todd Lincoln: Her Life and Letters*, 48, 56, 61; Ward Hill Lamon, *Recollections of Abraham Lincoln* (Lincoln: University of Nebraska Press, 1994), 21; Burlingame, *Abraham Lincoln: A Life*, 1:212.

39. Henry B. Rankin, *Intimate Character Sketches of Abraham Lincoln* (Philadelphia: J. B. Lippincott, 1924), 162; Wilson and Davis, *Herndon's Informants*, 643; Baker, *Mary Todd Lincoln: A Biography*, 152.

40. Turner and Turner, *Mary Todd Lincoln: Her Life and Letters*, 61–62; William Dickson to Abraham Lincoln with note from Annie Dickson to Mary Lincoln, May 21, 1860, Abraham Lincoln Papers, Library of Congress; Winkle, *Young Eagle*, 228, 279.

## WILLIAM H. HERNDON AND MARY TODD LINCOLN

*Douglas L. Wilson*

One thing that students of Abraham Lincoln are universally agreed on is that there was an antagonism between his wife, Mary Lincoln, and his law partner, William H. Herndon. How can it be doubted, when Herndon referred to her with such epithets as "she wolf" and "*the female wild cat of the age*" and she angrily denounced him as "a dirty dog"?[1] It seems unlikely that Herndon and Mary Lincoln would have been socially compatible, let alone friends, under any circumstances, but there can be little doubt they became antagonists because of their close personal relationships to Abraham Lincoln. This has led some biographers to see whatever enmity existed between them as being based on a kind of rivalry for Lincoln's attention.[2] Such characterizations are tantalizing, but Herndon's and Mary Lincoln's feelings toward each other would be of little consequence were it not for one thing: that it was Herndon who compiled much of the information on which our knowledge of Lincoln's life before the presidency depends. As a result, Herndon's information and opinions have assumed considerable weight in the scale of Lincoln biography, and the unflattering views he held on Lincoln's wife and his marriage raise the question of bias, of whether Herndon may have colored or falsified the picture to reinforce or confirm his own views.

Before the appearance of David Herbert Donald's biography of Herndon in 1948, one finds little concern among Lincoln students that Herndon may have tampered unfairly with the behavior and reputation of Mary Lincoln. A consensus had already formed among scholars that the incident reported in Herndon's biography in which Lincoln left Mary Todd standing at the altar probably never happened, but Herndon was not widely seen as a purveyor of misinformation and malice.[3] But as a result of Donald's superbly researched and influential biography, things have changed dramatically.[4] A recent statement chosen almost at random typifies the way this issue is nowadays perceived: "Herndon's biases included a hatred for Mary Lincoln, and he may have intentionally sought out respondents who would testify to a loveless Lincoln marriage."[5] That Herndon *hated* Mary Lincoln is currently a widely shared belief that has become axiomatic and is rarely questioned. It is something that self-respecting students of Lincoln's life are expected to know. Donald explained: "Herndon and Mary Todd had never got along. When Mary came to Springfield in 1837, Herndon had met her at a ball given by Colonel Robert Allen. He had asked the belle for a dance, and, thinking to compliment her, this youth just back from college tactlessly observed that the lady 'seemed to glide through the waltz with the ease of a serpent.' Miss Todd, never distinguished by a sense of humor, flashed back: 'Mr. Herndon, comparison to a serpent is rather severe irony, especially to a newcomer'—and she left him on the dance floor. Neither ever forgot that episode."[6]

Donald's conclusion that neither ever forgot the "serpent" incident, which he offered in 1948 as informed speculation, has been duly repeated ever since as established fact.[7] But is it? Is there, in fact, good reason for thinking that this incident was the starting point of a lifelong antagonism? A careful reading of this passage in Herndon's biography, along with other evidence, raises doubts. Near the beginning of his biographical collaboration with Jesse W. Weik, Herndon wrote him almost daily, sketching out the central characters and basic plot lines of Lincoln's early life. In one of these letters, he described the appearance on the Springfield scene of the Lexington belle, Mary Todd. "Let me give you an exact idea of Miss *Todd*—Mrs Lincoln afterwards. I said to you and now say to you that when Mrs Lincoln was a young and unmarried woman that she was rather pleasant—polite—civil—rather graceful in her movements—intelligent, witty, and sometimes bitter too: she was a polished girl—well educated—a good linguist—a fine conversationalist—was educated thoroughly at Lexington Ky: she was poor when she came here about 1839—a little proud—sometimes haughty. I have met Miss Todd many times at socials—balls—dances—& the like—have danced with her."[8] This would seem the appropriate moment for Herndon to have recalled and related the "serpent" debacle at Colonel Allen's, but he did not. In fact, in all the letters he wrote to Weik and others about his involvement in Lincoln's life—loquacious and repetitive letters that number in the hundreds—he never, to my knowledge, mentioned the serpent story. This strongly suggests that it may not have been until the biography was actually being drafted by Weik in 1887 and 1888 that Herndon recalled this colorful incident. It is introduced into the biography in chapter 9 following a quite positive depiction of Mary Todd at the time of her Springfield debut.

> The first time I met her was at a dance at the residence of Col. Robert Allen, a gentleman mentioned in the preceding chapter. I engaged her for a waltz, and as we glided through it I fancied I never before had danced with a young lady who moved with such grace and ease. A few moments later, as we were promenading through the hall, I thought to compliment her graceful dancing by telling her that while I was conscious of my own awkward movements, she seemed to glide through the waltz with the ease of a serpent. The strange comparison was as unfortunate as it was hideous. I saw it in an instant, but too late to recall it. She halted for a moment, drew back, and her eyes flashed as she retorted: "Mr. Herndon, comparison to a serpent is rather severe irony, especially to a newcomer."[9]

Far from being a story that puts Mary Lincoln in a bad light, this is a story that Herndon is telling on himself, for he acknowledges that he had inadvertently committed a gaffe, which he says he immediately regretted, and he pointedly gives Mary Todd the last word. The episode seems to be offered as an illustration of the newcomer's gifts: that she was graceful, an accomplished dancer, and quick-witted, and had a way with words. From the context and tone of this passage, it is hard to see that Herndon could have regarded his verbal slip about the serpent as a defining event in his relationship with Mary Lincoln.

If it seems unlikely that Herndon regarded Mary's retort as grounds for resentment, at least we can be sure that he remembered the incident, which is more than we know about Mary. In the absence of evidence that the "serpent" comment actually marked the beginning of a mutual antagonism, the notion that it *was* must be downgraded from fact to doubtful speculation. This is significant because the "serpent" incident is the only piece of evidence on offer in support of the existence of a longstanding antagonism between the two. Donald himself forthrightly admits as much: "During his partner's lifetime, Herndon managed to avoid hostilities with Mary Lincoln. There are no contemporary accounts of Mrs. Lincoln's cutting Herndon in Springfield or of her refusing to speak to him in the law office; such tales were spread by Mary's self-appointed defenders in the postwar period after she and Herndon had come to an open rupture. So far as can be judged from existing evidence, during Lincoln's Springfield years Herndon and Mary maintained restrained, if distant, relations."[10]

Donald adds as a qualification: "But Mrs. Lincoln never invited her husband's partner to her house for a meal." But this often-repeated circumstance is somewhat misleading, as Donald's source—one of Herndon's topical sketches—clearly shows. In drafting biographical material for the use of his collaborator, Herndon wrote: "Mr. Stuart said this to me, that 'I have been at Lincoln's house a hundred times and never was asked to dine. In Washington Mr. Lincoln never asked about any body— says Judge Davis, says so and never asked Davis to dine with him' though Davis was frequently at his house. I can say the same thing and so can all persons who ever visited that house, except on special occasions."[11] The point here is that if the experience of John T. Stuart, David Davis, and Herndon himself is indicative, the Lincolns did not socialize over dinner.

While close friends such as these were often in the Lincoln home, they were never invited to dine, except on special occasions.

What all this tells us is that, whatever the character of Mary and Herndon's mutual antagonism, its longstanding nature, reaching far back to their first acquaintance, is a presumption, not a fact. And we must recognize that, as such, it is largely a backward projection from later developments. This matters in the present discussion because Donald's positing of a longstanding antagonism is the ultimate platform on which the prevailing view concerning Herndon's "hatred" of Mary rests. Ruth Painter Randall, for example, has no doubt whatever that "Herndon wanted to believe the worst about Mrs. Lincoln," and her first item in evidence (and most of the rest) is taken directly from Donald: "From the first meeting there had been a mutual dislike."[12] Some years later, the editors of Mary Lincoln's letters concluded from Donald's account: "At a ball before her marriage he had told her, by way of clever compliment, that she danced with the ease of a serpent. She did not care for the comparison, said so, and from that moment on viewed Herndon with contempt."[13] Not to be outdone, Stephen B. Oates gave the screw yet another turn: "Herndon could never come to socialize in the Lincoln home, because Mary had nothing but contempt for him. According to Herndon's side of the story, he'd met Mary at a ball and was so enthralled with her graceful ways that he compared her to a serpent. He meant it as a compliment, but Mary disliked him in any case and took his remark as an outrageous and unforgivable insult."[14]

Donald, of course, is not responsible for the fanciful conjectures that have been embroidered onto his speculations. More recently, in his own biography of Lincoln, Donald allowed that Herndon had a "dislike, verging on hatred" for Mary Lincoln and implied that it was, indeed, of long standing.[15] But he did not gainsay his earlier characterization of the state of affairs that existed before 1866—"restrained, if distant, relations"—a characterization that seems hardly consistent with real hatred, on either side. Herndon's own reflection on the matter is actually quite generous:

"To me she was always kind and respectful," he says of this period, "and in return I respect[ed] her: she had much to bear."[16] If there had been hatred between these two before 1866, it is incumbent upon us to offer evidence of its existence as well as how and when it was displayed. This has yet to be done, and it needs to be emphasized that before 1866, in spite of widespread assumptions to the contrary, no factual basis for anything like hatred, on one side or the other, has ever been adduced.[17]

What difference does it make *when* their clear differences in temperament and outlook ripened into animosity? It matters because it bears on the question raised earlier about bias. Donald alleged that the kind of testimony and information Herndon gathered for his biography in 1865 and 1866 was directly related to his antipathy for Mary, whom Donald characterized in this context as "his old enemy." Herndon, he said, "built up a collection of tales concerning Mrs. Lincoln's unfortunate temper" and "harped on certain episodes in the Lincoln story—tales of the President's domestic infelicity, for example, to the neglect of other, and perhaps more important points."[18] At the time Donald made these charges, the materials on which they were based were largely inaccessible, but as they are now readily available, interested students can judge the matter for themselves.[19] There can be no doubt that Herndon believed Lincoln's marriage was unfortunate and that the anecdotes he collected tended to reinforce this idea. But if the implication is that Herndon unfairly loaded the dice against Mary in his investigations, I would certainly disagree, for it is hard to see that the stories Herndon collected, or his own view of Mary and the Lincoln marriage, differed materially from that of many of Lincoln's other close friends or, so far as we can gauge it, from that of Springfield generally. Paul M. Angle put the matter succinctly: "As to Lincoln's domestic difficulties, no fair-minded student can disregard what Herndon wrote. The supporting testimony of other contemporaries is too overwhelming."[20] What is important to emphasize here is that saying Herndon regarded Mary as his "old enemy" in 1866 amounts to stealing a march on the evidence, for it assumes what is yet to be proved.

It is not until late in 1866, after Herndon had collected the major share of his evidence, that we come to the first actual irruption of hostility. Herndon's collecting activities had been enormously productive, and by mid-November of 1866, the total number of his letters, interviews, and statements about Lincoln collected since beginning work in May the previous year was over four hundred.[21] One of his most important interviews, taken in September of 1866, had been with none other than Mary Lincoln. He had written her son Robert, requesting an interview, and Mary herself had responded with a very cordial letter, inviting Herndon to meet her in Springfield.

> The recollection of my beloved husband's *truly* affectionate regard for *you* & the knowledge, of your great love & reverence for the best man, that ever lived, would of *itself*, cause you, to be cherished with the sincerest regard, by my sons & myself. In my overwhelming bereavement, those who loved my idolized husband—aside from *disinterested* motives—are very precious to me & mine— . . . I have been thinking for some time past, that I would like to see you & have a long conversation—I write to [know?] if you will be in Springfield *next* Wednesday week—Sept—4th—if so—at 10 o'clock, in the morning, you will find me, at the St Nicolas Hotel.[22]

These compliments may have been so much eyewash, and her purpose in inviting Herndon to meet with her may well have been to convince him, which he says she tried to do, that "it was not usual to mention the facts, the history of the wife, in the biography of her husband, further than to say that the two were married at such time and place" and that he should leave her out of his biography.[23] But judging by Herndon's write-up of the interview, one of the most valuable he ever received, it must have gone well, for it indicates that Mary expressed herself on a wide range of subjects, including Lincoln's religion. She even imparted some highly confidential information about her family—such as the misbehavior of her niece in Washington and her husband's intention to dismiss her brother-in-law Ninian W. Edwards from his government post for stealing—all of which suggests that she spoke freely and trusted Herndon with sensitive information.[24]

Two months later, on November 16, Herndon delivered his fourth public lecture on his former law partner, revealing for the first time, in what was, even for him, baroque and extravagant language, the story of Lincoln's love for Ann Rutledge. Herndon began with the provocative statement: "Lincoln loved Anna Rutledge better than his own life." His thesis was that the sudden illness and death of the beautiful young woman Lincoln was engaged to in 1835—Ann Rutledge—gave him an emotional wound from which he never completely recovered and that was the root cause of his lifelong melancholy.

Herndon's revelations, and his highly conjectural interpretation of the episode's permanent effect on Lincoln, seemed to many observers, then and later, as heedlessly insensitive and deliberately hurtful. Isaac Phillips's complaint against Herndon was probably typical: "He was not a scrupulous man, and there is ample evidence in everything he wrote that he was a man of a coarse mind—a mind of the character that could not perceive those nice feelings and tastes that would be outraged by his disclosures. . . . A decent man would have been careful on these points."[25] Even those who harbored no love for Mary Lincoln probably reasoned that, in such a case, decency trumps history, regardless of the biographer's intentions.

But it is Herndon's *intentions* that concern us here. He thought he had discovered a previously unknown but critically important chapter in Lincoln's life, his tragic love affair with Ann Rutledge. This was an incident whose true import Herndon believed could only be grasped if one could recapture the context, by which he meant the natural setting, the pioneer culture, and the particular personal circumstances in which it took place. As he told Isaac N. Arnold at the time, the lecture was "an *attempt* to show the power & influence of mind—scenary—flowers, and mind on mind—Lincoln's mind."[26] This is why most of the lecture—about eighty percent of it—has nothing to do with the love affair per se but is given over to detailed descriptions of the natural setting and the pioneer culture of New Salem.

Herndon, of course, knew that he was treading on dangerous ground and inviting hostility in delivering this lecture, and hostility he certainly got. Because he had had it printed in advance as a broadside, it was rapidly reprinted in newspapers throughout the country, where the reaction was far from favorable. As Herndon certainly realized, he was violating accepted standards of taste and decorum just by disclosing such intimate matters as Lincoln's young love affair and his troubled bereavement. He must surely have been aware that by even suggesting, as he did, that Lincoln never again loved another woman as he had loved Ann Rutledge, he would deeply offend Mary Lincoln and members of her family. What he may not have been fully prepared for was the charge that he had deliberately betrayed the friend and partner he revered.

These charges came soon enough, and none with more force than those from Dr. James Smith, former pastor of the First Presbyterian Church of Springfield. In a letter to Herndon that Smith had widely published in newspapers, he spelled out Herndon's offenses: "I read [your lecture] with feelings of mingled indignation and Sorrow, because coming as it did from his intimate friend and law partner, it was calculated to do the character of that great and good man an incalculable injury, deeply to wound the feelings of his heart broken widow and her orphan boys, and to place that whole family both the dead and living, in their family relations, in a most unenviable light before the public."[27]

Herndon had not only offended his public and Lincoln's family, he had, as the Lincolns well knew, also recklessly overstepped his own knowledge in saying that Lincoln "*never* addressed another woman, in my opinion, 'yours affectionately.'"[28] It is not known when Mary Lincoln learned of Herndon's lecture, but her son Robert may have seen it first. Within a few days of the lecture, he wrote to his father's executor, Supreme Court Justice David Davis: "Mr. William H. Herndon is making an ass of himself." He continued: "If you have seen his lecture on 'Abraham Lincoln & Ann

Rutledge,' I have no doubt you will feel the impropriety of such a publication even if it were, which I much doubt, all true. His reflections, which make up a large portion, would be very ludicrous if I did not feel strongly that he speaks with a certain amount of authority from having known my father so long. Do you think it would be advisable to write to him? He is such a singular character that I am afraid of making matters worse, but I think something ought to be done to stop his present course."[29] After the lecture was published in the *Chicago Tribune*, Robert traveled to Springfield, possibly at the urging of his mother, to confront Herndon, who later said that Robert had come to fight, "but I kept my temper and he couldn't fight, because he had no one to fight with."[30] Upon his return, Robert wrote Judge Davis: "I have just returned from Springfield to see Mr. Herndon. We talked everything over in a very good natured way & I found that he really had no idea of conveying the impressions he does in his lecture and that the main trouble comes from his heaping words on words without much care in their selection."[31] But scarcely a week later, he was writing to John G. Nicolay with a draft of something he wanted Nicolay to revise and publish, for he believed "Herndon has so clearly falsified the record that I think it time he was squelched."[32]

Mary's first recorded reaction to what she considered Herndon's act of perfidy is in a letter of March 4, 1867, to Judge Davis, but it was apparently not her first letter to him on the subject: "Permit me to point your attention to another sentence in a lecture of the *distinguished* W H which is of great significance and indicates more clearly if possible, the malignity of *his* remarks, than any thing else. *He* pointedly says, 'for the last *twenty three years*, Mr Lincoln has known no joy,'—"[33] This is a reference to a little noticed remark in Herndon's first public lecture, delivered over a year earlier in Springfield on December 12, 1865. In a passage pertaining to Lincoln's habitual melancholy, Herndon had said: "His terrible gloom struck his friends and created a sympathy for him—*one means of his success. He was gloomy—abstracted and joyous—rather humorous by turns. I do not think he knew what joy was—nor happiness for more than 23 years.*"[34]

Whatever one may think of this allusive reference, Herndon was not attempting to mould the opinions of uninformed listeners, for he was here addressing a Springfield audience that was made up of the neighbors and fellow citizens of Abraham Lincoln and was thus capable of judging the aptness of such a statement. On the other hand, Mary Lincoln had every reason to be highly resentful of this remark, for simple subtraction would bring any listener or reader curious about the beginning of Lincoln's unhappiness to 1842, the date of her marriage.

Judge Davis seems to have attempted to ease her mind by playing down the importance of such an early romance as Lincoln's with Ann Rutledge, but Mary Lincoln had her own ideas: "As you justly remark, each & every one has had, a little romance in their early days—but as my husband was *truth itself,* and as he always assured me, he had cared for no one but myself, the false W. H. (au contraire) I shall assuredly remain firm in my conviction—that *Ann Rutledge,* is a myth—." In a postscript she added: "I would not believe an assertion of Herndon's if he would take a thousand oaths, upon the Bible—."[35]

Given the provocation and the well-known volatility of Mary Lincoln's temperament, this was a reasonably moderate response, but two days later she wrote again in a more animated state:

W H may consider himself a ruined man, in attempting to disgrace others, the vials of wrath, will be poured upon his own head. My love for my husband was so sacred and the knowledge it was fully returned so well assure, that if W. H—utters another word—and is not silent with his infamous falsehoods in the future, *his* life is not worth, living for—*I have* friends, if his *low* soul thought that my great affliction—had left me without them. In the future, he may well say, *his prayers*—"Revenge is sweet, especially to womankind but there are some of mankind left, who will wreak it upon him—He is a dirty dog & I [do not?] regret the article [by Dr. James Smith] was sent to the papers—it shows him forth, in his proper colors—& I think he will *rue* the day, he did not take your advice.[36]

At this point, we may safely use the word *hate* for what Mary Lincoln now felt for William H. Herndon.

But this is not the side of the equation that most concerns us. Up to the time of the Ann Rutledge lecture, while Mary Lincoln no doubt had serious misgivings about her husband's law partner, she had no known reason to hate him. Now she did, to be sure, but the question is, did Herndon have a prior reason to hate her? Certainly he had for a long time thought Lincoln's marriage unfortunate and a major source of unhappiness in Lincoln's life, which was doubtless why he dropped the offending remark in his discussion of Lincoln's melancholy. But this was hardly a reason to hate his wife, and nothing suggests that Herndon's fleeting and indirect reference to Lincoln's marriage was done out of hatred. In his own mind, he probably thought he was exercising restraint, as when he struggled in his second lecture to talk about Lincoln's life "domestically." In a section with this subtitle, he first wrote, "Home would have been to him Heaven and his wife and little ones angels but it ordained otherwise," then struck this out. Later he wrote: "O what a domestic life—what a domestic history[.] It is as terrible as death and as gloomy as the grave! Who shall write it Oh—policy—well," then struck that out. At the end of this section, realizing he had talked completely around the problem at the center, having said nothing whatever about Lincoln's wife, Herndon concluded: "I wish it were otherwise. I would change & alter here if I could this domestic touch. I cannot lie and I cannot escape his domestic life. It would be Hamlet played with Hamlet left out—Hamlet ignored."[37]

As this suggests, Herndon knew he was making a negative and unwelcome statement even in dodging the issue, but he thought it was something he was obligated to address. Herndon firmly believed, along with a number of Lincoln's closest friends, that Lincoln's unhappy marriage was a crucial factor in his becoming president. But Herndon differed from the others in undertaking to write Lincoln's biography, and in his belief that important factors in a great hero's career were "necessary truths," about which a conscientious biographer could not remain silent. A corollary to this doctrine was the belief that it was important that "necessary truths," particularly when they relate to problematical circumstances in the lives of great men, be first reported sympathetically by their friends, in order to forestall and offset the inevitable constructions that would be put on these same circumstances by their critics and enemies. I have described Herndon's doctrine of "necessary truth" its corollary, and its consequences elsewhere. Here it will perhaps suffice to say that Herndon's correspondence makes it clear that he was in great earnest about having to face up to "necessary truths," and the Ann Rutledge lecture in November 1866 was his first attempt to implement his theory and its corollary about timely and sympathetic public disclosure.[38]

It was, of course, a disaster. The adoring public, which had already elevated the martyred president to something like sainthood, was almost as shocked by Herndon's revelations and interpretations as the Lincoln family. Far from being grateful to Herndon for seeking out this unknown chapter in Lincoln's early life, showing how it related to and explained his temporary mental derangement and near atheism in New Salem, the public recoiled at his mentioning these unwelcome subjects at all. While the Ann Rutledge story would eventually find a sympathetic audience with the idolizing public, Herndon's bizarre presentation of so delicate a subject in 1866 probably led many to hope or believe, with Mary Lincoln, that it was merely a figment of Herndon's imagination.

Herndon refused to respond to the criticism publicly, but in his correspondence he defended his theory of "necessary truth" and his new disclosures. Isaac Arnold, a Chicago lawyer and congressman who was composing a life of Lincoln, wrote immediately to Herndon, who responded with a long list of intimate details from Lincoln's early life that the public (and Arnold) was unaware of, one of which concerned Mary.

> Did you know that all Lincoln's struggles—dificulties &c. between himself and wife were partly, if not wholy, caused by Mrs. L's cognition that Lincoln did not love her and *did love an other*. [Herndon

is here alluding to what Joshua Speed had told him about Lincoln's confrontation with Mary over his love for Matilda Edwards.³⁹] Lincoln told his wife that he did not love her—did so before he was married to her; she was cognizant of the fact that Lincoln loved an other. Did you know that the *Hell* through which Lincoln passed was caused by these things? Mrs. Lincoln's knowledge that Lincoln did not love her and did love another caused much trouble between them. . . . The world does not know her, Mrs. L's sufferings—her trials—and the causes of things. Sympathize with her. I shall never rob Mrs. Lincoln of her justice—Justice due her. Poor woman! She will yet have her rewards.⁴⁰

Herndon thought so well of his explanation of these matters to Arnold that he retained a copy of his letter and sent one a few days later to his young Philadelphia confidant, Charles H. Hart, a letter in which he acknowledges so directly what the result of his Ann Rutledge lecture had been on Mary Lincoln that it may indicate she had written him about it. [Y]ou will now begin to detect a purpose in my *4th* late, Lecture; . . . Mrs. Lincoln must be put properly before the world. She hates me yet *I can* and *will do* her justice; she hates me on the same grounds that a thief hates a policeman, who knows a dangerous secret, about him. *Mrs. Lincoln's domestic quarrels in my opinion sprang from a woman's revenge which she was not strong enough to resist.* Poor woman! The world has no charity for her, and yet justice must be done her—being careful not to *Injure* her husband. All that I know enobles both and their difficulties sprang from human nature—."⁴¹ In another letter to Hart a few weeks later, Herndon returned to the hostile reaction of Mary Lincoln: "Mrs Lincoln will scold me—poor woman, without knowing I am her friend, determined to put her right before the world for all time. She too has borne her cross; and she shall have justice if I live. . . . Mr & Mrs Lincoln's marriage was an unfortunate one, and I say to you that what *I know* and shall tell only ennobles both—that is to say it will show that Mrs L has had cause to suffer, and be almost crazed, while Lincoln *self sacrificed* himself rather than to be charged with dishonor."⁴²

We may dispute the adequacy of Herndon's theory of the Lincoln marriage given here to Arnold and Hart, but none of it goes to suggest that Herndon *hated* Mary Lincoln or that his real intention was, as had been urged, to get back at her.[43] On the contrary, he argued at the time that his Ann Rutledge disclosures—that Lincoln was traumatized by the loss of an earlier love—were necessary to lay the groundwork for a proper understanding of Lincoln's unhappy marriage, and that its unhappy character was not, as the public believed, solely the fault of Mary Lincoln.

One may, of course, doubt the sincerity of Herndon's protestations about the nature of his intentions and conjecture with Mrs. Randall that "Herndon hated Mrs. Lincoln, but in his own self-justifying mind he considered that, in bringing out his deductions from the supposed romance to explain the 'unhappy' marriage, he was doing justice to her."[44] But this requires the kind of "mud instinct" and "dog sagacity" about what went on in Herndon's mind that Mrs. Randall so deplores in Herndon himself. Donald, on the other hand, allows that Herndon's motive was not malicious. "His ideas may have been an unconscious rationalization of his dislike for Mary Lincoln, but there is no reason to think him insincere in believing that the Lincoln-Rutledge romance must be disclosed by a friend of the President in order to prevent hostile revelation at some later day."[45] Herndon's determination to act on his theory, regardless of short-term consequences, opens him to the charge of callousness and insensitivity, but hatred for Mary Lincoln and the wish to do her injury is something else.

Herndon's excuse to use hard words about Mary Lincoln would eventually come. Nearly seven years later, in 1873, the Reverend James Reed of Springfield delivered a lecture on Abraham Lincoln's religion, "The Later Life and Religious Sentiments of Abraham Lincoln." The lecture was in reaction to Ward Hill Lamon's 1872 biography, which gave much attention to Lincoln's "infidelity" as a young man on the basis of evidence collected by Herndon, and Reed sought to reclaim, at least for his later life, Lincoln's reputation as a Christian. Herndon was persuaded by his wife and others to reply to Reed, and on December 12, 1873, he delivered a public lecture titled "Lincoln's Religion." His most persuasive evidence that Lincoln was not a believer in Christian doctrines and that his religious views did not change while he lived in Springfield was a passage from his interview with Mary Lincoln, in which he reported her as saying: "Mr. Lincoln had no hope and no faith in the usual acceptation of these words, and Lincoln's maxim and philosophy were: 'What is to be will be, and no cares (prayers) of ours can arrest the decree.' Mr. Lincoln never joined any church. He was a religious man always, as I think. He *first thought*—to say think—about this subject was when Willie died—*never before*; he read the Bible a good deal about 1864. He felt religious, more than ever before, about the time he went to Gettysburg. Mr. Lincoln was not a technical Christian."[46]

Here it seems likely that Herndon had little or no idea that Mary Lincoln would take offense at his use of her testimony, for he said nothing disrespectful, and he was careful to portray her quite favorably: "Mrs. Lincoln is a close observer, a woman of intellect, a good judge of human nature and knew her husband thoroughly inside and outside."[47] What Herndon had not foreseen was that his lecture, which was printed the next day in full and widely circulated, created a firestorm of protest, not only in Illinois but around the country. As Donald reports, the Republican press, which saw anything tending to lower Lincoln's stature as a political liability, became actively aroused and "was uniformly hostile," loudly proclaiming Herndon a "Judas in Springfield."[48] Donald believed that, in view of her testimony's damning import, Mary had been "prevailed upon to denounce Herndon and repudiate the interview in which she had declared that Lincoln 'was not a technical Christian.'"[49] Her own letter, however, written a few days after the lecture and addressed to her cousin John T. Stuart, appears entirely voluntary. "With very great sorrow & natural indignation have I read of Mr Herndon, placing words in my mouth—*never once* uttered. I remember the call *he* made on me for a few minutes at the [St. Nicholas] hotel as he mentions, *your* welcome entrance a quarter of an hour afterward, naturally prevented a further interview with him. Mr Herndon, had always been an utter stranger to me, he was not considered an habitué, at our house. The office was more, in his line."[50] We should note in passing that this rare characterization of her relations with Herndon in Springfield, if spitefully dismissive, hardly sounds like a history of personal conflict, let along mutual hatred.[51]

The next day she wrote Stuart again: "Every word, Mr Herndon has stated as coming from me in a conversation held some years ago, is utterly false & has been entirely perverted. I hope you will kindly in my name, to parties interested pronounce it so." In her wrought-up condition, she returned to the note of revenge she had struck earlier with Judge Davis. "Cousin John, how can you all—the true friends of my dear good husband, allow such a wretched creature in your midst—A worse man I believe, had never lived. Pardon these lengthy notes, but let every one know, what false words he has attributed to poor unhappy me."[52] Three days later, the Springfield Republican newspaper announced triumphantly that Mrs. Lincoln had denied "unequivocally that she had the conversation with Mr. Herndon, as stated by him."[53]

This claim, of course, went well beyond what Mary Lincoln had written to Stuart, and Herndon, having apparently been shown the Stuart letter, was too good a lawyer not to know how to handle such contradictory statements. He composed a long public letter that appeared in several newspapers and was printed as a broadside entitled "Mrs. Lincoln's Denial, and What She Says."[54] In the letter, he explained the background of the matter and described his call on Mrs. Lincoln at the St. Nicholas Hotel. She at first demurred, according to Herndon, but "At my special request, and after some argument, she at last consented to give me a brief history of her life." Herndon then printed in full his write-up of the interview. He next pointed out that while it had been "telegraphed all over the country that no conversation ever took place," Mary nonetheless, "in the Stuart letter, expressly admits a conversation, and says that Mr. Stuart came into the room while I was taking down the substance of the conversation."

Having thus put his adversary on the horns of a dilemma, he turned to the matter of her alleging that his statements were false and perverted, noting that in this charge, "Her language is general and not specific." As a means of getting at what is actually false and perverted in his statement, he poses the issues as questions, which he does with devastating effect:

1st. Does Mrs. Lincoln mean to say that Mr. Lincoln had hope and faith in the Spiritual Unseen in the usual acceptation of these words? She knows better and so does the world. 2nd. Does she mean to say that Mr. Lincoln had no belief in nature's laws, or in other words substantially, "what is to be will be, &c. &c.?" 3d. Does she mean to say that Mr. Lincoln joined a church? 4th. Does she mean to say that Mr. Lincoln was not a religious man always, as she thought? 5th. Does she mean to say that Mr. Lincoln did not first think—to say think, about the subject of religion was when Willie died—never before? 6th. Does she mean to say that Mr. Lincoln did not read the Bible a good deal in 1864? 7th. Does she mean to say that Mr. Lincoln did not feel more religious than ever about the time he went to Gettysburg? 8th and lastly. Does she mean to say that Mr. Lincoln was a technical Christian and joined a church?

Mary Lincoln's mental health at this time was probably deteriorating and her behavior would soon force her son, on the advice of John T. Stuart and others, to have her committed. Her reaction to Herndon's public letter is probably another indication of this condition, for she immediately wrote Stuart to renew her denials. "When Herndon, presented his disagreeable self to me, at the time, he mentions, his appearance & the *air* he brought with him, were so revolting, that I could scarcely ask him to be seated—as it was, you came in about ten minutes afterwards—in *that* time, scarcely *notes* could be taken—every word the man *there*, in those two columns utters is a falsehood—so far as my conversation was concerned—The flowing bowl, must have been *entirely* exhausted—when he wrote that intellectual production."[55] In a postscript, she added, "Please deny to *every* one—that *the* interview never took place,"[56] but having second thoughts the next morning, she wrote Stuart again: "I have had a nights reflection over what I wrote you on yesterday concerning H[erndon] & think it is best—not to give the wretched, drunken madman so much importance, either to show my letter to any one or to say, I had *no such* interview—"[57]

Herndon had been firm in his public letter, as his honesty had been assailed and the Republican press had accused him of betraying his partner and friend. Nonetheless, he had deliberately kept his temper and avoided insulting language. Donald is convinced that Mary's accusation "was the signal for Herndon to loose all his long stored-up hatred for Mary Lincoln," whom Donald characterizes as the "most detested of his enemies."[58] But the existence of a long stored-up hatred still awaits proof, and Herndon's response simply does not bear the stamp of hatred, even though he regarded himself as the offended party. This was a circumstance noted at the time by his Springfield friends. William Jayne wrote to congratulate him, saying "you do not like a clod hopper call her a d—d old liar & hussey—but [instead acted] like a courtly gentleman & lawyer."[59]

Much has been made by Herndon's critics of the nasty things he later said about Mary Lincoln. To prove Herndon's "violent hatred"[60] of Mary, for example, Mrs. Randall simply pointed to Donald's finding that "since 1874 there had been in Herndon's mind no question of charity; he believed anything about Lincoln's wife that was bad. Some of his comments were unprintable."[61] Donald doesn't specify which remarks were unprintable, but the epithets he cites are these: "she wolf of this section," "soured . . . gross . . . material—avaricious—insolent," "a tigress," "like the tooth ake— kept one awake night and day," "terribly aristocratic . . . and haughty," "as cold as a chunk of ice," and "the female wild cat of the age."[62]

These examples of "hateful" language are certainly colorful and consistently negative. But as evidence of real hatred, they seem somewhat short of the mark. Surely not everyone who judged Mary on these grounds and found her wanting hated her. That Herndon's feelings towards her were decidedly mixed is suggested by the letters themselves. In spite of their being cited to prove that, after the lecture flap in 1874, Herndon had no charity for Mary, several of the letters from which these epithets are taken, all addressed to his collaborator Jesse W. Weik, contain passages that qualify these unflattering epithets and call Herndon's supposed hatred and lack of charity into question.

In the letter in which Herndon call Mary "soured . . . gross . . . material—avaricious—insolent," he also wrote, "This woman was once a brilliant *one*, but what a sad sight to see her in any year after 1862 and Especially a year or so before she died."[63] Lincoln, he wrote in another letter, "was not a judge of human nature. . . . *Mrs.* Lincoln used to help Lincoln from being imposed upon: he frequently said to her—What is your opinion of this man."[64] In the same letter, Herndon wrote: "Mrs Lincoln was a stimulant to Lincoln in a good sense: she was always urging him to look up—struggle—conquer. . . . [S]he was ambitious and helped Lincoln along in her own providential way, while she crushed his spirit in an other way: she was like the tooth ake—kept one awake night and day."[65] "She was a terrible woman," he allowed in another letter, "but I must give her credit for a keen insight into men and things. Had *hell* not got into her neck she would have led society anywhere: she was a highly cultured woman—witty—dashing—pleasant. and a lady, but hell got in her neck, which I will explain to the world sometime, if I live. This will be a curious history. When all is known the world will divide between Mr Lincoln & Mrs. Lincoln its censure as I believe."[66] A final example shows particularly well how the qualified meanings of epithets can be lost if cited in isolation: "I know that *Mrs* Lincoln acted badly, but hold your opinion for a while. I have always sympathized with Mrs. Lincoln. Remember that every Effect must have its Cause. Mrs. Lincoln was not a she wolf—wild cat without a cause."[67]

The failure to acknowledge such positive and even sympathetic comments deprives Herndon of the credit he is due for attempting to balance, in some degree, his accounts and descriptions of a woman he did not very much admire. The examples given above are, as indicated, all taken from the letters from which unfavorable epithets were culled to show his supposed hatred and lack of charity for Mary Lincoln, but in many other letters of this period he repeatedly tried to get his correspondents to understand what she had to contend with. Years after her death, in a letter to a trusted correspondent, former US senator Joseph S. Fowler, he speculated on what he thought may have been a major cause of Mrs. Lincoln's trouble: "Lincoln should never have married Mary Todd, ambitious to lead and Control Society: she was a woman of fine intellect—quick witted—sarcastic—aristocratic—refined. In fact she once was a lady, but unfortunately she fell from that high position, as I think, from the Excessive use of morphine."[68] Herndon's speculation may well have been prompted by his own wife's reported addiction to opium,[69] and he seems not to have ever mentioned this suspicion to his collaborator, or to anyone else that I am aware of. In this letter, he was clearly attempting to balance the publicly accepted picture of Mary Lincoln, which was highly unfavorable. "Mrs Lincoln was a better woman than the world gives her credit for. She was a whip and a sting to Lincoln's ambition—she urged him to go upward. I admit that *at times*, in her *after life*, that she was a she devil filled it may be with morphine. Let us be charitable for we are all weak creatures at best, no one knowing himself till conditions push him on to ruin. Bless this woman. She was Lincoln's best and wisest adviser when at herself and in her younger days. She had good judgements as to policies and a fine judge of human nature. She directed Lincoln rightly and kept him on that path."[70]

The account of Mary Lincoln in Herndon's 1889 biography is not extensive and, in the main, not highly prejudicial. There is, at the outset, a reference to the "tempestuous chapters of his married life," and we are told: "It is a curious history, and the facts, long chained down, are gradually coming to the surface. When all is at last known, the world I believe will divide its censure between Lincoln and his wife."[71] The section where Mary is featured most extensively tells not about the couple's marriage but about their troubled courtship. Lincoln is represented in this ordeal as an anguished suitor and very unwilling bridegroom, but the fault for all this is by no means laid exclusively at the feet of Mary Todd. A single paragraph, which includes Herndon's theory of Mary's supposed revenge, reports that the subsequent marriage was not happy, and ends with this: "Whether Mrs. Lincoln really was moved by the spirit of revenge or not she acted along the lines of human conduct. She led her husband a wild and merry dance. If, in time, she became soured at the world it was not without provocation, and if in later years she unchained the bitterness of a disappointed and outraged nature, it followed as logically as an effect does the cause."[72]

In a later chapter that attempts to "take a nearer and more personal view" of Abraham Lincoln, Herndon devotes several pages to his partner's domestic life, and the picture is not happy. Here Mary's difficulties with her husband, her servants, and others are outlined, mostly through anecdotes and the testimony of family and friends. Thus it is Mary's half sister who says that "she raised 'merry war' because he persisted in using his own knife in the butter, instead of the silver-handled one intended for that purpose."[73] It is Judge David Davis who is quoted as saying, "as a general rule, when all the lawyers of a Saturday evening would go home and see their families and friends, Lincoln would find some excuse and refuse to go. We said nothing, but it seemed to us all he was not domestically happy."[74] A letter from Lincoln to a newspaper editor is quoted to show that Lincoln, by his own admission, spoke "evasively" to his wife, rather than admit that he was responsible for subscribing to a newspaper she did not approve of.[75] Herndon plainly indicates that Lincoln was unhappy in his home life and often stayed away from home on that account, and he declares that, contrary to what some may insist, his account is not "too highly colored." But he concludes by emphasizing, as he did often in his own letters, that Mary Lincoln was not solely responsible for these difficulties. "In her domestic troubles I have always sympathized with Mrs. Lincoln. The world does not know what she bore, or how ill-adapted she was to bear it."[76]

Herndon's intention in discussing Mary Lincoln and the Lincoln marriage was to report on an important aspect of his subject's life, but it cannot be said that he presented a balanced picture. As Donald has pointed out, "Herndon's own testimony and the reminiscences he collected as to Mrs. Lincoln's temper and to occasional 'flare-ups' in the Lincoln home are supported by indisputable contemporary evidence. Mary Lincoln for years suffered from a mental ailment and eventually went insane. But Herndon did not have the whole story. Lincoln's letters to his wife, records of the Lincolns' participation in Springfield social life, reminiscences of many pleasant happenings in the house on Eighth Street are an equally important part of the record."[77] There is no doubt, as Donald shows, that Herndon's recollections and anecdotes, in attempting to demonstrate that Lincoln's marriage was troubled, tell an incomplete story and thus make for a "distorted portrait," but that is very different from saying that he acted from malice.

Did Mary Lincoln hate William Henry Herndon? The evidence suggests that she did with what appeared to her and many others to be good reason, but only after he published his offending Ann Rutledge lecture in November 1866. Did Herndon hate his partner's wife, and more importantly, did he frame, out of malice, a false and unfavorable picture of her? The current view that he did both, as I have tried to show, needs to be reconsidered, for it is almost entirely presumptive and is not based on established facts. Moreover, it often takes a form that verges on circularity: How do we know that Herndon hated Mary? Because he was out to get her. How do we know he was out to get her? Because he hated her. There is no factual basis for thinking that Herndon was openly or secretly hostile toward Mary Lincoln prior to 1866, or vice versa, and no evidence to contradict his claim that she was always kind to him and that he, in turn, respected her. The evidence of his letters that refer to her, almost all written after Lincoln's death, suggests that while he often faulted her for her aristocratic ways and violent temper and that he believed Lincoln's home life was a "domestic hell," his mature view of her was complicated and heavily qualified, conceding to her many good qualities and valuable contributions. In spite of his reputation as her sworn enemy who in later years engaged her in "open warfare,"[78] a consistent theme in Herndon's correspondence from 1866 on is that Mary Lincoln had been unfairly condemned as the sole source of difficulty in the Lincoln marriage, and that Lincoln, who was not an attentive and helpful husband, deserved a share of the blame. Herndon believed that they had married for the wrong reasons—she to land a successful politician and he to preserve his honor—and that this doomed their marriage. He further believed that she had changed over time—for the worse. They were not bad people, but they had a bad marriage. This caused Lincoln to be unhappy in his home life and Mary to sometimes behave as "the female wild cat of the age." In 1866, he had twice used a phrase that captures the essence of it: "what *I know* and shall tell only ennobles both—that is to say it will show that Mrs L has had cause to suffer, and be almost crazed, while Lincoln *self sacrificed* himself rather than to be charged with dishonor."[79]

### Notes

This article originally appeared in the *Journal of the Abraham Lincoln Association* 22 (Summer 2001): 1–26.

1. William H. Herndon (WHH) to Jesse W. Weik (JWW), January 16, 1886, Herndon-Weik Collection, Library of Congress; hereafter cited as H-W. Mary Todd Lincoln (MTL) to David Davis, March 6, [1867], Justin G. Turner and Linda Levitt Turner, eds., *Mary Todd Lincoln: Her Life and Letters* (New York: Alfred A. Knopf, 1972), 416; hereafter cited as Turner and Turner.

2. See Turner and Turner, 33. See also Charles B. Strozier, who speaks of "the triangular relationship of Lincoln, Mary, and Herndon," and who says that Lincoln's wife and his law partner, "like children in a situation of intense sibling rivalry, detested each other." *Lincoln's Quest for Union: Public and Private Meanings* (New York: Basic, 1982), 80, 81. See also David Herbert Donald, *Lincoln* (New York: Simon and Schuster, 1995), 160, 401.

3. There are, of course, some harbingers of Donald's view. See, for example, Ida M. Tarbell's review of Emanuel Hertz's *The Hidden Lincoln* in the *New York Times Book Review*, February 13, 1938, charging that Herndon "left no trace of kindness in the picture he drew of her [Mary Todd Lincoln] to Mr. Weik. He needed that picture for his thesis [i.e., his 'theory of Lincoln's melancholy']."

4. David Herbert Donald, *Lincoln's Herndon: A Biography*, (Knopf, 1948; reprinted New York: Da Capo, 1989). In the discussion that follows, I often differ with Professor Donald, but I wish to acknowledge that, like all who study Herndon, I am deeply in his debt. Both his doctoral dissertation (*Herndon: Lincoln's Law Partner*,

University of Illinois, 1946) and the published biography that emerged from it are models of skill and resourcefulness in research that have enabled and illuminated all subsequent studies.

5. Harold Holzer, book review, *Journal of Illinois History* 1, no. 2 (Winter 1998): 137.

6. Donald, *Lincoln's Herndon*, 188.

7. See notes 10, 11, and 12 below.

8. WHH to JWW, January 16, 1886, H-W.

9. William H. Herndon and Jesse W. Weik, *Herndon's Lincoln: The True Story of a Great Life* (Chicago: Belford, Clarke, 1889), 2:209; in Paul M. Angle, ed., *Herndon's Life of Lincoln* (1930; reprinted Cleveland: World, 1949), 166; and in Douglas L. Wilson and Rodney O Davis, eds., William H. Herndon and Jesse W. Weik, *Herndon's Lincoln* (Urbana: University of Illinois Press, 2006), 134.

10. Donald, *Lincoln's Herndon*, 189. In the nine years since the original publication of this article, I have seen only one reported instance of Herndon's having expressed his animosity toward Mary Lincoln prior to his partner's presidency. This was pointed out by Joshua Wolf Shenk in his fine and carefully researched study *Lincoln's Melancholy: How Depression Challenged a President and Fueled His Greatness* (New York: Houghton Mifflin, 2005), 296n. Shenk shows that Gibson Harris, who served as a law clerk for Lincoln and Herndon in the mid-1840s, recalled sixty years later that Herndon "cherished a strong dislike for . . . Mrs. Lincoln, and of this fact made no secret to the office-clerk" ("My Recollections of Abraham Lincoln," *Farm and Fireside*, December 1, 1904, 23).

11. "Lincolns Domestic Life," H-W Collection, Library of Congress.

12. Ruth Painter Randall, *Mary Lincoln: Biography of a Marriage* (Boston: Little, Brown, 1953), 37.

13. Turner and Turner, 33.

14. Stephen B. Oates, *With Malice toward None: The Life of Abraham Lincoln* (New York: Harper and Row, 1977), 74.

15. Donald, *Lincoln's Herndon*, 160.

16. WHH to Joseph S. Fowler, November 3, 1888, Ethan Allen Hitchcock Papers, Box 1, Library of Congress. I have here amended Herndon's "respect" to the past tense, which seems to be what he intended.

17. Donald says that Mary Lincoln snubbed Herndon during his only trip to the Lincoln White House and that he was "bitterly resentful." But Donald cites no evidence beyond a reference to Mrs. Lincoln in one of Herndon's letters as "a very curious—excentric—*wicked* woman" (Donald, *Lincoln's Herndon*, 153). This would certainly suggest that Herndon had credited the many stories making the rounds when he visited Washington about Mrs. Lincoln's improper behavior with Henry Wycoff, but how it would prove that Herndon was snubbed or that he was "bitterly resentful" is not evident.

18. Donald, *Lincoln's Herndon*, 188, 189, 196.

19. See Douglas L. Wilson and Rodney O. Davis, eds., *Herndon's Informants: Letters, Interviews, and Statements about Abraham Lincoln* (Urbana: University of Illinois Press, 1998); hereafter cited as *Herndon's Informants*.

20. Editor's preface, Angle, *Herndon's Life of Lincoln*, xliv.

21. This figure reflects dated items in the Herndon archive from May 1865 to mid-November and half the undated items known to have been collected no later than November 30, 1866.

22. MTL to WHH, August 28, [1867], *Herndon's Informants*, 326. MTL is confused about the date; this letter was written in 1866, but September 4 was a Tuesday.

23. "Mrs. Lincoln's Denial, and What She Says," printed broadside, Abraham Lincoln Presidential Library (formerly Illinois State Historical Library).

24. Mary Todd Lincoln (WHH interview), [September 1866], *Herndon's Informants*, 359–60.

25. Isaac N. Phillips to James R. B. Van Cleave, April 26, 1909, typescript, Abraham Lincoln Association Papers, Abraham Lincoln Presidential Library (formerly Illinois State Historical Library).

26. WHH to Isaac N. Arnold, November 30, 1866, H-W; copy made by WHH's copyist, John G. Springer.

27. Dr. James Smith to WHH, January 24, 1867, *Herndon's Informants*, 547.

28. Although very few letters from Abraham Lincoln to his wife are known, some are signed "Affectionately."

29. Robert Todd Lincoln to David Davis, November 19, 1866. Text interpolated from citations in John F. Goff, *Robert Todd Lincoln: A Man in His Own Right* (Norman: University of Oklahoma Press, 1969), 84; and Willard L. King, *Lincoln's Manager: David Davis* (Cambridge: Harvard University Press, 1960), 239.

30. WHH to JWW, December 1, 1888, H-W. The pages of this letter are out of order in the microfilm edition (Exp. 4:2410–13, 2322–25).

31. Robert Todd Lincoln to David Davis, December 8, 1866, in Thomas F. Schwartz, "'I Have Never Had Any Doubt of Your Good Intentions': William Henry Herndon and Ward Hill Lamon as Described in Correspondence from the Robert T. Lincoln Letterpress Volumes," *Journal of the Abraham Lincoln Association* 14, no. 1 (Winter 1993): 37.

32. Robert Todd Lincoln to John G. Nicolay, December 16, 1866, ibid., 39.

33. MTL to David Davis, March 4, 1867, Turner and Turner, 414.

34. WHH, "Analysis of the Character and Mind of Abm Lincoln," manuscript of WHH's first lecture on Lincoln, Huntington Library. The lecture was delivered December 12, 1865, in Springfield, Illinois.

35. MTL to David Davis, March 4, 1867, Turner and Turner, 414–15.

36. MTL to David Davis, March 6, 1867, Turner and Turner, 415–16.

37. WHH, "Analysis of the Character of Abrm Lincoln," manuscript of WHH's second Lincoln lecture, Huntington Library. The lecture was delivered December 26, 1865 in Springfield, Illinois.

38. See Douglas L. Wilson, "William H. Herndon and the 'Necessary Truth,'" in *Lincoln before Washington: New Perspectives on the Illinois Years* (Urbana: University of Illinois Press, 1997), 37–52.

39. See Joshua F. Speed (WHH interview), [1865–66], *Herndon's Informants*, 474–75, 477. See also Douglas L. Wilson, *Honor's Voice: The Transformation of Abraham Lincoln* (New York: Alfred A. Knopf, 1998), 220ff.

40. WHH to Isaac N. Arnold, November 20, 1866, copy enclosed in WHH to Charles H. Hart, November 26, 1866, Hart Papers, Huntington Library; hereafter cited as Hart Papers.

41. WHH to Charles H. Hart, November 26, 1866, Hart Papers.

42. WHH to Charles H. Hart, December 12, 1866, Hart Papers.

43. See Donald, *Lincoln's Herndon*, 188–91.

44. Randall, *Mary Lincoln*, 404.

45. Donald, *Lincoln's Herndon*, 220.

46. WHH, "Lincoln's Religion," *Illinois State Register*, December 13, 1873.

47. Ibid.

48. Newspaper headline cited in Donald, *Lincoln's Herndon*, 279.

49. Ibid. As with all Herndon's interview reports, the language here must be understood as substantive only, and not necessarily literal. There is evidence that "technical Christian" was one of Herndon's own terms, by which he meant someone who openly embraced Christian dogma. Even though its use here may have accurately reflected her meaning, Mrs. Lincoln may well have been justified in protesting that "technical Christian" was not her language.

50. MTL to John T. Stuart, December 15, 1873, Turner and Turner, 603.

51. For the qualification "spitefully dismissive," I am indebted to my colleague Rodney O. Davis.

52. MTL to John T. Stuart, December 15, 1873, Turner and Turner, 603.

53. *Illinois State Journal*, December 19, 1873, quoted in Donald, *Lincoln's Herndon*, 280.

54. According to Donald, Herndon's long letter, dated January 12, 1873, was first printed in the *Illinois State Register* on January 14 and in other papers soon thereafter (*Lincoln's Herndon*, 281n). For the broadside, which is the source of the text followed here, see the copy in the H-W Collection, Library of Congress. All quotations are from this copy.

55. MTL to John T. Stuart, January 20, 1874, Turner and Turner, 605.

56. Ibid., 606.

57. Ibid.

58. Donald, *Lincoln's Herndon*, 280.

59. Quoted in Donald, *Lincoln's Herndon*, 281.

60. Randall, *Mary Lincoln*, 38.

61. Ibid., 303.

62. Ibid., 303–4. The letters from which the quoted epithets are taken are WHH to JWW, December 1, 1885, January 8, 12, 15, 16, 1886, H-W.

63. WHH to JWW, January 8, 1886, H-W.

64. WHH to JWW, January 12, 1886, ibid.

65. WHH to JWW, January 12, 1886, ibid.

66. WHH to JWW, January 16, 1886, ibid.

67. WHH to JWW, January 16, 1886, ibid. It should be noted that the epithets "she wolf" and "wild cat" present here were not among those cited by Donald.

68. WHH to Joseph S. Fowler, November 3, 1888, Ethan Allen Hitchcock Paper, Box 1, Library of Congress.

69. Caroline Healey Dall, who stayed in Herndon's home in October 1866, wrote in her journal: "Nat the oldest son . . . explained the cloud hanging over Herndon's unhappy second wife. . . . He says she has always taken opium and this is the result—and the reason why the family has lost their status." Dall Papers, Bryn Mawr College Library. The reader should note that this portion of Dall's journal was reconstructed from her notes thirty years later and contains many known errors.

70. WHH to Joseph S. Fowler, November 3, 1888, Ethan Allen Hitchcock Paper, Box 1, Library of Congress.

71. *Herndon's Lincoln*, 2:205–6; Angle edition, 163.

72. *Herndon's Lincoln*, 2:230; Angle edition, 182.

73. *Herndon's Lincoln*, 3:427; Angle edition, 345.

74. *Herndon's Lincoln*, 3:425; Angle edition, 344.

75. *Herndon's Lincoln*, 3:429; Angle edition, 347.

76. *Herndon's Lincoln*, 3:433–34; Angle edition, 350

77. Donald, *Lincoln's Herndon*, 359.

78. David Donald, *Lincoln Reconsidered* (New York: Vintage, 1961), 43.

79. WHH to Charles H. Hart, December 12, 1866, Hart Papers.

## "I Am So Fond of *Sightseeing*"
### Mary Lincoln's Travels up to 1865

*Wayne C. Temple*

In Mary Ann Todd's era, many people were born and died in the same county—never having left its borders. However, Mary had an adventurous spirit and enough family money to travel. When just thirteen years of age, she would ride her white pony from her residence on West Main Street all the way out to Henry Clay's mansion—"Ashland"—on the Richmond Pike south of Lexington.[1]

After her mother died and her father, Robert Smith Todd, remarried and immediately started a second family, Mary sought every means to escape for long periods of time from home and her stepmother. We know that Mary and her older sister Frances Jane (March 7, 1817– August 14, 1899) were in Springfield, Illinois, on May 16, 1835, visiting the oldest sister, Elizabeth (November 18, 1813–February 22, 1888) who was married to Ninian Wirt Edwards. Both Mary and Frances witnessed a deed transaction on that date for their brother-in-law, Ninian.[2] Mary was just sixteen and a half years of age, and to reach Springfield from Kentucky required lengthy travels upon steamboats plying the Ohio, Mississippi, and Illinois rivers.

Again, in the summer of 1837, Mary Todd was with Elizabeth Todd Edwards in Springfield.[3] Once more, she travelled with sister Frances by water and the usual land connections. From numerous sources, it is known that Mary Todd came back to Springfield in October of 1839 to stay permanently with Mr. and Mrs. Ninian Edwards. Frances had married Dr. William Smith Wallace on May 21, 1839, and remained in Springfield, too.[4]

It should be assumed that some male certainly accompanied these girls on their travels. It is known that their father sometimes journeyed to Springfield. Perhaps he was one of those travelling companions.

During the summer of 1840, Mary Todd travelled up the wide Missouri River to vacation for several months with her uncle Judge David Todd, who resided at Columbia, Missouri. While there, she also boated up the Missouri to Boonville. She commented upon the charms of Boonville as well as St. Louis and declared that she could truly enjoy living in either place. She professed to Mercy Ann Levering on July 23, 1840, during her prolonged stay in Missouri, that "a life on the river to me has always had a charm." There was "so much excitement" in such a pleasant setting. She remained for a full week in Boonville attending parties and sightseeing before backtracking to Columbia and the eventual return trip to Springfield.[5]

On November 4, 1842, Mary Todd wed a tall, gangling trial lawyer who had no money to spend on a proper honeymoon. The newlyweds certainly spent the first night or so in Mary's bedroom in the Edwards home before securing a room at the Globe Tavern. Since their marriage was a spur-of-the-moment affair, Lincoln certainly had no time to secure boarding facilities beforehand. Their first lengthy excursion commenced on or about October 25, 1847, when Congressman Lincoln took his wife and family to Washington. No doubt they caught a stagecoach from Springfield so as to make a river connection to St. Louis, where they checked into Scott's Hotel on October 27. Awaiting them there was Joshua Fry Speed, Lincoln's oldest bosom companion. By the Mississippi River they travelled South to meet the beautiful Ohio and follow it upstream.

Since Speed had connected with the Lincolns at St. Louis, he certainly escorted them to Louisville. Speed was headed to "Farmington," his plantation near there. From Louisville, the Lincolns proceeded by railroad to Lexington, where they stayed with Mary's family for a period of time. Once more they made their way back to the Ohio River for a boat ride to Pittsburgh. From that point they took a stagecoach for a trip of less than one hundred miles to Cumberland, Maryland. After a tedious and bumpy journey, they engaged passage on a boat or barge for a smooth cruise down the Potomac River to Washington, where they arrived on December 2, 1847.[6]

Within a short time, the Lincolns took up quarters in Mrs. Anna G. Sprigg's boardinghouse across from the Capitol. With two very young and undisciplined children, the new congressman's wife and her spirited offspring must have created a few problems in Mrs. Sprigg's lodgings. Few members of Congress brought their families to Washington, and Mary Lincoln did not become a favorite of those on the premises. Long before April 16, 1848, she and the little boys had withdrawn to Lexington, Kentucky. In writing to his wife in the middle of April, Lincoln in great candor explained: "When you were here, I thought you hindered me some in attending to business." In somewhat of a chiding mood, Lincoln continued his letter by saying, "All the house—or rather, all with whom you were on decided good terms—send their love to you. The others say nothing."[7] Mary with the boys had most certainly travelled part of the way back to Lexington by water.

In the early part of June 1848, Mary Lincoln petitioned her doting husband for permission to return to Washington. Perhaps the Todd household in Lexington wished that her prolonged stay there would come to an end, or perhaps Mary sorely missed Abraham's comforting nature. Anyhow, on June 12, Congressman Lincoln replied to her urgent letter. "The leading matter in your letter, is your wish to return to this side of the Mountains," he surmised. "Will you be a *good girl* in all things, if I consent?" he questioned her. "Then come along," he said. From Mary's letter it appears that another of her uncles, James Parker of Missouri, would accompany her on the long journey.[8] He could assist her with the very young children, too. This trip, also, would be along the waterways with a few land connections.

Mary knew that the first session of the Thirtieth Congress would end on August 14, 1848, and that her Whig husband would be returning home to campaign for his party in the coming election. She practically begged him to take her on a roundabout route back to Springfield from Washington. "You know I am so fond of *sightseeing*, & I did not get to New York or Boston, or travel the lake route—" she hinted broadly.[9] Fortunately for Mary's intense desire to "sightsee," a prominent member of the national Whig Party in Boston invited Congressman Lincoln to come there and speak to the Massachusetts Whig State Convention opening on September 13. Such invitations would later be extended to him from several other Whig leaders in other cities of that state. Such a turn of events guaranteed that Mary would get to see those cities mentioned and sail through the Great Lakes as far as Chicago.

Lincoln remained in Washington franking political documents for the mails but finally quit and drew up a schedule for a lengthy odyssey—half vacation and half political. They planned to leave Washington on September 5 and proceed to New York City where they would visit the historic sites and other places. From there, the Lincolns departed on a boat to Norwich and by rail on to Worcester, by the twelfth. After making several speeches there and at New Bedford, they arrived in Boston, where he did speak on the fifteenth. Mary seems to have remained there while Lincoln travelled to other nearby cities to address political gatherings. Little Eddie, who suffered from chronic consumption, fell ill again and remained in Boston with his mother until sufficiently recovered for the lengthy, difficult voyage and land connections back to Springfield.

From Boston, the Lincoln family departed by train on September 23 bound for Albany, New York. By the following day, they would have reached Albany, where Thurlow Weed escorted Abraham to meet Millard Fillmore. From Albany they headed to Buffalo where they arrived sometime during the twenty-fifth. Here on Lake Erie, father Abraham sought passage to Chicago on Lake Michigan. There in the harbor lay the brand-new steamboat *Globe.* She had just entered lake service about July 1 that year. In length she ran to 251 feet with a saloon cabin approximately 190 feet long with luxury accommodations for first-class passengers. Her burden was thirteen hundred tons with a crew of twenty-five. "For speed, comfort and safety" no other vessel on the Great Lakes could compete with her. Lincoln always chose the very best for his "Molly." He purchased passage from the purser, and early on the morning of the twenty-sixth, the Lincolns mounted the gangplank and sailed away on this ship under the command of Captain James Sanderson, a dynamic sailor of great experience. At last, Mary was about to accomplish the third item on her travel wish list. Lincoln paid about ten dollars apiece for the tickets.

Under normal weather conditions, the *Globe* made the passage from Buffalo to Chicago in seven days. On this trip it would take her ten days. After the tenth of September, the Great Lakes experienced very heavy rain and high winds. It would be a "boisterous" crossing for the Lincolns. Mary, however, was generally a very good water traveler, rarely getting seasick.

On the early morning hours of September 29, the *Globe* steamed up the Detroit River, where the passengers observed the *Canada* stuck on a sandbar. During the previous night, her captain, H. Van Allen, had run her aground on Fighting Island. Lincoln watched as the *Canada*'s crew attempted to free her by forcing "all the loose planks, empty barrels, boxes, and the like" under the hull to buoy the ship higher in the water. It was this incident that inspired Abraham Lincoln to invent a method of getting ships off shoals and the like. Upon reaching home, he quickly fashioned two ship models which displayed the bellows and machinery that would float a vessel off an obstruction. One he kept and the other he took to Washington where he received a patent for his invention. In relating this incident, Billy Herndon got the ships mixed up. It was not the *Globe* that got stuck. Of course, Billy was not along on this voyage and merely surmised that it was the Lincoln's steamship that had suffered such a misfortune.

The next port of call for the *Globe* was Milwaukee, Wisconsin, which it reached on October 4. Passengers disembarked for a few hours on shore while the crew loaded and unloaded the freight. During the wee hours on the morning of October 6, the *Globe* docked at Chicago. The Hon. A. Lincoln "and family" quickly checked into the Sherman House on Clark Street near the steamboat landing. They would linger there to recuperate after the stormy voyage. However, that evening, Lincoln gave a political speech at the public square.

When the Lincolns arose early on the morning of October 7, Chicago still enjoyed wonderful fall weather. After packing up their belongings, the Lincolns headed by coach to the basin of the new Illinois and Michigan Canal, which had just opened for traffic on April 23 that year. It had four feet of water in it, sufficient depth for navigation of canal boats with their shallow draft. These crafts were pulled by horses or mules plodding along towpaths beside the canal. Passage cost four dollars per person, and it took twenty-two hours to reach LaSalle, which was the head of navigation for steamboats on the Illinois River. Father Abraham probably chose the *Chicago* under the command of Captain N. M. Wheeler. His ship carried no freight and made no stops between Chicago and LaSalle. This vessel could accommodate thirty-five passengers in quiet comfort. Lincoln always selected the best hotels and ships in order to please his aristocratic spouse. He, himself, couldn't have cared less, being used to very poor food and transportation while riding the circuit.

At breakfast time on Sunday, October 8, the *Chicago* drifted into the canal boat basin at LaSalle after a full day and night of travel. Certainly, the Lincolns next sought food and then walked about a half a block to the steam boat basin. Here with steam up were two steamboats: the *Domain* and the *Daniel Hillman*. Both left at about eight or nine for Peoria. By 5 P.M. both docked there on time. Just two blocks from the landing stood the Planter's House, a fine brick structure and Lincoln's favorite hostelry in Peoria. It had been constructed in 1840–41 and had the best accommodations in town. It also had another advantage; in its basement reposed the post office and the stage office from which the Lincolns would later depart.

After a good night's sleep, they arose late in the forenoon on the ninth. Congressman Lincoln informed the local Whigs that he could make a political speech favoring the election of General Zachary Taylor, their candidate for president. Quickly the Whigs printed handbills announcing that Lincoln would speak that night at the courthouse. When the speaking ended, Lincoln simply strode across the street to his hotel on Courthouse Square. He would need a good night's rest. Abraham, Mary, and the two boys had to be on the stage at 4 A.M. the following morning—October 10. Tickets cost approximately five and a half cents per mile, and the ride would be rough and tiresome in a crowded stagecoach. Gone were the more pleasant and restful days and hours on the waterways. Seventeen long hours later, the Lincolns arrived back in Springfield at 9 P.M. that day. At last, Mary could boast that she had travelled the Great Lakes and the Illinois and Michigan Canal, the latter a special interest of her husband, who had sponsored everything connected with internal improvements.[10]

When Mary's father, Robert Smith Todd (born February 25, 1791) died at 1 A.M. on July 17, 1849, at his farm, "Buena Vista," in Franklin County, Kentucky,[11] northwest of Lexington, one of his obstreperous sons, George, strongly objected to the provisions of Robert's will. Robert Todd's four daughters in Springfield—Elizabeth, Frances, Mary, and Ann—engaged Lincoln, their lawyer brother-in-law, to protect their monetary interests. So, sometime about the middle of October, Abraham, Mary, Robert, and Eddie commenced the long trek to Lexington, utilizing the steamboats on the Illinois, Mississippi, and Ohio Rivers.

When Robert's will was presented to the September term of the Fayette County Court, George pointed out that the will had only one witness. Two were required by law. So, the court declared that the estate be divided equally with the Widow Todd as administratrix who was now forced to liquidate her late husband's assets to obtain cash money. Robert had been a partner in Oldham, Todd, and Company, and his one-third share had to be sold, too. There were fourteen Todd children who now inherited part of the proceeds.

There is no record that Lincoln took part in the proceedings concerning the contested will. However, Robert S. Todd had previously sued Robert Wickliffe to recover property, and Lincoln assisted in handling this matter. A bill of reviver had been filed by Lincoln while he was in Springfield on October 2, 1849, on behalf of "Abraham Lincoln and Mary A. Lincoln, his wife; Ninian W. Edwards and Elizabeth P. Edwards, his wife," and the other legal heirs of Robert S. Todd—"who charge as in the original & cross bills of their ancestor." Wickliffe answered on October 11 that he did not recognize these heirs!

Thus matters stood when the Lincolns arrived in Lexington about October 20. Shortly afterwards, Lincoln the lawyer met with his local cocounsel, Judge George Robertson, who represented the Todds and had a small office on Jordan's Row. They commenced to take depositions from people that could prove the Todd claim. When the legal work was finished, the Lincolns departed from Lexington, before November 10, leaving the case of Todd's heirs versus Robert Wickliffe in the capable hands of Judge Robertson. They had vacationed in Lexington for several weeks.[12] Back they headed for Springfield, which they reached on the evening of November 15. A local newspaper estimated that they had been gone three or four weeks.[13] Abraham Lincoln's legal efforts had been in vain. Not only the lower court but also the court of appeals ruled against the Todds' claim.[14]

Mrs. Elizabeth R. Parker, Mary's widowed grandmother, died at the age of eighty, at 10:55 P.M. on January 22, 1850, at her residence on Short Street in Lexington.[15] She had given great solace to young Mary after her mother had passed away, and some of her estate might have descended to Mary. However, Lincoln did not make that long journey to the Bluegrass, as some authors have erroneously stated, to assist with any legal matters that might arise. He remained in Springfield with numerous law cases.

Despite having won his case for payment from the Illinois Central Railroad for successfully defending it against McLean County's taxation suit, the railroad delayed rendering Lincoln's extremely large fee. As a result, he certainly determined to travel to New York City to confront the home office. In doing so, Lincoln also provided Mary with a pleasant vacation of sightseeing, which she ever desired. They departed from Springfield on July 22, 1857. Arriving in Niagara Falls, New York, they registered at the Cataract House on July 24. Undoubtedly, husband and wife viewed the falls, rode one of the little excursion boats below the rapids, and toured nearby Canada, which Mary later mentioned as one of their stops. Onward they railroaded into New York City. After taking in the historic places there and about, they finally returned to Springfield about August 5.[16]

On the following month, Mary recalled her adventure to Emilie Todd Helm. "This summer," she wrote, "has strangely & rapidly passed away— some portion of it, was spent most pleasantly in traveling east[;] we visited Niagara, Canada, New York & other points of interest[;] when I saw the large steamers at the New York landing, ready for their European voyage, I felt in my heart, inclined to sigh, that poverty was my portion[;] how I long to go to Europe. I often laugh & tell Mr. L— that I am determined my next Husband *shall be rich*."[17] Such picturesque sights merely whetted her keen appetite for extensive travels in the future.

To accommodate all the Springfield citizens who wished to attend the last Lincoln-Douglas debate at Alton on October 15, the Chicago, Alton, and St. Louis Railroad assembled a special excursion train with half-price fares. When it left the station at Third and Jefferson that morning at 6:30, Mary Lincoln was aboard. Accompanying her was fifteen-year-old Robert, who was a member of the Springfield Cadets. Also aboard was the Merritt's Cadet Band. It was a merry trip of eighty-seven miles, which ended in Alton at 10:40. Mary immediately went to the Franklin House, where Abraham awaited her. The great discourse commenced at 1:30 with special seats provided for the ladies on the east side of city hall. Of the seven debates, this was the only one Mary Lincoln attended. At its conclusion, the special train departed for Springfield at 6:20 P.M. with Abraham, Mary, and Robert aboard. Happily, this time the Lincoln family was altogether in one place during that busy debate year of 1858. Without doubt, Mary had worn her very best dress.[18]

Imagine Mary Lincoln's pleasant surprise in the summer of 1859 when she learned that her husband and several of their close friends had been chosen to evaluate the extensive holdings of the Illinois Central Railroad. Then her mild surprise turned into pure delight when she discovered that the long, extended railroad trip of discovery could also include the wives as well. In total, the select party consisted of eighteen people, including Mr. and Mrs. Jesse K. Dubois; Mr. and Mrs. Thomas H. Campbell; Mr. and Mrs. Stephen T. Logan; Mr. John Moore; Mr. and Mrs. William Butler and others, such as Ozias Mather Hatch. Always eager for a travelling vacation, Mary, of course, gleefully joined Abraham in this merry group of fellow townsmen and women. They left Springfield by rail on July 14, 1859, and returned safely on the evening of July 22. In describing the work-and-play excursion of eleven hundred miles, Mary exclaimed, "*Words* cannot express what a merry time, we had, the gayest pleasure party, I have ever seen."[19]

Following his election to the presidency, Lincoln and Mary decided to travel to Chicago to meet the vice president–elect, Hannibal Hamlin, and attend to other business. Mary could shop and sightsee. They left on November 21, 1860, and checked into the Tremont House. On the following day, Mary saw the Wigwam, post office, custom house, and US courthouse. Then on Sunday, the twenty-fifth, they attended the St. James Episcopal Church with Isaac N. Arnold. After a most pleasant experience, they departed Chicago on the twenty-sixth for Springfield.[20]

Mary Lincoln, who always desired the finest and latest fashions in clothing, concluded that only in New York City could she assemble a suitable wardrobe for her new role as First Lady of the Land. So, on January 8, 1861, she departed by train for that city. Accompanying her were a brother-in-law—Clark Moulton Smith—and former congressman Amos Tuck of New Hampshire who had come out to Springfield seeking a federal appointment.[21] (President Lincoln later appointed him naval officer for the Port of Boston.)

She had managed to secure free railroad passes on the various lines, and on January 11 reached Albany.[22] On the following day, about noon, she steamed into New York City aboard "the Harlem cars from Albany, accompanied by Philip Dorsheimer, esq., the [New York] State Treasurer. From this city she [was to go]to Harvard to see her son."[23] There is no evidence that Mary went to Cambridge at this time.

A New York City reporter spotted her and minutely described her wearing apparel. "Her Dress," noticed the witness, "was a brown or oak-colored silk, with grayish flowers and leaves. It was made full, with flounces fitted well, hung gracefully about her person, and trailed just a trifle. Her bonnet was of black silk, trimmed with cherry ribbon, which, with a dark mixed shawl, neatly-fitted kid gloves, and a rich lavendar-colored parasol, completed her costume."[24]

Another publication learned that Mary was staying at the Astor House and bemoaned the fact that it did not know her mission in New York.[25] As if in answer to that question, another publication stated that she "will remain here for a few days, in order to make some needful purchases for the White House."[26] Actually, she embarked on "a series of giddy shopping sprees" where the many merchants supplied her desires with grants of credit."[27]

By January 22, she was residing in Warren Leland's Metropolitan Hotel, where on that date Robert Lincoln came down from Harvard to join her in sightseeing: the stock exchange, treasurer's office and "other public places."[28] On the next afternoon, both mother and son took their leave from New York City and started home. A reporter spotted them in Cleveland on the twenty-fourth taking "supper" at Wheeler's restaurant.[29] They rattled into Springfield on the Wabash Line during the evening of the twenty-fifth.[30] Robert was on a six weeks' vacation from college and would remain with his family and accompany them to Washington. That vacation was later extended by the college officials so that Robert could attend the inaugural events, etc.

At 8 A.M. on February 11, 1861, president-elect Abraham Lincoln departed from Springfield at the Great Western Railroad depot aboard a special train consisting of a passenger car, a smoking car, and a baggage car.[31] It was an "unpleasant cloudy rainy day," according to Henry C. Latham, and Lincoln had tears in his eyes as he closed his sentimental farewell remarks to his fellow citizens gathered around the station and the tracks.[32] Yet for security reasons, Mary Lincoln was not with him. She and the two younger sons, plus a couple of "domestics," would leave that evening and join him the following morning in Indianapolis.[33]

Now began a regal, twelve-day tour of 1,904 miles ending up in Washington. Despite the rigors of uncontrolled crowds at every railway stop, bad weather, and other distractions, Mary certainly felt like Julius Caesar returning to Rome after a successful military campaign. She had always wanted to be a president's wife, and now she was returning to be one. The Inaugural Special whistled its way through seven states plus the District of Columbia, where Mary slept in the finest hotels available, dined at the best of restaurants in the large cities, and caught glimpses of state capitols, city halls, and other historic sites. It was a triumphal line of march to Willard's Hotel and then on to the White House.

Just two days after the inauguration, a few of Mrs. Lincoln's "intimate Illinois friends" and her Todd relatives—especially her half sister, Margaret Todd, married to Charles Kellogg—invited her to accompany them on a visit to Mount Vernon. Of course, her celebrated presence would insure them of special treatment at the shrine. She agreed to go on March 9, but a severe storm prevented the trip.[34]

Having heard of the First Lady's interest in George Washington's estate, the officers of the Mount Vernon Ladies Association issued her an invitation on March 13. (This group still owns the home and grounds.) Marshal Ward Hill Lamon answered for Mary, stating that she would be there on the fifteenth.[35] Again, she did not go. Finally, on March 26, she and "a company of ladies and gentleman, visited Mount Vernon."[36] They steamed there on the Potomac aboard the *Thomas Collyer*. After looking at the mansion and the tomb, Mary and Margaret lunched on buttered bread and ham. Although Mary acquired photographs of the mansion and tomb, identified them in her own hand, and placed them in the family album, her only known written comment about this visitation was a letter to a friend on March 28. "One day this week," Mary confided, "we went down to Mt Vernon. A visit we can again pay, when you are with us."[37]

On the evening of May 9, 1861, Mrs. Lincoln held a reception where she appeared in "a very elegant blue silk [gown], richly embroidered, and with a long train; also point lace cape and a full set of pearl ornaments." Evidently, she was wearing apparel acquired during her January trip to New York. Now, she was preparing to return to New York for another shopping spree.[38]

At 10 A.M. on the following morning, Mary Lincoln, accompanied by Elizabeth Todd Grimsley (her cousin) and others, departed for New York.[39] That evening they alighted in Philadelphia. On the eleventh, Colonel Robert Anderson, also a member of the party, received an official reception at Independence Hall. Certainly, Mrs. Lincoln was along for this honor.[40]

Onward they sped to New York City, where they checked into the Metropolitan Hotel at 6:30 P.M. on May 11. Mr. William S. Wood escorted the First Lady's party on this trip. He was the same person who had arranged the grand inaugural trip in February, having previously worked for hotels and railroads. Mrs. Lincoln was reported in "the best of health and spirits, and is rejoicing at the opportunity of enjoying a couple of weeks' relaxation in New York, from the arduous cares and duties of the White House."[41]

Not being able to shop on Sunday, May 12, she and her guests created quite a sensation by walking into the Reverend Henry Ward Beecher's Plymouth Church during the service. The press noted that the congregation "was about equally divided between listening to the sermon and gazing at the unexpected distinguished visiters."[42]

Bright and early on the thirteenth, Mary "was busily engaged in 'shopping' the greater part of" the day. She examined carriages and bought one for $900 at Brewster's factory and then went to A. T. Stewart's and other dry-goods stores, "purchasing quite extensively."[43] On the following day, she "was engaged nearly all day . . . making extensive purchases at Lord & Taylor's and various other places about the city." Then that evening she attended Laura Keene's Theatre with friends to witness "The Seven Sisters," "Uncle Sam's Magic Lantern," "Beautiful Union Tableaux," and "The Birth of the Butterfly in the Bower of Ferns."[44]

In the forenoon of May 15, Mary made purchases at Lord and Taylor's and at Messrs. E. V. Haughwout and Company, where she ordered "a splendid [Haviland] dinner service for the White House, in 'Solferino' and gold, with the arms of the United States emblazoned on each piece." In addition, she ordered "handsome vases and mantle ornaments" for the Blue and Green Rooms. That afternoon she paid a visit to the famous *Great Eastern*, the largest ship afloat, and "was received on board with the most marked attention." That excursion and the intense shopping wore her out completely; so, she returned to the hotel and refused to see any visitors.[45]

Curious individuals besieged Mary Lincoln at the Metropolitan Hotel on the sixteenth, and some were even granted interviews. Yet in the forenoon she went for a carriage ride to the Brooklyn Navy Yard and the Green-Wood Cemetery. In the afternoon, she finished making purchases for the White House.[46] At 10:30 that night, the band of the Empire City Regiment serenaded "Mrs. President Lincoln" with popular and patriotic tunes, such as "Yankee Doodle." She appeared at her hotel window, bowed to the crowd, and threw a bouquet down to the band.[47]

At 11:30 A.M. on May 17, Mrs. Lincoln toured the Park Barracks where Colonel [Daniel Thompkins?] Van Buren, escorted her to view the troops. At noon she reboarded her carriage and drove to the Spingler Institute, where ladies were fashioning various articles for hospital use. Then at 5 P.M. she stepped onto the Fall River boat and sailed for Boston.[48]

On the morning of the eighteenth, Saturday, she reached Boston, received a reception at the Revere House, and proceeded on to see Robert Lincoln at Cambridge.[49] She and Mrs. Grimsley spent Sunday, the nineteenth, with him and returned to New York City on the afternoon of the twentieth and once more checked into the Metropolitan Hotel.[50] During the afternoon of the twenty-first, she departed for Washington, which she reached that night. She announced that she would receive visitors at the White House on Wednesday, the twenty-second.[51] It had been a twelve-day, prolonged journey of shopping and sightseeing.

When the hot, humid weather of Washington continued in August of 1861, "Mrs. President Lincoln," as some reporters called her, determined to seek a cooler clime. She needed some place that rivaled the resorts in Vichy, France, or the Isle of Wight off the English coast. As early as August 7, she revealed that she had chosen Long Branch, New Jersey, and would be going there soon.[52]

Finally, at 6:30 A.M. on August 14, she steamed out of Washington on a special train headed for Harrisburg and then New York City. John Milton Hay, assistant secretary to President Lincoln, had been assigned to conduct her, Mrs. Grimsley, and others to their destination.[53] Her fast engine put Mary into New York that very evening, where her party checked into the Metropolitan Hotel.[54] Robert Lincoln was already at this hotel awaiting his mother's arrival; he had secured a room there on the thirteenth.[55] Robert would spend vacation time with his mother.

A person in the news media reported that Mrs. Lincoln's "object in leaving the Presidential mansion for a brief season is to recruit her health, and to enjoy release from the arduous duties of her position." We, of course, know that she simply enjoyed travel and sightseeing. In the White House, she was waited upon hand and foot. Peering at the hotel registry, this reporter saw the entry for Mrs. Lincoln's party: "Three ladies [Mary Lincoln, Elizabeth Grimsley and Hannah Shearer], two children [Willie and Tad] and servant." Quickly Mary informed this news sleuth that she wished to avoid "all ostentatious display and excitement."[56]

Awaking in New York City on the fifteenth, Mary and her group of friends spent the entire morning shopping. They purchased clothing at Brooks Brothers and that afternoon took a drive around Brooklyn Heights and called upon Princess Clotilde (the eighteen-year-old wife of Prince Napoleon Joseph Charles Paul Bonaparte) at the New York Hotel.[57] As always, Mrs. Lincoln seems to have delighted in giving out false timetables for her travels. Robert, John M. Hay, Richard C. Meconkey—Robert's best friend and fraternity brother from Harvard—and O. Balstead, with his daughters, arrived at Long Branch on August 15 ahead of her. Robert informed the press that his mother should make her appearance the next day.[58] Meanwhile, John Hay was writing anonymous news stories for the *New York World* concerning the trip.

At 10 A.M. on the sixteenth, Mary Lincoln actually departed from the Metropolitan Hotel and headed for Long Branch.[59] Travelling like a queen on a special train in "a private car and heavily veiled," she, Willie, Tad, Mrs. Harrison Grimsley, and Mrs. John Shearer arrived there at 1 P.M. that day. Her escort on this leg of the journey was [Burnett?] Forbes, assistant to William S. Wood, and a Mr. Torrey who made the necessary railroad arrangements. She signed into the Mansion House operated by Mr. Samuel Laird and his wife, Sarah, a wealthy couple. Mary remained in her quarters that afternoon and dined privately that evening. To inquiring reporters, she divulged that she would remain about ten days.[60] Her appearance created great excitement all along the coast. Twenty-seven little girls dressed in white had met her at the station. The community even planned for "a grand ball" to be given later.[61]

At the Mansion House, Mrs. Lincoln occupied a suite of three rooms plus a private parlor—all completely refurbished—but Robert and Hay lodged in a private cottage attached to the hotel. On the seventeenth, two daughters of Judge James W. and Rhoda Elizabeth (Waterman) White called upon Mary Lincoln. These ladies were Mrs. Rhoda (White) Mack (about twenty and newly married) and either Jane C. White or Ellen G. White, both amateur singers. It is possible that their mother also accompanied her daughters to visit Mrs. Lincoln. James W. White (1807–June 12, 1867) married Rhoda Waterman (b. 1815) on September 29, 1834. James, a wealthy Irish lawyer, born on the "old Sod," became a judge on the New York City Superior Court and later carried on quite a correspondence with President Lincoln concerning the war effort. Mrs. Rhoda White became one of Mrs. Lincoln's few intimate, loyal, female friends, and they exchanged correspondence for many years. During a large portion of the day on the seventeenth, Mrs. Lincoln remained in her rooms, Hannah Shearer was ill, and John Hay departed for Washington. However,

Mary did witness an impromptu cricket match, "which was a novelty to her."[62] For the next three days, Mrs. Lincoln rarely left her rooms. But on the twentieth, Robert Lincoln and some of his college friends "went off crabbing."[63]

For several days, Master Tad Lincoln suffered from a severe cold, and his mother stayed in with him. But on the twenty-second, she went with former New Jersey governor William A. Newell to visit the Coast Guard station and in the afternoon hosted a reception. That night, there were fireworks, and instead of one, there were several grand balls. Mary Lincoln attended the one at the Mansion House, where the tickets were five dollars. She was dressed in "an elegant robe of white grenadine, with a long flowing train, the bottom of the skirt puffed with quillings of white satin, and the arms and shoulders uncovered, save with an elegant point lace shawl. She wore a necklace and bracelets of superb pearls, a pearl fan, and a headdress of wreathed white wild roses. Beyond all comparison she was the most richly and completely dressed lady present." Whenever Mary traveled, she took several trunks of clothes with her.[64]

As soon as Tad had recovered, Mary Lincoln and her friends departed very quietly on the afternoon of August 23 for New York City. She did admit that her husband was probably very lonesome, yet she continued her prolonged vacation. In New York, she took up apartments at the Metropolitan Hotel.[65] After John Hay left Mrs. Lincoln's entourage, John G. Nicolay seems to have replaced him.[66] Perhaps these secretaries assisted in obtaining free lodging and transportation for the First Lady. We know positively that she expected, demanded, and obtained free rooms and railroad passes for her many trips.[67]

Once back in New York from Long Branch, Mrs. President began a dizzying round of frantic shopping for herself and family.[68] Then, quietly, with little notice, Mrs. Lincoln and her travelling friends left New York and proceeded west with brief stops at Syracuse and Auburn, home of the Sewards. They arrived at Niagara Falls on August 29 and checked into the International Hotel. The clerk noted that her party consisted of

Mary; her sons, Robert, Willie and Tad; plus Mr. R. C. ("Dick") Meconkey; Mrs. Elizabeth Grimsley (who would leave Mary from here and return to Springfield, accompanied by her cousin, Brigadier General Charles Ferguson Smith); Mr. L. [N.] Fletcher, an attorney from Philadelphia; Mrs. Hannah Shearer; Mrs. Jane (Masterson) Watt—wife of the notorious White House head gardener, John Watt (1824–1892)—and servants.

Mrs. Watt was employed as the White House stewardess from June 1861 to February 1862. She drew $100 per month, which went back into Mrs. Lincoln's pocket. Perhaps this tour was a reward for giving up her salary. Even after Mrs. Watt lost her position, Mrs. Lincoln attempted to collect the nonexistent stewardess wages for herself![69]

As mentioned previously, Mary Lincoln had seen the falls on July 24, 1857. She enjoyed the repeat experience, and after sightseeing and partying, Mary and her company of merry vacationers returned to the Metropolitan Hotel in New York during the evening hours of September 2.[70] Two days later, on the fourth, she spent the whole day shopping.[71] At long last, Mary and her family departed from the Metropolitan at 7 A.M. on the fifth and started back to Washington by way of Philadelphia and Baltimore.[72] They arrived that evening. Mrs. Lincoln had been absent from the White House for twenty-three days. The president had sorely missed her succor and perhaps even his suppers.

While in New York, she had committed a mild social faux pas by attempting to board the USS *Monticello*, a cruiser, which housed male state prisoners captured at Cape Hatteras. The commanding officer denied her petition to board.[73]

Before September ended, Mrs. Lincoln was already contemplating a trip to Boston and a stay of two or three weeks at the Revere House.[74] And leave she did on November 4, "together" with John Watt, of all people.[75] That was a serious sexual-etiquette blunder, to say the least. They proceeded to New York and then on to Boston to visit Robert. While in Boston, she continued to buy items to refurnish the Executive Mansion. "She is determined to make the President's mansion as comfortable and elegant as possible during the winter."[76] John Watt later declared to Simon Cameron that he had "paid about \$700.00 for Mrs. Lincoln on one trip to Cambridge, Mass."[77] It was Watt who showed Mrs. Lincoln how to pad expense accounts and who enjoyed her complete confidence. She defended him to the very end until he and his wife were finally dismissed after a congressional investigation in February of 1862. Mrs. Lincoln did not return to Washington until November 13.[78] This blissful jaunt had lasted ten days.

Willie Lincoln's calamitous death on February 20, 1862, temporarily reduced Mary Lincoln's exuberant desire to travel. But the *New York Herald* announced on April 3 that the president and members of his family had paid a call to Mount Vernon on the previous day, going by ship. It should be assumed that Mrs. Lincoln was along. Then when hot, humid weather came to Washington, she escaped its affects by leaving on July 9 that year, with Tad and a few servants, for a stay at the Metropolitan Hotel in New York. On the next evening she was joined by Robert Lincoln, who was on vacation from Harvard.[79]

At noon on July 14, Mary, Robert, and their party were escorted by Captain William A. Murfey—purchasing officer of the US Military Railroad Department—out to the *J. C. Winants* for a sail to Flushing Bay, where the *Great Eastern* was anchored. Mary, of course, had previously been on this giant steamship. After her British Royal Navy captain entertained Mrs. Lincoln royally, the group proceeded to the *City of New York*, where lunch was served to them. Mary possessed a large penchant for ships and sailing. She relished being aboard them. Rufus F. Andrews, surveyor of the Port of New York and a Lincoln appointee, managed her itinerary.[80] Again, at 10 A.M. on the following day, she and others boarded the *Winants* at Spring Street for a voyage up the East River, past the *Great Eastern* and on to the lightship off Sandy Hook and returned to port later that evening.

On several different days—as usual—Mary Lincoln divulged to reporters that she would sail up the Hudson to call upon Brevet Lieutenant General Winfield Scott. In the previous month on June 24 and 25, President Lincoln had been at the US Military Academy in order to consult with General Scott, who resided there in retirement. Great crowds had greeted Lincoln at Cozzen's Hotel, where he stayed. This time, numerous locals again assembled around this same hotel to welcome Mrs. Lincoln on several different days when newspapers announced that she would be there. They were greatly disappointed each time by her nonappearance. Even her husband was misled by those newspaper reports of her intended itinerary. He wired her on July 13, 1862, and sent it to West Point, saying: "I am here, and well. How are you?"[81]

On the morning of July 16, Captain Frank E. Howe, a wealthy politician who had entertained Robert Lincoln at Hamilton House on Staten Island, took Mary to inspect the government hospitals.[82] (On June 11, Howe had been commissioned as an assistant quartermaster of volunteers.) Then she visited the New England Soldiers' Relief Association at 194 Broadway and signed the visitor's book.[83] Finally, shortly after 7 A.M. on July 17, Captain William A. Murfey, "acting under special orders from the War Department," conveyed Mrs. Lincoln, Robert, and Tad on a private railway car to Jersey City, where it was connected to a fast train leaving for Washington.[84] Her personal escort had once resided in Chicago and perhaps had met Mr. Lincoln previously.[85] On this trip, Mary Lincoln had been gone for nine days.

Despite the fact that the president was harried every day with the war going badly, his wife deserted the Executive Mansion with Tad and Elizabeth Keckly and fled north to the Metropolitan Hotel in New York, where she checked in on the evening of October 20, 1862.[86] When Abraham Lincoln did not write to her, she remarked that she would "be charitable enough to impute your silence, to the right cause."[87] One of the causes was Major General George B. McClellan and his inaction!

Ever since Mary Lincoln had arrived at the Metropolitan Hotel, she often kept an open house for distinguished visitors who called at her suite. Among them were the Honorable John Van Buren (1810–1866), son of former president Martin Van Buren, and Samuel J. Tilden (1814–1886), an important Democratic politician and lawyer who favored the Union and who ran for president in 1876. On the twenty-fifth, the US Band from the Brooklyn Navy Yard serenaded her with a concert beginning at 10 P.M. [88]

By the twenty-eighth, she had resumed her "shopping excursions."[89] On the twenty-ninth, she went aboard the USS *North Carolina* commanded by Rear Admiral Hiram Paulding.[90] On the thirty-first, she again engaged in extensive shopping for most of the day before Colonel Daniel Craig McCallum (1815–1878) dropped in to see her. He was another officer who could facilitate her travel plans; a Scotsman, he was the military director and superintendent of the railroads of the United States. With him was the familiar Captain W. A. Murfey.[91]

At long last, Mary and Tad got to see Lieutenant General Scott, who happened to be in New York City with Brigadier General Robert Anderson on November 1.[92] It is certain that on November 3 Elizabeth Keckly was still with Mary in New York.[93]

After several false starts, on November 7, Mary and Tad departed on the Lake Shore route to Boston under the guidance of Captain and Mrs. W. A. Murfey. No doubt Captain Murfey arranged the transportation. Mrs. Lincoln took rooms at the Parker House. She came to visit with Robert at Cambridge.[94]

A brigade band serenaded Mrs. Lincoln at her hotel on the evening of November 10. It played operatic and popular airs, and Mrs. Lincoln appeared at her window several times to wave to the musicians with her handkerchief. Some in the crowd, however, "had the bad taste to cheer" for McClellan and Burnside![95]

After spending several days with Robert, the First Lady returned on the thirteenth to the Metropolitan Hotel in New York.[96] There, she resumed holding court for the "*elite* of the city."[97] Again, she repeatedly gave out reports that she would leave for home on this day or that but did not depart. Sometimes she would explain that the weather had not been conducive for travelling.[98]

It would seem that nine-and-a-half-year-old Tad grew bored with his mother's high society routine. Anyhow, he had a wealthy adult friend who operated a tobacco shop in Philadelphia. This was Gustav Edward Gumpert (1835–1883), who picked him up and took him on a trip of their own to Baltimore, where they lodged at Barnum's Hotel. When Mary finally determined to return home, she wired Mr. Gumpert on the twenty-sixth and asked him to bring Tad to New York "immediately." On this trip or one in 1864, Tad was photographed with Gumpert.[99]

With Tad in tow, Mrs. Lincoln left the following morning at 7 A.M. on the New-Jersey Central Railroad in a private car provided by the efficient W. A. Murfey, who would escort them to Washington. Their route would be through Philadelphia and Baltimore. That evening they steamed into Washington; "few upon the train . . . knew that this distinguished lady was among the passengers."[100] She had been absent from the Executive Mansion for thirty-nine days.

As Tad Lincoln's tenth birthday approached, Mrs. Lincoln suggested to the president that they go on a military expedition to celebrate it. Such an excursion would also relax Abraham, who totally agreed with her. Therefore, the president wired Major General Joseph Hooker on April 3, 1863, that he and a few close friends would visit his headquarters on the following day, Tad's actual birth date. Quickly a small party was invited. Dr. Anson Gordon Henry, whom Lincoln had appointed surveyor general of Washington Territory, was lingering in Washington and was "ordered" by the president to join them. In turn, Henry suggested they include his good friend, Attorney General Edward Bates. Lincoln also asked Noah Brooks, a personal friend from California, and Captain Medorem Crawford of Oregon, assistant quartermaster, who had been assigned by the secretary of war to the Overland Emigrant Escort Service to guard civilians travelling to the Pacific coast. On that long trail from June 16, 1862, until October 30 that year, he had commanded a company of fifty mounted soldiers armed with rifles and revolvers but was now back in Washington.

At 5 P.M., at sunset, on the fourth, the president, his wife, Tad, Henry, Brooks, Crawford, and Bates left from the navy yard on the *Carrie Martin*, the president's steamer at that time. Upon entering camp, they discovered that Hooker had erected large hospital tents for their housing: one for the Lincolns and the second for the others. A third tent supplied some unnamed purpose, perhaps for toilet facilities. Mrs. Lincoln seemed not to mind such crude accommodations and enjoyed herself greatly. Tad— ever the lively sprite—clad in a gray suit, with boots and spurs, rode in the several reviews of the troops with his father. He also "rambled about among the tents examining the quarters of the staff, and watched . . . the orderlies and sentries with a curiosity somewhat amusing."

Bates and Crawford left the Army of the Potomac on the eighth and returned to Washington. But the others stayed until April 10, when they departed on the *Carrie Martin* for home. Lincoln had thoroughly examined the various army corps and acquired about a week of much needed rest.[101]

By June 8, 1863, Mary Lincoln and Tad were lodging at the Continental Hotel in Philadelphia.[102] Evidently, Tad had taken a real, working service revolver with him on this trip. He delighted in playing soldier and had several uniforms, a rifle, and a sword, too. Anyhow, the president had had an ominous dream about some misfortune falling upon Tad and wired Mary on June 9 suggesting that she "better put 'Tad's' pistol away."[103] On June 16, she and Tad were still in Philadelphia, and Abraham asked if she were coming home or not. He predicted—incorrectly, of course—that the Confederate raid into Pennsylvania would not amount to anything![104] She then departed on a special car for Baltimore, which she reached late in the evening of June 18. She had several friends with her and soon left there for places farther north.[105] Nevertheless, she was back in Washington by July 1.[106]

On the following morning about 10 A.M., while Mary Lincoln was travelling as the only passenger along the Rock Creek Road toward the White House from the Soldiers' Home, the coachman's seat "became detached from the carriage in some way, precipitating the driver to the ground"; following this equipment failure, she jumped out when the frightened horses ran off. The mishap occurred near where the road bent around Mount Pleasant Army Hospital, which consisted of large buildings and tents and curved into Fourteenth Street. Farther south along Fourteenth Street was the Carver Army Hospital, which was close to where Mary actually landed on the ground. Physicians and surgeons from Carver immediately rushed to her aid. The one who personally took care of her head wound has until now been completely lost to the Lincoln story. A local newspaper frustrated historians by printing his first name as his last.

This good Samaritan was Dr. Judson C. Nelson (June 3, 1824–July 11, 1895), of Truxton, New York, who had been commissioned as surgeon of the Seventy-Sixth Regiment of New York Volunteers on January 17, 1862, but who at the time of Mary's accident was an acting assistant surgeon and assigned, as of January 1863, to the US General Hospital Department in Washington.

Mary suffered several bruises and a severe cut to the back of her head. After treatment, Dr. Nelson drove her home to the Executive Mansion. No broken bones were discovered.[107] However, her suffering greatly distracted the president while the horrific Battle of Gettysburg raged on.

Knowing that Robert would read of his mother's misfortune, Lincoln wired him the next day, saying: "Don't be uneasy. Your mother very slightly hurt by her fall."[108] But the laceration to her head became infected. On July 9, surgeons opened the scalp when pus collected there in a large amount.[109] This turn of events—or the simmering unrest in New York over the conscription act—caused the president to telegraph Robert on July 11 while he sojourned at the New York Fifth Avenue Hotel: "Come to Washington."[110] On that same day, the press learned that Mrs. Lincoln was better and no "fears are entertained in regard to her final recovery."[111] This head injury, however, caused her to postpone for some days her usual escape from Washington summers.

By July 20, Mrs. Lincoln—healed or not—had determined to shun Washington and head north to the White Mountains of New Hampshire. Robert would join her later.[112] However, it would appear that he did not completely relish spending the whole summer with her. In the late afternoon of July 26, Robert had slipped off and arrived at Fort Monroe aboard the US gunboat *Ella* with Secretary Seward, his son Frederick, and others. The *Ella* was their floating domicile.[113] Mary waited and waited for Robert to join her in New York, and when he did not appear promptly, she wired the White House on July 28, asking: "Did Robert leave this morning for New York[?] I hope the President is well[;] answer this immediately." As ordered, Lincoln replied that same day: "Bob went to Fort-Monroe & only got back to-day. Will start [him] to you at 11 a. m. to-morrow."[114]

With his family and most of the office staff away on vacation, the president slouched into his usual relaxed mode. Judge Edwards Pierrepont called at the Executive Mansion and "found Lincoln lying on a sofa, in a sort of yellow linen dressing-gown and embroidered slippers."[115]

Leaving her usual vacation hub of New York City sometime after July 29, Mary and her two boys travelled to Boston. From there, they proceeded to Center Harbor on Lake Winnipesaukee, New Hampshire, where they arrived on the evening of August 3, 1863. They spent two days at the Kearsarge House, a boarding house charging a mere $1.50 per day in North Conway and operated by Samuel W. and Eliza Thompson. On the fourth, they crossed the Saco River to see the "Cathedral," "Echo Lake," the "Motes," "Diana's Bath," and "Hart's Ledge" in the Notch Mountains. Mrs. Lincoln "expressed herself more than delighted with the elegant and unobtrusive attention which the guests at North Conway" gave her. That evening, they attended the "Academy of Music" in that village. The weather was most pleasurable, and gentlemen from Boston put their carriages "at the disposal of the Presidential party."

On the fifth, they departed in the morning in "a handsome 'turnout'" (carriage) with "an old and popular driver in charge." Their destination was the Glen House at the foot of Mount Washington. It sat at 1,632 feet above sea level, also in North Conway, and owned by the noted couple Joseph M. and Catherine W. Thompson, whose huge and plush wooded structure with its own telegraph office was valued at $40,000 or more. Its parlor, measuring 100' by 60', was the largest of any American hotel. Guests dined elegantly in an enormous hall on extravagant multicourse meals served by a whole throng of waiters. A horde of "domestics" took care of the rooms, which could shelter three hundred guests and were always filled to overflowing in August.

From the front door of the Glen House on the sixth of August, Mary and Robert, accompanied by "several great men," unnamed, boasting LLD and other degrees, ascended Mount Washington, lying in the Presidential Range to an exciting lookout place managed by John R. Hitchcock: the two-story Tip Top House, with walls of granite piled extremely thick to withstand violent weather conditions. It offered a fantastic view of the whole area of the White Mountains and a fine luncheon of ham, fish, bread, coffee, tea, milk, and so on. It housed seventeen tiny bedrooms, too.

The Lincolns that day were among the 130 who made the steep and hazardous eight-mile ride up the Carriage Road in four-or-six-horse stage-coaches. It being the date that President Lincoln had declared a National Thanksgiving Day to commemorate Union victories, the Stars and Stripes were hoisted upon Summit Rock. At 6,288 feet, Mount Washington was the tallest point in New Hampshire, and was wildly strewn with uneven rocks, making walking extremely difficult. Mary was there for "dinner," perhaps meaning "lunch," where "noted gentlemen made appropriate speeches."

On the following day, Mary again joined a group headed up to Tip Top House. Upon both occasions, a journalist using the initials J. H. S. and being a correspondent from the *Boston Journal*, encountered the First Lady. Fortunately, he compiled a full description of her: "she is a lady of medium size, rather round favored, and quite fleshy. She was dressed in a dark chequered riding habit, dark bonnet and veil. She has a very fair, cheerful, smiling face, which does one good to look upon. She is quite light complexioned, has blue eyes and dark auburn hair, and on the whole, as might be hoped and expected of a President's wife, has a very easy, agreeable way." On the other hand, Robert was depicted as "dark complexioned."

On this trip, she collected "a piece of rock" as a souvenir. Called "Franconia brecia," this granite was a conglomerate with embedded elements that gave a white appearance when exposed to sunlight. Thus, the term White Mountains.[116]

Another neighboring and unusual landmark they explored was "The Flume," a granite gorge in the Franconia Range Notch where Mary, Robert, and Tad were photographed on a very narrow wooden walkway with about eleven others in their tour, all properly attired in suits, hats, long dresses, and bonnets.

On August 11, Mrs. Lincoln and sons checked into the Profile House at Cannon Mountain. It was "crowded to suffocation," and many visitors could not even rent a cot. Mary had come to observe the famous "Old Man of the Mountain," a natural formation that resembled the profile of a human head jutting out from the cliff, hence the name of the hotel. She did not mingle with the other guests except to travel to points of interest in that region. "Probus," a correspondent for the *Boston Journal*, declared that her arrival was the major event of the summer. (Unfortunately, this national treasure fell in May of 2003.)

From the Profile House, Mrs. Lincoln immediately returned to Boston and checked into the Revere House on August 13. It would seem that the aged Brigadier General Joseph Gilbert Totten (1788–1864), stationed in Washington as the chief engineer of the regular army, had been along on this excursion. He also checked in on that date.[117]

From Boston, Mary went back to New York City. After several days there, the press corps finally discovered her presence on August 2, when she openly expressed a desire to investigate the French frigate *La Guerriere* lying in the harbor. The admiral welcomed her aboard with full naval honors.[118]

Then on August 24, she left New York for Manchester, Vermont. Robert did not go with her; by August 17 he had returned to Washington.[119] (As late as August 31, the president thought Mary was in Manchester, *New Hampshire*. He telegraphed her at that location.)[120] In her large party were Brigadier General and Mrs. Abner Doubleday. They arrived on the ten o'clock train the following day and immediately checked into the

Equinox House.[121] The general was footloose; Major General George Gordon Meade had relieved him of battlefield command right after Gettysburg, and Doubleday was without another assignment. Typical of the First Lady, Mary now importuned her husband to find a position for him. The president sidestepped her request by replying on September 3 that the "Secretary of War tells me he has telegraphed Gen. Doubleday to await further orders."[122]

Manchester, in the cool, picturesque Green Mountains of Vermont, served as the center for Mrs. Lincoln's wide peregrinations. Robert, too, fell in love with this location, and here he constructed his beloved "Hildene" years later. After two weeks of delightful vacationing, "enjoying themselves," Mrs. Lincoln and the Doubledays departed Manchester on September 7.[123] They were headed back to New York City.

When the Polish uprising broke out, Russia feared that Great Britain would join the fight against her. Therefore, she sent a large squadron of her warships to New York where, if necessary, they could attack British shipping in the Atlantic. These battleships arrived one or two at a time.[124] The frigate *Osliaba* docked on September 11, 1863, while Mrs. Lincoln sojourned in New York. It was a huge vessel with a crew of 450 under the command of Captain Boutakoff.[125] With her complete fascination with ships, she determined to tour the *Osliaba*. Therefore at 2 P.M. on September 16, she was piped aboard with a small group of her sycophants, including Baron d'Ostensachen, the consul general of Russia. They inspected the very impressive ship with a promenade that ended in the captain's cabin, where an exquisite "repast was spread out." Here, Mary offered a toast: "The health of the Emperor of Russia." The captain replied with: "The President of the United States." After about an hour the visitors departed. Mrs. Lincoln relished the fact that she was the first wife of a US president to trod the decks of a Russian man-of-war.[126]

While Mary continued her lengthy residence at the New York Fifth Avenue Hotel, the president informed her that he did not know of any sickness in Washington and wanted to see her and Tad.[127] As if to comply with her husband's wishes, on September 21, she wired Edward McManus at the Executive Mansion that he should inform Colonel Daniel C. McCallum, director of military railroads, to send a "special car" to New York and to have her favorite "Green Car" at Philadelphia ready to take her on home. She reported "a very bad cold," but that Tad was well.[128]

However, Mary did not leave New York as she had indicated.[129] Those special cars stood empty in the stations. Instead, on September 24, she boarded the *J. C. Winants* and steamed up the Hudson to West Point, where she landed and received a salute of fifteen guns. She proceeded to the library and then to the Cozzen's Hotel, where she dined with Lieutenant General Winfield Scott. Accompanying her were Major General John Adams Dix, commander of the Military District of New York, and Rufus F. Andrews. Following this social call, they returned to New York.[130]

That same day, another segment of the Russian fleet floated into New York, but there is no reference that she went to view them.[131] By the twenty-sixth, reporters learned that Mrs. Lincoln finally was preparing to return to Washington. One of them informed his readers that she had been gone for many weeks and had visited not only the White Mountains of New Hampshire but also the Green Mountains of Vermont and added the news that she had again spent time at Niagara Falls.[132] New York news-hawks had previously missed that last excursion. Mary later confessed that she "always returned to Niagara with renewed interest."[133]

At long last, Mary reappeared in Washington on the evening of September 28, where the president was still residing at Soldiers' Home.[134] She had been gone for seventy-one days. Secretary William O. Stoddard reported, "The return of Mrs. Lincoln, to resume her wifely care of the President's valuable health, seems to have already given a more cheerful look to his Excellency's care-worn face."[135]

At noon on November 18, 1863, President Lincoln set out on a special train of four cars to dedicate the cemetery at Gettysburg.[136] Mrs. Lincoln did not accompany him. Tad was ill.[137] When Lincoln came back to Washington, he was already suffering from a case of smallpox. The indisposition hung on and became quite serious. John Hay noted on November 26, "The President quite unwell." He was "sick in bed. Bilious."[138] By the thirtieth, the press revealed that he was "considerably improved, and he will very soon be able to attend to his official duties."[139] But the president was not fully recovered on December 1.[140] In fact, he was even "unable to leave his chamber" on December 4. [141]

Despite his severe indisposition, Mrs. Lincoln had taken her leave of Washington on the previous day and checked into the Metropolitan Hotel in New York on the evening of December 3. She reported herself tired with a "severe headache."[142] She had always been plagued by head-aches. On the sixth, she wired her suffering husband and inquired about Tad's and his health. She promised to return, "without fail," on December 8. [143] This time she kept her word and left at 8 A.M. A carriage awaited her at the depot in Washington that night.[144] She had been absent six days. Two days after her return, the president felt well enough to spend "several hours in his office."[145] And on the eighteenth, a Washington correspondent divulged that the president had occupied the last four nights at Ford's Theatre watching James H. Hackett perform in *Henry IV* and *The Merry Wives of Windsor*.[146] Mary's presence seems to have hastened his recovery.

With cold weather upon her, Mary remained in Washington and hosted a brilliant reception on January 9, 1864, from 1 to 3 P.M. To greet the foreign diplomats and "a host of brigadiers," Mrs. Lincoln appeared in her wintery finery: a gown of "black velvet, corded with white, postillion back, trimmed with black-thread lace over white silk, and pellarine collar of white point lace. Her headdress was of white and black flowers with jet and pearl ornaments. Her gloves were white, stitched with black." Her morning dress was lined with ermine and fur.[147] Certainly, her outfit—or the material for it—had been selected in New York during her shopping tour in the previous month.

To consult with a dressmaker in Baltimore, Mrs. Catherine C. Sum-wault at Sixty-Six South Sharp Street, Mary left Washington on April 20,

1864, on her special Green railroad car. President Lincoln, himself, gave the time of Mary's arrival to Mrs. Sumwault and signed the telegram: "Mrs. Lincoln." The First Lady landed in Baltimore at noon that same day. How long she remained is unknown.[148]

To supplement her extensive wardrobe for future functions, Mrs. Lincoln with Tad departed from Washington aboard the evening train on April 27. She arrived at 5 A.M. the following morning, where Warren Leland had a carriage waiting at the depot. It conveyed them to his Metropolitan Hotel, at that time on Duane Street. There, she immediately wired her husband for an extra fifty dollars.[149]

"Business being the object of her visit," a newsman revealed, "she devoted the whole of her time to it. Milliners, dressmakers, mantua makers and other *artistes* versed in the mysteries of female attire were consulted . . . in reference to a suitable outfit for the approaching fashionable campaign, when the dog star will be in the ascendant, and *winter apparel at a discount*." She shopped from early in the morning until late in the evening on Broadway. Her trunks were certainly filled when she returned to Washington at 7 P.M. on May 1 and declared her mission completely accomplished.[150] She had been gone five days.

A Philadelphia committee in charge of a gigantic Sanitary Fair fundraiser convinced the president to leave his ever-demanding duties at the White House and appear at their event. It would be one of the very rare occasions when Lincoln travelled out of Washington to participate in a civilian event. And it would also be a unique happening when the president accompanied his wife and Tad on a train ride to the North. Husband and wife invited a very select few to accompany them. Prominent among them was Mr. Cuthbert Bullitt, a Union man from New Orleans whom Lincoln had appointed US marshal for Louisiana. This little party departed on a special train from Washington at 7 A.M. on June 16, 1864, bound for Philadelphia, which they reached at 11:30 A.M. and took up quarters in the Continental Hotel. After lunch, Lincoln proceeded to Logan Square Fairgrounds at 4:15. There he spoke to aid the US Sanitary Commission's war efforts. He also made an address at the Union League and from the balcony of his hotel. After a night's rest, he departed from Philadelphia at 8 A.M. on June 17 for Washington.[151]

However, Mary did not return with her husband. John Hay noted cryptically on June 20 that Mary Lincoln "is in the North."[152] Actually, Mary had immediately left Philadelphia after the events there, but Tad remained in town for a while with his good friends: Gus Gumpert and Colonel Thomas H. Sweney. Mary went on up to New York, where she secured a room at the Fifth Avenue Hotel. Either Gumpert or Sweney later conducted Tad home to Washington, where he arrived on June 19.[153] On the very next evening, Tad put on his "Lt. Col.'s" army uniform and with his favorite pony on board, left with his father on an ordinance steamer, the USS *Baltimore*, for a visit to Grant's army. They returned on June 23.[154]

Meanwhile, Mrs. Lincoln had shifted her location to Boston and Cambridge where on June 24, she attended Robert's Senior-Class-Day festivities at Harvard. The actual graduation ceremonies did not occur until July 20, and there is no indication that either Mary or Robert were present for that. (Robert was still in Washington as late as July 18.)[155]

A rumor then emanated from Washington that President and Mrs. Lincoln were scheduled to spend a week's vacation at Manchester, New Hampshire, after Robert received his bachelor of arts degree.[156] Of course, the president never left Washington. After further vacationing—some said at Long Branch again—Mary Lincoln was back in New York by June 29, where her husband informed her that Tom Cross was moving the household effects out to the Soldiers' Home.[157] Robert and Mary said goodbye to New York and returned to Washington on July 2, where they reoccupied their summer quarters for the first time that year.[158] Mary had been gone for seventeen days.

To confer with Lieutenant General Grant, President Lincoln departed on the steamer *Baltimore* for Fort Monroe on July 30. Mrs. Lincoln and a few of her lady friends went along, but they did not leave the ship when it docked. Mary related that she merely wanted to experience the cool breezes on the river to refresh herself. All came back to Washington on the morning of August 1.[159]

To avoid the heat and humidity of the nation's capital, Mary—as usual—entrained with Robert and Tad on the evening of August 15, bound for New York, said to be on their way to Saratoga.[160] A prying reporter spotted Robert Lincoln at the Astor House in New York on August 18.[161] And Mrs. Lincoln signed the guest register at the Equinox House in Manchester, Vermont, on August 24.[162] From there, she went off to Lake George, where she was discovered on August 27. Meanwhile, folks at Saratoga Springs anxiously awaited her expected arrival there.[163] But by the thirtieth, Mrs. Lincoln denied that she ever intended to stop at Saratoga Springs.[164] Robert separated from his mother and Tad somewhere along the line and left New York on August 31 for Washington.[165] Mrs. Lincoln's complete whereabouts are not known, but she was still in Manchester, Vermont, on September 8. On the following day, while Lincoln was in the White House and Mary gone, he was nearly asphyxiated due to a gas leak in his office.[166] Mary and Tad at last came home on the evening of September 15, 1864, and returned to the Soldiers' Home.[167] She had been absent for precisely one month.

For the White House's New Year's reception on January 2 in the Blue Room, Mrs. Lincoln appeared in "heavy purple brocade silk, trimmed very richly with velvet, surmounted by a beautiful black lace shawl, gloves, head dress and jewelry." Those attending the second inauguration of President Lincoln at the Capitol could again witness the costly results of his wife's previous shopping trips to New York. She was now dressed in her well-known "black velvet robe, trimmed with emine."[168]

At the gala inaugural ball on March 6, her gown was of "white satin, richly embroidered, and [she] wore a point lace shawl. Her necklace and earrings were of diamonds. Her hair was arranged with a fall of curls and with silver ornaments and white artificial flowers." Such finery "assured all observers that she was the wife of the President."[169] That last comment would have pleased Mary Lincoln no end. At her next reception on the eleventh, a reporter disclosed that "Madam Lincoln, dressed very becomingly, received her visitors with courteous cordiality, and was assisted by Mr. Lincoln."[170]

Noah Brooks saw by March 22, 1865, that President Lincoln's health had "been worn down by the constant pressure of office-seekers and legitimate business."[171] Mary also worried about his physical well-being and thought a "change of air & rest may have a beneficial effect on" him.[172] Mrs. Julia Grant, likewise, heard of Lincoln's weariness—perhaps from Captain Robert Lincoln who was on Lieutenant General Grant's staff—and reasoned that a relaxing vacation with the Army of the Potomac would aid his recovery.[173] She convinced her husband to invite the commander-in-chief down to his headquarters. Grant telegraphed his personal invitation on March 20, saying, "Can you not visit City Point for a day or two?" President Lincoln gleefully answered that same evening, saying he had already thought of making the trip.[174] Mary, naturally, was eager for another sight-seeing outing.

At noon on March 23, 1865, the president, Mary, and Tad sailed from Washington on the *River Queen*, commanded by Captain William Bradford. Captain Charles Bingham Penrose was ordered by Secretary Stanton to accompany the Lincolns as their personal armed escort. On board were some White House servants and two black females who were permanent crew members in charge of housekeeping chores. For protection, the USS *Bat*, under command of Lieutenant Commander John S. Barnes, sailed with the *River Queen* from the Sixth Street Wharf. The *Bat* was a steel-hulled man-of-war with cannons and extremely fast. In addition, there was the *Columbus*, which transported escort soldiers and the necessary horses.[175]

The following day at noon, the Lincolns docked at Fort Monroe. From there they proceeded up the James River to meet Grant at City Point, which they reached at 8:30 that evening.[176] At breakfast time on the twenty-fifth, Robert Lincoln came aboard the *River Queen* to see his parents. He informed his father that there was "a little rumpus up the line" just south of Petersburg. Immediately, the president insisted upon going to the battle site.

About noon, the Lincolns departed by train for the front. At the end of the line, the men mounted horses while Mrs. Lincoln and Mrs. Grant rode forward in an army ambulance. When their attendant, Lieutenant Colonel Adam Badeau of Grant's staff, casually mentioned that only one woman, Sally (Carroll) Griffin, wife of Brigadier General Charles Griffin, remained with the Army of the Potomac by special permission of President Lincoln, Mary flew into a rage, threatened to get out of the vehicle and confront her husband about this matter. She shrieked that she never allowed any woman to see her husband alone. Mary embarrassed all who saw and heard her tantrum.

On March 26, the Lincolns and the Grants went to review the troops in the Army of the James, commanded by Major General Edward Otho Cresap Ord. Again, the wives were riding in an ambulance and arrived late at the passing of the troops for the president. There, Mary observed that Mary Ord, wife of the commander, was riding on horseback near the president. The First Lady flew into another terrible rage, even blaming Captain Barnes, who happened to be riding near Mary Ord. She screamed to the captain that in the future she did not want any woman to even set foot on the *River Queen,* and that included Mrs. Grant. That evening, the president learned of his wife's despicable tirade when she even demanded that he censure Captain Barnes, too.

After having acted like an ass and a jealous fool on March 26, Mary Lincoln finally felt ashamed. For five days after that second outburst she shut herself up in her quarters aboard the *River Queen* and refused all visitors. It was probably her husband who suggested, or even demanded, that she return to the Executive Mansion. Anyway, on April 1 at noon she departed City Point on the USS *Monohassett,* a common army transport steamer used for troop movements. Lincoln wired both Stanton and Alfonso T. Donn, doorkeeper at the White House, to have a closed carriage waiting for Mary at the Arsenal Wharf at 8 a. m. on April 2. Tad Lincoln remained with his father at the front.[177] When she arrived home, Mary telegraphed Abraham of her safe arrival, saying that she missed him and Tad and hinted that she would like to return to City Point on April 5 with "a little party."[178]

Evidently, Mary Lincoln regained her composure after a few days back home in Washington. Having learned that Petersburg and even Richmond had fallen, she determined to pay those conquered cities a visit. Without hesitation, she asked her husband's permission to return to City Point. He replied: "Come down as you proposed."[179]

Mary quickly assembled a little gaggle of congenial, doting friends: Senator Charles Sumner, Senator James Harlan, his wife and daughter; the Marquis de Chambrun; and Elizabeth Keckly, Mary's dressmaker and confidant who had once lived in Petersburg. At 11 A.M. on April 5, they departed again on the *Monohassett*—a ship disliked by Mary—and sailed into Fort Monroe at 4 A.M. on the sixth. By noon, they had steamed into City Point and transferred onto the president's luxurious *River Queen*. In the afternoon, the president allowed his wife and party to commandeer his ship to convey them to Richmond in style. Mary recounted, "We had a gay time I assure you."[180] That night outside of Richmond they slept aboard their vessel and cruised back to City Point at 9 A.M. on the seventh, having had "a charming time." At noon, a special train carried them to Petersburg. This time, Lincoln accompanied them. They were back at City Point by evening.[181]

To celebrate the capture of Richmond, Mrs. Lincoln arranged a grand soiree aboard the *River Queen* for the evening of April 8, the president's last night at City Point. Mary's exclusive invitation list to this bon-voyage party brazenly excluded the visiting vice president, Andrew Johnson, and especially Julia Grant. When the gala celebration—complete with a military band—ended at 10 P.M., the *River Queen* cast off her mooring lines and departed for Washington, escorted and guarded by the *Bat*. At Fort Monroe, the tiny flotilla docked temporarily to receive supplies, mail, and telegraphic messages. From there, the voyage continued in a restful, happy manner. The long cruel war was nearly over.[182]

Those eighteen days at the front were certainly the president's best vacation of his entire presidency. At 6 P.M. on April 9, Palm Sunday, the *River Queen* nosed into her dock at Fifth Street in Washington. One reporter who witnessed his arrival testified, "The president is looking much better for his extended absence from the capital."[183] Later that evening, a most-welcomed telegram informed Lincoln that Lee had surrendered; a perfect ending for a very blissful day of sailing.

Mary had been thrilled with pure delight to have made a triumphal parade through both Petersburg and the fallen Confederate capital city. It was her last dynamic excursion as the reigning First Lady. The untimely and tragic death of her husband on April 15, 1865, propelled Mary Lincoln into a complete physical collapse. B. B. French, commissioner of public buildings, thought she "exhibited all the symptoms of madness." He declared her "a most singular woman." For thirty-eight days she remained in the White House with her unstable mind "unhinged" from her ailing body.[184]

Finally, with Robert's guidance and the medical assistance of Dr. A. G. Henry, a physician friend from Springfield days, plus Elizabeth Keckly, William H. Crook, and Thomas Cross—all three of the latter had worked at the Executive Mansion—Widow Lincoln, clothed in black, and her entourage, with Tad in hand, were driven to the Baltimore and Ohio train station in Washington on the evening of May 22. Mary's destination was not her family home in Springfield but rather a hotel in Chicago. All of those mentioned above would accompany her there. Keckly ministered tenderly to Mrs. Lincoln's physical needs. Cross and Crook were along to take charge of the travel details, which included her many packing boxes and trunks—provided free to her by the government. (These items of freight were to be deposited temporarily in a Chicago warehouse.)[185] These two men also watched over the rambunctious Tad, keeping him entertained and safe.

At 6 P.M., Mrs. Lincoln's travelling companions mounted her favorite Green Car, which had been chartered for her last ride on the rails as an official function. It was connected to the end of the rolling stock with an observation car coupled to it. Commissioner French was perhaps the only government official who appeared at the station to see her off. Mary Lincoln seemed "in a daze" and almost in "a stupor." With a mournful blast from its whistle, the locomotive headed northeast to Relay House, where those passengers proceeding on west were transferred to B. and O.'s "Express Train."[186] It proved a most difficult time for Mrs. Lincoln. She later confided to the Reverend Noyes W. Miner that she had no memory of the days that followed the assassination. They had completely flown from her mind.[187]

At about 4:00 P.M. on May 23, Mary Lincoln's party rolled into Pittsburgh and transferred to another rail line.[188] They had been en route for a tiring twenty-two hours. From there, they continued on the tracks of the Pittsburgh, Fort Wayne and Chicago Railroad, bound for the "Windy City," which they finally reached at noon on the twenty-fourth. That last leg of the journey had taken twenty hours. The suffering widow had spent a long forty-two hours on the road. From the train station, Mary was driven immediately to the Tremont House, where she engaged a suite of rooms numbered 32 and 34 on the second floor. She desired to receive no visits for "a day or two," and then only from "personal friends."[189]

Now began seventeen years of lonely widowhood. But her travelling and wandering days were far from over. However, that is another tale, which cannot be told here.

### Notes

The quote that serves as the title of this essay is from Mary Lincoln's letter to her husband, May 1848.

Special thanks to Michael Burkhimer, Teena D. Groves, Judith Ann Harwood, Beverly Hickox-Whitton, Stacey Skeeters, and Sunderine Temple.

1. Katherine Helm, *The True Story of Mary, Wife of Lincoln* (New York: Harper and Brothers, 1928), 1.

2. Sangamon Co. Deed Record H, 310–11, MS., IRAD, UIS.

3. Mrs. Lincoln's interview with William H. Herndon, which he published as "Mrs. Lincoln's Denial, and What She Says," Broadside, January 12, 1874, MA. Hist. Soc.

4. Parish Register, 1838–1905, 274, MS., St. Paul's Episcopal Procathedral, Springfield, IL.

5. Justin G. Turner and Linda Levitt Turner, *Mary Todd Lincoln: Her Life and Letters* (New York: Alfred A. Knopf, 1972), 14–15.

6. Previous authors have merely speculated as to their route to Washington. However, I have found a contemporary account of Lincoln making just such a journey. See Wayne C. Temple, "Lincoln's Route to Washington from Springfield in 1848," *Lincolnian*, 24, no. 6, 7–8 (July–August 2005). Certainly, their 1847 trip would have been by the same route that Lincoln, himself, took the following year. See also Temple, *Lincoln's Connections with the Illinois and Michigan Canal* (Springfield: IL Bell, 1986), 27–28.

7. Roy P. Basler, Marion Dolores Pratt, and Lloyd A. Dunlap, eds., *The Collected Works of Abraham Lincoln* (New Brunswick: Rutgers University Press, 1953), 1:465.

8. Ibid., 1:477–78. Uncle Parker was headed to Philadelphia by way of Washington.

9. Turner and Turner, *Mary Todd Lincoln*, 37–38.

10. Temple, *Lincoln's Connections with the Illinois and Michigan Canal*, 30–54.

11. Entry in Levi Owen Todd's family Bible, photocopy in possession of the author. The body was buried on his farm and later, on December 8, 1849, transferred to the Lexington Cemetery. Previous authors not having access to this primary record show Robert dying on the sixteenth.

12. William H. Townsend, *Lincoln and His Wife's Home Town* (Indianapolis: Bobbs-Merrill, 1929), 205–24.

13. *Illinois Daily Journal*, November 19, 1849, 3, col. 1.

14. Townsend, *Lincoln and His Wife's Home Town*, 222n27.

15. Death entry in Levi Own Todd's family Bible.

16. William. E. Baringer, ed., *Lincoln Day by Day* (Washington: Lincoln Sesquicentennial Comm., 1960), 2:198–99.

17. Turner and Turner, *Mary Todd Lincoln*, 49–50.

18. Newspaper accounts in Edwin Erle Sparks, ed., *The Lincoln-Douglas Debates* (Springfield: IL State Hist. Library, 1908), 449–50, and photo facing page 498; for proof of Mrs. Lincoln's attendance, see Gustave Koerner, *Memoirs* (Cedar Rapids: Torch, 1909), 2:66–67; for proof that Robert was along, see his letter to Horace White, Washington, DC, December 31, 1910, White MSS, Abraham Lincoln Presidential Library.

19. Baringer, *Day by Day*, 2:256; Turner and Turner, *Mary Todd Lincoln*, 57–58; Basler et al., *Collected Works*, 3:393.

20. Baringer, *Day by Day*, 2:298–99; Wayne C. Temple, *Abraham Lincoln: From Skeptic to Prophet* (Mahomet: Mayhaven, 1995), 86.

21. Springfield report in *Chicago Tribune*, January 9, 1861, 1, col. 2.

22. *New York Tribune*, January 12, 1861, 4, col.1.

23. Ibid., January 14, 1861, 5, col. 5; Chicago *Tribune*, January 17, 1861, 2, col. 7.

24. *New York Tribune*, January 14, 1861, 2, col. 5.

25. *Frank Leslie's Illustrated Newspaper*, 11, no. 146 (January 26, 1861).

26. *New York Herald*, January 14, 1861, 5, col. 2.

27. Turner and Turner, *Mary Todd Lincoln*, 69.

28. *New York Herald*, January 23, 1861, 8, col. 4; *Frank Leslie's Illustrated Newspaper*, 11, no. 163 (February 2, 1861).

29. *New York Herald*, January 24, 1861, 8, col. 5; *New York Tribune*, January 28, 1861.

30. *Illinois State Journal*, January 28, 1861, 3, col. 2.

31. *New York Tribune*, February 12, 1861, 5, col. 3.

32. Entry of February 11, 1861, in diary of Henry C. Latham, in *Bulletin of the Abraham Lincoln Assoc.*, 52, no. 8 (June 1938).

33. *New York Tribune*, February 13, 1861, 5, col. 4. One of the "domestics" was William H. Johnson, a mulatto who helped with the children, and another was Ellen Shehan, a seamstress, etc. For the mention of "domestics," see *Illinois State Journal*, February 11, 1861, 2, col. 1.

34. *New York Herald*, March 7, 1861, 1, col. 3; March 10, 1861, 1, col. 2.

35. Reproductions of the letters in *The Lounge Lizard*, 2d Ser., 2, no. 2, 4–5 (February 2009).

36. *New York Herald*, March 28, 1861, 1, col. 4.

37. Dorothy T. Muir, *Presence of a Lady: The Story of Mount Vernon during the Civil War* (Mount Vernon: Mount Vernon Ladies' Assoc., 1974), 21; Mark E. Neely Jr. and Harold Holzer, *The Lincoln Family Album* (New York: Doubleday, 1990), 17–18, 75; Turner and Turner, *Mary Todd Lincoln*, 81–82. Her friend was Hannah Shearer.

38. *New York Tribune*, May 10, 1861, 5, col. 2.

39. Ibid.

40. Ibid., May 12, 1861, 4, col. 5.

41. *New York Herald*, May 11, 1861, 1, col. 1; May 12, 1861, 1, col. 5.

42. Ibid., May 13, 1861, 5, col. 5; *New York Tribune*, May 13, 1861, 5, col. 5.

43. *New York Tribune*, May 14, 1861, 8, col. 5.

44. Ibid., May 15, 1861, 5, col. 1. For the program, see ibid., May 14, 1861, 2, col. 1. Doors opened at 7:30; play, at 8 PM.

45. Ibid., May 16, 1861, 8, col. 4.

46. Ibid., May 17, 1861, 4, col. 6.

47. Ibid., May 17, 1861, 5, col. 6; *New York Herald*, May 17, 1861, 4, col. 6.

48. Ibid., May 17, 1861, 4. col. 6; May 18, 1861, 8, col. 1.

49. Ibid., May 19, 1861, 5, col. 4; *New York Herald*, May 19, 1861, 1, col. 4.

50. Ibid., May 21, 1861, 8, col. 4; *New York Herald*, May 21, 1861, 4, col. 5.

51. *New York Tribune*, May 21, 1861, 8, col. 4; *New York Herald*, May 20, 1861, 1, col. 1.

52. *New York Herald*, August 7, 1861, 4, col. 5.

53. *New York Herald*, August 14, 1861, 1, col. 1; 4, col. 6.

54. Ibid., August 15, 1861, 5, col. 1.

55. *New York Tribune*, August 14, 1861, 3, col. 4.

56. *New York Daily Tribune*, August 16, 1861, 5, col. 6.

57. *New York Herald*, August 16, 1861, 5, col. 5. This royal couple had visited the White House on August 3 that year as private citizens.

58. Ibid., August 16, 1861, 5, col. 5.

59. Ibid., August 17, 1861, 5, col. 1.

60. Ibid., August 17, 1861, 5, col. 2; US census 1860, Long Branch, Monmouth, Co., NJ, 119, 11. 36–37; Michael Burlingame, ed., *Lincoln's Journalist* (Carbondale: Southern Illinois University Press, 1998), 93–99.

61. *New York Tribune*, August 18, 1861, 3, col. 4.

62. Ibid., August 18, 1861, 5, col. 1; *New York Herald*, August 18, 1861, 4, col. 6. Hannah Shearer had once lived across the street from the Lincolns in Springfield but now resided with her husband, a physician, in a hotel at Wellsboro, Tiogo Co., Pennsylvania, although she owned $10,000 in real estate from a previous marriage. US census 1860, Wellsboro, PA, 742, 11. 35–38. Mrs. Shearer and her two young sons had joined Mrs. Lincoln's travelers in Philadelphia.

63. *New York Herald*, August 19, 1861, 5, col. 3; August 22, 1861, 2, cols. 4–5.

64. Ibid., August 23, 1861, 4, col. 6; August 24, 1861, 8, cols. 3–4; Burlingame, *Lincoln's Journalist* (Carbondale: Southern Illinois University Press, 1998), 93. This dress is certainly the one shown in photos nos. MLO-13–0-19 by Lloyd Ostendorf. For Mrs. Lincoln's trunks, see Turner and Turner, *Mary Todd Lincoln*, 95.

65. *New York Herald*, August 25, 1861, 2, col. 4, 5, col. 5.

66. Burlingame, *John Hay's Civil War Correspondence* (Carbondale: Southern Illinois University Press, 2000), 12, 216n54.

67. Turner and Turner, *Mary Todd Lincoln*, 94.

68. *New York Herald*, August 28, 1861, 4, col. 6.

69. Chicago *Tribune*, September 2, 1861, 2, col. 2; Burlingame, *John Hay's Correspondence,* 20, 186, 217, 219; *New York Herald*, August 25, 1861, 2, col. 4; Elizabeth Todd Grimsley, "Six Months in the White House," *Jour. IL St. Hist. Soc.*, 19, nos. 3–4, 72 (October 1926–January 1927).

70. *New York Tribune*, September 5, 1861, 5, col. 6.

71. *New York Herald*, September 5, 1861, 4, col. 6.

72. Ibid., September 6, 1861, 8, col. 4.

73. Mrs. Maria Lydig Daly in Harold Earl Hammond, ed., *Diary of a Union Lady, 1861–1865* (New York: Funk and Wagnalls, 1962), 53.

74. Turner and Turner, *Mary Todd Lincoln*, 104.

75. Burlingame, *John Hay's Correspondence*, 14.

76. *New York Herald*, November 5, 1861, 1, col. 2; *Frank Leslie's Illustrated Newspaper* 13, no. 3 (November 23, 1861).

77. Turner and Turner, *Mary Todd Lincoln*, 103n5.

78. Baringer, *Lincoln Day by Day*, 3:76.

79. *New York Herald*, July 10, 1862, 4, col. 6; July 11, 1862, 5, col. 4.

80. Ibid., July 14, 1862, 5, col. 2; July 15, 1862, 8, col. 4. Murfey was born in Rhode Island but commissioned from Wisconsin on April 14, 1862.

81. Ibid., July 16, 1862, 6, col. 6; Basler, *Collected Works Supplement* (Westport, CT: Greenwood, 1974), 141.

82. *New York Herald*, July 16, 1862, 6, col. 6. There is no record that Howe was a colonel in the US Army as the newspaper indicated.

83. Item for sale by Parke-Bernet Galleries at auction on December 3, 1957.

84. *New York Herald*, July 18, 1862, 4, col. 4.

85. *Chicago Tribune*, July 17, 1862, 4, col. 1.

86. *New York Tribune*, October 21, 1862, 5, col. 2.

87. Turner and Turner, *Mary Todd Lincoln*, 139, 140.

88. *New York Herald*, October 24, 1862, 8, col. 5; October 25, 1862, 5, col. 3. After Willie's death, Mrs. Lincoln refused to allow the Marine Band to play on the White House grounds until May 15, 1863.

89. Ibid., October 29, 1862, 4, col. 6.

90. Ibid., October 30, 1862, 1, cols. 2–3.

91. Ibid., November 1, 1862, 5, col. 3.

92. Ibid., November 2, 1862, 4, col. 5; Turner and Turner, *Mary Todd Lincoln*, 139–40.

93. Turner and Turner, *Mary Todd Lincoln*, 140–41.

94. *New York Herald*, November 8, 1862, 8, col. 6; November 10, 1862, 1, col. 6.

95. Ibid., November 14, 1862, 5, col. 4.

96. Ibid., November 13, 1862, 5, col. 5.

97. Ibid., November 18, 1862, 1, col. 2.

98. Ibid., November 20, 1862, 5, col. 5; November 23, 1862, 5, col. 2; November 25, 1862, 5, col. 4.

99. Turner and Turner, *Mary Todd Lincoln*, 142. For the story of Tad and his photograph with Gumpert, see Gustav Gumpert, "Tad Lincoln and Gus Gumpert," *Jour. IL State Hist. Soc.* 48, (Spring 1955). Another close Philadelphia friend of young Tad was Colonel Thomas Worthington Sweney (May 22, 1812–April 7, 1872), who had been the Colonel of the Ninety-Ninth Pennsylvania Infantry from November 7, 1861, until January 24, 1862, when discharged for "physical inability." He was a wealthy real estate agent who became a US assessor of internal revenue from 1863 to1866 by presidential appointment. Roger D. Hunt, *Colonels in Blue: The Mid-Atlantic States* (Mechanicsburg, PA: Stackpole, 2007), 160.

100. *New York Tribune*, November 27, 1862, 5, col. 3; November 28, 1862, 4, col. 6; *New York Herald*, November 27, 1862, 1, col. 5; November 28, 1862, 5, col. 3.

101. A. G. Henry to his wife, Washington, April 12, 1863, Henry Papers, Abraham Lincoln Presidential Library; Noah Brooks, *Washington in Lincoln's Time* (New York: Century, 1895), 47; Burlingame, *Lincoln Observed* (Baltimore: Johns Hopkins University Press, 1998), 35–45; Howard K. Beale, ed., *The Diary of Edward Bates* (Washington: US Govt. Print. Office, 1933), 287; O. R., Ser. I, 50:153–55; *New York*

*Herald*, April 10, 1863, 1, col. 5, April 11, 1863, 6, col. 6; *National Intelligencer*, April 14, 1863, 1, col. 5; Wayne C. Temple, *Dr. Anson G. Henry* (Bulletin no. 43 of Lincoln Fellowship of Wisconsin, 1988). In the following year, the *Carrie Martin* went to Grant when Lincoln got the new *River Queen*.

102. Turner and Turner, *Mary Todd Lincoln*, 152 and n2.

103. Basler et al., *Collected Works*, 6:256.

104. Ibid., 6:283.

105. Clipping from the *Baltimore American* dated June 20, reprinted in *New York Herald*, June 22, 1863, 5, col. 4.

106. Turner and Turner, *Mary Todd Lincoln*, 153.

107. *New York Herald*, July 3, 1863, 4, col. 5, July 4, 1863, 4, col. 5; *Frank Leslie's Illustrated Newspaper* 16, no. 259 (July 18, 1863). The reporter called him "Dr. Judson." See Richard Palmer's article at <http://www.bpmlegal.com/76NY/truxdoc.html>. President Lincoln blamed not only the loose driver's seat but also the condition of the roadway at that spot. On July 17, 1863, he dashed off a memorandum: "The place on the road near Mt. Pleasant Hospital ought to be repaired." Basler, *Collected Works Supplement*, 194.

108. Basler et al., *Collected Works*, 6:314.

109. *New York Herald*, July 11, 1863, 1, col. 6. Surgeons with their dirty hands and instruments often caused infection to develop.

110. Basler et al., *Collected Works*, 6:323. The draft riot started on July 13.

111. *New York Herald*, July 12, 1863, 5, col. 2.

112. Burlingame, *John Hay's Civil War Correspondence*, 45.

113. *New York Herald*, July 29, 1863, 4, col. 5.

114. Turner and Turner, *Mary Todd Lincoln*, 157; Basler et al., *Collected Works*, 6:353.

115. Robert C. Winthrop Jr., *A Memoir of Robert C. Winthrop* (Boston: Little, Brown, 1897), 229. These slippers are without question the same ones that Mrs. Lincoln gave to Alexander Williamson after the president's death. In turn, Williamson presented them to President Rutherford B. Hayes, and they are now in the Hayes Presidential Center at Fremont, Ohio. See Wayne C. Temple, *Alexander Williamson: Friend of the Lincolns* (Lincoln Fellowship of WI, Special Publication no. 1, 1997), 35, for a photo of them.

116. "X.Y.Z." to the *Boston Journal*, Kearsarge House, August 4, 1863, clipping; "J.H.S." to the *Boston Journal*, Mt. Washington, August 7, 1863, clipping. Samuel C. Eastman, *Eastman's White Mountain Guide* (Concord, NH: P. B. Cogswell, 1863), passim; Randall H. Bennett, *Images of America: The White Mountains* (Charleston, SC: Arcadia, 1994), 2, 29, 30, 33, 38, 50, 51, 77; US census 1860, Success, Coos, NH, 1071, 11.20–28; US census 1860, Conway, Carroll Co., NH, 937, 11.2–3; Lincoln issued his Proclamation of Thanksgiving on July 15 to be observed on August 6, Basler et al., *Collected Works*, 6:332–33; family members generally described Mary's hair as "chestnut" in color.

117. "Probus" to the *Boston Journal*, Profile House, August 12, 1863, clipping; Basler et al., *Collected Works*, 6:371–72; Turner and Turner, *Mary Todd Lincoln*, 154 and n4, 687, 690; photo in Neely and Holzer, *The Lincoln Family Album*, 90; *Boston Morning Post*, August 14, 1863, 4, col. 4.

118. *New York Herald*, August 22, 1863, 4, col. 6.

119. Ibid., August 27, 1863, 6, col. 5.

120. Roy P. Basler and Christian O. Basler, eds., *Collected Works Second Supplement* (New Brunswick, NJ: Rutgers University Press, 1990), 79.

121. *Manchester Journal*, August 25, 1863, 2, col. 4; *New York Herald*, September 1, 1863, 1, col. 3.

122. Basler et al., *Collected Works*, 6:431. In December, Doubleday was ordered to sit on court-martial cases.

123. *Manchester Journal*, September 8, 1863, 2, col. 3.

124. Nikolay Andreyevich Rimski-Korsakov, *My Musical Life* (New York: Alfred A. Knopf, 1942), 40–45. He was a midshipman on the *Almaz* at this time.

125. *New York Daily Tribune*, September 12, 1863, 6, col. 1.

126. Ibid., September 18, 1863, 2, col. 6; *New York Herald*, September 17, 1863, 7, cols. 2–3.

127. Basler et al., *Collected Works*, 7:469, 471.

128. Turner and Turner, *Mary Todd Lincoln*, 157.

129. Basler et al., *Collected Works*, 6:474, 478.

130. *New York Herald*, September 26, 1863, 3, col. 6.

131. *New York Daily Tribune*, September 25, 1863, 4, col. 1; September 26, 1863, 4, col. 1.

132. *New York Herald*, September 26, 1863, 3, col. 6.

133. Turner and Turner, *Mary Todd Lincoln*, 690.

134. *New York Herald*, September 29, 1863, 3, col. 5.

135. Burlingame, ed., *Dispatches from Lincoln's White House* (Lincoln: University of Nebraska Press, 2002), 177.

136. *New York Herald*, November 20, 1863, 4, col. 1.

137. Turner and Turner, *Mary Todd Lincoln*, 158.

138. Michael Burlingame and John R. Ettlinger, eds., *Inside Lincoln's White House* (Carbondale: Southern Illinois University Press, 1997), 118; Burlingame, *John Hay's Correspondence*, 70.

139. *New York Herald*, December 1, 1863, 4, col. 5.

140. *New York Daily Tribune*, December 2, 1863, 1, col. 5.

141. *New York Herald*, December 5, 1863, 6, col. 6.

142. Turner and Turner, *Mary Todd Lincoln*, 159.

143. Ibid.

144. Ibid., 160; *New York Herald*, December 9, 1863, 1, col. 4; 1, col. 1.

145. *New York Herald*, December 11, 1863, 3, col. 3.

146. Ibid., December 19, 1863, 2, col. 5.

147. *Gloucester (MA) Telegraph*, January 16, 1864.

148. Basler, *Collected Works Supplement*, 239.

149. Turner and Turner, *Mary Todd Lincoln*, 175; *New York Herald*, May 9, 1864, 5, col. 3. Mary purchased mainly on credit, and some merchant, perhaps, demanded payment before extending more credit.

150. *New York Herald*, May 2, 1864, 4, col. 5. Emphasis on the winter apparel added by the author.

151. Ibid., June 16, 1864, 5, col. 1; June 17, 1864, 1, col. 5. Baringer, *Day by Day*, 3:265–66.

152. Burlingame, *John Hay's Correspondence*, 85.

153. Basler et al., *Collected Works*, 7:401.

154. *National Intelligencer*, June 23, 1864, 1, col. 4; June 25, 1864, 1, col. 2.

155. Basler et al., *Collected Works*, 7:406; *New York Herald*, July 21, 1864, 1, col. 6.

156. *New York Times*, June 29, 1864, 2, col. 3.

157. Basler et al., *Collected Works*, 7:417; John S. Goff, *Robert Todd Lincoln* (Norman: University of Oklahoma Press, 1969), 59.

158. *New York Herald*, July 3, 1864, 5, col. 1.

159. *Correspondence of B. F. Butler* (Norwood, MA, 1917), 4:566; "Castine," Washington, August 1, 1864, in *Sacramento Union*, August 29, 1864; Turner and Turner, *Mary Todd Lincoln*, 178.

160. *New York Herald*, August 16, 1864, 4, col. 5.

161. Ibid., August 18, 1864, 4, col. 5.

162. Hotel Register, MS, courtesy of Astri, the concierge, at the Equinox.

163. *New York Herald*, August 29, 1864, 4, col. 5.

164. Ibid., August 30, 1864, 5, col. 2.

165. Burlingame, *With Lincoln in the White House*, 155.

166. Donald B. Cole and John J. McDonough, eds. *Benjamin Brown French: A Yankee's Journal* (Hanover, NH: University Press of New England, 1989), 456; Basler et al., *Collected Works*, 7:544.

167. Willard A. Cutter to George Cutter, Washington, DC, September 17, 1864, Willard A. Cutter Coll., Allegheny College, Meadville, PA. Pvt. Willard A. Cutter was in Co. K, 150th Pennsylvania Inf. stationed at the Soldiers' Home to guard the Lincolns, and he thus witnessed their comings and goings.

168. *New York Herald*, January 4, 1865, 4, col. 6; March 6, 1865, 5, col. 2.

169. Ibid., March 8, 1865, 5, col. 2.

170. Ibid., March 12, 1865, 5, col. 1.

171. Burlingame, *Lincoln Observed*, 175–76.

172. Turner and Turner, *Mary Todd Lincoln*, 209.

173. John Y. Simon, *The Personal Memoirs of Julia Dent Grant* (New York: G. P. Putnam's Sons, 1975), 141–42.

174. *O. R.*, Ser. I, 46, Pt. 3, 30.

175. For a detailed account of this trip, see Wayne C. Temple, *Lincoln's Travels on the River Queen* (Mahomet: Mayhaven, 2007).

176. *New York Herald*, March 24, 1865, 1, col. 5, March 26, 1865, 4, col. 4, March 27, 1865, 1, col. 5.

177. For the best study of this sorry incident, see Temple, *Lincoln's Travels on the River Queen*, and Donald C. Planz, *The Petersburg Campaign* (Lynchburg: H. E. Howard, 1989). Donn's name is often spelled "Dunn."

178. Mary Lincoln to Abraham Lincoln, Washington, April 2, [1865], telegram, MS, Abraham Lincoln Presidential Library, Springfield.

179. Basler, *Collected Works Supplement*, 285.

180. Turner and Turner, *Mary Todd Lincoln*, 220.

181. Marquis Adolphe de Chambrun, *Impressions of Lincoln* (New York: Random House, 1952), 77–78.

182. Ibid., 83; Planz, *The Petersburg Campaign*, 84–88.

183. *National Intelligencer*, April 10, 1865, 2, col. 1; *New York Herald*, April 10, 1865, 4, col. 6; *Washington Star*, April 10, 1865, 2, col. 2.

184. Cole and McDonough, *Benjamin Brown French*, 479.

185. Turner and Turner, *Mary Todd Lincoln*, 236.

186. *New York Herald*, May 23, 1865, 1, col. 6; B. and O. schedule printed in the *Daily National Intelligencer*, February 24, 1865, 4, col. 1; Margarita Spalding Gerry, ed., *Through Five Administrations: Reminiscences of Colonel William H. Crook* (New York: Harper and Brothers, 1910), 70–71; Elizabeth Keckley, *Behind the Scenes* (New York: G. W. Carleton, 1868), 203–4, 210. Keckly actually signed her name without the second "e."

187. N. W. Miner, "Mrs. Abraham Lincoln: A Vindication," MS, Abraham Lincoln Presidential Library, Springfield.

188. *Pittsburgh Gazette*, May 24, 1865, 1, col. 5. This paper falsely thought "that Marshal Lamon accompanied the family."

189. *Chicago Times*, May 25, 1865, 3, col. 4. Crook erroneously remembered the travel time as fifty-four hours. Gerry, *Through Five Administrations*, 70–71. His book is very unreliable.

## Fashion Plate or Fashion Trendsetter?

*Donna McCreary*

Mary Lincoln was known to have enjoyed fine horses, a good joke, and an exquisite wardrobe. As a member of the aristocratic Todd family, Mary was raised as a member of the social plane where ladies were concerned about the width of their ribbons, the length of their skirts, and the latest Parisian fashions.[1]

As First Lady, she was both criticized and revered for her lavish gowns and elegant laces. Despite the criticism, Mary understood fashion and how a woman's attire depicted not only society's vision of women but also reflected a woman's view of herself. Mary was known to seek the finest fabrics, laces, and trims, and to haggle for the best prices possible. Because she was the wife of a president, reporters followed her on shopping sprees for peeks at her purchases or interviews with sales clerks who had sold the goods. Descriptions and illustrations of Mary's gowns were often published on the front pages of newspapers. Did Mary merit this attention because she was a fashion trendsetter? Or did she merit it because she wore the finest of what was considered fashionable? Or both?

The Roman statesman and author Seneca once said: "We live not according to reason, but according to fashion." For the Victorians, especially Victorian women, fashion ruled their lifestyle. The manner in which a lady walked, sat, stood, moved, and behaved was controlled by her dress and undergarments. Fashion served as a window to the woman's sphere, or at least the male designers' version of it. Men often viewed women as frail, fragile, delicate, and helpless and designed clothing that ensured that image. A boned corset "extended not only over the bosom but also all over the abdomen and back down to the hips" thus controlling a woman's posture.[2] Tight, skin-hugging sleeves prevented her from raising her arms. Early Victorian women wore clothing that shut them away from others and protected them from the masses. Nearly every inch of a woman's being was covered in cloth; even her face was protected from wayward stares by poke-bonnets, veils, and fans. According to the male fashion designers, a woman's place in public view was clear—she was not to be seen.

In America's infancy, fashion influence was primarily British. However, during the Revolutionary War, those who wished to be both fashionable and patriotic wore finery from Paris. When Philadelphia, Pennsylvania, became the capital of the new republic's government, it also became the fashion capital of the new country. For where power and money flow, people come, and fashion flourishes.[3]

For this reason, in 1828, a self-educated French immigrant named Louis A. Godey arrived in Philadelphia. He worked as a "scissors editor" until 1830, when he began publishing his first and most successful publication—*Godey's Lady's Book*.[4] Within six years, *Godey's* had the largest circulation of any magazine in America. Under the editorship of Sarah Josepha Hale, the magazine continued to reach a record number of subscriptions. No matter where a woman lived in American, she could subscribe to the magazine and keep abreast of the latest fashion advice, cooking instructions, household management guides, and rules of social etiquette. Mary would have been familiar with *Godey's* whether she was a young belle in Lexington, a young mother in Springfield, or the wife of the president in Washington. Women studied issues of *Godey's Lady's Book* examining the hand-tinted fashion plates that were published in each issue. These plates depicted groups of wealthy women performing leisurely activities. Women were shown horseback riding, ice skating, dancing, and playing musical instruments. They were reading, doing hand sewing, conversing with one another. Groups of women were depicted at the sea shore, at parties, and at other desirable places. Background images showed elegant curtains and furnishings, and opulent décor. This was the image of the wealthy, the famous, and the aristocratic women of society. With the rise of the middle class, and the ability to transport goods westward, thousands of women strived to create images in their own homes and wardrobes that had previously been reserved for the elite. In Europe, shopgirls, seamstress, and other members of the middle class made every effort to own at least one silk dress.[5] Just as modern women often search for a less expensive dress similar to a designer gown, Victorian women did the same. When English women searched for a similar, but less expensive, copy of Queen Victoria's cashmere shawls, they found the Paisley mill near Glasgow created ones that were close to the quality of the originals. Increasing her popularity among the middle class, Queen Victoria lent her cashmere shawls to the mill to use as patterns.[6] American women followed the example of their European counterpart and created opulent designs in their own homes and wardrobes. Mary Lincoln was one of those women.

Mary's interest in fashion developed when she was a child. It was an era when garments were made entirely by hand. It was a daunting task for every married woman to provide her family with clothing. In addition to the family's clothing needs, she was required to provided bed coverings, curtains, table clothes, napkins, and all other linens. In the Todd household, the skilled hands of the "sewing woman" (a slave servant) were not capable of providing all of the garments required by the large family. The Todd daughters, including Mary, learned to sew, embroider, and knit. After finishing her school lessons, one of Mary's nightly tasks was to knit "ten rounds of sock."[7] Mary honed her sewing skills early in her life and much of her time was occupied with the task. In an early letter written while visiting her cousin Ann in Missouri, Mary wrote to her friend Mercy Levering, "I have scarce a leisure moment to call my own, for several weeks this fall a formidable supply of *sewing*, necessary to winter comfort, engaged our constant attention."[8] Family legends of the young Miss Todd include stories about costumes made from sheer embroidered pink muslin, layers of white organdy, billowing lace, blue satin sashes, leghorn hats, and feathered headdresses. These were elegant garments worn by women of the elite social set.

The first recorded attention Mary gave to fashion occurred when she was about ten years old. This was the romantic era of fashion. Garments of pink, azure blue, myrtle green, jonquil, and marshmallow were made from soft fabrics such as batiste and chintz. A fashionable bodice had a high waist, wide shoulder lines, and large upper sleeves. Skirts were ankle-length and gently pleated. Lower hems were trimmed with flounces, a padded roll at the hem, or other three-dimensional decoration. A single fine reed (the same type used by milliners when making drawn-silk bonnets) was basted on the inside of the skirt to keep the skirt from wrapping around the wearer's legs. Done properly, the effect was lovely and balanced the hemline with the wide shoulder and sleeve design.[9] Although called a "hooped skirt," this was not the hoop crinoline of the Civil War era.

Mary became frantic for one of these newest fashionable "hooped" skirts. According to her stepcousin Elizabeth Humphreys, Mary knew that if she asked for one, her request would be denied. How to obtain one caused her great worry until "at last she hit upon an expedient." She planned to visit a neighbor, Mrs. Hostetter, one Saturday afternoon and ask for branches from her weeping willow tree. That night, working by the light of a single candle, the two giggling girls sewed branches into their dress hems. The task had taken them nearly all night. After breakfast the next morning, they hurriedly dressed into their remade frocks. As they raced out of the house on their way to Sunday school, Mary's stepmother, Betsy, stopped Elizabeth, who had almost made it to the front door. Mary, who was already on the street, was called back.

Betsy knew at once what the girls had done. They stood before her "a burlesque on vanity, two of the most grotesque figures her eyes ever fell upon in hoops that bulged in front and at the back, while they fell in at the sides the narrow white muslin skirts stretched to the bursting point."[10] The girls had basted the branches into the skirts just as they came off the tree with one end being very large and the other being very small.

Mary's temper flared because she felt they were unjustly treated when told they looked like frights and to return to their room to change into suitable attire for church. A few weeks later, her bitter disappointment was appeased when her father returned from a business trip to New Orleans. He brought with him several yards of lovely sheer embroidered pink muslin—enough for Mary and Elizabeth to each have a new frock. For the first time, Mary was allowed to determine the fashion of her own clothing. She supervised the details and made sure the "sewing woman" followed her every detail creating a fashionable new dress.[11] Miss Todd had become aware of fashion.

Attention to fashion details stayed with Mary throughout her life. Years later, her older sister Frances stated that Mary was "one of the best seamstresses I ever knew. She made all her clothes and her children's clothes; and they were better made than most anyone else's."[12] Mary's skill as a seamstress and her love of fashion made her wardrobe spectacular. It was a time-consuming task, and many women delighted at the news of a new machine to help with the chore. It is not known if Mary owned a sewing machine in Springfield. Oral history includes stories that Mary and other ladies gathered at the home of a neighbor woman to take advantage of the one she owned. Sadly, the name of the neighbor and any collaborating evidence has been lost. With many relatives and friends in Springfield, it is probable she had access to a machine even if she did not personally own one. A machine was given to Mary by the Wheeler and Wilson Sewing Machine Company of Chicago to be used at the White House, but it is doubtful she found time to use it. It was described as being "mounted in a solid rosewood full case," and "richly silver plated and ornamented with inlaid pearl and enamel." Similar machines manufactured by the same company were set to the English Duchess of Sutherland and the Russian Duchess of Constantine.[13]

In 1846, Elias Howe invented and received a patent for a lock-stitch sewing machine. He traveled to Europe hoping to find financial support for his machine, and upon his return to America, found others manufacturing better machines. Howe may have created the infant industry, but it was Isaac Singer's creation of a sewing machine for home use that gave women the ability to keep their wardrobes fashionably current. The initial $100 purchase price prevented many households from obtaining sewing machines, so Singer developed a payment plan. By allowing women to pay a little every month, he soon had placed Singer sewing machines in most American homes. By the mid-1850s, women were sewing quilts, linens, and clothing by machine. Seamstresses could manufacture clothing faster, and more women made their own dresses. Trims such as machine-made lace were easily available to the home seamstress. Suddenly, fashion was no longer just for the wealthy. Fashion was now affordable and had become equally important to both upper- and middle-class women no matter where they lived.

As the wife of a successful attorney and sometimes politician, Mary wanted to dress her best. Abraham and Mary had different views of what was suitable fashion. For Lincoln, the home in Springfield was the best place he had ever lived. The Lincoln family was doing well financially, his clothes were tailor made, and his home was far removed from the dirt and puncheon floors of his youth. He did not care if his coat was a little worn, his shirt slightly mussed, or his trousers worn at the knees. Mary did care, and she tried to ensure that Lincoln was professionally dressed—at least on the streets of Springfield. Mary loved her husband, family, and home. Early in her marriage, she knew the financial burdens of the family. They were not poor, but they were not as financially stable as some of her relations in Springfield, and certainly not as wealthy as the family she had left behind in Kentucky. Mary had every desire to dress and live as well as her sisters, who had also moved and married in Springfield. To do so, she often searched for ways to economize while maintaining the proper image for society.

Store records from Irwin and Company indicate Mary bought "thirty yards of calico cotton purchased on July 3, 1844, two months after the Lincolns moved into their own home at the corner of Eighth and Jackson streets."[14] The record indicates that the thirty-yard purchase consisted of two separate pieces of fabric, and therefore, two separate calico designs. Mary was about to embark on a few major sewing projects. Some historians have speculated that Mary was making curtains and other items needed for a new home.[15] Lengths of calico may have been suitable to hang in the windows of a sod home on the prairie or the log cabin in the forest (and even their usage there is questionable), but it was not suitable for the windows of an urban home. Most Victorian homes had upholstered chairs and sofas covered with expensive damask cloth. Chair covers, slip covers, and curtains, made from matching fabric, were used to protect upholstered furniture from damaging sunlight and dirt. While not as inexpensive as common calico, chintz was the most popular fabric used for summer curtains and furniture coverings. Wealthier families often hung lace curtains or sheers and used a finer fabric such as silk for their summer furniture coverings. In the winter, a housewife changed her curtains to a heavier fabric to help keep out cold drafts. Moreen (a cheaper woolen fabric), velvet, or damask was often seen at the windows of urban homes during winter months.[16] The Todd home in Lexington, Kentucky, used silk damask curtains in their parlors.

Frequently used to make quilts, children's clothing, men's drawers, work shirts, and ladies' day wear, calico cotton was a common cloth with a small print on one side of the fabric. Its average cost was twenty cents per yard. Irwin's store ledger indicates that Mary paid just eight cents per yard—she had a bargain![17] No one knows why Mary paid such a small amount for the fabric. Perhaps it was substandard fabric or old merchandise, or perhaps Mary was able to haggle for a lower price. Thirty yards of fabric in two prints provided her with enough fabric to make two day dresses for herself and some clothing for her young son. If she was lucky, and if she used calico from another purchase, she may have had enough fabric to make a small quilt. Mary had many wardrobe needs for her family; the fabric was soon put to use. Little Robert, who was nearly one year old, would have required several changes of clothing per day. In a letter to her husband, Mary made reference to children requiring many changes of clothing, "particularly in summer."[18] Soon Robert would be potty trained, learn to walk, and find mischief in the yard. Until he reached the age of five or six, a young boy wore a dress similar to little girls' frocks. These were usually made of cotton so they could easily be washed. As every mother knows, children and their clothing are in constant need of soap and water.

Mary could have easily used some of the calico fabric to make a day wrapper for herself. A wrapper was a "loose-fitting garment worn by women of all social levels while they were at home. It resembled a loose or unfitted day dress since it preserved the same fashionable shape. It could be tied at the waist, buttoned down the front, or belted, and some had a set of drawstrings at the waist to add more fit."[19] Wrappers were often worn by women while working in the home and in the garden. Because of their loose fit, a wrapper allowed a woman to raise her arms to reach higher shelves, to bend to clean under a bed, and to stoop to pull weeds from a garden. Wrappers were also the chosen robe of women who were "in the family way." A sunbonnet made from the same fabric would have protected Mary's face from sunburn when outside working her in yard and garden.

Other fabric purchases from Irwin's store were for "muslin, cambric, gimp, whalebones, and corset lace." These indicate that Mary was improving her wardrobe, and probably those of her husband and young son, by manufacturing proper under garments.[20] Mary used the whalebone in a new corset. Muslin may have used for a new chemise and drawers. Cambric was most often used to make petticoats and was sometimes used for a chemise. It is possible Mary used some of these fabrics to make nightclothes. Later purchases from Irwin and Company included tweed, muslin, flannel, Irish linen, gingham, pearl buttons, assorted threads, and ribbon. Store records also indicate purchases for "kid slippers, a Neapolitan bonnet, a parasol, collars, suspenders, shoes, and boots."[21] As her budget allowed, Mary used finer fabrics for her wardrobe and household linens. A nicer wardrobe indicated a higher level on the social plane, and one's social plane was extremely important to Victorians. To the Victorian eye, first appearance and the way one was dressed made a lasting impression, and proper Victorian ladies wanted to leave a positive lasting first impression. Women paid attention to the details of their attire and their accessories, for one mistake could lead to social ostracization. As one French author wrote, "Those who do not wish to be taken as belonging to the vulgar, prefer to risk a wetting rather than be looked upon as pedestrians in the street, for an umbrella is a sure sign that one possesses no carriage."[22] The practicality of carrying an umbrella was ignored for the sake of appearances. No one wanted to be considered "vulgar," especially women such as Mary Lincoln. Her sister Elizabeth frequently reminded Mary that she was born a Todd, and therefore had standards to maintain.

The earliest image existing of Mary Lincoln is a daguerreotype that was taken sometime between June and December of 1846. Several photographers visited Springfield in the 1840s. (See figure 1 in the essay by Harold Holzer also included in this volume.) It is believed Abraham and Mary Lincoln visited one of the temporary studios of photographer N. H. Shepherd to have companion images taken. If the likeness was taken before her birthday on December 13, Mary would have been twenty-seven years old when photographed. According to Robert Todd Lincoln, the original daguerreotypes hung on walls in the Lincolns' Springfield home.[23]

According to fashion historians, "Never before or since has Western women's costume expressed respectability, acquiescence and dependence to such a degree as the 1840s."[24] Even though Mary's dress appears to be quite fashionable in her photograph, there are aspects about her that seem to indicate an unconventional woman. Fashions of the 1840s helped hide and protect women. When outside, women were completely covered and wore a long shawl or mantle over their gowns. Heads were covered. When outside, a poke bonnet was worn, which prevented onlookers from seeing the wearer's face. Indoors, even a young woman was expected to "wear a cap as soon as she had children."[25] Yet, here is Mary Lincoln, the young mother of two small boys, wearing nothing on her head with her face fully visible. She wears no shawl to cover her dress. She appears respectable, but it is doubtful she was either quiet or dependent. Her face is open to the camera as if almost to say, "My husband has just been elected to Congress—and here I am."

For her photograph, Mary probably chose to wear one of her more fashionable dresses. In the mid-1840s, "there was a marked taste for materials with horizontal stripes," and Mary's fabric choice depicts that taste.[26] The round dress was fashionable, and skirts were worn very full. Fullness was achieved by wearing layers upon layers of petticoats. The layers began with a "knee-length petticoat of some stiff material called a 'crinoline' which was composed of horsehair warp and wool weft." This was covered with four to six plain petticoats often made of muslin for the summer months and flannel (for warmth) in the winter. These petticoats were never to be seen. However, a young lady who was dancing or walking may have lifted her skirt with discretion to show the outmost petticoat. Only it was decorative. Generally made of fine cambric, it was often "elaborately embroidered or trimmed with embroidery, crochet, or lace to a depth of six or eight inches above the hem."[27]

As many as seven widths of fabric (fifteen to thirty inches wide) would be used in a skirt with no flounces. A large amount of fabric was needed to supply a lady with the number of petticoats and the proper skirt circumference worn by fashionable women. This style of skirt was sometimes decorated with "rows of ornamental buttons, running down the whole length in the center of the dress.[28] The photo shows two rows of large, ornamental buttons on Mary's skirt. The large buttons in center front appear to be somewhat shaped like sunflowers. The companion buttons in a row to the right side of the skirt also appear floral in design. Most likely, a third row of the smaller floral buttons, not visible in the photograph, was on the skirt's left side. A more appealing visual effect would have been achieved by having more than two rows of buttons.

Her bodice was made with a wide neckline to visually balance the width at the hem of the skirt, and a traditional hook-and-eye back closure. Fashion designers wished to create an image that women had drooping shoulder lines. Sleeve designs perpetuated this image by pulling shoulders down and pulling a woman's arms against her torso. Sleeves remained very tight in the mid-1840s; they were cut on the bias and slightly gathered at the elbow thus preventing movement. Mary's sleeves followed the fashion by having a dropped shoulder line and by being fashionably tight fitted. They were finished with white ruffles at the wrists. Separate cuffs or ruffles could easily be removed and washed and would save wear on the edges of the fashion fabric of the dress. Silk, like this dress, would generally not be washed. The waist of the dress was low and pointed at the center front. Mary wore a ribbon cincture at the waist. An elbow-length, lace-trimmed, sheer bertha pulled close at the neckline with a brooch complimented Mary's ensemble.

The 1840 fashion magazines wrote that these new tight designs were convenient for wear. However, considering the number of underclothes, the tight corsets, the boned bodice with back-fastenings of hooks and eyes, the restricting sleeves, and the weight of petticoats, it seems strange that women's dress should be praised for its convenience."[29] A woman's attire was heavy, hot, and cumbersome. She was in constant peril of catching skirt hems on fire at fireplace hearths and cook stoves. Layers of petticoats often became tangled around a woman's legs and feet, and if a woman was not careful, improperly fitting undergarments could land at her feet at the most embarrassing moments.

During the next decade, women's fashion changed considerably. Gone were the pale shades of the 1840s. Due to the invention of chemical dyes, fabric could now be obtained in bright colors. Made from a by-product of burning coal, the first aniline dye was developed in 1856. It produced the color mauve. The colors alizarin and indigo were soon to follow. In 1860, aniline dyes were developed in the colors of magenta and solferino. In England, magenta was used for "dresses, petticoats, bonnets, and stocking, as well as ribbons; it was described as the queen of colors."[30]

The most fashionable women of the era dressed in printed fabrics that took advantage of the new dyes. Fabric patterns included a bold mix of floral sprays and colorful geometric stripes.[31] Turkey red was often used as a background color for prints featuring leaves, geometric shapes, and wavy lines. Wide stripes and plaid were extremely popular.

A lady's face could be seen in public for they were no longer half hidden by the projecting bonnet brim. By the middle of the decade, the bonnet brim was pushed back, and the front half of the wearer's head was exposed. Women could go bare-headed indoors, and an evening headdress could consist of a simple wreath of flowers.[32] Flowers worn at the back of the neck indicated a lady was single. Married women such as Mary Lincoln wore a floral diadem.

During this era, women were no longer completely hidden by their wardrobe. The drooping self-effacing attitude of the forties was gone. Bodices were still tight, but the tight, plain sleeve was gone. Pagoda sleeves came into vogue. These were wide and bell shaped, giving the wearer more freedom of movement. They were often trimmed with elaborate ribbons, ruching, or bows. Removable white undersleeves were worn with pagodas. In theory, undersleeves could be easily removed if they became soiled or were accidentally dipped into the gravy bowl during dinner. They served their purpose with pagoda sleeves but were rendered useless with other sleeve designs. By the end of the decade, some dresses were fashioned with a wide sleeve that was "slit open and hung down in such a way that it was difficult to take up a glass of wine without dipping the sleeve in one's plate."[33]

As ridiculous as this sleeve design was, nothing was as ridiculous as the ever-widening skirt. Actually by 1850, skirts were slightly less full than those of the 1840s. But fashion changes quickly. In 1853, the report came from Paris that "skirts become wider and wider."[34] The skirt width at the hem had become so large that instead of gathering the skirt at the waist, deep pleating was the most common manner of forming the waistline. Layers of petticoats were worn to achieve the desired width. For an even wider effect, three to five flounces adorned the skirt. Flounces were embroidered or had stripes woven into the material. Alternating rows of flounces made from contrasting colors were also used.[35] Both designs would have given an illusion of wider fabric.

To achieve the desired width of fan-shaped skirts, women donned layers of starched and flounced petticoats. One observer commented, "Many belles now wear fourteen [petticoats] in evening dress. They go to a ball standing up in their carriages and stand between the dances, for fear of crushing their dress and fourteen petticoats."[36]

To elevate the problem, by the middle of the decade, some women were wearing pneumatic tubes. The garment was described as being made of an "airtight material with a small nozzle for the insertion of a bellows for inflating it, and a larger aperture for the escape of air when the wearer wishes to sit down."[37] Whether a lady carried a bellows for inflating the tubes as the night progressed, or whether she chose to allow her gown to go flat is not known. The idea was cumbersome, and the noise generated by the whoosh of escaping air would have been most unladylike.

To enable a lady to widen her skirts without returning to multiple layers of petticoats, the crinoline was invented in 1856. This undergarment was "an open cage of metal hoops graduated in circumference and held at intervals by vertical tapes attached to a waistband, which allowed for skirts of even greater width at the hem, as well as increased comfort for the wearer."[38] It allowed women's limbs to be free of the confining petticoats and allowed air to circulate under her skirt. In wintertime, not so much air circulation was desired, and many women chose to wear a warm under petticoat or flannel drawers for insulation.

The crinoline was an improvement, but it also created new problems for a woman. If the wearer sat down incorrectly, the crinoline would tilt up. If she stood too close to a piece of furniture, it would tilt back. Tables laden with brick-a-brac were in danger of being knocked over by a wide hoop. Walkways became congested with the width of the crinoline. A hostess had to add more seating when entertaining, for sofas that had held two or three guests comfortably in the mid-1850s, now held only one lady and her crinoline. The dangers involved in wearing a crinoline included entanglement in carriage wheels and the fear of being blown off of one's feet during a strong wind with embarrassing consequences. Such was the case with the Duchess of Manchester, who caught her hoops when climbing over a stile and landed upside down, exhibiting a pair of scarlet knickers.[39]

However, the greatest threat to a woman's life was the danger of fire. Lightweight fabrics, especially tulle and muslin, worn in evening attire were most flammable. Homes were heated by open fires or iron stoves. Lighting was gaslight or candlelight—all of which could quickly ignite fabric that touched it. If a woman's clothing were to catch fire, she could not be rolled in a carpet to extinguish the flames because the crinoline still allowed air to flow. People throughout the world were shocked when they read of the catastrophe at the cathedral in Santiago, Chile, in early December 1863. Over two thousand women were burnt to death as the vast quantities of fabric fed the flames.[40]

Despite the dangers and possible embarrassments of wearing a crinoline, every lady of status was properly attired for social functions and whenever seen in public. Mary Lincoln was no exception. As a child in Springfield, Emily Huntington (later Mrs. John Todd Stuart Jr.) lived across the street from Mary's sister Elizabeth Edwards. In her 1918 memoirs, Emily wrote of watching Mrs. Lincoln walking home after visiting Elizabeth. "She had on [a] beautiful summer lavender dress with a long train and I distinctly remember to this day with what fascination I watched her train swish from side to side, leaving a long serpentine trail behind her."[41] Mary's skirt swished from side to side because she wore a crinoline.

Emily's memory of Mary's costume brings credence to the humorist of the nineteenth century who often poked fun at women's fashions. It was said that "trailing skirts gave rise to the story that the municipal authorities found it an unnecessary expense to employ street cleaners for doing what ladies so kindly performed gratis."[42] Despite jokes and ridicule of the style, women still wore the fashion of the day.

Little is written about Mary's fashions during her life in Springfield. Her sister Elizabeth Edwards commented that "it has always been a prominent trait in her character to accumulate a large amount of clothing."[43] When younger half sister Emilie came to visit, she remembered Mary making a lovely lavender brocade gown and a floral evening dress. Emilie offered no descriptions of Mary's gowns but was "struck with her exquisite taste in dress."[44] That Mary made the gowns indicates that in the mid-1850s, she was still manufacturing her own clothing. That may have changed by the end of the decade. In April of 1859, Mary mentioned "her seamstress" when writing to a friend. It is not know if the seamstress made Mary's dress, Abraham's suits, or both.[45]

In 1860, America elected Abraham Lincoln as president. Because the public wanted to know something about Mrs. Lincoln and the boys, Mary and her two youngest sons posed for a photograph at the studio of Preston Butler in Springfield. (See figure 3 in the essay by Harold Holzer also included in this volume.) Since this was the public's first image of Mary, it is most likely that she chose to wear her best dress, bonnet, and mantle (a loose, cape-like garment). It is possible the photo was slightly rushed in the activity after the election, for the trio does not appear to be posed at all. They simply stand in front of the camera with a simple painted backdrop and no props. Willie is looking in another direction. Mary holds Tad's hand as if he may bolt in another direction if she let go.

In this photograph, Mary wears a silk skirt with two deep flounces. Large flounces were not only popular; they indicated the wearer could afford the extra fabric required to make them. The geometric pattern consists of small and large diamond shapes as well as a horizontal strip. The fabric's design is printed "en disposition" and was manufactured specifically to be used as flounces. The color of Mary's dress is not known; however, it was fashionable for such fabrics to be printed with a Turkey-red background.[46] The bodice of the dress is not visible, but white undersleeves can be seen under the dark colored mantle, which is trimmed with elaborate ribbons. She wears a white lace-trimmed collar, which was probably fastened with a brooch. Her bonnet is trimmed with lace, flowers, and leaves. The bonnet ribbons are two-toned and coordinate with the ribbons on her mantle. Dark wrist length gloves complete the ensemble. It is not difficult to imagine that after the photograph was taken, Mary gathered her sons to leave the studio and return to the sidewalk, clearing a wide path with her hooped skirt.

The Lincolns arrived in Washington surrounded by friends and family. There had been threats of assassination against Lincoln's life. The air was filled with fear and anticipation while the streets were filled with spectators and soldiers. Seven states had declared secession, and the Confederate States of America was already in place with Jefferson Davis as its chosen president. Lincoln believed it would be best for "our women to remain indoors . . . as the bullets may be flying."[47] Mary would not hear of hiding on such an important day as her husband's inauguration. The family would present a united front. Mary, her sons, Mrs. Grimsley (Mary's cousin), Elizabeth Edwards, and other Todd family relatives occupied the diplomatic gallery during the inaugural ceremony.

That evening, the public gleaned their first impressions of Mary as she attended the Inaugural Ball. Newspapers had reported only her presence at the inauguration ceremony—not her attire. Reporters were quick to comment on her costume for the ball. She was "superbly dressed in a low-necked, blue water silk trimmed with Alençon lace and a blue ostrich feather in her hair which was exceedingly becoming."[48] Her costume was described as being of good taste. Mary was described as being "evidently a lady of refinement, of tact, and taste."[49] Critics had thought because the Lincolns were from the West, that Mary would be uncouth and unfit to host Washington society entertainments. Mary desired to prove them incorrect. And at least for tonight, Mary was once again the belle of the ball.

Fashion had changed considerably for women during the previous five years. Some observers thought most of the changes were improvements that helped shape a woman's figure. With the invention of the crinoline and other garments, fashion was supposed to be easier to wear. All observers did not agree. Oscar Wilde commented, "Fashion is a form of ugliness so intolerable that we have to alter it every six months."[50] At the onset of the Civil War, skirts had reached their maximum hemline circumference of five and a half to six yards. The front was flattened, thus moving more of the skirt towards the rear, sometimes in a train for fancy dress. One Parisian fashion journalist wrote: "All robes continue to be spread out like fans. Observe I say fans, *not* bells; the bell-shaped is now absurd."[51] To emphasize the width of the hem even more, flounces or horizontal ribbons trimmed the lower portion of the skirt. A modern fashion designer commented: "In difficult times, fashion is always outrageous."[52] She was referring to the fashions in the first half of the twentieth century, but she could have easily have meant the mid-nineteenth century. These were difficult times, and the ridiculous fashion prevailed. For skirts, the wider the better seemed to be the normal, not the absurd in the latest fashions.

It is certain that as skirts widened and dress trims became more elaborate, the cost of a fashionable lady's wardrobe increased. The wider the skirt, the more fabric was used. The more fabric used, the wealthier the lady. Mary exhibited this philosophy when wearing double layered skirts for day wear and long trains for evening attire. "One observer commented, "If ladies' dresses continue to increase in breadth, it will be absolutely necessary to widen all the public thoroughfares. Perhaps it is the spirit of exclusiveness which has induced the leaders of fashion to surround themselves with barriers of barége and similar outworks to keep the common herd at arm's length—or rather at petticoats' breadth."[53] To keep the general public at petticoats' breadth was one of the reasons for the fashion.

During the onset of the Civil War, the population of Washington swelled as thousands of people needed to support military operations and the war effort arrived in the city, and they often looked for some form of free entertainment. The White House was expected to maintain the tradition of holding free public receptions almost every week during the winter months. There was no crowd control, and often public gatherings attracted as many as three thousand or more people. Some newspapers were quick to criticize Mary for holding the receptions during the war. The money could surely be spent in a better manner—such as feeding soldiers instead of politicians. Others criticized her if she did not hold free receptions for the public because they helped boost the morale of military personnel. Besides, these receptions were traditional—some dating back to the administration of George Washington. Mary found that traditions in any social sphere are difficult to break. Those who came expected to shake hands with the president, and Lincoln often complained his hands were swollen after shaking the hands of so many guests. Mary stood slightly to Lincoln's right—often on the other side of Benjamin French. She was not required to shake everyone's hand, for this was an era when cleanliness was not a requirement for attending public events. Mary may not have been aware of germs carried by people, but she and other ladies were aware of the dirt. Those who had traveled the dirt roads by horseback (or even via carriage) were often dusty, and they smelled worse. Due to the lack of available sanitation, the general public was filthy. Mary's petticoat circumference, and the train trailing behind her, allowed guests to come close, but not too close.

Another fashion accessory that helped keep the unwashed at bay was a pair of gloves. Since ladies were required to wear gloves for all social activities except eating, they were a necessary accessory to a lady's wardrobe, and ladies often owned several pairs. How many gloves were needed? Apparently Mary Lincoln believed a lady could never have too many pairs of gloves. According to Judge David Davis, after the president's death, he was presented with a bill from Mr. Perry, a merchant of Washington, for three hundred pairs of kid gloves. These were purchased by Mary during the first four months of 1865. Judge Davis told Mr. Orville Browning about this bill and others that he refused to pay.[54] He offered no explanation for refusing payment. Did he think it was fraudulent? Had Mary already paid the bill? Was there a mistake in the number of gloves purchased? Were the gloves returned? Whatever the reason, we only know that Mary purchased several pairs of gloves in the beginning of 1865. To the modern shopper, the thought of three hundred pairs of gloves is outrageous. To the Victorian lady, it was a large amount, but not necessarily completely outlandish. French kid gloves were made to fit the hand tightly, like a second skin so that the fingernails showed through. These gloves were packaged and sold by the dozen.[55] If Mary truly did buy three hundred pairs of gloves, she purchased twenty-five dozen—still more gloves than most women would purchase. Assuming these were ladies' gloves and not a combination of men's and ladies' gloves, the question is why would she purchase so many pairs?

Traditionally, the president and his wife, or other female relative, would hold large public receptions every week during the winter months. Another public reception was held on New Year's Day. These were described as "throwing open the Presidential mansion to every one high or low, gentle or ungentle, washed or unwashed who chooses to go, and the net result is always a promiscuous, horrible jam, a species of social mass meeting."[56] Crowds of three thousand or more people attended. One crowd was so large that windows were used as exits. They came to see the president, to meet his wife, and to shake their hands. Lincoln was known to wear several pairs of gloves at each reception, putting on a clean, fresh pair as one pair became too soiled to offer to a lady's hand.[57] In addition to receptions, the Lincoln's greeted guests at smaller levees, state dinners, and private entertainments.

Kid gloves were not laundered; a soiled pair was discarded. If Mary used ten pairs of gloves per week (which is not an outrageous number considering her social calendar) by purchasing three hundred pairs of gloves over four months, she had truly only purchased a seven month supply. If Lincoln had not have been assassinated, many more public receptions would have been held in Washington to celebrate the end of the Civil War. Mary would have used many more pairs of gloves when shaking the hands of her "soldier boys" as they returned home dusty and dirty from battle. Maybe the purchase of three hundred pairs of gloves was outrageous and evidence of mania. Or, perhaps she did have actual use for them. The modern historian will never know. It is known that Mary followed society's rules for dress—including the use of proper accessories.

Honoré de Balzac, the nineteenth-century writer, believed a woman's attire was "a permanent revelation of her most secret thoughts. . . . Dress is a sort of symbolical language, the study of which it would be madness to neglect. To a proficient in the science, every woman walks about with a placard on which her leading qualities are advertised . . . . Upon the whole a prudent and sensible man may safely predicate of the inner lining from the outer garment, and be thankful that he has this, at least, to go by."[58] Every lady of status was properly attired for social functions; Mary was no exception. She agreed with Balzac's comment that a lady's costume was her placard. She understood a lady's costume was scrutinized by members of her community and was an indication of her ability to possess social graces.

As the wife of a president, Mary expected to dress like Republican royalty. Her position caused newspaper reporters to record details of her attire, her jewelry, and her manner. Other presidential wives had led the fashion scene for Washington society, and Mary had every reason to believe she would do the same. When first arriving in Washington, Mary "would have joined a society pledged to use no foreign dress goods, laces, or ornaments during the War, if Mr. Lincoln and his Secretary of the Treasury had not condemned the project, declaring that the Government needed the revenue coming from the importation of these luxuries. They thus made the wearing of rich clothing a patriotic duty."[59] Mary needed no encouragement to fulfill her patriotic duty. If wearing costly goods and fashions would help the Union, she was proud and willing to do her part. She commented to her dressmaker, Elizabeth Keckley, "I must dress in costly materials. The people scrutinize every article I wear with critical curiosity."[60] Mary had a statement to make, and she allowed her wardrobe to convey the message that she was educated, well mannered, politically informed, and patriotic.

Mary's wardrobe and accessories received both praise and criticism. Some comments, while at first appearing to be complimentary, had a negative twist to them as well. Such is the case as one observer quoted in a Lexington, Kentucky, newspaper. Mrs. C. thought that Mrs. Lincoln was "very gorgeous, she stuns me with her low-necked dresses and the flower beds which she carries on her head."[61] Another observer, Oregon's Senator Nesmith commented, "The weak minded Mrs. Lincoln had her bosom on exhibition and a flower pot on her head, while there was a train of silk or satin, dragging on the floor behind her of several yards in length, as I looked at her I could not help regretting that she had degenerated from the industrious and unpretending woman that she *was* in the days when she used to cook old Abe's dinner, and milk the cows with her own hands."[62] Senator Nesmith apparently was not a connoisseur of ladies' fashions. Perhaps Oregon's distance from the fashion center on the East Coast prompted his fondness for a farm-wife's wardrobe. One can only imagine how this comment was received by Mrs. Nesmith, especially if she was a subscriber to *Godey's Lady's Book*!

Mr. Lincoln frequently praised Mary for her wardrobe. While in Springfield, Mary once reminded Lincoln to dress for a party, and he replied, "Fine feathers enough on you to make fine birds of both us. Those posies on your dress are the color of your eyes." Mary was pleased he had noticed.[63] For a White House reception, Mary chose a rose-colored, moiré gown. Mrs. Keckley fashioned the dress in her shop, but Mary made several suggestions for alterations. When the president entered the room, he told his wife, "I declare, you look charming in that dress. Mrs. Keckley has met with great success."[64] While Lincoln was pleased with most of the gowns fashioned by Mrs. Keckley, at least once, he slightly disapproved. As the fashion called for a lower décolletage, Mary's dresses followed the fashion. Mrs. Keckley commented that Mary "had a beautiful neck and arm, and low dresses were becoming to her." Lincoln somewhat disagreed when he saw Mary wearing a white satin gown trimmed in black lace. He exclaimed, "Whew! Our cat has a long tail tonight. Mother, it is my opinion, if some of that tail was nearer the head, it would be in better style."[65]

It seems that almost everyone, friend and foe, enjoyed discussing Mary's wardrobe. Julia Taft, the older sister of Tad and Willie's playmates, recalled how Mary was very particular about her wardrobe. Julia's mother, Mary Taft, had purchased a new bonnet from a local milliner. It was "lavishly trimmed with purple ribbon embroidered with small black figures. When Mrs. Taft wore the bonnet to a concert at the White House, Mary took Mrs. Taft aside to speak with her privately. As she explained, the milliner had made her a bonnet with the same ribbon but did not have enough for the strings. Mary wanted her strings to match. An agreement was made between the two women and the milliner. Mrs. Taft gave up her strings, and her bonnet was retrimmed. Both women seemed very pleased with the exchange. Mary received the bonnet ribbons she wanted, and Mrs. Taft had a more beautiful bonnet than at first. Not long after the incident, Julia reported to her mother that Mrs. Lincoln had worn "those strings which were on your bonnet at first." Mrs. Taft quickly and sharply reproved her daughter. "Never let me hear you make any remark about Mrs. Lincoln's clothes, Julia. The wife of the President should be above petty gossip." Sadly, neither the rest of Washington society nor the press agreed with Mrs. Taft.[66]

By the early 1860s, the busy, large-scale prints and complex striped backgrounds were no longer the fashion. They were replaced with heavier dress fabrics, which, if solid in color, where elaborately trimmed. Mary's wardrobe consisted of gowns made of exquisite fabrics. Embroidered fabrics, silk brocades, deep-piled velvets, and cashmere were some of her favorites. These were trimmed with imported fine laces and floral displays. Mrs. Swisshelm noticed Mary's attire and her "full share of the general love of personal adornment."[67] Mary's photographs give evidence of her love for personal adornment and her commitment to patriotic duty through her wardrobe.

For critics who thought that Mrs. Lincoln had previously looked as if she had a flowerpot on her head, in one photo she gave them reason to think she had attached a rosebush to her bosom. Fashion advisors in that year suggested for evening attire, a young woman should wear a wreath with a cache-peigne of flowers behind. It was suggested a matron wear a diadem of flowers, feathers, or gauze and gold cable cord twisted together in her hair.[68] Mary's most popular choice was the matronly crown of roses or other flowers.

*White Silk with Ruffles—First Half of 1861.* Photograph by Mathew Brady. Washington, DC, 1861. (Library of Congress)

In the photograph, Mary wears a diadem of flowers consisting of a large cabbage rose in the center and smaller roses on the side. A smaller flower, which could be hydrangeas or sweet william, is used to fill in areas of the headpiece. Instead of a small bouquet at the center front bodice, Mary wears a garland of flowers that begins at the center front of the bodice, extends diagonally to the left, and continues onto the skirt to slightly below her left knee. The garland is made primarily of rosebuds and also includes flowers at each end that appear to be the size and shape of a dogwood blossom. The dark green leaves appear to be something such as Italian ruscus. These offer a contrast for the colorful flowers against the white fabric of the gown.

Mary's gown is a two-piece evening dress made of white silk. Keeping with the style of the era, her evening bodice has a low décolletage. It also features an elongated center point at the bodice waist. There is a hook-and-eye back closure. Two ruffles made from silk fabric with small bouquets of printed flowers enhance the bodice neckline and cover the short sleeves. Each sleeve also has two ruffles made from the same floral material.

The gored skirt is made with a small train that would have swayed gently as a lady walked and dusted her floors behind her. Mary's choice of a white dress indicates this dress was worn primarily for a receiving line and perhaps a grand march in the carpeted East Room of the White House. The bottom of the skirt is decorated with five rows of three-inch ruffles made from the same floral print fabric as the bodice ruffles. Each ruffle was sewn on to a cord in a casing, gathered, and then sewn to the skirt. The bottom ruffle would have been placed on the skirt first, and following ruffles would be placed farther up the skirt until complete. The top edge of the top ruffle was covered with a white silk ribbon, or ruching, for a finished look.

Mary was attired in a fashion such as this one when Elizabeth Keckley described her by saying, "No queen, accustomed to the usages of royalty all her life, could have comported herself with more calmness and dignity than did the wife of the President. She was confident and self-possessed, and confidence always gives grace."[69]

Willie Lincoln died at 5 P.M. on February 20, 1862, from bilious fever, which was probably either typhoid or acute malarial infection. While both parents were thrown into a deep depression and grief over the loss of the boy, it was Mary's wailing for Willie that could be heard throughout the White House. Willie's body lay in state in the Green Room. His funeral, the first White House funeral for a child, was held in the East Room—the same room where, just days before, Mary and others had danced. Mary remained in seclusion for days, unable even to gather the strength to attend her son's funeral.[70]

Robert sent word to his Aunt Elizabeth Edwards to come to help care for Mary. The day of Willie's funeral, Elizabeth boarded a train in Springfield and headed east for Washington. The eldest of the family, Elizabeth had been like a mother to Mary after the death of their own mother. Robert believed if anyone could help Mary through this difficult period of grief, it was Elizabeth Edwards.

By February 28, Elizabeth had arrived in Washington, where she found Mary "utterly unable to control her feelings."[71] Mary had confined herself to her room and her bed. She was so distraught that she was unable to take care of Tad, who was suffering from the same illness that had taken Willie. By March 2, Tad was feeling better but was still ill. Elizabeth knew that her presence was soothing to Mary. In a letter to her daughter, Elizabeth explained how a little more than a week after Willie's death, she had compassionately "persuaded" Mary "to put on the *black dress*, that so freshly and painfully reminded of the loss, that will long shadow her *pleasures*. Such is her nature, that I can not realize that she will forgo *them* all, or even long, under existing circumstances."[72]

Elizabeth was wrong, for Mary would remain in mourning beyond the expectations of society. All receptions were cancelled for the remaining year, as were the band concerts held on the White House lawn. The public could not be pleased. People had earlier criticized Mary for holding public receptions during wartime, and now they complained about the lack of entertainment. A compromise was reached, and the Marine Band performed in Lafayette Square, across from the White House.[73]

With her sister by her side, Mary slowly regained her composure. By March 20, newspapers reported that Mrs. Lincoln had been confined to her room since her son's death but now was "almost back to normal health," and by March 21, she was receiving visitors other than her family members.[74] Having relatives cheered Mary and helped her regain health and strength, and after Willie's death, she was blessed with having an abundance of family surround her. One observer noted the White House had guests and that Mrs. Lincoln was surrounded by "a dozen Todds of the Edwards breed."[75] By the end of Elizabeth's visit, Mary was once again sending floral bouquets to friends, and accompanying the president on carriage rides to the Navy Yard. Elizabeth and her entourage of Edwardses had accomplished their mission and left Mary, still a grieving mother, but better able to handle her situation.

During the summer months, the Lincoln family moved into the Anderson Cottage at the Soldiers' Home. There they were just a short carriage ride away from the dirt, disease, and din of the city, but still far enough away to leave some of their problems in Washington. When Laura Redden visited, Mary was wearing "deep black." Mary was still in her first stage of mourning.[76]

Exactly how long did Mary continue to wear mourning attire for Willie? Some historians believe that she emerged from her mourning around 1864, or even as late as 1865. Others believe that she remained in mourning and only put aside her mourning attire for special occasions such as the wedding reception for General Tom Thumb and Lavinia Warren. In 1864, Walt Whitman often saw the Lincolns as they rode from the Soldiers' Home to the city. He commented that Mary was "in complete black with a long crape veil" typical of mourning attire.[77] Mary did exceed the one year socially required mourning period a mother observed for her child, but it is unclear for how long. There were other deaths for Mary to mourn.

Two of her half brothers and a brother-in-law were killed in battle during the course of the war. Samuel died in April 1862, just under two months after Willie's death. By the end of the summer, Mary's youngest half brother, Alexander, had also died. It is doubtful Mary would have donned mourning attire for any of these relatives as they were both Confederate soldiers. Even if she mourned for them in her heart, the public would have been endlessly critical if she had mourned them publicly. However, she did have other relatives, those who supported the Union, who died during this time. Her brother Levi died in the latter part of October 1864, and it is probable Mary donned mourning attire in memory of him. Victorian mourning customs required Mary to observe three months in deep mourning, two months in full mourning, and one month in half mourning for a sibling. It is likely Mary was mourning her brother when Walt Whitman wrote of her attire.

Just as Mary would have been making the transition from deep mourning to full mourning attire, two more family members passed away. On January 5, 1865, Harrison Grimsley, the husband of Mary's cousin Elizabeth, died. Elizabeth and Mary were cousins, friends, and confidents. Elizabeth had traveled to Washington with the Lincoln family and had stayed for six months. Even though the Grimsleys lived in Springfield, it is likely that Mary wore some form of mourning for her cousin-in-law. Her mourning for Harrison was quickly overshadowed when Elizabeth's father passed away just four days after her husband. Dr. John Todd was Mary's closest blood relative in Springfield; he had been a surrogate father to her in many ways. She quickly donned crape and was once again in deep mourning. Some historians have referenced Mary's purchase of mourning attire during this period as an omen for event yet to unfold. However, this was not why Mary purchased the clothing. Rather, with the death of three close male relatives within three months, by early 1865, Mary was thrown into a perpetual state of morning. And the worst was yet to come.

Different mourning rituals were expected to be followed for each family member. For the Victorian woman, mourning was more than a ritual, it was often a way of live. When a woman became a widow, she was expected to cancel all social engagements within twenty-four hours. She dressed in black from her head to her toe with the most suitable color being "dead black." Undergarments were white, but some women trimmed them with black ribbon or embroidery to show that her grief had penetrated to the innermost sanctuaries. Widows were expected to wear deepest mourning for at least a year. Most etiquette books advised women observe this stage of mourning longer. This period of mourning was followed by at least another full year of full mourning and six months of half mourning. A woman was expected to wear black for a minimum of two and a half years. Some women chose to continue wearing mourning for the rest of their own lives. Mary was one of those women.

Lincoln's assassination plunged Mary into her deepest affliction. Consumed with grief, she was unable to find the composure to attend her husband's funeral. She remained in her upstairs bedroom allowing few people to enter. Those who did enter mostly heard "the wails of a broken heart, the unearthly shrieks, the terrible convulsions, the wild, tempestuous outbursts of grief from the soul."[78] For the next five weeks, Mary remained in the White House, grieving the loss of her husband, being comforted by her sons, and packing boxes and trunks to leave the White House.

Mary did not feel she could ever return to Springfield, so she decided to reside in rented rooms in Chicago. There, Mary observed the rules of mourning and stayed as far removed from society as possible. She rarely ventured into the city streets, received few callers, and called on no one. At this time in her life, Mary undoubtedly cared nothing about fashion.

Slowly, Mary did begin to receive visitors and venture out into the Chicago stores. She felt that people were looking at her clothing and making comments. And, they probably were, for to the Victorians, appearance meant so very much. And widows of high social status were expected to maintain the latest fashions. Those fashions were just expected to be made of proper fabrics and shades of black. In Mary's case, her appearance as a properly dressed widow helped bolster Lincoln's memory. If "the clothes make the man," in this case, the widow's clothes make the memory.[79] Mary felt that had she been dressed inappropriately while walking in the social districts or stores of places like Chicago and New York, people would stare and speak in hushed tones. It was with this in mind that Mary wrote to Elizabeth Keckley in December 1867, "I am positively suffering for a decent dress. I see Mr. A. [unidentified] and *some* recent visitors eyeing my clothing askance. . . . Do send my black merion dress to me very soon; I must dress better in the future."[80]

For most of her remaining years, Mary wandered. She traveled to various parts of the United States including Florida, New York, Wisconsin, and Kentucky. At least once, she visited Canada. Years earlier, Mary had written to her sister Emilie that she longed to go to Europe. As a widow, she traveled and resided there. But no matter where Mary she went, she could escape neither the memories of happy times nor the pain of her present. She needed something in life that gave her joy, and she found it through shopping.

Mary purchased items for herself, a home she did not live in, and gifts for friends and family. By doing so, she also kept abreast of the latest fashions. In 1869, while traveling in Europe, Mary wrote to her daughter-in-law Mary Eunice Harlan directing her to take some of the best dresses that were stored away in her trunks in her Chicago home, and use them. She wrote of a white crape shawl and a muslin dress with narrow flounces and encouraged Mary Harlan Lincoln to "have this made over for yourself—in Europe—those dresses are so much worn." Mary also asked her daughter-in-law to use the white paisley shawl, an ermine cape, velvet cloaks, camel hair dress shawls, and countless laces.[81]

Never having had a daughter of her own, and now having a daughter-in-law and a granddaughter, Mary showered them with gifts while she was abroad. In France, Mary purchased a white hat; from Italy came a set of malachite jewelry. Other gifts included a lovely apple-green-and-white silk dress, a green silk walking suit, striped blue-and-white foulard costume, evening dresses, a brown shawl, a white Shetland shawl, jewelry, and many other fashionable gifts. Mary also sent gifts for her daughter-in-law's mother, and two parasols were sent to the baby's nurse—to be use when walking little Miss Lincoln. Precious and expensive gifts for little Mary "Mamie" Lincoln included dresses, caps, baby shawls, baby bonnets, embroidered cloak, shoes, and exquisite pieces of jewelry. Mary's letters are filled with descriptions of items purchased for her granddaughter, her daughter-in-law, and other family members.

Mary was keeping abreast of the latest fashions and observing what European women were wearing. In addition to sending expensive gifts to her daughter-in-law, Mary sent fashion advice. She explained what colors were popular, what styles of dresses were fashionable, and what type of jewelry should be worn. Robert was concerned about the cost of everything his mother was purchasing. From the tone of one of Mary's letters, his wife must have also expressed her concerns. "Robert writes that you were quite frightened, about the baby clothes—Certainly they were made of the simplest materials & if they were a little trimmed there was certainly nothing out of the way—the *baby* is *not* supposed to be able to walk out in the street this winter & being carried in a nurse's arms, certainly a simple embroidered cloak—is not too much, for people in *our station* of life—The very *middle classes* in Europe, dress their children quite as much & as I do not consider ourselves in that category, I would not care what the MEAN & ENVIOUS, would say."[82]

Mary Lincoln enjoyed shopping—and much has been written about that—for her it was almost an art form. She sought the best items, bargained for the best prices, and demanded the best customer service. A few of Mary's costumes have become famous because she wore them for a photo sitting, and some are known because they have been displayed in museums. While a few historians have commented about Mary's love of floral headdresses or her love of beautiful clothing, most historians do not examine how Mary's dress related to the fashion of the era. Were her dresses outstanding because they were different and more elaborate than everyone else's?

Mary did dress in the latest fashions of her day. Her costumes could be found on the pages of *Godey's Lady's Book* and other fashion publications.

Mary did not create new standards of fashions but rather was the perfect model for what was fashionable. As a member of the aristocratic Todd family, and then the wife of the president of the United States, Mary had a social station to maintain, which included an obligation to dress impeccably.

## Notes

1. Nineteenth-century grammar did not intertwine the words *fashion* and *style*. According to an 1860 edition of Noah Webster's *Dictionary, fashion* was either "the form of a garment; the cut or shape of clothes" or "the prevailing mode of dress of ornament." *Style* did not refer to clothing or attire. Its definition included "a manner or form" regarding writing, speaking, entertaining, music, and other fine arts. However, in letters to her milliner, Mary Lincoln did use the word *style* when referring to how something was made. The author has used Victorian definitions for fashion and style in this chapter.

2. C. Willett Cunnington and Phyllis Cunnington, *The History of Underclothes* (New York: Dover, 1992), 148.

3. Robert Whitworth, "Fashion Capital of the New Republic," *Early American Life* 36, no. 1 (2005): 25.

4. Ibid., 32.

5. Gernsheim, Alison, *Victorian and Edwardian Fashion: A Photographic Survey* (New York: Dover, 1981), 27.

6. Ibid., 30.

7. Katherine Helm, *The True Story of Mary, Wife of Lincoln.* (New York: Harper and Brothers, 1928), 21.

8. Justin G. Turner and Linda Levitt Turner, *Mary Todd Lincoln: Her Life and Letters* (New York: Alfred A. Knopf, 1972), 20.

9. Donna McCreary, *Fashionable First Lady: The Victorian Wardrobe of Mary Lincoln* (Charlestown: Lincoln Presentations, 2007), 3.

10. Helm. *True Story of Mary,* 28.

11. Helm. *True Story of Mary,* 29–30.

12. *Lincoln's Marriage, Newspaper Interview with Mrs. Frances Wallace, Springfield, IL September 2, 1895,* Lincoln Collection, Abraham Lincoln Presidential Library.

13. "A Present to Mrs. Lincoln," *Chicago Tribune,* January 24, 1861.

14. Henry Pratt, "The Lincolns Go Shopping," *Journal of the Illinois State Historical Society,* 1955, 66–81; *John Irwin and Co. Ledgers* 1 (July 3, 1844): 10.

15. Thomas J. Dyba and George L. Painter, *Seventeen Years at Eight and Jackson: The Lincoln Family in Their Springfield Home* (Lisle: TLC, 1982), 11.

16. Stuart Stark, <www.oldhouseliving.com>.

17. Barbara Brackman, *America's Printed Fabrics, 1770–1890* (Lafayette: C and T, 2004), 51; and Pratt, "Lincolns Go Shopping," 67.

18. Turner and Turner, *Mary Todd Lincoln*, 37.

19. McCreary, *Fashionable First Lady*, 33.

20. Pratt, "Lincolns Go Shopping," 66–67.

21. Dyba and Painter, *Seventeen Years at Eight and Jackson*, 10–11.

22. Alison Gernsheim, *Victorian and Edwardian Fashion: A Photographic Survey* (New York: Dover, 1972), 26.

23. Lloyd Ostendorf, "The Photographs of Mary Todd Lincoln." *Journal of the Illinois State Historical Society* 63, no. 3 (1968): 274.

24. Gernsheim, *Victorian and Edwardian Fashion*, 25.

25. Ibid., 29.

26. C. Willet Cunnington, *English Women's Clothing in the Nineteenth Century* (New York: Dover, 1990), 146.

27. Cunnington and Cunnington, *History of Underclothes*, 145.

28. Cunnington, *English Women's Clothing*, 143.

29. Gernsheim, *Victorian and Edwardian Fashion*, 31.

30. Cunnington, *English Women's Clothing*, 208.

31. Brackman, *America's Printed Fabrics*, 31

32. Gernsheim, *Victorian and Edwardian Fashion*, 40–41.

33. Ibid., 43.

34. Cunnington, *English Women's Clothing*, 177.

35. Gernsheim, *Victorian and Edwardian Fashion*, 42.

36. Ibid., 44.

37. Ibid., 44.

38. Jo Anne Olian, *Eighty Godey's Full-Color Fashion Plates 1838–1880* (New York: Dover., 1998), 5.

39. Gernsheim, *Victorian and Edwardian Fashion*, 47.

40. Ibid.

41. Emily Huntington Stuart, *Some Recollections of the Early Days in Springfield and Reminiscences of Abraham Lincoln and Other Celebrities Who Lived in That Little Town in My Youth* (IL: DAR Genealogy Records, 1940–1941), 1086.

42. Gernsheim, *Victorian and Edwardian Fashion*, 27.

43. Jason Emerson, *The Madness of Mary Lincoln* (Carbondale: Southern Illinois University Press, 2007), 24.

44. Helm, *True Story of Mary*, 106.

45. Turner and Turner, *Life and Letters*, 55.

46. Brackman, *America's Printed Fabrics*, 67.

47. McCreary, *Fashionable First Lady*, 28.

48. Ibid., 30.

49. *The New York Times*, March 5, 1861, Abraham Lincoln Presidential Library.

50. Fashion Institute of Design and Merchandising. <www.educators.fidm._just-foreducation>.

51. Gernsheim, *Victorian and Edwardian Fashion*, 45.

52. Fashion Institute of Design and Merchandising. <www.educators.fidm._just-foreducation>.

53. Cunnington, *English Women's Clothing*, 185.

54. Michael Burlingame, *At Lincoln's Side: John Hay's Civil War Correspondence and Selected Writings* (Carbondale: Southern Illinois University Press, 2000), 187.

55. Gernsheim, *Victorian and Edwardian Fashion*, 42.

56. McCreary, *Fashionable First Lady*, 62.

57. Ibid., 111.

58. Gernsheim, *Victorian and Edwardian Fashion*, 31–32.

59. Jane Grey Swisshelm, "Tribute to the Dead," *Chicago Daily Tribune*, July 20, 1882, 7.

60. Elizabeth Keckley, *Behind the Scenes* (Salem: Ayer, 1868), 149.

61. *(Lexington) Kentucky Observer and Reporter*, February 15, 1862.

62. Ruth Painter Randall, *Mary Lincoln, Biography of a Marriage* (Boston: Little Brown, 1953), 221.

63. Helm, *True Story of Mary*, 109.

64. Keckley, *Behind the Scenes*, 88.

65. Ibid., 101.

66. McCreary, *Fashionable First Lady*, 36.

67. Swisshelm, "Tribute to the Dead," 7.

68. Cunnington, *English Women's Clothing*, 244.

69. Keckley, *Behind the Scenes*, 89.

70. Philip B. Kunhardt Jr., Philip B. Kunhardt III, and Peter W. Kunhardt, *Lincoln: An Illustrated Biography* (New York: Random House, 1992), 174.

71. Letter, Elizabeth Edwards to Julia Edwards Baker, March 2, 1862, Manuscript Department, SC 445, Abraham Lincoln Presidential Library and Museum, Springfield, IL.

72. Ibid.

73. Randall, *Mary Lincoln*, 297.

74. Earl Schenck Miers, ed., *Lincoln Day by Day: A Chronology 1809–1865* (Dayton: Morningside House, 1991), 102.

75. Ibid., 104.

76. Randall, *Mary Lincoln*, 296.

77. Ibid., 342.

78. Keckley, *Behind the Scenes*, 191.

79. McCreary, *Fashionable First Lady*, 125.

80. Keckley, *Behind the Scenes*, 466.

81. Mark E. Neely and Gerald R. McMurty. *The Insanity File: The Case of Mary Todd Lincoln* (Carbondale: Southern Illinois University Press, 1986), 154.

82. Ibid., 174.

## THE REPORTS OF THE LINCOLNS' POLITICAL PARTNERSHIP HAVE BEEN GREATLY EXAGGERATED

*Michael Burkhimer*

During the early months of 2001, an ugly rumor spread across the Internet. The source of the rumor was of all places the *Sunday Times* of London. The article, entitled "Spielberg Shows Darker Side of Saintly Lincoln," claimed the famed director would soon make a film that would show Lincoln as "a manic depressive racist who nearly lost the American Civil War."[1] The movie supposedly would be based on a yet unpublished biography of Lincoln by Doris Kearns Goodwin. Soon posts on Civil War sites across the Internet were abuzz with condemnation of both Spielberg and Goodwin. Not surprisingly, Goodwin heatedly denied that there was any truth in the story.[2] The controversy quickly died down.

Almost unnoticed in all the back-and-forth was the second part of the original story. Along with Lincoln's supposed racism, the movie would focus on the Lincoln marriage. The story falsely claimed that Goodwin called it a "political alliance" and stated, "I doubt whether Lincoln would have made it to the White House if she had not used her connections and acumen to spur his ambition and ease the way."[3] The most likely reason this part of the rumor was ignored was because it has increasingly come to be the orthodox view of the Lincoln marriage. Since the 1990s, a steady drumbeat of biographers and apologists for Mary Lincoln have called attention to her political skills and emphasized the notion of a political partnership as a strong facet of the Lincoln marriage. That this idea, which gives an increased role for Mary in the rise of Lincoln to the presidency, is a standard part of her biography is not surprising because as one Lincoln scholar has said, "Even more than is normally the case, Mary's biographers have been her champions."[4] But as will be seen, the idea of a true political partnership is not one that can ultimately stand on the evidence.

The view of Mary's importance in Lincoln's political career was first widely aired by Mary Lincoln historian Jean Baker in a lecture at Gettysburg in 1999. The lecture was published in essay form as "Mary and Abraham: A Marriage" in Gabor Boritt's 2001 volume of essays, *The Lincoln Enigma: The Changing Faces of an American Icon*. In the essay, Baker elaborates on three areas of "congeniality" in the Lincoln marriage: sex, children, and politics. In the area of politics, Baker writes, "This was a couple that transformed a mutual interest in public events into a love affair." She also relates, "At home Lincoln received not only the applause that a typical wife might bestow; he received heartening reinforcement as well as intelligent discussion of ambitions that were mutual."[5]

It was a film documentary that gave this idea the widest audience. David Grubin's 2001 documentary *Abraham and Mary: A House Divided* had a number of Lincoln authorities making the case for Mary's political acumen. Linda Levitt Turner, editor of a collection of Mary's letters, made that point, and the late famed Lincoln author David Herbert Donald stated flatly, "They worked as a team politically."[6] In an interview, the director of the film said of Mary, "She was an aristocrat, a southerner who grew up with slaves. He was a backwoods guy who was, who really had no polish, who had to learn how to move in society as it were. When he met her, she was the one who was connected, who knew important political figures, and she kind of put a polish on him."[7]

The apotheosis of Mary as a political partner thesis was reached in 2008 with the publication of Daniel Mark Epstein's *The Lincolns: Portrait of a Marriage*. This book-length study of the Lincoln marriage highlights two themes. According to Epstein, "After my research, I reached two conclusions that shaped my portrait of the marriage. First, these two people loved each other deeply, from the time they met in Springfield in 1839, until his assassination in 1865. The second is that Mary was extremely interested in Abraham's career and speeches; whenever they could, the two of them talked about these things. She was a strong political partner for him."[8]

Throughout the book, Epstein time and time again emphasizes this partnership. Yet the evidence does not bear the weight of this interpretation. For instance, he claims that Lincoln would not have given his famous Cooper Union speech without checking it with Mary for, "Lincoln would not have left Springfield before hearing his wife's opinion of so important a speech any more than he would have left without the approval of his wardrobe and grooming."[9] One looks in vain in the historical record for any evidence for this and the other times Lincoln supposedly went over his speeches with Mary. It says something for the strength of the political partnership thesis that it can be asserted and accepted as a given without the hard facts to back it up.

As the Lincoln bicentennial approached, more attention naturally turned to Mary Lincoln. In the popular media, she was Lincoln's political partner, and there was nary a word of dissent. A *Newsweek* article about an exhibit on Mary at the Lincoln Library at Springfield states, "Mary Todd Lincoln gentrified her husband—and told him he would be president. He read all his speeches to her."[10] The article then quotes Mary's most prominent biographer as saying, "This was a political marriage. It's sort of like Bill and Hillary—a sense that this is something we can do together."[11] Another biographer agrees and states, "She was his political adviser all the way through. . . . She saw the greatness that Abraham Lincoln would become."[12] Journalist Anna Quindlan thought that Mary's real tragedy was that she was not alive today because "calculating and ambitious, she might have dreamed of being president instead of marrying one."[13]

This interpretation of Mary has even spilled over into fiction. M. Kay duPont's *Loving Mr. Lincoln: The Personal Diaries of Mary Todd Lincoln* emphasizes Mary's political skills. In the imagined diary, Mary tells Lincoln to run against the normal Whig ticket in 1843. She says, "Run against him anyway. I will help you. We'll write your speeches together." Later in the 1850s, Mary again is helping Lincoln by ghostwriting letters for him. She tells the reader, "Of course all the letters are signed 'A. Lincoln' but we are collaborating and I'm writing many."[14] In Barbara Hambly's *The Emancipator's Wife*, Mary again is the secret to Lincoln's literary skill: "From such discussions, and reading the newspapers, she was often able to help Lincoln hone his speeches."[15] In the novel *Mary*, Janis Cooke Newman has Mary as the reason for Lincoln's antislavery stance. It is she who pushed Lincoln to take a more antislavery stance after the Kansas-Nebraska Act in 1854. She even makes Lincoln go to hear an antislavery speech and makes sure he is near the speaker so he will become inspired.[16] As will be seen, this is the exact opposite of what happened; it was Lincoln who first supported the Republican Party and its antislavery platform. Mary followed Lincoln, not the other way around.

Before a judgment is given on the merits of the supposed political partnership of the Lincolns, a distinction in the definition of political partnership needs to be made. The question of what it means can be asked many ways. Did Lincoln and Mary share a strong political ambition for Lincoln's career? Did Lincoln's marriage further his political career? Did Lincoln and Mary share political views? Did Lincoln listen to, and more importantly, follow Mary's political advice? Did the Lincolns collaborate on his speeches? All of these questions deal with the definition of political partnership, and all need to be answered in order to judge the thesis in a rational manner.

The first question was whether Lincoln and Mary shared a strong political ambition for Lincoln's career. The answer would have to be a resounding yes. There are a number of sources that point to both of their ambitions. The story is often told of Mary Todd bragging as a child that she would marry the president. Naturally one could see this as a later interpolation in the record, given the historical events. However, there are multiple attestations to it. Elizabeth Keckley, Mary's seamstress in Washington, states that one of Mary's sisters remembered Mary making a commotion as a young child. Mary was told to be quiet by her grandmother and was asked what would become of her if she kept acting like this. Mary replied, "Oh I will be the wife of the President someday."[17] The sister above was probably Elizabeth Edwards. She told the same story to William Herndon, Lincoln's law partner and biographer. "She was an extremely Ambitious woman in Ky & often Contended that she was destined to be the wife of some future President—Said it in my presence in Springfield and Said it in Earnest."[18] She also once said, "I would rather marry a good man—a man of mind—with hope and bright prospects ahead for position—fame & power than to marry all the houses—gold and bones in the world."[19] There can be little doubt that from an early age, Mary was ambitious politically for her future husband.

Mary's ambition could lead to extremely spiteful and petty behavior. When Lincoln lost an election to the Senate in 1855, a disappointed Lincoln was quick to publicly congratulate the winner, Lyman Trumbull, at a reception that night. Trumbull's wife, Julia, had been Mary's bridesmaid and had helped bring the Lincolns back together after an initial breakup. As one of Mary's biographers relates, "Thereafter Julia and Mary were enemies and Mary dismissed her intimate friend as 'ungainly,' 'cold,' 'unsympathizing,' and 'unpopular,' even a 'whited Sepulchre,' by which she conveyed the idea that Mrs. Trumbull was dead to her."[20] The contrast against the magnanimity of Lincoln, who went on to have a fruitful political relationship with Trumbull, couldn't be more striking.

Lincoln's own political ambition cannot be in doubt at all. We have the all too familiar quote from William Herndon, "That man who thinks Lincoln sat down calmly and gathered his robes about him, waiting for people to call him, has a very erroneous knowledge of Lincoln. He was always calculating, and planning ahead. His ambition was a little engine that knew no rest."[21]

In fact, Lincoln historian Mary Neely Jr. could state in 1995, "But the fact remains that politics came first. He ran for the Illinois legislature in 1832, when he was only 23 years old. That was long before he decided to become a lawyer (he was still considering becoming a blacksmith at the time). And it was years before he married Mary Todd. Politics was his first love."[22]

The record then supports the notion that both Lincoln and Mary Todd were ambitious politically from an early age. In that sense it was a true political partnership. The record also states that one's ambition was not dependent on that of the other. One cannot say that Mary fueled Lincoln's ambitions in politics. What can only be said is that she did not discourage Lincoln in this area because she wanted him to succeed as much as he did.

Did Lincoln's marriage further his political ambitions? He was certainly marrying into a politically influential clan. The Edwardses, Lincoln's future in-laws, had a long history of prominence in the state. Yet it seems that Lincoln's marriage actually had a detrimental effect on his political career, at least in the short run. In early March of 1843, the Whigs had set up a convention to nominate a candidate for Congress. This was a few short months after Lincoln's marriage. Congressman was a job Lincoln sorely wanted. He lost the nomination to his friend Edward Baker, and Lincoln felt he knew why. He wrote another friend, "It would astonish if not amuse, the older citizens of your Country who twelve years ago knew me a stranger, friendless, uneducated, penniless boy, working on a flatboat at—ten dollars a month to learn I have been put down as the candidate of pride, wealth, and aristocratic family distinction."[23] A scholar who studied Lincoln's quest for Congress concluded, "Thus Lincoln saw his association with the wealthy Edwards family, and his marriage to Mary Todd (herself of a wealthy, aristocratic family related to the Edwardses), turning out to be political liabilities rather than assets."[24] Rather than spurring Lincoln on through a political partnership, his political career stalled immediately after his marriage.

Those who rate high the importance of Mary's polishing Lincoln's manners and dress have to remember what Lincoln's political success was often based on. Lincoln never campaigned on the grounds that he was the most learned or polished candidate for office. As late as 1860, he was running as the "Rail-Splitter" even though that was a life he had left far behind. From his earliest political campaign Lincoln stressed, "I was born and have remained in the most humble walks of life. I have no wealthy or popular relations to recommend me."[25] Friends remember Lincoln campaigning with such homely phrases as, "My politicks are short and sweet, like the old Womans dance."[26] Lincoln was also not afraid to get dirty while campaigning. One early associate related that during harvest time in Lincoln's second campaign, he was introduced to some men working in the field. They told him they would not vote for a man unless he could keep up with them in their work. Lincoln said, "Boys if that is all I am sure of your votes."[27] Lincoln then proceeded to work alongside the men, and the associate thought Lincoln did not lose a single vote with the farmers.[28] It was this retail style of politics that Lincoln excelled in that made his early success possible, not any supposed polish that Mary gave him.

There is an even larger problem with the "polishing" part of the argument. It speaks well of the strength of Lincoln's 1860 presidential campaign that the "Rail-Splitter" image of an always rustic Lincoln still sticks to him in historical interpretation. The idea that Lincoln needed polishing in order to succeed is false. Lincoln was no hayseed from the frontier when he met Mary Todd. He had taught himself law and was law partner with a congressman. He had already been elected three times to the legislature, and so well thought of by his colleagues that he was elected as the Whig Party floor leader. He was seen as a rising man. He was already showing signs of his talent as a writer in speeches like the lecture he delivered at the Young Men's Lyceum in 1838.[29] All of this happened before he ever met Mary Todd. He may have been rough around the edges at times, but he was good enough to succeed in his profession and to become well liked by many around him.

Ironically, it also appears Mary never succeeded in her mind of polishing Lincoln. As one Mary Lincoln scholar writes, "Yet despite his earnest and best efforts, Lincoln's dress consistently fell below his wife's standards, dragging him down a social notch or two in her eyes. 'Why don't you dress up and try to look like somebody?' she would say, a particularly pointed barb at his origins."[30] Her lack of success here may have been fortunate for Lincoln politically in that he could have never pulled off his "Rail-Splitter" campaign had he been an aristocrat in dress and manner.

Mary Lincoln biographer Catherine Clinton has offered some strong evidence of Mary's polishing when she quotes Edward Everett's comment that Lincoln's polish "may be credited to the influence of his wife."[31] Everett spoke before Lincoln at Gettysburg. He was the main speaker on the occasion of Lincoln's Gettysburg Address. However, Everett did not really know Lincoln. He ran against Lincoln in 1860 as the running mate of John Bell of the Constitutional Union Party. Again the strength of the 1860 campaign image of Lincoln comes into play. Everett, a Harvard professor, suspected no doubt to find Lincoln a backwoods buffoon. When he didn't find that in Lincoln, he naturally assumed his aristocratic wife was the reason. It is certain that Mary added to Lincoln's manners in many ways but most likely less than has been alleged.

There is even strong doubt that Lincoln and his wife agreed on politics throughout the marriage. When they first met, they were both ardent Whigs. Mary Lincoln was a neighbor of Lincoln's political idol Henry Clay, perhaps the supreme Whig, when she was younger. In 1840, Lincoln was out campaigning for the Whig candidate, William Henry Harrison, for president. Mary was also involved in the campaign. She wrote a friend, "This fall I became quite a politician, rather an unladylike profession, yet at such a crisis, whose heart could remain untouched while the energies of all were called in question?"[32] Jean Baker recounts some of Mary's activities during this period. "She was among the women who crowded into the offices of the *Sangamon Journal* to hear Harrison's chances, and she also watched parades, listened to speeches, and talked issues."[33]

If Lincoln and Mary were both Whigs in their courtship and early marriage, what made them so? Lincoln was a Whig because he believed in the party's commitment to internal improvements and banks. He saw the "right to rise" as being an important point in the American dream. Lincoln author Gabor Boritt states, "The key to Lincoln's economic persuasion was that all people should receive a good, full, and ever increasing reward for their labors so that they might have the opportunity to rise in life."[34] A developed country would allow the many to do this. After two flatboat journeys down the Mississippi, Lincoln saw the need for improvements of waterways. Lincoln faced economic hardships growing up. He saw that the policies of Andrew Jackson and the Democrats were holding back development and forcing future generations to live as he had.

Mary Lincoln's allegiance to the Whig Party is easier to explain. She was a Whig because her father was a Whig and because of her family's connection to Henry Clay.[35] There is nothing in the record that states any reason for her party affiliation beyond those two rather unsophisticated reasons. She was eager for the election of William Henry Harrison as president, "a cause that has excited such deep interest in the nation and one of such vital importance to our prosperity."[36] However, she does not explain why it is so vital, and there is nothing in the record to suggest any meaningful grappling with the issues. As Jean Baker admits, "Nowhere in her 600 surviving letters is there a reasoned exposition of her political views."[37] Mary should not be judged harshly for this, as politics were not seen as a women's profession. Even Mary herself in the above quoted letter calls her interest "unladylike." Still this does not bode well for the contention of the political partnership between the Lincolns.

If Lincoln and Mary Todd got married agreeing in politics, did the situation ever change? There is strong evidence that it did. When the Whig Party was falling apart in the early 1850s, there were a number of parties that vied to be the major opposition to the Democrats. Many Whigs became Republicans; many others became members of the American Party, better known as Know-Nothings. The reason that anyone is discussing Lincoln today is because he made the choice to stand against the spread of slavery with the Republican Party following the passage

of the Kansas-Nebraska Act, which allowed slavery to spread into ter-
ritories in which it had previously been banned. He went against many
of his former colleagues including John Todd Stuart and Usher Linder.[38]
It was this decision that ultimately put Lincoln in the White House and
ended the peculiar institution. Apparently, he made this choice against
the advice of his wife.

When Lincoln was supporting the Republican candidate Frèmont
for president in 1856, Mary Lincoln was supporting the anti-immigrant
Know-Nothing candidate, Millard Fillmore. In a letter she wrote to her
half sister Emile Todd Helm that year, she stated, "My weak woman's
heart was too Southern in feeling, to sympathize with any but Fillmore.
I have always been a great admirer of his, he made so good a President &
is so just man & feels the necessity of keeping foreigners within bounds.
If some of you Kentuckians, had to deal with the 'wild Irish' as we housekeepers are sometimes called upon to do the south would certainly elect
Mr. Fillmore next time."[39]

Compare the sentiments expressed above with what Lincoln wrote a
year earlier. In a letter to his best friend, Joshua Speed, Lincoln wrote,
"I am not a Know-Nothing. That is certain. How could I be? How can
anyone who abhors the oppression of Negros be in favor of degrading
classes of white people?"[40] The Lincolns had parted ways politically with
the end of the Whig Party. As Lincoln knew, and apparently Mary did
not, suppressing Hibernians was not the pressing issue for the country
in the 1850s; it was stopping the spread of slavery. Mary Lincoln came to
support her husband politically because of their mutual ambition, and
she later came to adopt Republican principles. However, these two letters,
by themselves, show that a political partnership never existed in the way
that Mary Lincoln's apologists would have one believe.

The strongest case made for Mary Lincoln's political partnership is
that she regularly gave advice to Lincoln on matters of public policy and
especially patronage. How accurate is this characterization? Not very,
according to Lincoln scholar Charles B. Strozier. In discussing Mary's

possible influence on Lincoln's views towards African Americans, Strozier states, "Actually, she exerted little influence on Lincoln in regard to this or any other political subject."[41] Lincoln's ideas on this subject were long held and were not shaped by Mary. Lincoln could say in 1864, "I am naturally anti-slavery. If slavery is not wrong, nothing is wrong. I can not remember when I did not so think, and feel."[42] Apologists for Mary Lincoln may be hard pressed to come up with an example that contradicts Strozier.

It is true that Mary Lincoln often gave Lincoln political advice. The record is very full of examples of her providing this to him. In her memoir, Elizabeth Keckley devotes a whole chapter to this, entitled "Candid Opinions."[43] Here, Keckley remembers Mary Lincoln as being against a host of people associated with Lincoln in his cabinet and the military. She was particularly hard against Secretary of State Seward. Even in her drives around Washington, she ordered the coachman to avoid the street on which Seward lived.[44] Keckley remembers, "She but rarely lost an opportunity to say an unkind word of him."[45] Lincoln seemed to listen to all of this in a somewhat patronizing way but never acted on her advice. It is true that she saw that Chase was not loyal. Lincoln of course knew this already, as it would seem most people in Washington did. Mary Lincoln seemed to be against Chase mainly because of her jealousy of his daughter.

Did Lincoln have to read his speeches to Mary, and did she change them when she didn't agree with the speech as Epstein and others claim? There is not a shred of evidence this is so. Douglas Wilson has done the most extensive work on Lincoln's writing. He has found revealing insights into the process of Lincoln's revising.[46] The sixteenth president truly was a master of the English language. There is no hint in any of his research that Mary had anything to do with his speeches or had to fix up his prose. In her voluminous letters she never makes that claim. We have only the one public incident of her comments on one of his speeches. When Lincoln spoke at a Sanitary Fair in 1864, his wife remarked to him in front of a friend, the future governor of Illinois Richard Oglesby, "That was the worst speech I ever listened to in my life. How any man could get up and deliver such remarks to an audience is more than I can understand. I wanted the earth to sink and let me go through."[47]

One could also make a strong argument that at times in his presidency, Lincoln's wife made herself a distinct liability. Her behavior was at times an embarrassment for him. The famous City Point episode is the best example. Mary Lincoln berated officers and their wives mercilessly when she arrived in City Point, Virginia, to visit the army with her husband in 1865. Even stalwart apologist Ruth Painter Randall was forced to admit, "The First Lady remained in this abnormal state of mind the rest of the day, berating Lincoln in the presence of others, creating scenes and acting out like what she was, a woman temporarily out of her mind."[48] The record shows that Lincoln's closest associates found her hard to deal with. Lincoln secretary John Hay wrote to his friend in April 1862, "The Hell-cat is getting more Hell-cattical day by day."[49] These and other examples of Mary Lincoln's behavior in the White House do not come from political enemies. The apologist for Mary must deal with the good probability that instead of helping Lincoln's presidency as a political partner, she hindered it.

Perhaps even worse, any historical interpretation of Mary that sees her as contributing to Lincoln's political career opens the door to look into her public corruption and how that hindered Lincoln as president. For example, after Lincoln was elected president many felt the way to get influence was to flatter and bribe Mary. When one man gave Mary a diamond brooch in order to get a job, a visitor found Mary having a fit on the floor. As Lincoln scholar Harold Holzer relates, "Lincoln remarked despairingly to his guest, 'she will not let me go until I promise her an office for one of her friends.' Mary's 'fit continued until the promise was obtained.'"[50] The release in 1994 of suppressed portions of intimate family friend Senator Orville Browning's diary has shown even more evidence of corruption. One notable passage states that a corrupt associate of Mary had "suggested to Mrs. Lincoln the making of false bills so as to get pay for private expenses out of the public treasury and had aided her in doing so . . . that the President had to be informed of it, at which he was very indignant, and refunded what had been thus filched from the government."[51] This is hardly the actions of a political partner.

The greatest scandal involving politics and Mary is the furnishing of parts of Lincoln's 1861 message to Congress to the press. The *New York Herald* printed portions of it prematurely. There was a lot of finger pointing, and an obviously false story was given by one of the coconspirators to protect the real guilty party. According to the suppressed portions of Browning's diary, it was Mary who furnished the material, thus undermining Lincoln's presidency, mostly likely in exchange for bribes or gifts.[52] Even a man who was originally sympathetic to Mary early in Lincoln's term, Benjamin French, the commissioner of public buildings, was forced to change his mind by the time she left Washington. He wrote in his journal in regards to her corruption, "She is a most singular woman, and it is well for the nation that she is no longer in the White House. It is not proper that I should write down, even here, all I know! May God have her in his keeping, and make her a better woman."[53]

Why then the emphasis on Mary's political contribution to the marriage if the evidence is so weak? It is a fairly new phenomenon. In 1987 Jean Baker had written of Mary, "She left no published work. She joined no reform movements, nor was she a clandestine supporter of unpopular social causes. She said nothing about women's issues and very little about slavery."[54] What changed? The answer may lie in the very negative scholarship that appeared about Mary in the 1990s. The publishing of the unflattering material on Mary in the Herndon-Weik manuscripts by Douglas Wilson and Rodney Davis as well as highly critical books like Michael Burlingame's *The Inner World of Abraham Lincoln* may have caused an inevitable reaction, and since the story of a political partnership is indeed an appealing one that plays to the American sense of fair play and invokes genuine sympathy for the second-class status of women in nineteenth-century America, it found a ready audience among the public. There are of course external factors outside of Lincoln scholarship that have given the theory more plausibility with the public than it deserves, such as the welcome acceptance of feminism by the majority of Americans and the rise of skilled female political figures such as Hillary Clinton.

It also appears that the natural result of all this is that the kernel of truth of the Lincolns' mutual ambition is being expanded far more than the evidence warrants. This has a snowball effect of making Mary's contribution more and more important as time goes by in historical and popular interpretation. A recent biographer can say, "No one could doubt that her coaching and scheming helped Lincoln attain his nomination as a presidential candidate."[55] It is though possible to doubt this because Lincoln's nomination more likely had to do with a number of things such as geography, availability, his Cooper Union speech, his innate political ability, as well as other factors.

Another example of placing too much interpretative significance on a small bit of evidence is the importance given to Lincoln saying to his wife on the night of his election to the presidency, "Mary, Mary! We are elected!"[56] What Lincoln said could be taken a number of ways. It is not clear that it means that Lincoln was saying that the election was a joint undertaking in which she was a full partner. It could more likely mean that as Lincoln's spouse, she was to take joy in his election, especially since she shared his ambition. In either case, the comment is simply not the smoking gun that it is made out to be for the political partnership thesis.[57]

Considering her temperament and interaction with other people, it is hard to see Mary succeeding in politics even today, when her gender would not disqualify her. A reading of her writings shows that Mary was intelligent and highly educated. However, she lacked the personal magnetism that Lincoln and other politicians have. It is hard to see Mary employing the self-deprecating humor that Lincoln used to his advantage so well. Her habit of holding grudges would have served her ill by preventing her from working with people across the aisle. She simply lacked the necessary skills to succeed as a politician. Her often quick and mercurial temperament would have been a distinct liability. A politician must know how to build coalitions and co-opt the opposition. As David Donald remarked over fifty years ago, "The secret of Lincoln's success is simple: he was a skilled operator of the political machine."[58]

In the final analysis, to paraphrase Mark Twain: The reports of the Lincolns' political partnership have been greatly exaggerated. Mary Lincoln was a product of her times. Yes, she shared a strong political ambition with her husband and was eager for him to succeed. Beyond that, there is no evidence of a true political partnership. To try to turn Mary into an Eleanor Roosevelt or an Abigail Adams would be unhistorical. Besides Lincoln really needed no help when it came to politics, since all concede he was a master in its practice. As Pennsylvania Republican boss Alexander McClure said, "If Abraham Lincoln was not a master politician, I am entirely ignorant of the qualities which make up such a character."[59]

### Notes

This essay first appeared in an abbreviated form in Michael Burkhimer, "Mary Todd Lincoln: Political Partner?" *Lincoln Herald* 105, no. 2 (2003): 67–72.

1. John Harlow, "Spielberg Shows Darker Side of Saintly Lincoln," *Sunday Times*, World News, March 18, 2001.

2. Doris Kearns Goodwin, "Abe Lincoln and the Truth Get Mugged at the Click of a Mouse," *Los Angeles Times*, editorial, April 1, 2001.

3. Harlow, *Sunday Times*, March 18, 2001.

4. William Hanchett, "Lincoln and the Tripp Thesis, Part Three," *Lincoln Herald* 111, no. 2 (2009): 79.

5. Jean Baker, "Mary and Abraham: A Marriage," in Gabor S. Boritt, ed., *The Lincoln Enigma: The Changing Face of an American Icon* (Oxford: Oxford University Press, 2001), 36–55.

6. *The American Experience—Abraham and Mary Lincoln: A House Divided*, videocassette, directed by David Grubin (PBS Home Video, 2001).

7. Rafeal Epstein, "Abraham Lincoln Labeled a Racist in New Book," *World Today*, <http://www.abc.net.au/worldtoday/stories/s262349.htm>, accessed November 19, 2011.

8. Daniel Mark Epstein, "What's New in *The Lincolns, Portrait of a Marriage?*" *Amazon.com Review*, <http://www.amazon.com/Lincolns-Portrait-Daniel-Mark-Epstein/dp/0345478002/ref=sr_1_1?ie=UTF8&s=books&qid=1257215048&sr=1-1>, accessed November 19, 2011.

9. Daniel Mark Epstein, *The Lincolns: Portrait of a Marriage* (New York: Ballantine, 2008), 247.

10. Karen Springen, "Hellcat or Helpmate: The Mary Todd Lincoln Saga: A New Exhibit Examines a Controversial First Lady's Troubled days," *Newsweek*, September 19, 2007, <http://www.newsweek.com/id/41140/page/1>, accessed November 19, 2011.

11. Jean Baker, as quoted in ibid.

12. Catherine Clinton, as quoted in ibid.

13. Anna Quindlan, "The Other Lincoln," *Newsweek*, February 21, 2009, <http://www.newsweek.com/id/185921/page/1>, accessed November 19, 2001.

14. M. Kay duPont, *Loving Mr. Lincoln: The Personal Diaries of Mary Todd Lincoln* (Atlanta: Jedco, 2003), 65, 178.

15. Barbara Hambly, *The Emancipator's Wife* (New York: Bantam Dell, 2008), 343.

16. Janis Cooke Newman, *Mary* (Orlando: Harcourt, 2007), 204–6.

17. Elizabeth Keckley, *Behind the Scenes; or, Thirty Years a Slave, and Four Years in the White House* (New York: New York Printing, 1868), 228–29.

18. Elizabeth Edwards to William Herndon, 1865–1866, in Douglas L. Wilson and Rodney O. Davis, eds., *Herndon's Informants: Letters, Interviews, and Statements about Abraham Lincoln* (Urbana: University of Illinois Press, 1998), 443.

19. Mary Lincoln, as quoted in Michael Burlingame, *The Inner World of Abraham Lincoln* (Urbana: University of Illinois Press, 1994), 308–9.

20. Jean Baker, *Mary Todd Lincoln: A Biography* (New York: W. W. Norton, 1987), 150.

21. William H. Herndon and Jesse W. Weik, *Herndon's Life of Lincoln* (Cleveland: World, 1942), 304.

22. Mark Neely Jr., "Lincoln's First Love," *Civil War Times Illustrated* 34, no. 5 (1995): 45.

23. Abraham Lincoln to Martin M. Morris, March 26, 1843, in Roy P. Basler, Marrion Dolores Pratt, and Lloyd A. Dunlap, eds., *The Collected Works of Abraham Lincoln* (New Brunswick: Rutgers University Press, 1953), 1:320.

24. Donald E. Riddle, *Lincoln Runs for Congress* (New Brunswick: Rutgers University Press, 1948), 64.

25. "Communication to the People of Sangamo County," March 9, 1832, in Basler et al., *Collected Works*, 1:8–9.

26. Abner Y. Ellis to William H. Herndon, 1866, in Wilson and Davis, *Herndon's Informants*, 171.

27. Rowan Herndon to William Henry Herndon, ibid., 8.

28. Ibid.

29. "Address before the Young Man's Lyceum of Springfield, Illinois," January 27, 1838, in Basler et al., *Collected Works*, 1:108–15.

30. Jennifer Fleischner, *Mrs. Lincoln and Mrs. Keckly: The Remarkable Story of a Friendship between a First Lady and a Former Slave* (New York: Broadway, 2003), 152–53.

31. Edward Everett, as quoted in Catherine Clinton, *Mary Lincoln: A Life* (New York: Harper, 2009), 210.

32. Mary Todd Lincoln to Mercy Levering, December 15, 1840, in Justin G. Turner and Linda Levitt Turner, *Mary Todd Lincoln: Her Life and Letters* (New York: Albert A. Knopf, 1972), 21.

33. Baker, *Mary Todd Lincoln*, 86.

34. Gabor S. Boritt, "Lincoln and the Economics of the American Dream," in Gabor S. Boritt, ed., *The Historian's Lincoln: Psuedohistory, Psychohistory, and History* (Urbana: University of Illinois Press, 1988), 88.

35. Turner and Turner, *Mary Todd Lincoln*, 7.

36. Mary Todd Lincoln to Mercy Levering, December 15, 1840, in Turner and Turner, *Mary Todd Lincoln*, 21.

37. Baker, *Mary Todd Lincoln*, 134.

38. For a discussion of this, see Don E. Fehrenbacher, *Prelude to Greatness: Lincoln in the 1850s* (Stanford: Stanford University Press, 1962), 19–47.

39. Mary Todd Lincoln to Emile Todd Helm, November 23, 1856, in Turner and Turner, *Mary Todd Lincoln*, 46.

40. Abraham Lincoln to Joshua F. Speed, August 24, 1855, in Basler et al., *Collected Works*, 2:323.

41. Charles B. Strozier, *Lincoln's Quest for Union: Public and Private Meanings* (New York: Basic, 1982), 95.

42. Abraham Lincoln to Albert G. Hodges, April 4, 1864, in Basler et al., *Collected Works*, 7:281.

43. Keckley, *Behind the Scenes*, 127–37.

44. Burton J. Hendrick, *Lincoln's War Cabinet* (Boston: Little, Brown, 1946), 187.

45. Keckley, *Behind the Scenes*, 130.

46. See Douglas L. Wilson, *Lincoln's Sword: The Presidency and the Power of Words* (New York: Albert A. Knopf, 2006).

47. Mary Lincoln, as quoted in Carl Sandburg and Paul M. Angle, *Mary Lincoln: Wife and Widow* (New York: Harcourt, Brace, 1932), 112.

48. Ruth Painter Randall, *Mary Todd Lincoln: Biography of a Marriage* (Boston: Little, Brown, 1953), 336.

49. John Hay to John G. Nicolay, April 19, 1862, in Tyler Dennett, ed., *Lincoln and the Civil War: In the Diaries and Letters of John Hay* (New York: Dodd and Mead, 1939), 41.

50. Harold Holzer, *Lincoln President-Elect: Abraham Lincoln and the Great Secession Winter 1860–1861* (New York: Simon and Schuster, 2008), 238.

51. Orville H. Browning, as quoted in Michael Burlingame, ed., *At Lincoln's Side: John Hay's Civil War Correspondence and Selected Writings* (Carbondale: Southern Illinois University Press, 2000), 186.

52. Michael Burlingame, *Abraham Lincoln: A Life* (Baltimore: Johns Hopkins University Press, 2008), 2:274.

53. Benjamin French, as quoted in "Mary Todd Lincoln's Unethical Conduct as First Lady," in Burlingame, *At Lincoln's Side*, 195.

54. Baker, *Mary Todd Lincoln*, xiv.

55. Catherine Clinton, "Wife versus Widow: Clashing Perspectives on Mary Lincoln's Legacy," *Journal of the Abraham Lincoln Association* 28, no. 1 (2007), <http://www.historycooperative.org/journals/jala/28.1/clinton.html>, accessed November 19, 2011.

56. Epstein, *The Lincolns: Portrait of a Marriage*, 267; 266–81.

57. See Springen, "Hellcat or Helpmate."

58. David Donald, *Lincoln Reconsidered* (New York: Vintage, 1989), 65.

59. Alexander McClure, *Lincoln and Men of War Times* (Philadelphia: Times, 1892), 85.

# A Psychiatrist Looks at Mary Lincoln

*James S. Brust, MD*

I have practiced psychiatry full time for over forty years. That is my profession and main role—what I do most and know best. My interest in historical research and writing grew out of collecting nineteenth-century prints and photographs. These are my leisure activities, and for a long time I went out of my way never to mix vocation and avocation. For example, when asked by research colleagues at the Little Bighorn Battlefield for my psychological analysis of George Armstrong Custer, I would find a way to politely decline.

And then along came Mary.

Settling down to lunch one day in June of 2006, I opened *American Heritage* and was quickly drawn to an article titled "The Madness of Mary Lincoln."[1] I read it twice before I got up from the table. Most people in this country are familiar with Mary Todd Lincoln but know only a tiny bit about her. I was no different. But suddenly I was reading vivid, detailed descriptions of symptoms and situations very familiar to me as a practicing psychiatrist. Mary Lincoln had a significant psychiatric illness, most likely bipolar disorder. She required hospitalization and improved while she was there. For me there was no "controversy" about her condition and need for treatment. Everyone could understand that aspect of Mrs. Lincoln if her story were told with proper psychiatric perspective, which, it occurred to me, I might help provide. The author of the article,

Jason Emerson, was working on a book on this topic. Overcoming my own resistance to mixing psychiatry with historical research, I contacted Jason, who accepted my offer to assist.[2]

Any attempt to study Mary Lincoln from a psychiatric point of view must include an examination of general attitudes and perceptions regarding mental illness, both past and present. Psychiatry has always been viewed differently from other medical specialties. The brain is both more complex and less accessible than other organs of the body; its workings more mysterious and difficult to understand. The symptoms associated with conditions classed as "mental" illnesses are more personal and emotional, affecting essential aspects of an individual's identity and personality. If the heart beats irregularly or blood sugar is elevated, we can usually be objective. But that is more difficult when thoughts and feelings become abnormal.

The earliest explanations of mental illness were supernatural, with madness seen as a punishment from the gods or possession by demons. People so afflicted became the province of the clergy, with uncertain benefit and occasional excesses like executions for witchcraft. Later views would see mental illness as unbalanced bodily "humours," an excess of passion or failure of reason.[3] But into the twentieth century, each evolving theory provided little in the way of improved treatment, yet still left a stigma on those seen as suffering from "madness" or "insanity" or whatever word was being used to connote serious mental illness. Such individuals were not fully accepted. Regardless of their social class, if they had significant psychiatric illness, they would be viewed as being "different from" or "less than" others—even a president's wife or widow. This stigma against mental illness was powerful and pervasive in Mary Lincoln's time and sadly continues into the present. As a psychiatrist, I see it every day, and it must be kept in mind whenever the psychiatric aspects of Mrs. Lincoln are discussed.

Also important in the history of mental illness in general, and the story of Mary Lincoln in particular, are asylums for the care of the insane. "Asylum" means a place of protection and refuge, and such facilities should have provided acceptance and support, though in the early days they often fell short. Asylums began to proliferate in the late eighteenth century, with a renewed effort to be therapeutic and to alleviate or even cure mental illness. As the nineteenth century progressed, however, such care was not to be the case for the vast majority of patients because public facilities became so overfilled and physically taxed they could be little more than warehouses.[4]

Of course there were private sanitariums that were not overcrowded and could be beneficial, such as Bellevue Place in Batavia, Illinois, where Mrs. Lincoln was sent in 1875. Living in comfortable quarters in a beautiful rural setting, she received special attention from the superintendent and his family, and the most humane treatment.[5] So it was not the actual events of her four months at Bellevue Place that were so repugnant to her, to some of her family and friends, and to her "supporters" both then and now. It was the *symbolism* of it, because one remanded to any asylum was branded as "mad" or "insane" and hence stigmatized in a way so awful that over one hundred and thirty years later there are many who still argue that it never should have happened. This dramatic impact of her hospitalization is further verified by the frequent use of the term "insanity episode" to describe it. If Mary Lincoln was "insane" (that is, psychiatrically ill) in 1875, then she was also ill at other times, and we should speak of "insanity episode*s*." But all focus seems to be on the one that led to hospitalization. How ironic that the place meant to be helpful and accepting, which might have countered stigma, ended up increasing it.

What are we speaking of when we refer to serious and stigmatizing illnesses known by such words as "madness," "insanity," "craziness," or "derangement"? None of these terms are still used in psychiatry or medicine, though all remain in our language, loaded with negative connotation. The modern word that most closely corresponds to these older ones is "psychotic," which means unable, at times, to tell what is real from what is not. Such patients might have delusions (fixed beliefs in things that are impossible, or known to be untrue by all other observers) or hallucinations (sensations seeming to be external but actually arising in the individual's own brain, such as hearing voices when no one is talking, or seeing things that are not there). Those suffering from delusions and hallucinations are certain they are true and will not accept any logical alternative explanation. Also included among the more serious psychiatric conditions are two severe disorders of mood. One is the extreme sadness of depression so profound that the person is rendered unable to function, or possibly driven to suicide. The other mood disorder is a manic state, with emotions often being euphoric, accompanied by excitement or agitation that impairs activities and interactions, and likewise makes normal function impossible. Both severe depression and mania are often accompanied by delusions. Manic patients are often paranoid (as Mary Lincoln was at times)[6] and can show a full range of psychotic symptoms. Even patients in the depressed state can have delusions, usually negative towards themselves. They may believe that they have done something wrong, have a deadly illness, or, in Mrs. Lincoln's case, that she was impoverished.[7] These, then, were the conditions whose sufferers were most stigmatized, and most likely to end up in asylums where they were tended to by the psychiatrists of that era who were known as "alienists."[8]

Of course there were more minor psychiatric ailments such as anxiety and depression that was not disabling. In the nineteenth century, these might be classed as "nerves" or "nervous illness." They were seen as physical or medical conditions and not nearly as stigmatized as psychotic illnesses. Since those afflicted were not sick enough to require institutionalization, they were not treated by the asylum-based psychiatric profession,[9] but by general medical doctors or neurologists. An informal distinction has existed through the ages separating serious forms of mental illness from their less dramatic and disabling counterparts. Simply put, it was better to suffer from "nerves" than "madness" or "insanity."

Where does Mary Lincoln fit in this psychiatric spectrum? Other qualified physician-writers have tried to diagnose Mrs. Lincoln with varied conclusions. Their work is well thought out and generally accurate, though often not providing a complete understanding of all facets of her psychiatric symptoms.

W. A. Evans, MD, assisted by five psychiatrists, published a book in 1932 titled *Mrs. Abraham Lincoln: A Study of Her Personality and Her Influence on Lincoln.*[10] His goal was a "study of her personality," a term he defined broadly to include not only her basic traits, but also intelligence, emotions, physical characteristics, and illnesses. His work contained fascinating biographical information on Mrs. Lincoln, and an interesting discussion of her medical conditions. But as a psychiatric study of Mary Lincoln, it is handicapped by several factors. Terminology has changed so much in the years since Evans wrote this book that it is hard to correlate his wording to modern psychiatric thought. More importantly, though he acknowledged that delusions and hallucinations were prominent in Mary Lincoln's illness, he explained them away as being either near-normal or associated with her Spiritualism. Finally, in his efforts to "understand Mrs. Lincoln and be just to her," he seemed to go out of his way to defend rather than diagnose her. Dr. Evans's emphasis on Mrs. Lincoln's psychological and emotional state is laudable, but his study fails to deal fully with the seriousness of her most severe psychiatric symptoms.

In January 1941, Dr. James A. Brussel, then an army psychiatrist who would later gain fame for his use of psychiatric profiling to solve criminal cases, published a study of Mary Lincoln.[11] Using the evidence available to him, Brussel did not find a major psychiatric diagnosis such as manic-depressive illness or schizophrenia. He concluded that Mrs. Lincoln suffered from migraine, which explained her seeming psychiatric symptoms, including visual hallucinations and certain delusions. Migraine can cause visual abnormalities that include seeing colors and patterns. While these have sometimes been called hallucinations, they are vague in form, and those experiencing them know they are inside their own brain. The visual hallucinations of psychotic illness are very different, with specific objects "seen" and firmly believed to exist in the external world. In day-to-day practice, psychiatrists and neurologists have no problem differentiating one from the other. Certain of Mrs. Lincoln's apparent delusions have likewise been attributed to migraine.

She told Dr. Willis Danforth that wires and springs were being pulled out of her head and eyes, and some have taken these statements as figurative descriptions of migraine headache pain. But she attributed them to an "Indian spirit" who was also removing her scalp and bones from her face.[12] In full context these sound like literal beliefs that were delusional. Migraine cannot explain the full range of Mary Lincoln's psychiatric symptoms.

In 1966, UCLA psychiatrist John Suarez, MD, published a case history of Mary Lincoln.[13] He focused on Mary's early personality traits, and the dynamics of her relationships with family members throughout her life. He wisely expressed trepidation at the prospect of establishing a firm psychiatric diagnosis. He concluded that as a result of the repeated stresses in her life, Mrs. Lincoln developed a "paranoid psychosis . . . that had manic, schizophrenic and involutional features." He also noted that the depressions she suffered when she lost her sons and husband were "clearly pathological in severity and duration." All told, Suarez's description of an illness that was at times psychotic, at times manic, and at times severely depressed is consistent with current concepts of bipolar disorder. Also noteworthy in Dr. Suarez's study are his observations that Mary Lincoln's commitment was necessary, and her hospitalization helpful.

In a 1999 article, physicians Norbert Hirschhorn and Robert G. Feldman presented and studied a most important primary source document—the report of a medical examination of Mrs. Lincoln by four prominent physicians conducted in New York City on January 1, 1882, and subsequently submitted to Congress in support of her request for an increase in her pension. It was preserved in the *Congressional Record*.[14] In a careful study of the 1882 report, Hirschhorn and Feldman concluded that Mary Lincoln had tabes dorsalis, which is a complex of symptoms affecting certain nerves in the body. It can be caused by a number of different illnesses. By that late stage of her life, Mrs. Lincoln had many medical complaints, among them various pains, difficulty walking, and disturbances of vision, all of which could be caused by tabes dorsalis.

Hirschhorn and Feldman's conclusion that Mary Lincoln had tabes dorsalis is astute but raises some interesting and potentially troubling questions. What illness caused this syndrome in Mrs. Lincoln? There was a school of thought in the nineteenth century that tabes dorsalis could be caused by certain spinal injuries. By the 1880s, support for that etiology was fading, but Mrs. Lincoln had been involved in a carriage accident in 1863 and reported having hurt her back in two separate falls in France in 1879 and 1880,[15] so the 1882 evaluators favored injury to her spine as the cause. In doing so, they skirted around the ever-increasing awareness that tabes dorsalis was more frequently associated with late stage syphilis. Given the fact that the 1882 medical report was intended to support a petition for an increase in Mary Lincoln's pension, and no definitive test for syphilis existed as yet, it is not surprising that the examining physicians leaned away from that diagnosis.

The possibility that Mrs. Lincoln had syphilis presented Hirschhorn and Feldman with a dilemma similar to that faced by the 1882 examiners, but by the time they were writing in 1999, other causes of tabes dorsalis had been identified. The most notable of these is diabetes, and they settled on that as the cause. I agree with them and find no strong evidence that Mary Lincoln had syphilis, though at least one modern author, Deborah Hayden, is convinced that she did, as was William Herndon in the 1860s.[16] Hirschhorn and Feldman made a good case that Mary Lincoln had tabes dorsalis, but the more important question for this study is whether that condition, be it from diabetes or syphilis, could account for her psychiatric symptoms. These authors were mindful of the difficulties of establishing a psychiatric diagnosis from the historical record alone but did state that symptoms of tabes dorsalis were "misinterpreted as madness" in Mrs. Lincoln. A specific point was made of a feature of tabes dorsalis known as Argyll Robertson pupils, in which the pupil of the eye no longer constricts in response to bright light.[17] Hirschhorn and Feldman offered this as an explanation of Mary Lincoln's tendency to stay in a darkened room using only candlelight in the final years of her life. Finally, they added that the more bizarre symptoms seen prior to Mrs. Lincoln's 1875 commitment may have had their roots in a posttraumatic stress disorder (PTSD) triggered by the tenth anniversary of President Lincoln's death.

As excellent as the Hirschhorn and Feldman study is, I doubt that tabes dorsalis could account for the full picture of Mary Lincoln's psychiatric symptoms. It would not cause her paranoid delusions, auditory hallucinations, or delusions of poverty. And patients with Argyll Robertson pupils, even if sensitive to bright sunlight, can come out of their darkened rooms at night, which Mary Lincoln did not, making it more likely that she chose isolation because she was depressed. As to the possibility of posttraumatic stress disorder, given the awful events of April 14, 1865, it was likely present to some degree, but the key element in a formal diagnosis of that condition is the persistent reexperiencing of the traumatic event, which is not described in the historical record of Mrs. Lincoln's symptoms. Moreover, delusions and hallucinations are not usually part of PTSD.[18]

If we can establish a diagnosis for Mary Lincoln, it might help us to understand her, but is it even possible to do so for someone who lived so far in the past? We might look first at how we diagnose people in the present. Historically, medical diagnosis was completely "clinical"—based solely on direct and personal interaction between the doctor and the patient and their family. The physician would talk to the patient, obtain a description and history of the illness and symptoms, physically examine the person, and then, if possible, corroborate or augment that information with family or other observers. Most fields of medicine have benefitted from impressive advances in diagnostic technology through the twentieth and into the twenty-first century. We now have sophisticated analysis of blood and bodily fluids, ever sharper pictures obtained by X-ray and other imaging techniques, and even direct visualization of internal body spaces with scopes and catheters. But the brain yields up its secrets much more grudgingly. Though there has been progress, such technologies have not yet proved applicable to psychiatric diagnosis, which continues to be almost completely clinical. Without a major boost in diagnostic acumen from laboratory and imaging, we still rely on talking to, interacting with, and observing people. This has helped to keep psychiatry a truly interpersonal discipline but has left it vulnerable to criticism that it is somehow not the equal of other medical fields and, therefore, more readily undervalued or ignored.

If psychiatric diagnosis requires direct contact and observation, how do we attempt it on someone who has been dead for over a century? We could only do so with great trepidation. We cannot conduct a psychiatric interview on Mrs. Lincoln, and there is no one alive who can describe her to us from personal observation. But we are not totally without information. Mary Lincoln was a person of interest and at times controversy as a president's wife and widow, and more was written about her than would be the case for most nineteenth-century Americans. And we have the additional benefit of surviving medical records.[19] We must be aware of the limitations of such a backward-look diagnosis, but we do have some information to base it on.

In an earlier essay[20] I discussed the multiaxial diagnostic system currently used in psychiatry, which considers factors such as personality traits, coexisting medical illnesses, and psychosocial stressors. These are of great significance in the complex case of Mary Lincoln, especially the multiple losses she endured. But they engender far less controversy, so I will not repeat that discussion here. It has become clear to me that when psychiatry is considered in regard to Mrs. Lincoln, the debate centers on whether or not she had a major mental illness that included psychotic thinking (delusions and hallucinations) and potentially dangerous behaviors—the kind of disorder that would necessitate psychiatric hospitalization for her own safety. Do we have evidence for such a condition?

There can be no question that Mary Lincoln suffered from depression, which she acknowledged herself, speaking of April as her "season of sadness." Other observers who noted her depression made no mention of it being limited only to a certain month, so likely it could occur at any time of the year. One of her closest family members, sister Elizabeth Edwards, with whom she lived at various times, said of Mary, "it is impossible to prevent frequent reactions to extreme sadness." Two of her physicians also observed depression. Dr. Willis Danforth, who treated her in 1873, described "melancholia" as one of her symptoms, and Dr. Louis Sayre, who usually emphasized her physical symptoms, said that Mrs. Lincoln was suffering from "great mental depression" upon her return from France to the United States in October (not April) of 1880.[21] Discussions of Mary Lincoln's mental health often center on grief, and depression is expected after a loss, of course. But the severity and duration of her symptoms following President Lincoln's assassination and the deaths of sons Eddie (1850), Willie (1862), and Tad (1871) exceeded the usual grief reaction.[22] Also of note is her tendency to stay in darkened rooms in the later years of her life, which was more likely a sign of depression than the product of any abnormality of her eyes. The next important consideration is whether Mary Lincoln was at times psychotic, that is suffering from delusions and hallucinations. The presence of psychosis greatly increases the severity of an illness, the potential for dangerous behavior, and the need for intervention. The earliest documentation of such symptoms in Mrs. Lincoln was in 1863, even before her husband's assassination. Her half sister Emilie Todd Helm noted in her diary that Mary spoke of nighttime visits from her son Willie, who had died the year before. Mary's descriptions were vivid and detailed: "He lives[,] Emily. . . . [H]e comes to me every night and stands at the foot of my bed. . . . [L]ittle Eddie is sometimes with him and twice he has come with our brother Alec." She not only "saw" Willie, she also "heard" him ("he tells me he loves his Uncle Alec and is with him most of the time"). And all of this was related to Mrs. Helm with "eyes [that] were wide and shining."[23] While it may be tempting to dismiss these visions as dreams, or as fantasies fueled by Spiritualism, the repetitive and dramatic nature of these symptoms, and Mary Lincoln's unquestioning belief in them, make it far more likely that they were hallucinations.

Psychotic symptoms would be described again in Mrs. Lincoln even before the remarkable events of 1875. According to family friend Isaac N.

Arnold, from the time of Tad's death in 1871, Mrs. Lincoln "had various hallucinations." During the same period of time her personal nurse stated that Mary "had strange delusions," including a preference for candles since she believed gas to be the invention of the devil. By 1873, Mary was telling her physician, Dr. Willis Danforth, that an Indian spirit was removing her scalp and the bones of her face, and pulling wires out of her eyes and steel springs out of her head. Dr. Danforth concluded these symptoms "were indications of mental disturbance."[24]

The psychotic symptoms described in 1875 that led to Mary Lincoln's commitment were even more dramatic. She rushed from Florida to Chicago based on the delusional belief that her son Robert was gravely ill. She spoke of a "wandering Jew" who had stolen her pocketbook on the train. She thought the city of Chicago was on fire, heard "strange sounds," and feared that she was in danger from a man who was "going to molest her." She was described by hotel employees as "excited, agitated, restless and nervous," and "complain[ing] frequently that people were speaking to her through the wall." She told Dr. Danforth that she had been poisoned on the train from Florida. All told, the evidence that Mary Lincoln suffered from psychotic symptoms seems clear, particularly during her 1875 episode.[25]

Mrs. Lincoln's episodes of significant depression accompanied by psychosis would be sufficient evidence of a major psychiatric illness, which in current terminology would be called major depressive disorder with psychotic features.[26] But there were other symptoms as well. Prominent in the story of Mrs. Lincoln was her extravagant spending of money, often on unnecessary items. Her sister Elizabeth Edwards noted Mary's spending habits, telling Robert that "it has always been a prominent trait in her character to accumulate large amounts of clothing." At her commitment hearing in 1875, five Chicago merchants testified that Mrs. Lincoln, in the weeks since her arrival from Florida, was making large and "reckless" purchases—hundreds of dollars worth of lace curtains, watches, jewelry, soaps, and perfumes—all items she had little or no use for as she was living in a hotel and always dressed in mourning black without jewelry.[27]

Spending of this kind is a symptom not usually associated with depression, but rather with what we now refer to as mania or a manic state. If Mary Lincoln experienced manic episodes, our diagnostic speculation turns in an important new direction, toward what for years was known as manic-depressive illness but is now called bipolar disorder, a condition characterized by episodes that can take two distinct forms, sometimes manic and at other times depressed, though there can even be a mixture of the two.[28] Mary Lincoln was depressed at times, but did she have evidence of sustained spells of any other abnormal or troubling mood? The official diagnostic criteria for a manic episode require a "distinct period of elevated, expansive or irritable mood lasting at least a week." There is little in the historical record to support sustained elevated or expansive mood in Mrs. Lincoln, but irritable spells would not be hard to imagine.

Mood abnormality, by itself, is not enough to diagnose a manic state, so even if we accept sustained irritability, other symptoms would be required. One, "engaging in unrestricted buying sprees," is well documented in Mary Lincoln, and a case can be made that she showed another symptom of mania, "inflated self esteem or grandiosity." Benjamin French, commissioner of public buildings, referred to Mrs. Lincoln as "The Queen," and a number of people felt she acted as if she were royalty.[29] Other symptoms of a manic state include decreased need for sleep, being more talkative than usual, racing thoughts, and distractibility. We have no specific descriptions of these in Mrs. Lincoln; they may have been present, but no firsthand account has survived that might prove it. These are things we would ask her about if we could, but of course we cannot, and not surprisingly, any attempt to diagnose her by strict current criteria will fall short. But still, there are many interesting diagnostic signs worth considering.

For example, another characteristic of bipolar disorder is that it tends to be intermittent rather than chronic, at least until its late stages. The episodes, whether manic or depressed, occur on a periodic basis, perhaps with a regular cycle, but then remit, leaving the affected individual relatively normal until the next spell. Mary Lincoln seemed fine at times, and even her son Robert noted that her episodes tended to "blow over."[30] As mentioned, she herself saw her depressions as cyclical, coming in April, which she referred to as "my season of sadness." April, of course, was the anniversary of President Lincoln's assassination, and near in the calendar to the February deaths of sons Willie (1850) and Eddie (1862). Though we know she was likely depressed at other times as well, her self-described cycle also points toward bipolar disorder.

So we have evidence of depression, mania, and psychosis, of a relapsing-remitting course, and even of a regular cycle. All of this is consistent with bipolar disorder. Another factor we look for is a family history of the illness. Mary Lincoln's full sister, Elizabeth Edwards, once again proves to be a helpful informant, by revealing that her daughter Julia (Mary's niece) first showed signs of "insanity" at age thirteen, and "at the birth of each child, the same symptoms were shown, and severely felt."[31] Since the niece's symptoms were described as "insanity," they must have been severe. The picture described sounds consistent with full-blown postpartum psychosis, rather than milder postpartum depression, and women with such episodes in their childbearing years often turn out to be bipolar with spells of illness later in life.[32] The likelihood that niece Julia Edwards Baker suffered from bipolar disorder is strengthened by knowledge that she engaged in "risqué" behavior in 1864 and was involved in a scandal in 1872.[33] While details are not known, it seems quite possible these events involved sexual indiscretion, and hypersexual behavior is another sign of a manic state.

There is further evidence of serious psychiatric illness in Mary Lincoln's family. One of Mary's brothers, Dr. George Todd, was "given to moods of deep melancholy," while another brother, Levi Owen Todd, died in an insane asylum. Also institutionalized were niece Mattie Todd and a grandniece (the daughter of Mary's nephew Albert Edwards). Another grandniece, Nellie Canfield, committed suicide, and fourteen members of her family were said to have been in asylums.[34] Together, these cases point toward an inheritable, biological component to Mary Lincoln's mental illness.

Bipolar disorder has a high suicide rate, and Mary Lincoln tried to ingest a lethal dose of laudanum the day after her commitment hearing. Like so many aspects of this story, those who wish to minimize her psychiatric illness can speculate that she was not seriously trying to kill herself. But a well-researched and thought-out study by physician Norbert Hirschhorn has shown that this was, indeed, a serious attempt to end her life.[35]

As I have acknowledged, I cannot "prove" that Mary Lincoln had bipolar disorder, but for all of the reasons presented, I think it quite possible that she did. If accurate, what can that tell us about her? First, it shows us she had an *illness*. One of the most extreme criticisms occasionally leveled at psychiatry is that mental illness does not really exist, but is just a construct of society to deal with individuality or deviance, or an invention of psychiatrists to insure their influence and income.[36] But the illness we now call bipolar disorder has been described for some twenty-five hundred years. Though given different names through the ages, there is evidence of a consistent clinical entity whose essential features have been described similarly for centuries. It is not unique to a certain individual or specific period of time.[37] Given this historical stability, it is a "real" illness.

Establishing a diagnosis can tell us something about the cause of that illness. Those interested in Mary Lincoln, and horrified by the stigma of major mental illness, have tried to "defend" her from such a diagnosis. This is still the case in the twenty-first century as it was in the nineteenth. But in defending Mary Lincoln, they overlook a factor that might place her symptoms in a more favorable light. Based on emerging scientific knowledge of the chemicals that mediate brain function, research studies that reveal evidence of an inherited pattern to major psychiatric illnesses, and the development of medications that can enter the brain and improve psychiatric symptoms, these psychotic illnesses are now thought to be based in brain chemistry, not personal weakness or failure. Though episodes may be precipitated or worsened by unhappy life events, they will not occur at all unless the individual has the necessary biological and biochemical vulnerability. And internal shifts in brain chemistry in those with such biologically based susceptibility can even cause illness at times when there has been no unusual stress or unhappiness in their lives, leaving others puzzled about why they got sick for "no reason." Since these physical and chemical factors in the brain are beyond conscious control, the affected individual can neither cause nor cure the symptoms themselves, and the episodes of illness are not the person's "fault." So to say that Mary Lincoln or anyone else demonstrated abnormalities of thought, mood, or behavior brought on by such illness is not a personal criticism but a blameless explanation.

Finally, a diagnosis tells us something about the expected course or prognosis of that illness. As noted, bipolar disorder can completely remit, even for extended periods of time, though other episodes will eventually follow. This is a more favorable outlook than many other major psychiatric conditions, which can become chronic. Sadly, though, bipolar disorder tends to worsen over time, the episodes becoming more frequent and more severe, even to the point of no longer fully remitting. This seems to have been the case for Mrs. Lincoln in the last two years of her life.

If we acknowledge the severity of Mrs. Lincoln's symptoms at the time of her commitment in 1875, we can see a major level of psychiatric illness. Her delusions and hallucinations caused erratic, irrational, and potentially dangerous behavior. Fearing she had been robbed on the train to Chicago, and thinking she was in danger from one or more "strangers," she felt a need to protect her money by carrying thousands of dollars in cash and bonds in her pockets, making her a target for anyone wishing to rob her. She believed the city was on fire, which led to fears that she might jump from a window. Hospitalization was necessary to protect her from these frightened responses to her delusions and hallucinations. Yet despite the fact that acceptance of her condition helps explain much of her behavior in a way that does not leave her personally blameworthy, and even though she actually improved at Bellevue Place once she finally got there, the stigma is so strong that some simply do not want to see her as having had a psychiatric illness, and seek another explanation.

One such alternative view is that Mary Lincoln had no significant mental illness at all but was simply the victim of her powerful and unfeeling son Robert and others, operating in a male-dominated society, who wished her out of the way in order to stifle her assertiveness, silence her outspoken nature, or steal her money. Jean H. Baker, in *Mary Todd Lincoln: A Biography* (1987) was a prominent proponent of this viewpoint.[38] Though there are ample firsthand descriptions of Mary Lincoln's psychotic symptoms at the time of her commitment in 1875, Baker declares them unreliable, the products of Robert Lincoln's influence and money. She says: "Robert carefully organized his case, rounding up doctors, hotel maids, waiters and store clerks to testify against her," tipped "the small time merchants . . . two weeks' wages," and paid "fifty dollars apiece" to the doctors who "were [his] friends and would say what he directed."[39] So in a few sentences written over one hundred years later, multiple statements and descriptions, many given under oath, are dismissed despite the fact that not a single one was ever recanted or proved false.

Baker's other focus is on her perception of the unfairness of Mary Lincoln's insanity trial. I would agree that an open trial before a jury is an awkward way to rule on commitment, and the very use of the terms "trial" and "verdict" add a very negative slant to what is meant to ultimately be a helpful process. It is doubtful that a private person like Robert Lincoln would have chosen that route if he had any other choice. But it was an improvement over the ultrasexist Illinois system it replaced,[40] and the proceedings were conducted under the rules set forth by law. The all-male nature of the proceeding does not automatically invalidate the findings, any more than Robert Lincoln's supposed wealth proves that he bribed all the witnesses. And in further regard to this notion that it was sexism and not psychosis that caused Mrs. Lincoln to be committed to Bellevue Place, it is interesting to note how many of the witnesses who left descriptions of her psychiatric symptoms were women, including close relatives such as sister Elizabeth Edwards and half sister Emilie Todd Helm, who could not have been controlled by Robert. Even Myra Bradwell, Mary Lincoln's chief defender, told Mary's psychiatrist Dr. R. J. Patterson "that she had no doubt that Mrs. Lincoln was insane and had been for some time"; she simply doubted the need to keep her in an asylum.[41]

Feminist concerns that Mary Lincoln's troubled circumstances may have been gender related are understandable. She was of symbolic importance as the widow of a revered and martyred president, and as a high-profile woman in an age when women were not usually in the public eye. Robert Lincoln was concerned about family legacy and may have been worried about the view others had of his mother's behavior. The sexist nature of society at that time might have judged Mary more harshly because she was a woman, and given Robert more power because he was a man. The possibility of mistreatment based on gender, combined with the stigma against mental illness, could create a blind spot in which psychiatry would be rejected as a form of sexist oppression. This should not be the case. Sexism and psychiatric illness can coexist; they are not mutually exclusive. If the true goal of historical inquiry is to understand multifaceted situations as fully as possible, then the psychiatric component should be included as one piece among others that can provide a more complete understanding of this complex figure.

There are other alternative explanations sometimes offered to explain Mary Lincoln's psychiatric symptoms, but they may be difficult to evaluate for those without a background in the mental health professions. Many people have no experience with serious or psychotic-level mental illness at all and may never have seen a person suffering from such a condition. It is good for them, of course, if mental illness has never touched their friends or loved ones, but this lack of familiarity is a definite handicap in understanding the realities of evaluating and dealing with psychiatric illness—then or now. Without knowledge of the full range of psychiatric illnesses, it is hard to know how they differ in their causes and symptoms. For example, Mary Lincoln's mental or emotional difficulties are usually attributed to grief. She was cruelly aggrieved by the death of three of her four sons, and the assassination of her husband as he sat by her side.

But grief alone, either at the time or anniversary of a loss, causes a different symptom picture. Though it creates great sadness, it would not cause the delusions and hallucinations she suffered in 1875 and other times.

Other explanations have been put forth to account for Mrs. Lincoln's 1875 illness. One is migraine, but as discussed earlier in this essay, that condition cannot fully account for her psychiatric symptoms. Another sometimes offered is misuse of chloral hydrate or some other sedative substance.[42] Chloral hydrate is not without potential for danger or abuse, but here too, the symptom picture is wrong. If overused, chloral hydrate would cause excessive sedation or sleepiness, not excitement or agitation, and not delusions or hallucinations. If a person were addicted to chloral hydrate or a similar compound, then stopped it suddenly, there could be withdrawal symptoms, including a brief delirium with visual hallucinations, but it would run its course in days and not last from March to May as Mrs. Lincoln's symptoms did in 1875. And it is unlikely she was misusing chloral hydrate at the time of her hospitalization, as her medical records at Bellevue Place make no note of any withdrawal after she arrived.[43] So most likely the psychotic illness she suffered from in 1875 was just that, a psychotic illness akin to the ones we continue to see in psychiatry today.

All of this might be relatively clear, but sadly, the stigma surrounding mental illness skews the viewpoint of many observers. Both in the past and in the present, it creates a crucial dilemma—does one accept the illness and fight the stigma, or so fear the stigma that they deny the illness? I see this with patients and their families all the time, and I fear that some who study Mary Lincoln feel it as well. So perhaps a closer look is in order. Stigma means a mark of shame, but where or what is that shame as regards psychiatric illness? This stigma is not the product of rational thought, but rather arises from misunderstanding and fear, which we should be able to counter. I offer interesting points of view on denial of illness and undeserved stigma from two women who have achieved admirably despite suffering from and requiring treatment for major psychiatric illness.

The first is Elyn R. Saks, a professor of law at the University of Southern California, who, by her own acknowledgment, suffers from schizophrenia, which is definitely a major psychiatric illness. In a thoughtful essay in the *American Journal of Psychiatry*, she discussed how, for many years, she denied her illness. She alternately tried to convince herself that "everyone's mind contained the same chaos, violence, confusion and scary beliefs that mine did," or that she really was not mentally ill, or that she, herself, simply chose to have the symptoms. With treatment she came to accept her mental illness. And, her most important observation: "with this acceptance, paradoxically, my illness came to define me much less."[44]

The second is actress Carrie Fisher, widely known in our popular culture for her portrayal of Princess Leia in the *Star Wars* movies. She openly discussed her bipolar disorder in a recent autobiography, which she ended with some very straightforward remarks about her condition and reactions to it: "One of the things that baffles me . . . is how there can be so much lingering stigma with regards to mental illness, specifically bipolar disorder. In my opinion, living with manic depression takes a tremendous amount of balls. Not unlike a tour of duty in Afghanistan (though the bombs and bullets, in this case, come from inside). At times, being bipolar can be an all-consuming challenge, requiring a lot of stamina and even more courage, so if you're living with this illness and functioning at all, it's something to be proud of, not ashamed of."[45]

Their message is clear—failing to accept the reality of illness is neither helpful nor wise. In most fields of medicine, people would readily acknowledge the need to recognize and treat diabetes, or high blood pressure, or a lump in the breast. The same should be true in psychiatry. It is unnecessary to avoid Mrs. Lincoln's psychiatric symptoms. We can better honor her for bearing the burdens she faced if we fully acknowledge those burdens, including her psychiatric illness.

There is one final factor of absolutely overriding importance that must be kept in mind when evaluating the events leading to Mary Lincoln's hospitalization. When someone becomes severely ill, as Mrs. Lincoln did in 1875, *something* has to be done. That is the bottom line, then or now. No matter how disinclined such a person or their family might be to turn to psychiatry, they have a crisis and must seek help from a professional person who knows what to do. Until such an unhappy moment arises in any of our lives, it is easy to think that it never will. But if your mother had terrifying paranoid delusions, heard frightening voices, and reacted in ways that put her in danger, you would have little choice but to turn to the psychiatric profession. That is what happened to Robert Lincoln's mother in 1875 and he had no choice either.

### Notes

1. Jason Emerson, "The Madness of Mary Lincoln," *American Heritage* 57, no. 3 (June/July 2006): 56–65.

2. Jason Emerson, *The Madness of Mary Lincoln* (Carbondale: Southern Illinois University Press, 2007). I served as psychiatric consultant for this book and contributed an essay that appeared as an appendix titled "The Psychiatric Illness of Mary Lincoln," 185–90.

3. On societal views of mental illness, see Roy Porter, *Madness: A Brief History* (Oxford: Oxford University Press, 2002).

4. On asylums see Edward Shorter, *A History of Psychiatry* (New York: John Wiley and Sons, 1997), 4–22, 33–68.

5. Mark E. Neely Jr., and R. Gerald McMurtry, *The Insanity File: The Case of Mary Todd Lincoln* (Carbondale: Southern Illinois University Press, 1986), 38–39; Emerson, *The Madness of Mary Lincoln*, 71–72.

6. Neely, *Insanity File*, 6–8, 11–12; Emerson, *The Madness of Mary Lincoln*, 40, 44, 46.

7. Emerson, *The Madness of Mary Lincoln*, 23, 28–29, 45.

8. The term "psychiatry" dates to the early nineteenth century but was not frequently used in the United States until the twentieth century. Before that, those who treated the mentally ill often referred to themselves as "alienists" because they treated mental alienation. See Shorter, *A History of Psychiatry*, 17. For ease of understanding, I will use the terms psychiatry and psychiatrists throughout this essay.

9. The degree to which psychiatrists in the United States in the nineteenth century were asylum based is reflected in the name chosen for their first professional organization, the Association of Medical Superintendents of American Institutions for the Insane, founded in 1844. This became the American Psychiatric Association in 1921.

10. W. A. Evans, *Mrs. Abraham Lincoln: A Study of Her Personality and Her Influence on Lincoln* (New York: Alfred A. Knopf, 1932). This book was reprinted in 2010 by Southern Illinois University Press with an informative foreword by Jason Emerson.

11. James A. Brussel, "Mary Todd Lincoln: A Psychiatric Study," *Psychiatric Quarterly* 15, supplement 1 (January 1941): 7–26.

12. Neely, *Insanity File*, 11; Emerson, *The Madness of Mary Lincoln*, 40.

13. John M. Suarez, "Mary Todd Lincoln: A Case Study," *American Journal of Psychiatry* 122, no. 7 (January 1966): 816–19.

14. Norbert Hirschhorn and Robert G. Feldman, "Mary Lincoln's Final Illness: A Medical and Historical Reappraisal," *Journal of the History of Medicine and Allied Sciences* 54, no. 4 (October 1999): 511–42.

15. Emerson, *The Madness of Mary Lincoln*, 16, 129.

16. Ibid., 230 n. 75 contains a summary of published thought on the possibility that Mary Lincoln had syphilis.

17. In the normal eye, the pupil will constrict in response to bright light (sometimes called the light reflex), or when focusing on a near object (also known as accommodation). Argyll Robertson pupils no longer constrict in response to light but still react to accommodation. This symptom was named for Scottish ophthalmologist Douglas Argyll Robertson (1837–1909), who described it in 1869.

18. American Psychiatric Association, *Diagnostic and Statistical Manual of Mental Disorders*, 4th ed., text revision (Washington, DC: American Psychiatric Association, 2000), 463–68, hereafter cited as *DSM-IV-TR*.

19. Rodney Ross, "Mary Todd Lincoln: Patient at Bellevue Place, Batavia," *Journal of the Illinois State Historical Society* 63, no. 1 (Spring 1970): 5–34 contains a transcription of Mrs. Lincoln's daily patient notes while at Bellevue Place, and Hirschhorn and Feldman, "Mary Lincoln's Final Illness," contains the 1882 medical evaluation submitted to Congress.

20. Brust, "The Psychiatric Illness of Mary Lincoln," 185–86.

21. Emerson, *The Madness of Mary Lincoln*, 40, 103, 129, 174.

22. *DSM-IV-TR*, 740–41.

23. Katherine Helm, *The True Story of Mary, Wife of Lincoln* (New York: Harper and Brothers, 1928), 227. "Uncle Alec" was Mary's youngest half brother, Lieutenant Alexander H. Todd, who was killed while serving with Confederate forces at Baton Rouge, Louisiana, in August of 1862; see Stephen Berry, *House of Abraham: Lincoln, and the Todds; A Family Divided by War* (Boston: Houghton-Mifflin, 2007), 126–28.

24. Neely, *Insanity File*, 6, 11; Emerson, *The Madness of Mary Lincoln*, 33, 40.

25. Emerson, *The Madness of Mary Lincoln*, 44–46 gives a good description of Mary Lincoln's symptoms between March and May of 1875.

26. *DSM-IV-TR*, 349–56.

27. Neely, *Insanity File*, 15–16; Emerson, *The Madness of Mary Lincoln*, 24, 45–46.

28. *DSM-IV-TR*, 357–62. The terms *manic depressive illness* and *bipolar disorder* had not yet come into use during Mary Lincoln's lifetime, but for ease of understanding, I will use them.

29. Emerson, *The Madness of Mary Lincoln*, 25.

30. Ibid., 46.

31. Ibid., 101.

32. *DSM-IV-TR*, 422–23.

33. Michael Burlingame, *Abraham Lincoln: A Life* (Baltimore: Johns Hopkins University Press, 2008), unedited manuscript on the Knox College website <http://www.knox.edu/Academics/Distinctive-Programs/Lincoln-Studies-Center/Burlingame-Abraham-Lincoln-A-Life.html>, 538–39, accessed August 5, 2010.

34. Ibid., 535–40.

35. Neely, *Insanity File*, 34–35; Emerson, *The Madness of Mary Lincoln*, 67–70; Norbert Hirschhorn, "Mary Lincoln's 'Suicide Attempt': A Physician Reconsiders the Evidence," *Lincoln Herald* 104, no. 3 (Fall 2003): 94–98. Laudanum is a liquid medication containing various forms of opium. Like other narcotics, it is usually taken to relieve pain, but since an overdose can cause fatal suppression of breathing, laudanum ingestion was a frequent method of suicide in the nineteenth century.

36. Shorter, *A History of Psychiatry*, 274–77.

37. For a good review of the history of manic-depressive illness/bipolar disorder, see Frederick K. Goodwin and Kay Redfield Jamison, *Manic-Depressive Illness* (New York: Oxford University Press, 1990), 56–61, 70.

38. Jean H. Baker, *Mary Todd Lincoln: A Biography* (New York: W. W. Norton, 1987).

39. Ibid., 317–18, 323–24.

40. Neely, *Insanity File*, 19–21; Emerson, *The Madness of Mary Lincoln*, 55–56.

41. Ross, "Mary Todd Lincoln: Patient at Bellevue Place," 32, quote from patient record entry for August 6, 1875.

42. Baker, *Mary Todd Lincoln: A Biography*, 324, 331, 345; and Catherine Clinton, *Mrs. Lincoln: A Life* (New York: HarperCollins, 2009), 300, 304–5. Chloral hydrate was the first sedative synthesized in the laboratory (1832) and was used extensively in psychiatry beginning in the late 1860s. Though it has largely been replaced by other agents, it remains available today and I still prescribe it on rare occasion. See Louis S. Goodman and Alfred Gilman, *The Pharmacological Basis of Therapeutics*, 3rd ed. (New York: MacMillan, 1965), 131–34; and Shorter, *A History of Psychiatry*, 198–99.

43. Ross, "Mary Todd Lincoln: Patient at Bellevue Place," 26–34.

44. Elyn Saks, JD, "Some Thoughts on Denial of Mental Illness," *American Journal of Psychiatry* 166, no. 9 (September 2009): 972–73. On schizophrenia, see *DSM-IV-TR*, 297–317.

45. Carrie Fisher, *Wishful Drinking* (New York: Simon and Schuster, 2008), 159.

## "I Miss Bob, So Much"
### Mary Lincoln's Relationship with Her Oldest Son

*Jason Emerson*

Leo Tolstoy's famous adage, "Happy families are all alike; every unhappy family is unhappy in its own way," is one of the great truisms in world literature. When considering the happiness or unhappiness of the Lincoln family—particularly the relationship between Mary and her oldest son, Robert—it is necessary to keep this apothegm in mind because the connection between mother and son is not only incredibly complex, but often misunderstood. Quite simply, Mary's relationship with Robert was one of the closest and most important of her entire life. It went beyond the typical mother-son experience and into nearly unparalleled areas of triumph and tragedy, death and murder, fame and infamy, and, ultimately, arrest and insanity. But how and why did Mary and Robert turn from a nearly inseparable closeness to a five-year rift that ended only months before Mary's own death in 1882?

Mary Lincoln is a difficult woman to understand, as nearly all of her biographers have discovered. Perhaps the most quoted assertion to this effect was by Elizabeth Keckley, Mary's White House seamstress, who wrote, "I never in my life saw a more peculiarly constituted woman. Search the world over, and you will not find her counterpart."[1] Unfortunately, Mary's actions during her life were so interesting, sometimes notorious, and even bizarre, that most books about her rarely delve beyond the obvious and ubiquitous surface.

Mary is a different woman to each new generation of historians. To the Victorians of the late nineteenth century she was a mere side character; to the modernists of the early-to-mid-twentieth century she was a loving and attentive wife and mother; to the postmodernists of the late twentieth and early twenty-first centuries she was (and is) a feminist icon superior in political skill and intellect to her husband. Robert Lincoln is generally disregarded by Lincoln scholars—who typically see him as an aristocratic prig who knew nothing about his famous parents' lives and cared even less—and so interpretations of his life are negligible. The portrayal of Robert as a person and as his mother's son has—like his mother's image—changed with the times, and his most distinguished and recognized characterization today is in the postmodernist epithets of misogynist, racist, and rapacious aristocrat.

To understand the Mary-Robert relationship requires recognition of the four distinct periods of Mary Lincoln's adult life, and the realization that she was a different person during each different period: the Springfield years (1839–1860), the Washington years (1861–1865), the postassassination years (1865–1875), and the postinsanity years (1875–1882). Just as Mary Lincoln was a different person in each of the different periods of her life, so her relationship with Robert was vastly different in each period as well.

The Mary Todd with whom Abraham Lincoln fell in love and whom he eventually married was one of the shining lights of Springfield society—and remained so until the family's departure for Washington in 1861. She was beautiful and intelligent, vivacious and witty, and full of charm, grace, and culture. As one young lawyer wrote in 1840, "She is the very creature of excitement."[2] Conversely, she had a mercurial temper, could be biting and sarcastic, and was occasionally petulant and selfish. But the Springfield years were arguably the happiest of her life, and she was remembered there more for her genial and attractive attributes than for her negative ones.

Both Mary and Abraham loved children—one of the characteristics they shared—and their family started quickly with the birth of their son Robert Todd Lincoln on August 1, 1843, only nine months after the wedding. Robert was followed three years later by second son, Edward Baker "Eddie" Lincoln. Mary, typical of any mother, coveted her children and her role as mother, as the few existent stories of Robert's infancy illustrate. One neighbor recalled that baby Robert suffered from the diarrheal disorder called "summer complaint," for which his mother would adamantly drive around the streets of Springfield every day in the cool of the morning with him on a pillow to help him get well.[3] One of the Lincolns' hired girls remembered how Mary Lincoln once refused to invite her cousin to a party because the cousin had "intimated that Robert who was a baby was a sweet child but not good looking."[4]

Abraham and Mary adored and indulged their children—to the point of spoliation; their parental philosophy was, in fact, to "Let the children have a good time."[5] While Abraham Lincoln was universally characterized as "the very best kindest father I ever saw," and spent as much time as possible with his sons, he typically was away from home for six to eight months of the year on business.[6] Even though this was not an extraordinary situation at the time (other lawyers and judges "on the circuit" lived the same way), and Mary had numerous family and friends in Springfield for support, still she was, as one of her biographers accurately characterized, a single parent most of the time.[7] As a consequence, Mary had the primary responsibility to raise (and discipline) the children: teach them manners, social etiquette, reading, writing, and other early and necessary life lessons.[8]

Biographer Gamaliel Bradford once wrote, "It is with her children that Mrs. Lincoln is most attractive"—but it was also where she was most vulnerable.[9] The stories of her terror, even paranoia, of Robert's being injured or killed are famous: Whenever she could not find her oldest son, she would run through the streets screaming, "Bobbie is lost! Bobbie is lost!" and once when she found him playing in the lye in the privy, she became hysterical and ran into her front yard screaming, "Bobbie will die! Bobbie will die!"[10] In an age of high infant mortality, Mary's fear is understandable, and unfortunately it came to fruition all too soon with the death of three-year-old Eddie in 1850 from tuberculosis.[11]

Eddie's death was the catalyst that enabled an extraordinary closeness between Mary and her six-year-old son, Robert. Not only did Mary cling ever tighter to her surviving son, but Robert also gave his mother comfort—especially as the "man" of the house when his father was gone. In fact, Abraham Lincoln left home for nearly eight weeks only two months after Eddie's death, leaving Robert alone to cope with his mother's bereavement.[12] It may have been during this period that Robert's great humor and storytelling ability—so like his father and often commented upon by friends and observers in his later years—developed in order to help his mother smile.[13]

Ten months after Eddie's death, the third Lincoln son, Willie, was born, and three years later followed the final son, Tad. Robert, older than his brothers by seven and nine years respectively, was somewhat apart from them. While Willie and Tad were best friends, Robert's natural companion, Eddie, was gone; and instead his close companion at home became his mother. Mary and Robert shared many interests and activities in common. They both loved reading literature and poetry; they took piano lessons together and shared a skill and interest in the French language, in which both were fluent and Mary most likely began Robert's instruction. Mary was a highly educated woman and encouraged and assisted Robert's education in Springfield during the years 1850–1859.[14]

During these years of his childhood and adolescence, Robert was not only the oldest son but acted as his mother's social and intellectual companion, and also in many ways her protector. When his father was gone Robert was the man of the house; he not only did the male chores but also acted as an anodyne to his mother's emotionalism. Mary was a highstrung woman (a Todd family trait) and suffered from many fears (both rational and irrational). Many of her terrors occurred at night, when she feared burglars, and when she was particularly afraid of lightning and thunderstorms. When Robert was a child and his father was away, a local neighbor boy often would stay at the Lincoln home. As Robert grew older, he became the calming presence to his mother when her fears gripped and overpowered her.

When sixteen-year-old Robert left home in summer 1859 to attend school in the East, Mary felt "quite lonely" at her oldest son's leave-taking. "It almost appears as if light and mirth, had departed with him," she wrote.[15] Two months later she wrote, "I miss Bob, so much, that I do not feel settled down, as much as I used to and find myself going on trips quite frequently."[16] Traveling was actually another interest mother and son shared, and while Robert was away at school over the next five years, it would be their main recreation together. They made plans to travel to the White Mountains of New Hampshire in summer 1860—Mary missed Robert so much she was "*wild* to see him" after their separation of "almost *a year, a long year,*" she lamented that June—but the presidential campaign interposed.[17]

It was not until January 1861 that Mary finally saw her oldest son again. By then, Robert was a student at Harvard College, Abraham Lincoln had been elected president, and Mary was the First Lady-to-be. Mary traveled to New York City in order to purchase new clothing befitting her role as First Lady, and Robert, whose college term had just ended, met his mother there. The two shopped together for a few days (stylish clothing was another interest they shared) and returned together to Springfield to prepare for the inaugural journey to Washington.[18]

From the middle-class days as Springfield housewife and mother and the heady days of the presidential election season, the reality of life in the White House was something of a rude awakening for Mary Lincoln. Washington was not a welcoming town for the "Rail-Splitter's" wife: To the North she was a Southern sympathizer; to the South she was a traitor; to the easterners in the capital she was an uncouth western rube. She simply could do nothing right. As one biography of her astutely observed,

"No president's wife in history had a more turbulent career in the White House than Mary Todd Lincoln. None took up her duties under more difficult circumstances; none was so consistently criticized, none so vulnerable to criticism."[19] Her years as First Lady turned her from a genial (although temperamental) wife and mother of three to the eccentric, infamous, criticized, accused, abused, and harassed woman she is better known as today.

One way for her to escape all the Washington invective was to travel, and her oldest son often was her companion. Robert met his mother during many of her trips to New York, Philadelphia, and Boston, where the two would not only spend hours together shopping in the most fashionable stores, but also entertaining with social, political, and military leaders. Mary also visited Robert at Cambridge when she could, at least once a year. Every summer, mother and son spent one to two weeks traveling around New England on vacation: in August 1861 to Long Branch, New Jersey, for two weeks; in 1862 to New York City for one week; in 1863 to the White Mountains of New Hampshire for one week; and in 1864 from Boston to New York City to Manchester, Vermont, for a total trip of about ten days.

Robert also visited the White House during every break from school he had, where he spent time with friends and family. "Robert will be home from Cambridge in about six weeks and will spend his vacation with us," his mother wrote in anticipation in May 1862. "He has grown and improved more than any one you ever saw."[20] As the summer of 1862 neared its end, Mary told a friend that Robert was "very companionable," and she lamented, "I shall dread when he has to return to Cambridge."[21] Robert's friend Richard Meconkey, who spent much of July 1861 at the White House, said that he and "Bob" took a carriage ride with Mrs. Lincoln every afternoon, and that she and her oldest son loved to play practical jokes on each other. "Mrs. Lincoln is a 'perfect brick,'" Meconkey wrote, "generally up to some joke upon us, and you may bet that we reciprocate a little."[22]

One of Mary's pleasures as Robert grew older was to look for the right girl and attempt to make a marital match for him. Her preferred

Washington belle was Mary Eunice Harlan, the beautiful and cultured daughter of Iowa senator James Harlan. "Mary is tremendously in love with Senator Harlan's little daughter," President Lincoln once supposedly said. "I think she has picked her out for a daughter-in-law. As usual, I think Mary has shown fine taste."[23] Another reminiscence states that Mary Lincoln first saw Mary Harlan at an opera and said, "I should like Robert to marry just such a girl as that," to which her husband observed to Senator Charles Sumner, "My wife is a great matchmaker. She will make a match between Harlan's daughter and Bob; see if she don't."[24] The First Lady often invited the entire Harlan family on outings with her as a way to get Robert and Mary together. It worked well. Robert invited Mary to attend his Harvard graduation, he escorted her to his father's second inaugural, and, in 1868, he married her.

But for all of this mother-son closeness, Robert still was a young adult (he turned twenty in August 1863) and a college student and had his own ideas and opinions and wanted his own personal time to himself. In fact, much of his time with his mother was curtailed by or shared with time with his friends. When Robert accompanied his mother to Long Branch, New Jersey in summer 1861, he invited a group of college friends to go with him; they shared an apartment adjacent to Mary's hotel and spent more time with each other than with the First Lady. When Robert spent summers in the White House, he often brought friends home with him, such as Dick Meconkey or Clinton Conkling, and spent much time with presidential secretary John Hay. When Robert escorted his mother and brother Tad to Manchester, Vermont, in summer 1864, he spent only one night with them at the Equinox House before abandoning them for his college friends at Saratoga, New York.

Robert's increasing age and independence led to typical family disagreements as well. The major dispute between Mary and her oldest son was her refusal to allow him to join the Union army at the outbreak of the war. Mary was terrified that Robert would be killed in battle, and after losing son Eddie in 1850, she told her husband she could not bear to lose another.[25] Lincoln told his wife not to be so selfish, but, understanding her emotional frailty and anxiety, he acquiesced to her wishes. Robert deeply resented and was embarrassed by his parents' decision. Administration critics around the country called Robert a coward and a shirker. He continued to ask for permission to enlist every year he was in college, but after his brother Willie's death in 1862, Mary's panic at the thought of losing Robert was nearly insurmountable. It was only at the war's end when Robert was allowed to join, but even then he was placed in a safe general staff position.

Another famous disagreement between Mary and Robert occurred in February 1863, when the First Lady hosted a party in honor of General Tom Thumb, the well-known dwarf. "Tom Thumb had been caressed by royalty in the Old World, and why should not the wife of the President of his native country smile upon him also?" Mary supposedly asked. To Robert's New England Victorianism, however, the entertainment was undignified, even ridiculous, and he refused to attend. "My notions of duty, perhaps, are somewhat different from yours," he told his mother. Mary's White House seamstress, Elizabeth Keckley, commented on the incident, "Robert had a lofty soul, and he could not stoop to all the follies and absurdities of the ephemeral current of fashionable life."[26]

In July 1863, Robert again snubbed his mother when he neither came home nor telegraphed her in the wake of a serious carriage accident she suffered that turned out to be an act of sabotage.[27] The president telegraphed Robert at Cambridge not to worry, "Your mother very slightly hurt by her fall"; but when Robert did not come immediately to see his mother and ignored the missive, his father irritably remonstrated, "Why do I hear no more of you?"[28] Robert arrived at the White House the next day, but the emotional damage to his mother had been done.

Throughout the entirety of the war, even though Robert was away at school, he was aware of the negative publicity about his mother, such as the accusations that she was a Rebel spy and that she accepted bribes and gifts in exchange for political favors, and the criticisms of her penchant for shopping and owning fine goods in a time of war.[29] Some incidents utterly humiliated Robert, such as on one trip to City Point when Mary lashed out in a verbal harangue at a general's wife for riding too close to the president.[30] Mary Lincoln had always had a vicious temper and a wicked tongue, which Robert knew all about from his childhood, but suffering the vagaries of Washington—the negative press, social and political snubs, the accusations, the preoccupied husband, the death of her son Willie—clearly made things worse for Mary. Robert later said his mother never fully recovered from the head injury she received after her carriage accident, but he believed that it was his father's murder that truly unhinged his mother's mind.

The night of April 14, as the mortally wounded Abraham Lincoln lay comatose in the Petersen House attended by doctors, Mary Lincoln was either in the sickroom or in the front parlor, sobbing and hysterical. Robert spent the majority of the evening comforting his mother. After the assassination, Robert Lincoln, age twenty-one, found himself returned to his previous occasional childhood role as the head of the family. The difference in 1865, however, was that Robert was a grown man and his mother was an emotionally distraught—even disturbed—widow. The social mores of the time required that Robert be more than a son and traveling companion to his mother—he was duty-bound to care for her and to protect her as his father would if he were alive. This was a duty Robert took very seriously because he believed deeply in the Victorian honor code of the day—a belief system if not instilled then certainly inculcated into him during the five years he lived in New England during his higher education.

Robert sacrificed whatever plans for the future he had considered and instead moved with his mother and younger brother, Tad, to Chicago. There he resumed his law studies (begun at Harvard) at the University of Chicago, and also clerking at the law office of Scammon, McCagg, and Fuller. Mary was proud of and also felt guilty over Robert's dedication to her. "Poor Robert, has borne his sorrows, manfully, yet with a broken heart," she wrote. When Robert was invited on a trip to Cuba with a friend, he decided it was his "duty" to stay in Chicago and continue his studies in order to begin his career—and thereby take better care of his family—as soon as possible.[31]

Robert was no selfless saint, as no young man of twenty-one is, and at times he clearly resented the changes in his life. When the family first moved to Chicago in May 1865, Robert was not happy by the cramped accommodations at their hotel in Hyde Park. "I presume that I must put up with it, as mother's pleasure must be consulted before my own. But candidly, I would almost as soon be dead as be compelled to remain three months in this dreary house," he told Elizabeth Keckley.[32] He moved into his own apartment as soon as he could, although he visited his mother and brother every Sunday.

Over the next ten years, Mary Lincoln considered her oldest son to be a blessing to her—in 1871 she called him "all that is noble and good"—and showered him with all the love and generosity she could.[33] She loaned him money, postponed her European trip with Tad to attend Robert's wedding to Mary Harlan in 1868, sent her son and daughter-in-law money and gifts from Europe, and as they were setting up their new house, told them to take and use anything of hers that was in storage in Chicago. Mary's letters are filled with lavish praise over her son; and she more than once bestowed upon him the greatest compliment during her widowhood she could give, such as when she declared in 1868, "Robert grows every day, more and more like his father."[34]

For his part, Robert Lincoln did his duty by taking care of his father's will and papers (assisting estate administrator David Davis); he took charge of Tad's education and became the boy's mentor, even idol. He tried to help his mother with her estate and investments by suggesting stocks and bonds for her, by advising her against buying her Chicago home (which she eventually sold because she could not afford), and by preventing her purchase of a second Chicago house after he (who was a real estate and insurance lawyer) read the proposed lease and pointed out its numerous flaws. While Mary and Tad were in Europe, Robert and his wife kept a constant correspondence with his mother, always telling her of their love and encouraging her to come home and live with them in Chicago. He also named his first daughter Mary after his mother.

After Tad Lincoln died at age seventeen in 1871, Mary was distraught and depressed. She had now lost three sons and her husband, and felt like heartache and tragedy were to be her lot in life. "Ill luck presided at my birth," she told her daughter-in-law, "certainly within the last few years it has been a *faithful attendant.*"[35] Robert invited his mother to live with him and his wife, which she did for about six months, until the two Marys had a falling out. Apparently, Mary Todd Lincoln was so demanding, commanding, and even spiteful towards her daughter-in-law and the way the house was run that the only way Robert could end the trouble was to send his mother away.[36] During these years Mary Lincoln's physical and mental health continued to deteriorate, and when she left Chicago in 1872, a concerned Robert hired a nurse to accompany his mother and act as her caregiver and companion, which she was for the next three years. She spent the next three years traveling the United States, visiting health spas and Spiritualist retreats.

By March 1875, Mary Lincoln was suffering from mental troubles including hallucinations, delusions, paranoia, and depression. Her statements and actions had become so bizarre and worrisome to her son that he consulted seven of the region's best medical experts and three of his father's closest friends seeking advice. They all advised him that his mother was insane and needed medical treatment.[37] Since Mary did not believe herself insane and would not acquiesce to medical treatment, thirty-one-year-old Robert Lincoln followed Illinois's legal strictures for the situation: He had an arrest warrant sworn out for his mother and had her brought to court to stand trial for insanity. Although Mary was given no notice or warning of that legal action against her, Robert did arrange for her to have an attorney in court.[38]

Mary's insanity trial lasted for three hours, during which time eighteen witnesses—doctors, hotel employees, and shopkeepers—testified that she was mentally impaired and needed medical treatment. In addition to the testimony of her primary physician, Dr. Willis Danforth, the most damning testimony against her came from her son, Robert. Pale and teary-eyed, breaking down in tears more than once, Mary's last living son told the court of his mother's eccentric behaviors and statements, that he was in constant anxiety for her safety, and that he had "no doubt" she was insane. "She has been of unsound mind since the death of father; has been irresponsible for the past ten years," he said.[39] The jury took less than ten minutes to declare Mary Lincoln insane and a fit person to be committed to a sanitarium for medical treatment. Robert was subsequently named the conservator of his mother's estate, and had total control of her property and finances.

Robert Lincoln—and all of his advisors—honestly believed his mother was insane, and he took this legal action in order to protect her from herself and from other people. Robert's attorney, B. F. Ayer, said during the trial that Robert's actions were taken "through feelings of concern for his mother's safety," and that Mary Lincoln's friends and family "feared some harm might befall her unless she is placed under restraint."[40] Mary Lincoln, however—who for years had suffered from paranoia and delusions about money and finances—saw the entire trial as a nefarious plot by her traitorous son to lock her up and steal her money. This belief festered in her mind like a cankerous sore until the pain of it finally overwhelmed her, causing a severe, nearly irretrievable, rift in their relationship.

During the one-year period from May 1875 to June 1876, while Mary was legally insane and Robert acted as her conservator, their relationship bottomed out—all because of Mary's paranoia and mania concerning money. She wanted control of her estate, which Robert could not legally give her and, despite his attempts, could find no one to take his place as conservator. After four months in Bellevue Place sanitarium, Mary lived with her sister and brother-in-law, the Edwardses, in Springfield, and they often were the intermediaries between mother and son. They constantly informed Robert of his mother's needs and desires, and especially of her anger at him. Robert accommodated his mother on nearly everything she wanted, sending her money and personal possessions she demanded—everything except control of her estate—to which as his uncle eventually told him, "Your mother for the last two or three weeks has been very much embittered against you, and the more you have yielded the more immeasurable she seems to be." It was around this time that Mary said she hired two men to murder her son; and she also carried a pistol in her pocket and declared she would shoot Robert if he ever came in her presence again.[41]

Mary became so intractable and agitated, and then so bent on resuming her shopping and spending sprees, that Robert threatened to send her back to the asylum. He told his uncle, "[My mother] has always been exceedingly generous to me," for which he was grateful, "but being grateful merely will not discharge my duty to her even if necessary against her will."[42] In the end, he decided (and was advised by David Davis) to allow his mother leeway and eventual freedom from legal restraint. Mary Lincoln's second trial, in June 1876, declared her restored to reason. Robert did not fight the trial or any of the judgments. Although he did not consider her returned to sanity, he did this to appease his mother, to avoid open conflict with her, and to rid himself of the onus of further conservatorship.

When Mary was released, she quickly fled to Europe in a self-imposed exile. Part of the reason she left America was that she could not stand the way everyone looked at her as if she were insane; but the main reason was that she feared her son would commit her again. (Robert later said he never would do so, because "the ordinary troubles and distresses of life are enough without such as that."[43]) So Mary secretly fled Springfield for New York, boarded a steamer, and returned to Pau, France, which she had visited previously with Tad, and stayed there for the next four years.

Mary was so angry and bitter over what her son had done that she refused to communicate with him, and even avoided writing his name, generally referring to him only as "RTL," "that one," or one of numerous epithets such as "monster of mankind." She credited her separation from

Robert as contributing to her tranquility, writing in 1876, "I am allowed tranquility here and am not harassed by a demon."[44] Their estrangement was so thorough that in 1877, Robert even admitted to a correspondent that he did not know his mother's address, only that she was "somewhere in Europe."[45]

Mary's antipathy for her son did not extend to her granddaughter, Mary, to whom she continually sent gifts from her European exile. Robert believed these packages offered a hope that one day his mother would forgive him. When his aunt Elizabeth Edwards suggested to Robert in 1879 that he send a letter to his mother to help repair the family breach, Robert replied, "I am afraid a letter from me would not be well received. If I could persuade myself otherwise, I would write to her at once and not think I was making any concession, for I have not allowed her anger at me to have any other effect upon me than regret that she should so feel and express herself towards me." But he also admitted that his mother's animosity towards him was very "distressing," and he hoped one day it would end.[46]

It took two more years, but Mary and Robert's reconciliation finally did occur in May 1881—after five years of estrangement. Mary was then living at the Edwards home in Springfield, after returning to the United States in October 1880 due to deteriorating health.[47] She did not inform her son of her return. Robert was at that time President James A. Garfield's secretary of war and in mid-May left Washington for an official visit to Fort Leavenworth, Kansas. He stopped in Springfield from May 26 to May 27 on his way west, and spent an entire day with his mother at the Edwards home.[48]

The origin of this meeting is unknown, but it is logical that Elizabeth Edwards was the architect. She was the mother figure who understood her stubborn younger sister, and the matriarch who respected Robert and always regretted the mother-son rift. Elizabeth was in fact probably the only person who *could* have brought them together; and she had for years had been urging both sides to mend fences. While Robert had been willing, Mary never was. But by spring 1881, sick, lonely, missing her granddaughter, and perhaps finally softening in her anger at her son, Mary Lincoln relented. Whatever occurred at this meeting has gone unrecorded, but it resulted in Mary's forgiveness.

Tradition erroneously holds that Robert was in the city on a personal visit and brought his daughter, Mamie, with him—Mary Lincoln's little namesake whom she adored—as a way to help smooth the peace. This is a case of historical hearsay, and primary evidence proves it a myth. Historians W. A. Evans and Carl Sandburg began the Mamie story in separate 1932 biographies, both without citation. Sandburg's account was especially egregious, however, as he claimed Robert's entire family went to Springfield to see Mary. The newspaper accounts and Robert's letters prove this untrue. In 1953, Ruth Painter Randall, who cited Evans, repeated the Mamie story, and it has been considered authentic by subsequent historians.[49]

For the rest of Mary's life, Robert (usually with his family) visited his mother every few weeks; when Mary stayed in New York City for medical treatment from October 1881 to March 1882, she saw her son every week.[50] Just as he had after his brother Tad's death in 1871, in 1881 Robert invited his ailing mother to live with his family in Washington, and to allow him to help pay her bills. She refused the offer because he was a grown man with a family and she did not want to intrude.[51] One thing that Robert and his wife Mary did do for his mother, however, was to get her government pension increased.

After the assassination of President Garfield, Congress granted the president's widow, Lucretia Garfield, a lifetime pension based on the Mary Lincoln precedent. But instead of the $3,000 Mary Lincoln received in 1870, Lucretia Garfield was given $5,000. Although ill and ailing, Mary Lincoln was insulted and incensed at the disparity, and was roused for one final battle with the Congress in order to get paid on par with Mrs. Garfield. She began to write letters and make requests of congressional Republicans for parity in her widow's pension. But it was Mary Harlan Lincoln, supported by her husband, Robert, who succeeded in getting her mother-in-law's money. Robert's wife approached Cyrus Field—the man responsible for achieving a hugely successful subscription fund for Mrs. Garfield—to lobby Congress for the increase in Mary Lincoln's pension to $5,000 per year.[52] Legislation "for the relief of Mrs. Lincoln"—sponsored by Senator John A. Logan of Illinois and supported by Secretary of War Lincoln—was passed without any controversy.[53] It not only increased her annual pension but also paid her $15,000 in back payments.[54]

Mary Lincoln died of a stroke on July 16, 1882. A few days earlier, her health had declined so dramatically that her death seemed imminent. Her son, Robert, was telegraphed and kept constantly updated on her critical condition. Robert, assisted by his Aunt Elizabeth, planned his mother's funeral as close as possible to her final wishes, which she had written out for him in 1874.[55] His mother's body was laid out for private viewing for family and friends in the parlor of the Edwards home, the same room in which she was married, in a white silk dress.[56] Mary's funeral was held in the First Presbyterian Church of Springfield on Wednesday, July 19, and was characterized as nearly the largest funeral in the city's history, second only to that of her husband.[57] Robert attended with his aunts and uncles, as well as some personal Chicago friends, but without his family.[58] Mary's casket, accompanied by an enormous funeral cortege of citizens and admirers, was conveyed to the Lincoln tomb in Oak Ridge Cemetery. There it was placed in crypt number 4, alongside her sons Eddie, Willie, and Tad, and her beloved husband.

Robert Lincoln had spent his entire adult life trying to protect his mother from the selfish motives of untrustworthy people. He warned her about questionable business investments, shady Spiritualist mediums, and general unsavory companions. After her death, Mary's last surviving son had one final act of protection to undertake. The night before the funeral, Robert met with his cousin John Todd Stuart, who also was chairman of the Executive Committee of the National Lincoln Monument Association. Robert feared for the safety of his mother's remains, feared someone would attempt to steal her body as they had attempted to steal her husband's six years earlier, so he arranged with Stuart to have his mother's body secretly removed from the crypt and buried next to his father in the basement of the tomb, where he had been secretly buried in 1879.

At 10 P.M. on the night of July 21, two days after Mary Lincoln's burial, eight members of the Lincoln Guard of Honor—the men sworn to protect the remains of Abraham Lincoln—gathered at the Lincoln monument. They removed Mary Lincoln's coffin from crypt number 4, carried it down into the catacombs of the Lincoln tomb monument, and buried it under the dirt floor beside the remains of her husband. Upon learning that the reburial had been completed, Robert wrote a letter of thanks to the men of the Lincoln Guard of Honor, stating that they had "laid me under a great obligation by carrying out the wish I expressed . . . that my mother's body should be placed beside my father's, so that there can be no danger of a spoliation. It is a great satisfaction to know that such an act is now impossible, and I think it will be best that no change should be made for a long time to come."[59]

## Notes

1. Elizabeth Keckley, *Behind the Scenes; or, Thirty Years a Slave, and Four Years in the White House* (New York: G. W. Carleton, 1868), 182.

2. James C. Conkling to Mercy Ann Levering, September 21, 1840, Folder 1, Box 1, Conkling Family Papers, Manuscripts Division, Abraham Lincoln Presidential Library.

3. Statement by Emily Huntington Stuart, quoted in Beulah Gordon, untitled unpublished essay, 7, Mary Todd Lincoln Vertical File, Sangamon Valley Collection, Lincoln Library, Springfield, IL.

4. Harriet A. Chapman, interview by Jesse Weik, 1886–1887, Douglas L. Wilson and Rodney O. Davis, eds., *Herndon's Informants: Letters, Interviews, and Statements about Abraham Lincoln* (Urbana: University of Illinois Press, 1998), 646.

5. Julia Taft Bayne, *Tad Lincoln's Father* (1931; reprinted, Lincoln: University of Nebraska Press [Bison Books], 2001), 47.

6. Robert later wrote about his father's constant absences, stating, "During my childhood and early youth he was almost constantly away from home, attending court or making political speeches." Frances Todd Wallace, interview by William Herndon, 1865–1866, Wilson and Davis, *Herndon's Informants*, 485; Robert T. Lincoln to Josiah G. Holland, June 6, 1865, Robert Todd Lincoln Family Papers, Manuscripts Division, Library of Congress.

7. Jean Baker, *Mary Todd Lincoln: A Biography* (New York.: W. W. Norton, 1987), 120.

8. Lincoln's absence from home upset Mary a great deal. She once told a neighbor that if her husband stayed home "as he ought to" she could "love him better." James Gourley, interview by William Herndon, February 9, 1866, LN 2408, 2:124–30, Ward Hill Lamon Papers, Huntington Library, San Marino, CA.

9. Gamaliel Bradford, *Wives* (New York: Harper and Brothers, 1925), 30.

10. Elizabeth Lushbaugh Capps, "Early Recollections of Abraham Lincoln," n.d., Reminiscences Folder, Lincoln Collection, Abraham Lincoln Presidential Library.

11. Eddie died on February 1, 1850, after a fifty-two-day struggle. It was one month before his fourth birthday. US Census 1850, Mortality Schedule for Springfield, Sangamon Co., IL, 787, MS., Illinois State Archives; *Illinois Daily Journal*, February. 2, 1850; Abraham Lincoln to John D. Johnston, February 23, 1850, Roy P. Basler, Marion Dolores Pratt, and Lloyd A. Dunlap, eds., *The Collected Works of Abraham Lincoln* (New Brunswick, NJ.: Rutgers University Press, 1953–55), 2:76–77. For an excellent summary of Eddie's life and death see, Harry Pratt, "Little Eddie Lincoln—We Miss Him Very Much," *Journal of the Illinois State Historical Society* 47 (1954): 300–305.

12. Earl Schenck Miers, *Lincoln Day by Day* (Dayton: Morningside, 1991), 2:27–34.

13. This is a common role oldest children take on upon the death of a younger sibling. One well-known modern example is former president George W. Bush's role as family clown, which developed at age seven after the death of his three-year-old sister Robin from leukemia. His father, George H. W. Bush, was often away on business, and George W. used humor to ease his mother's suffering. Bill Minutaglio, *First Son: George W. Bush and the Bush Family Dynasty* (New York: Three Rivers, 1999), 45–47.

14. Mary once boasted to a friend in 1853 that ten-year-old Robert was studying Latin and Greek. Mary Lincoln to Margaret W. Preston, Springfield, IL., July 23, 1853, Box 48, Wickliffe-Preston Papers (63M349), Special Collections and Digital Programs, University of Kentucky Libraries.

15. Mary Lincoln to Hannah Shearer, Springfield, August 28, 1859, Justin G. Turner and Linda Levitt Turner, *Mary Todd Lincoln: Her Life and Letters* (New York: Alfred A. Knopf, 1972), 58.

16. Mary Lincoln to Hannah Shearer, Springfield, October 2, 1859, ibid., 59.

17. Emphasis in original. Mary Lincoln to Adeline Judd, Springfield, June 13, 1860, Turner and Turner, *Mary Todd Lincoln*, 64.

18. "Personal," *Chicago Tribune*, January 17, 1861, 2; Mercy Levering Conkling to Clinton Conkling, Springfield, January 19, 1861, and Clinton Conkling to Mercy Levering Conkling, New Haven, January 20, 1861, and James Conkling to Clinton Conkling, Springfield, January 30, 1861, Folder 15, Box 1, Conkling Family Papers, Abraham Lincoln Presidential Library; Julia Jayne Trumbull to Walter Trumbull, Washington, January 30, 1861, Walter Trumbull Papers, Rare Book, Manuscript, and Special Collections, Duke University, Durham, NC; "Personal," *Chicago Tribune*, January 17, 1861, 2; "From New York," *Hartford Daily Courant*, January 23,

1861, 3; "Return of Mrs. Lincoln," *Illinois Journal*, January 28, 1861, 1; "The Incoming Administration," *New York Herald*, February 1, 1861, 5.

19. Turner and Turner, *Mary Todd Lincoln*, 77.

20. Mary Lincoln to Julia Sprigg, May 29, 1862, first published in Carlos W. Goltz, *Incidents in the Life of Mary Todd Lincoln: Containing an Unpublished Letter* (Sioux City, IA: Deitch and Lamar, 1928), 35. Goltz also printed his interview with Mrs. Sprigg from January 1928, when she was age seventy-six, see pages 47–54. See also Turner and Turner, *Mary Todd Lincoln*, 127–28.

21. Mary Lincoln to Mrs. Charles Eames, Soldiers' Home, July 26, 1862, Turner and Turner, *Mary Todd Lincoln*, 131.

22. Exactly what some of these jokes were, Meconkey does not state. Richard Meconkey to Jennie Johnson, Executive Mansion, Washington, July 28, 1861, Florence Bowen Jacobs Murtagh Collection, MG4.23, Chester County Historical Society, West Chester, PA.

23. Katherine Helm, *The True Story of Mary, Wife of Lincoln* (New York: Harper and Brothers, 1928), 274–75.

24. Reminiscence of Mrs. William Preston, printed in "Mrs. Lincoln's Ambition," untitled, undated newspaper clipping in Box 74, Randall Family Papers, Manuscripts Division, Library of Congress. See also Miriam Elkins to James Gordon Bennett, February 23, 1865, James Gordon Bennett Papers, Duke University, Durham, NC.

25. By 1863, after the death of numerous family members in the war and of her son Willie in 1862, Emily Todd Helm, Mary's sister, told the president that Mary's mental state seemed so precarious that she felt that "if anything should happen to you or Robert or Tad it would kill her." Helm, *True Story of Mary*, 225–26, 229–30; Keckley, *Behind the Scenes*, 121–22.

26. Keckley, *Behind the Scenes*, 122–24.

27. "Serious Accident to Mrs. Lincoln," *Washington Evening Star*, July 2, 1863, 2; "Accident to Mrs. Lincoln," *(Washington, DC) National Intelligencer*, July 3, 1863, 3; Anna L. Boyden, *War Reminiscences; or, Echoes from Hospital and White House* (Boston: D. Lathrop, 1887), 143–44.

28. Basler et al., *Collected Works*, 6:314, 323, 327.

29. For an examination of Mary's questionable actions as First Lady, see Michael Burlingame, "Mary Todd Lincoln's Unethical Conduct as First Lady," in *At Lincoln's Side: John Hay's Civil War Correspondence and Selected Writings* (Carbondale: Southern Illinois University Press, 2000), 185–203.

30. Adam Badeau, *Grant in Peace from Appomattox to Mount McGregor: A Personal Memoir* (Hartford: S. S. Scranton, 1887), 356–60.

31. Mary Lincoln to Anson G. Henry, July 26, 1865, and to Mary Jane Welles, October 14 and December 6, 1865, Turner and Turner, *Mary Todd Lincoln*, 263, 277, 294.

32. Keckley, *Behind the Scenes*, 212–13.

33. Mary Lincoln to Eliza Stuart Steele, Chicago, May 23, 1871, Turner and Turner, *Mary Todd Lincoln*, 588.

34. Mary Lincoln to Jesse K. Dubois, Cresson Penn, July 26, 1868, Lincoln Collection, Abraham Lincoln Presidential Library, quoted in Thomas F. Schwartz and Kim M. Bauer, "Unpublished Mary Todd Lincoln," *Journal of the Abraham Lincoln Association* 17, no. 2 (Summer 1996).

35. Emphasis in original. Mary Lincoln to Mary Harlan Lincoln, letter fragment, Folder 1, Box 1, Mary Todd Lincoln Insanity File, Lincoln Financial Foundation Collection, Allen County Public Library, Fort Wayne, IN.

36. Robert Lincoln to Elizabeth Edwards, August 7, 1875, 133–39, vol. 1, microfilm reel 1, Robert Todd Lincoln Letterpress Books; "Clouded Reason," *Chicago Tribune*, May 20, 1875, 1; "Mrs. Lincoln," *Chicago Inter Ocean*, May 20, 1875, 1.

37. For the full examination of these events, see Jason Emerson, *The Madness of Mary Lincoln* (Carbondale: Southern Illinois University Press, 2007), and Mark E. Neely Jr. and R. Gerald McMurtry, *The Insanity File: The Case of Mary Todd Lincoln* (Carbondale: Southern Illinois University Press, 1986).

38. Isaac N. Arnold, a former congressman and longtime friend of Abraham Lincoln.

39. "Clouded Reason: Trial of Mrs. Abraham Lincoln for Insanity," *Chicago Tribune*, May 20, 1875, 1; "Mrs. Lincoln: The Widow of the Martyred President Adjudged Insane in County Court," *Chicago Inter Ocean*, May 20, 1875, 1.

40. "Mrs. Lincoln," *Chicago Inter Ocean*, May 20, 1875, 1.

41. Ninian Edwards to Robert Lincoln, Springfield, December 22, 1875, Folder 17, Box 2, Mary Todd Lincoln Insanity File.

42. Robert Lincoln to Ninian Edwards, Chicago, December 21, 1875, Folder 2, Box 2, Mary Todd Lincoln Insanity File.

43. Robert Lincoln to Elizabeth Edwards, April 18, 1879, Robert Todd Lincoln Correspondence, Lincoln Financial Foundation Collection at Allen County Public Library, Fort Wayne, IN.

44. Mary Lincoln to Myra Bradwell, Pau, France, December 1, 1876, Pritchard, "The Dark Days of Abraham Lincoln's Widow," 9:1–4, Folder 5, Container 8, Part 2, Robert Todd Lincoln Family Papers, Library of Congress.

45. Robert Lincoln to Reverend Henry Darling, November 15, 1877, Folder 38, Box 6, Lincoln Collection, Miscellaneous Manuscripts, Department of Special Collections, University of Chicago Library.

46. Robert Lincoln to Elizabeth Edwards, April 18, 1879, Robert Todd Lincoln Papers, Allen County Public Library, Fort Wayne, IN.

47. "Sarah Bernhardt Beset," *(New York) Sun*, October 28, 1880, 3; "Mrs. Lincoln's Illness," *New York Times*, October 31, 1880, 5.

48. Untitled article, *Illinois State Journal*, May 27, 1881, 6, and May 28, 1881, 4, 6; Robert Lincoln to Sally Orne, Washington, June 2, 1881, Robert Todd Lincoln Papers, Abraham Lincoln Presidential Library.

49. W. A. Evans, *Mrs. Abraham Lincoln: A Study of Her Personality and Her Influence on Lincoln* (New York: Alfred A. Knopf, 1932), 53; Carl Sandburg and Paul M. Angle, *Mary Lincoln, Wife and Widow* (New York: Harcourt, Brace, 1932), 158; Ruth Painter Randall, *Mary Lincoln: Biography of a Marriage* (Boston: Little, Brown, 1953), 440.

50. Robert Lincoln to Sally Orne, Washington, June 2, 1881, Robert Todd Lincoln Papers, Abraham Lincoln Presidential Library; Robert Lincoln to Benjamin Richardson, June 3, 1881, Robert Todd Lincoln Letterpress Books, 4:6:376. Abraham Lincoln Presidential Library.

51. "Mrs. Lincoln: Broad Denial of the Stories Set Afloat by Dr. Sayre," *Chicago Tribune*, November 24, 1881, 3; "Mrs. Lincoln: She Corrects Some Reports Concerning Her Financial Condition," *Illinois State Journal*, November 29, 1881, 1.

52. "Mrs. Lincoln in Want," *New York Times*, November 23, 1881, 5; "Mrs. Lincoln," *Chicago Tribune*, November 24, 1881, 3. There was one newspaper article written, purporting to be based on an interview with "a member of the family of Mrs. Lincoln," which stated that Robert "has done all he could quietly do" to defeat her 1881 pension bill, just as he tried to defeat her 1870 pension. In both cases, the article stated, Robert thought the pension unnecessary because his mother had plenty of money on which to live, and her beliefs in her poverty were just a symptom of her insanity. "Mrs. Lincoln's Whims," *Chicago Tribune*, February 7, 1882, 11.

53. US House member William M. Springer, a Democrat from Springfield, Illinois, also furthered Mary's cause when he requested Sayre and three other eminent physicians—experts in ophthalmology, neurology, and kidney diseases—examine the widow's case and give a report of her physical condition to Congress. The physicians declared she suffered from chronic inflammation of the spinal cord, chronic disease of the kidneys, and commencing cataract of both eyes; the effects of her maladies would be ultimate paralysis of her lower limbs and loss of eyesight. They declared her condition would never improve considering its nature and her age. Mary Lincoln to Noyes W. Miner, January 3, 1882, Turner and Turner, *Mary Todd Lincoln*, 711; "New York: The Health of Mrs. Abraham Lincoln Not Improving," *Chicago Tribune*, January 15, 1882, 6; *Congressional Record*, 47th Cong. 1st sess., 1882, 13:402.

54. President Arthur signed the bill on February 2, 1882. *Congressional Record*, 47th Cong. 1st sess., 1882, 13:578, 652, 705–6, 882; "Mrs. Lincoln's Needs," *New York Times*, January 25, 1882, 3; "Coke's Bill," *Chicago Tribune*, February 3, 1882, 2; "Notes from Washington," *New York Times*, February 3, 1882, 1; "Mrs. Lincoln's Pension," *New York Times*, March 17, 1882, 5.

55. "Mrs. Lincoln's Health," *New York Times*, July 16, 1882, 7; "Mary Todd Lincoln," *Illinois State Journal*, July 17, 1882, 6; "Secretary Lincoln," *Illinois State Journal*, July 18, 1882, 4; "Awaiting the Burial," *Illinois State Journal*, July 18, 1882, 6; Mary Lincoln to Robert Lincoln, August 1874, Lincoln Collection, Abraham Lincoln Presidential Library, published in Thomas F. Schwartz, "'My Stay on Earth, Is Growing Very Short':

Mary Todd Lincoln's Letters to Willis Danforth and Elizabeth Swing," *Journal of Illinois History* 6, no. 2 (Summer 2003): 130.

56. "Awaiting the Burial," *Illinois State Journal*, July 18, 1882, 6; Dorothy Meserve Kunhardt, "An Old Lady's Lincoln Memories," *Life*, February 9, 1959, 59–60; "Mrs. Lincoln's Funeral," *New York Times*, July 18, 1882, 1; "Dust to Dust: The Body of Mrs. Abraham Lincoln Consigned to the Tomb," *Chicago Tribune*, July 20, 1882, 7.

57. "The Funeral," *Illinois State Journal*, July 19, 1882, 6; "Laid to Rest: The Last Sad Rites Paid to the Remains of Mary Lincoln," *Illinois State Journal*, July 20, 1882, 1.

58. Robert's wife and children were in Colorado at the time, and although they returned to Chicago at Robert's request, Mary Harlan Lincoln, who was described as an "invalid" for much of her life, was too ill to attend. Historians long have claimed that Mary Harlan's absence at the funeral was the final slight of a long-insulted daughter-in-law, but the historical evidence is clear that Mary Harlan was a physically frail woman—same as her mother—and the year 1882 was especially bad for her. Robert's law partner, Edward Isham, characterized Mary Harlan as "for years an invalid." "Isham and Lincoln," *Chicago Tribune*, November 24, 1883, 8.

59. Robert Lincoln to Clinton L. Conkling, Washington, July 26, 1882, printed in John Carroll Power, *History of an Attempt to Steal the Body of Abraham Lincoln* (Springfield, IL: W. W. Rokker, 1890), 87; Robert Lincoln to John T. Stuart, Washington, July 26, 1882, Box 1, Stuart-Hay Family Papers, Abraham Lincoln Presidential Library; for Power's description of Mary's reburial, see *History of an Attempt*, 86–87. Mary's secret reburial was unknown to the public until the remains were again moved in 1887. "Illinois' Hallowed Spot," *Chicago Inter Ocean*, April 15, 1887, 1; "Lincoln's Body," *Morning Oregonian*, April 15, 1887, 1.

## Mary Lincoln among the Novelists
### Fictional Interpretations of the First Lady

*Richard W. Etulain*

Fiction and history, argued Lincoln scholar Donald Fehrenbacher, are closer neighbors than many historians and biographers realize. "Both are constructs of factual materials," wrote Fehrenbacher, "shaped and cemented with imagination." And the best of the novels about Lincoln, even when sometimes containing factual errors, nourished "interest on a broad front" and had "a vitality that stimulates remembrance."[1] In the end, historical fiction, like works of history, not only helped one to understand events and people of the past; in Fehrenbacher's view, it also animated self-understanding and, perhaps, clarified the future.

What Fehrenbacher asserted a generation ago about historical fiction in general and about Abraham Lincoln specifically provides helpful guidance for examining and evaluating novels about his wife, Mary Lincoln. Even when sometimes containing factual mistakes, fiction about Mrs. Lincoln still illuminates her life, suggests reasons for her controversial actions, and supplies imaginative, cathartic lessons of understanding for own lives.

Unfortunately, the first fictional treatments of Mary Lincoln were not very promising. Cloying sentimentalism, shaky historical research, and stereotypical characterizations marred the initial novels. Most of the best Mary Lincoln fiction did not appear until the early twenty-first century. Altogether, fewer than ten full-length adult novels on Mary Lincoln have been published. In addition, she appears in several other novels as the supporting heroine or villainess in fiction about her husband, Abraham Lincoln. A few young adult novels have also featured Mary Lincoln. One suspects that other authors, realizing the complex and frequently negative turns in her married life, shied away from her as a subject for their fiction. Moreover, Mary's life after the assassination of her husband in 1865 until her death in 1882 was so depressing that it did not lend itself to fictional treatments popular with numerous readers.

The initial Mary Lincoln novels appeared in the late 1920s. At the end of the first book-length work of fiction about Mary, Bernie Babcock's romantic, sentimental *Lincoln's Mary and the Babies* (1929), a minor character asks, "What kind of woman is Mrs. Lincoln? Tell me about her?"[2] Although that important question serves as the central query of Babcock's novel, the work is too flawed and limited in characterization, analysis, and plot to deal adequately with that significant query. Still, the question about Mary's character—her personality and actions—is pivotal to most fiction about her. The best of the Mary Lincoln novels provide abundant background for understanding the people and forces that shaped the young Mary Todd before her marriage to Abraham Lincoln in 1842.

In *Lincoln's Mary and the Babies*, Babcock displays a good deal of Lincoln research—she authored several other fictional works about Abraham and Mary Lincoln—but here she fails both as a *historical* novelist and a historical *novelist*. Her limitations as historian and writer are doubly unfortunate because this was the first widely circulated novel about Mary Lincoln.

Babcock begins with the Lincolns off scene. Two neighbor ladies, Betty Bradley and Almyra (Miry) Spear hold opposite views of their close-at-hand neighbors, the Lincolns. A kindly lady taking care of her elderly father, Betty loves everything about the Lincolns, choosing to overlook the boyish antics of Willie and Tad and speaking well of Mary and Abraham. But Miry sees Abraham as an ugly, uncouth man; Mary as "a cat," a "Tartar [Lincoln] tied himself to"; and the "babies," the two boys, well "all they lacked of being imps [was] tails and horns" (11, 12).

In these two protagonists and their contrasting points of view, the author attempts to introduce complexity, historiographical difference. But the women and their opposing perspectives are, unfortunately, so stereotypically and superficially portrayed they cannot carry their intended ambivalence. Betty Bradley, winsome and warm, and Miry Spear, a "nasty gossip" woman, are little more than cardboard characters, unable to project any thoughtful, analytical portraits of the Lincolns.

Then Babcock takes Bradley and Spear offstage and spotlights Abraham and Mary in their Springfield home in the 1850s. The author rearranges chronology, bringing together events separated by several years, but she now allows the Lincolns to speak for themselves rather than through the words of the two neighbors. Nonetheless, the superficial characterizations, wobbly plot, and "history lite" undermine Babcock's attempts to "get inside" Mary Lincoln and her family.

Most of the novel's plot treats Mary Lincoln's life as wife and mother in the decade from the mid-1850s through her husband's assassination. However, Babcock does not allow Mary much leeway in acting out her character; rather, Mary and other characters *tell* us what she's like. Mary particularly recounts why she needs fine clothes and why she wants Lincoln to succeed, and Abraham explains directly and explicitly why Mary has trouble with alienating servant girls, Washington wives, and other would-be acquaintances. He also speaks to her—in fact (out of character) preaches to her—about the meaning of Christianity absent from her unkind and negative attitudes toward persons such as Seward, Stanton, and Andrew Johnson (on one occasion called Andrew Jackson). In telling too much and showing too little, Babcock breaks a cardinal law of appealing historical fiction.

The historical events the author chooses to emphasize and those she omits provide intriguing insights into her sense of fictive history. We get several familiar scenes: Mary's drive to enlarge her Springfield home, her conflicts with Lincoln's law partner Billy Herndon, her difficulties with overspending in the White House, and her desire to keep Robert out of the army. But we get almost nothing on her difficulties with her family's Southern roots and Confederate activities, her fraudulent actions to cover up her overspending, and her several embarrassments of Lincoln in her public actions.

In the end, Babcock's novel also fails as satisfactory historical fiction because the author is unable to give us enough of Mary Lincoln and her times. We see too few of her actions, encounter too few scenes dramatizing and defining her character. Similarly, her conversations are rarely introspective or suggestive, too often blasts of sharp criticism and blatant negativity toward less-than-elites and minorities. The author suggests some of the pressures of the Civil War, particularly through the statements and monologues of President Lincoln, but Mary rarely interacts with the shifting opinions about slavery, secession, the union, and emancipation that raged in the decade covered in this novel.

Published about the same time as Babcock's novel, Honoré Willsie Morrow's hybrid work, *Mary Todd Lincoln: An Appreciation of the Wife of Abraham Lincoln* (1928), illustrates some of the challenges lying in wait for writers attempting to treat Mary Lincoln in biography and fiction.[3] Morrow's book is not entirely fiction or wholly traditional biography. Contemporaries could have termed it a "novelized biography"; later commentators might have described it as "creative nonfiction." Morrow was already known for the first of her fictional triplex about Abraham Lincoln: *Forever Free* (1927). *With Malice Toward None* (1928) and *Last Full Measure* (1930), the second and third parts of what became the *Great Captain* trilogy, drew on her extensive Lincoln research for this curious sketch of Mary.[4] It was not a successful work.

Morrow's book wobbles indecisively in its intensions and outcome. As Morrow tells us, once she turned up considerable information on Mary Lincoln, she chose "to translate" those findings "into my own vernacular." That meant she decided to turn "some of the [historical] episodes into dialogue"; she "made some 'miniatures' of [Lincolns'] children, based on authentic material"; and she "took some of the episodes out of the past tense and put them into the present." Finally, other events were kept "authentic" "but fictionalized as to conversations and continuity" (11). Reevaluating her research, Morrow gave in to her desire to enhance the narrative power of those facts; she "was ready to discard my abortive biography and write Lincoln's wife into the novel" (12). Almost, but not quite. Instead, she moved to a treacherous and unsatisfactory middle ground—producing neither novel nor traditional life story. "That's the rub," to employ some of Mr. Lincoln's favorite words.

Morrow's work betrays her uncertainty about format. She shuffles together bits and pieces of her research, quoting extensively from books and newspaper articles about Mary Lincoln, Abraham Lincoln, and their son Tad. But this "appreciation" fails because the author has not found a satisfactory structure through which to organize her material. Morrow also moves too easily into questionable generalizations. Early on, she asserts, "I am firmly convinced that without the influence and inspiration of Mary Lincoln, the world never would have known Abraham Lincoln, for he never would have reached the White House without her" (13). A provocative but unprovable assertion. And later: "Had there been no Mary Todd, there would have been no Lincoln the Emancipator" (206). Most historians and biographers would argue that the pressures of the Civil War and Lincoln himself, much more than his wife, were the forces bringing about the Emancipation Proclamation.

Morrow's "creative" or fictionalized biography is deeply flawed, illustrating a central dilemma facing all historical novelists. Once a fiction writer has uncovered considerable factual material, how faithful must the author remain to those facts? Could the research be used for fictional purposes, with recorded conversations, events, and ideas being combined with imagined scenes and characters? As one leading specialist in historical fiction discerningly notes, this is a major question facing workers in the field of historical fiction.[5] Honoré Willsie Morrow could not make up her mind on this dilemma in her "appreciation" of Mary Lincoln, with the book suffering from her indecision. Indeed one wonders whether the book would have been published had the author not already been recognized as a writer of western and Lincoln fiction, and even more importantly, had her husband not been the owner of William Morrow and Company, the publisher of this book.[6] If this work on Mary Lincoln is ultimately unsuccessful, her other historical fiction on Abraham Lincoln was not. Those were some of the best early novels about the sixteenth president.

Anne Colver's *Mr. Lincoln's Wife*, which first appeared in 1943 and then in revised form in 1965, resembles the work of her predecessor Babcock more than the later and more significant novel *Love Is Eternal* (1954), by well-known biographical novelist Irving Stone.[7] Colver's novel is much less a historical work than Stone's and more akin to the domestic—even sentimental—fiction of Babcock. Most of all, Colver focuses primarily on the family life of Mary and Abraham Lincoln, with a minimum of contextual history surrounding those two lives.

In a brief introduction, "Note from the Author," Colver tells readers Mary Lincoln "is not a character to be idealized." Her temper flared too often, her emotions were too mercurial, and her tongue too sharp. No one ought to understand Mary without accepting these limitations, Colver adds. On the other hand, Mary loved Abraham and her four boys; she pushed her reluctant husband toward his successes, and she often smoothed over Lincoln's social gaucheries. Overall, Mary "followed [Abraham's] fate and found herself eventually lost in its vast and lonely shadow" (7). In short, the heroine of *Mr. Lincoln's Wife* is a tension-filled figure, swinging from emotional downers to ebullient uppers.

Colver begins in medias res, opening with Mary Todd's months of staying in Springfield with her sister Elizabeth before she meets Abraham. Mary's previous years in Kentucky are resurrected in brief flashbacks of rumination. In these opening scenes, the youthful Mary seems to live little beyond pretty new dresses, parties, and seeing Mr. Lincoln, who is portrayed as a strange, backwoods, and reclusive man. The distaste of Elizabeth and her husband, Ninian Edwards, for the awkward and unpromising Lincoln, as well as the author's glancing treatment of pretty

Matilda Edwards's visit to Springfield and Lincoln's possible interest in her, provide the prefatory conflicts on which later chapters play.

Colver stays close to the story of Mary and Abraham. After the first episodes of courtship, several chapters on homemaking, parenthood, and family life follow. If the opening sections focus on Mary's experiences—and that emphasis continues throughout the novel—the second half of the story reveals much more about the inner and outer dimensions of Abraham's personality and actions. Although Mary believes she will be able to smooth off Abraham's several rough edges, her married older sister Frances communicates a widely known and accepted truth when she tells Mary: "Once she's married, I daresay Mary will discover it's not as easy as it looks to change a husband" (58). It is a difficult lesson Mary learns after many false moves, and flat failures.

On the other hand, in the second half of the book, it is Abraham who becomes a calming influence on Mary. Even though he fails to respond to all her emotional needs, Mary realizes repeatedly how much her calm husband defuses and dissolves conflicts and issues that repeatedly set her on edge. Abraham plays with the boys when they've run Mary up the wall, he finds time to ask her about her problems when he's trying to steer the whole country through troubled waters, and he counsels her when critics and journalists attack her as a Southern spy, a spendthrift, and an emotional wreck. Gradually, as the novel progresses, Colver provides additional glimpses of the emotional center of Abraham Lincoln.

The author's choices of what historical scenes to emphasize and which to omit reveal a good deal about her intentions. We get much about Stephen Douglas and his comely second wife, Adelle; extensive discussions of the Lincolns' reactions to the Civil War; more than passing depictions of the Lincolns' stay at the Soldiers' Home on the edge of Washington; Mary's trips away from the capital; and her dilemmas in reacting to the Southern branches of her family. But the Lincolns' stay in Washington during his congressional period, the years of the Kansas-Nebraska upset, the Peoria Speech, and the Senate contest of 1855—indeed the entire period from

1846 to 1858—receive only passing mention. Nor does Colver say much about the Fort Sumter, the Emancipation Proclamation (the author incorrectly states it freed all slaves), the Gettysburg Address, or Lincoln's numerous conflicts with Republican Radicals. Interestingly, while dealing with Mary's overspending for White House refurbishing and on her own clothing, the author does not mention Mary's huge emotional explosion when she discovers that Mrs. Ord has ridden beside Lincoln as he reviewed Union troops. The author also chooses to depict the Lincolns' oldest son, Robert, as stuffy, self-centered, and much too critical of his mother's overindulgences.

Colver utilizes two interesting narrative tricks to help power her fictional narrative. One, she frequently ends chapters with interest-whetting mistaken notions or actions by Mary and Abraham. Mary thinks, for example, that the conflicts she experiences with negative residents of Springfield will dissolve when she gets to Washington, where people will love her and her family. She finds just the opposite, with even more criticism and snubs. The second technique is the telling use of foreshadowing; later events hinted at through an imagined scene or statement: Lincoln tells Mary he's all right after a dangerous incident; he's evidently "bulletproof" (308).

Seen whole, Colver's novel is diligently domestic, devoting much more space to the color and style of hundreds of Mary's dresses than to her well-known interests in political, cultural, and economic activities. Undoubtedly, these emphases appealed to feminine readers, emphasizing Mary's private activities as wife and mother rather than her public activities. In this way, Colver's work follows the Babcock and Morrow traditions rather than serving as precursor to the trends that surfaced in later fiction about Mary Lincoln.

Only a quarter of a century separated the works of Bernie Babcock and Honoré Willsie Morrow (and roughly a decade, the work of Colver) from Irving Stone's well-known *Love Is Eternal: A Novel about Mary Todd Lincoln and Abraham Lincoln* (1954), but a giant chasm divides their fictional purposes and achievements.[8] The works of Babcock, Morrow, and Colver, primarily stereotypical volumes of sentimental fiction and novelized biography, looked backward more than forward. But *Love Is Eternal* and other novels by Irving Stone were emblematic of a new genre of biographical fiction that surfaced in the later twentieth century. No one in Stone's time became a more skilled practitioner of this literary type than he. His biographical novels of major historical figures such as Vincent van Gogh, Jessie Benton Frèmont, Michelangelo, Sigmund Freud, Charles Darwin, and Jack London illustrated his skill in blending biographical-historical facts and imagined scenes and created conversations. Stone's novels were works of thick description adumbrating the even more popular historical fiction of James Michener and the later novels of Gore Vidal and William Safire treating Abraham and Mary Lincoln.

The plot of *Love Is Eternal*, told primarily through Mary Lincoln, runs rapidly and revealingly through her childhood, adolescence, and early twenties. Fictionalized history abounds. Stone lards his narrative with large doses of Mary Todd's family heritage, the social and physical layouts of Lexington, Kentucky, and Springfield, Illinois, and the state and national political maneuverings that enriched the careers of Henry Clay, Abraham Lincoln, Stephen A. Douglas, and several others in the 1840s and 1850s. He also moves well beyond any previous novelist in portraying Mary Lincoln on several historical platforms dramatically acting out her imagined thoughts and conversations.

*Love Is Eternal* devotes about three-quarters of its 430 pages to the years prior to Lincoln's presidency. In depicting the full generation of Mary and Abraham's lives between the early 1840s and the presidency beginning in 1861, Stone provides lengthy discussions of slavery in the South, Northern antislavery attitudes, Whig and Republican politics, and the rapidly evolving social scene of Springfield. Likewise, the treatment of Mary and Abraham's complex, troubled, and convoluted romance is shot through with twists and turns and mistaken notions of the "Fatal First" experience that historians have recently clarified.[9]

Stone does not shy away from the conflicts that complicated the Lincolns' early marriage and that continued into the White House. Mary's excessive social ambitions and Abraham's parallel withdrawal tendencies vex husband and wife, but the "Love Is Eternal" theme keeps Mary, for the most part, agreeable and willing to compromise. She gives way in this novel more often and much less traumatically than in other accounts more critical of her.[10]

The major challenge for historical novelists surfaces early and often in Stone's work. How much will the author follow historical facts, how much will he embroider those facts, and when will he imagine conversations and events not a part of the historical record? Stone chooses a compromise path: He relies heavily on events like Abraham's speeches, travels, and friendships known to be true, but he also creates conversations either dubious or absent from the historical record. For instance, Lincoln's statement about his autobiography—"There is not much of it for the reason, I suppose, that there is not much of me"—is here attributed to a conversation with Mary (286), but most scholars cite it as Lincoln's response to one of his campaign biographers. Similarly, in this novel, in the aftermath of the Lincoln-Douglas debates, Abraham tells his wife: "I'm glad we made the race, Mary: it gave us a hearing on the great and durable question of the age" (273). That response is usually credited to a letter Lincoln wrote to a close political friend. And most blatantly, Stone steals the words of Lincoln's famous letter to Horace Greeley and shoves them into another conversation with his wife: "Nobody knows better than you, Mary, that my paramount object in this struggle has been to save the Union, and not either to save or destroy slavery. . . . If I could save the Union without freeing *any* slave I would do it, and if I could save it by freeing *all* the slaves I would do it; if I could save it by freeing some and leaving others alone I would also do that" (373).[11] These egregious misattributions of conversations and sources likely still set the teeth of scholars on edge.

In all, Stone's Mary Lincoln is neither a troublemaking wife nor a carping, impossible First Lady, two of the major personality flaws negative novelists and biographers attribute to her. True, the heroine of *Love Is Eternal* is too socially conscious, overspends budgets in renovating the White House, and loses control of herself in jealous reactions following a head injury suffered in a carriage accident. But she is a loving wife and diligent mother and committed to helping the needy and caring for wounded soldiers. Usually, Stone provides a balancing redeeming quality for each of Mary's imperfections. Sometimes the author excessively stirs the emotions of his female protagonist, often presents a very negative picture of Robert Lincoln, and occasionally telescopes too severely the presidential period, especially the years of 1863 to 1865. But he also makes apt uses of historical backgrounds, portrays discerningly specific events in the Lincolns' lives, and paints a sparkling portrait of Mary's love for and aid to her husband. Love is indeed eternal—and overarching—in Irving Stone's depiction of the Lincolns.

For the most part, historical novelists abandoned Mary Lincoln from the late 1950s into the next century. No major novel on Mary appeared during these years. Not even much fiction was written about her husband.[12] Perhaps "the 60s" and the Cold War, with their emphases on social activism and international politics, turned writers to other subjects. But the oversight was corrected after the year 2000. Indeed, several novels about the First Lady appeared in the opening decade of the twenty-first century. Although not all were first-rate novels, most were among the best fictional portraits of Mrs. Lincoln.

M. Kay duPont utilized an unusual storyline for fiction about Mary Lincoln although one quite familiar to other historical novelists. A long-lost Mary Lincoln diary is discovered and becomes the source for duPont's novel *Loving Mrs. Lincoln: The Personal Diaries of Mary Todd Lincoln* (2003).[13] This storytelling technique allows the author to utilize a first-person perspective, which she adheres to throughout her novel.

Indeed, the author relentlessly rides this interpretive horse. Early on, Mary Todd is set on marrying a president and living in the White House. In her courting and early married days, she vows to smooth over

Abraham's blemishes and spark his ambition for high office. But she also incessantly worries about social acceptance, her husband's lack of drive, and her growing inability to control her tongue, mother her children, and rein in her buying binges. These desires and character flaws, most historians, biographers, and novelists agree, seemed part of Mary's DNA. But duPont's excessively explicit emphases on these characteristics leaves one puzzled about why the author feels so driven to stress these difficulties on nearly every page. The overemphasis on this handful of personal traits undermines the aesthetic quality of the novel, making the author more than Mary Lincoln the mistress of the plot.

DuPont reveals—perhaps more than she realizes—the shortcomings of her approach to historical fiction in a brief preface, "To the Readers." The author asserts that her people are all real, the events she includes "actually happened on or about the dates recorded here," and most of Abraham and Mary's conversations recorded here "are documented," but they "may not have said those words to each other.". When the author uses the notably important words Abraham Lincoln wrote to Horace Greeley or delivered at tipping point events in his presidency and credits them to conversations between Mary and Abraham, she distorts history (as Stone had earlier) and, quite possibly, the relationship between the First Lady and the president. Similar problems arise when the author misdates the Louisiana Purchase, incorrectly has John C. Frèmont a presidential candidate in 1848, misfires on the facts of the Mexican War controversy, and mistakenly has Lincoln going to church on the Good Friday he was assassinated. These misuses of facts and the glaring errors undermine the author's credibility.

Clearly, duPont does not oversimplify Mary's complexities or gloss over her large faults. True, in the roughly twenty-five years she knew Abraham Lincoln, Mary came to love and cherish her husband. Yet she could add measurably to his difficulties and demanding life with her tart tongue and misguided opinions. The author also suggests, with no evidence on which to base her assumptions, that the Lincolns enjoyed a rich sexual life until Abraham's obsession with the Civil War and Mary's mental and physical difficulties foreshortened their bedroom gymnastics. The deaths of her two sons Eddy and Willie, her growing inability to halt excessive shopping, and her increasing drug use led to Mary's rapid decline in the White House. One day up and a week down becomes the pattern of duPont's Mary. On occasion, the First Lady realizes that she has "been blind and selfish" (305), but mostly she is self-absorbed, defensive, and sightless concerning her faults. Begun with such warmth, vivacity, and love, her life spirals downward in depression and near defeat with the Lincolns on their way to Ford's Theater.

Two years later, Barbara Hambly's *The Emancipator's Wife: A Novel of Mary Todd Lincoln* (2005) moved well beyond the less polished *Loving Mr. Lincoln*.[14] The longest and best of the Mary Lincoln novels, Hambly's work is a sophisticated piece of historical fiction. A gifted stylist and imaginative storyteller with narrative skills honed from writing dozens of popular novels, Hambly adeptly utilizes her six hundred oversized pages to provide a provocative portrait of Mary Lincoln.

Of all the Mary Lincoln novelists, Hambly furnishes the fullest coverage of Mary's earlier years. In doing so, she stresses those experiences that shaped Mary's later life. She lost her much-loved mother while still a girl, never connected with her stepmother Betsy, and developed detrimental defense mechanisms that surfaced more frequently and negatively in her adult years. Feeling great need to be seen and heard, Mary broke Southern social customs by expressing her strong opinions in male gatherings; pushed for education and books beyond her peers; and rationalized her behavior when she lied, stole, spent lavishly, and exhibited numerous temper tantrums. These were early evidences of the actions that so undermined Mary's reputation and skewed her desires during her quarter century of marriage.

In the opening sections of her novel—and frequently thereafter—Hambly uses several devices to suggest the continuities in Mary's life. Over time we see the gradual emergence of character defects in a youthful

Mary that became near disastrous in the later, depressing years of her life after the assassination. Unable to hold in her temper, bite her tongue, and control her undisciplined and erratic spending habits; and relying increasingly on prescribed and home remedies to counter her headaches, depression, and anxiety, Mary alienates family and friends and numbs her sensitivities through excessive drug use. Through flashbacks, interior monologues, and stream of consciousness scenes, the author posits a mature and then elderly Mary Lincoln suffering increasingly from the imperfections of her earlier girlhood, teenage years, and early adulthood. A key sentence illuminates these continuities: "And as usual when she [Mary] felt fear, it transformed itself into anger" (202).

Since Hambly generally sticks close to the known facts of Mrs. Lincoln's life, it is all the more startling when she moves daringly beyond previous novelists and most historians and biographers in one scene. Worried that the indecisive Lincoln will hesitate once more and leave her unwedded, Mary plans and carries out her seduction of him. Then, uneasy about the result of their sexual encounter, she tells him, well before she could know with certainty, that she is "with child" (240). Concerning this controversial scene, in a brief appended author's note, Hambly asks, "Did Mary Todd entrap Abraham Lincoln into marrying her?" "Looking at the manipulative chicanery she later indulged in," the author continues, "I can only say I wouldn't put it past her" (607–8). Even more questionably, Hambly asserts "that lie" of premature pregnancy forced Lincoln to marry Mary, which led to another controversy. Much later, in a dreamlike backward look, Mary wonders if her first son, Robert Todd Lincoln, knowing about the lie and the forced marriage, concludes that his entrapped father never loved him as a firstborn offspring deserved. No previous historian, biographer, or novelist has attempted to forge all these controversial connections. Instead, most would agree with Mary Lincoln's most recent biographer when she writes of a possible seduction: "this indiscretion is not impossible, but it reflects character assassination more than reasonable speculation."[15] Nor does the biographer speculate about "the lie's" impact on Robert.

Another technique Hambly uses illustrates the distance between many historians and novelists in their handling of time sequences in their stories. The plot of *The Emancipator's Wife* alternates from Chicago in the mid-1870s, when Mary is institutionalized in a home for the insane, then back to her younger and White House years, and then her return to Chicago. Perhaps Hambly wants to suggest the continuing impact of Mary's experiences and character flaws; possibly she also desires to illustrate the ways Mary's mind, often beclouded by overdoses of prescriptions and home remedies, works in juxtaposing past and present. Granted, this fluidity of time sequences implies how, for example, the deaths of three sons and the tragedy of her husband's assassination continue to bludgeon and misshape Mary's shaky mental condition. But the sharp shifts back and forth also disrupt historical continuity and, in the end, detract more than they add to Hambly's otherwise superb historical novel.

One year later, another writer, Janis Cooke Newman, in her novel *Mary: Mrs. A. Lincoln* (2006), painted Mary Todd as an even more conniving seductress.[16] When Abraham seems unable to move toward the marriage Mary so much wants, she invades his bachelor digs on a late New Year's Eve and seduces Lincoln. He's so discombobulated from her headlong actions that he fails to show up the next day at the Edwardses (Mary's sister and brother-in-law). He is unable to admit to their clandestine actions and to ask for her hand in marriage, thus giving new, enlarged meaning to the famous "Fatal First" of 1842 that has generated so much discussion among Lincoln scholars. After several more months—during most of which Lincoln stays away from the passionate Mary—they once again enjoy sexual union in the front room of Dr. Anson G. Henry, Lincoln's close friend and doctor. Newman's heroine is convinced that the second tryst produced Robert, their first son, nine months later.

Newman relates Mary's revealing and sometimes racy story in the first person. Through this intimate narrative perspective, the author paints the most assertive, pushy protagonist of the entire coterie of fictional Mary Lincolns. In virtually every paragraph, Mary defines herself by her strong opinions and controversial actions—this through conversations, internal monologues, or stream of consciousness thinking. We learn, at length, what she thinks about her husband, three boys, and dozens of friends and enemies.

Newman's stories about Robert Lincoln are particularly negative, sometimes exceptionally hostile. He is never treated as a sympathetic character, rather in fact frequently extensively savaged. Robert upbraids his mother for her flirtations, her housekeeping failures, and her tendency to bruise and even break his rigid sense of decorum. Historical evidence does not sustain the incessant, harsh criticism that washes over Robert here.

Newman also utilizes the back-and-forth storyline that Hambly and other novelists employ. Readers are transported back from events during Mary's three to four months in the Bellevue Place sanitarium, where Robert had her committed after several madcap actions, to events in her girlhood, tragedies in the White House, and events beyond. For the most part, the transitions work, although the chapters about Bellevue lack the liveliness of Mary's earlier history. Newman tries, rather unsuccessfully, to create stories about imagined residents of the asylum, perhaps, to add color and action missing from Mary's diurnal activities there.

Newman's Mary is a woman of unbridled intensity married to a relentlessly rationalistic man. Her passion, physical and emotional, scares her husband, and as a president overwhelmed with war, he pays increasingly less attention to his needy wife. His growing inattentions impel her toward the tawdry affair she consummates with wily William Wood, commissioner of buildings in Washington, DC, and a notorious purveyor of crooked patronage. Because the author tells her story so thoroughly through the I-Mary narrator, we get little of Abraham Lincoln—less here than in other major novels about Mary Lincoln. Moreover, the descriptions of Lincoln, especially his grief over the loss of Willie and less over Eddie, seem flat, with little illumination of his inner character. Indeed, unless a reader is entirely drawn to reading about Mary's self-absorption (and there was much of this factually and even more here fictionally), Newman's story is too one-dimensional to draw readers as much as to Stone's *Love Is Eternal* or Hambly's *The Emancipator's Wife*.

Seen more positively, Newman's *Mary: Mrs. A. Lincoln* remains the fullest and most revealing interpretation of the inner life of Mary Lincoln. Even though much of the inward skies of Mary's heart and mind are imagined more than based on factual research, a large part of Newman's treatment of Mary's mental imbalances, drug overdoses, and untoward actions ring true. Remembering that this is a work of fiction, one can congratulate Newman for her probing portrait, keeping in mind that the insights of her leading character owe more to the author's imagination than to historical facts.

During the twentieth century, authors of adolescent fiction also use Mary Lincoln or Mary and Abraham as subjects for their novels. Generally, most of these novels for children and young adults differ so markedly from other historical novels dealing with the Lincolns that comparisons are not easy to make. A recent example—Ann Rinaldi's *An Unlikely Friendship: A Novel of Mary Todd Lincoln and Elizabeth Keckley* (2007)—illustrates the large challenges and the dilemmas of writing historical fiction for teenagers.[17]

Rinaldi, a veteran writer of nearly twenty books for teen readers, clearly knows how to tell stories for her age group. In a note (237–41), the author recounts how she was struck with the stark differences between the earlier years of Mary, who was pampered and a member of the social elite, and the traumatic, formative experiences of Elizabeth (Lizzy) Keckley (or Keckly) as a mulatto slave girl. The author set out to depict the startling disjunctions of childhood and youth in these two women who become friends in the White House. She devotes about a hundred pages of her 240-page novel to Mary's years before her marriage and about ninety pages to Lizzy's life before 1861. Surprisingly, although the title suggests a novel about the "friendship" of the two women, only twenty to thirty pages deal with that friendship.

Rinaldi follows a familiar path in her treatment of Mary Todd. She stresses Mary's sense of loss after her mother's death; her falling out with her stepmother; and her dependence on the household slave Mammy Sally, her maternal grandmother, Grandma Parker, and her father (less so here) to protect her from life's challenges and crises. Rinaldi also makes much of Mary's growing sympathy for slaves, her desire to gain an education, and her dream to make something of herself. But we get little of her temper, her overspending, her out-of-control emotions, and certainly nothing of her bedroom life.

This inattention to Mary's early flaws ill prepare one for the bad-tempered, intemperate, and spendthrift sprees of the Mary who serves as First Lady. Other novelists, biographers, and historians have done a better job of depicting the prepresidential downside of Mary's life, helping readers to understand why the deaths of two sons, the assassination of her husband, and the incessant pressures of the White House threw her off track. Conversely, Rinaldi is more successful in showing how Lizzy Keckley learned to discipline herself and to rise above multiple disappointments before she met Mary and became her seamstress and her close friend and confidant.

Indeed, what Rinaldi leaves out of her story of Mary Lincoln is as revealing as what she includes. In this novel, Mary's initial years are primarily ones of sunshine and little rain—at least much less rain than falls on her in other fictional and historical accounts. In addition, the author omits the dark side and later negative impact of Elizabeth Keckley's book *Behind the Scenes, or, Thirty Years a Slave, and Four Years in the White House* (1868) on her friendship with Mrs. Lincoln.[18] That work, because of its realistic depiction of Mary's persisting problems, and the inclusion of personal letters from Lincoln to Keckley, immediately ended their contact. Indeed, the friendship terminated on a sour, negative note, but that unfortunate ending is not mentioned here.

Finally, Rinaldi frequently tips her hand that she is writing for adolescent readers in the tone and content of her work. In doing so she clarifies the distance between her fiction and that of other historical novelists writing about Mary Lincoln. Rinaldi particularly plays up the rites of passage from young girl to adolescent to young adult in the lives of both heroines. The transitions are more shocking for Lizzy, having to face slavery, her mixed race and uncertain class status, and, most of all, the sexual abuse forced on her. For Mary the moves from much-loved girl to abandoned teenager (by her stepmother and less so by her father), and the loss of other support leave her an uncertain and emotionally marked young woman. These dramatic challenges are ones young readers undoubtedly identify with when they too feel the threats of change, lack of acceptance, and even violence.

At this point a few general comments about Mary Lincoln novels are in order. When seen in chronological and comparative perspectives, this cavalcade of Mary Lincoln fiction takes on larger historiographical meaning.

Surprisingly few novels about Mary Lincoln have been published. Less than ten have appeared since the initial novels about her came out in the late 1920s. But even this small number of novels followed patterns of American historical fiction and fiction about Abraham Lincoln in the twentieth century. The first novels about Mary Lincoln—those by Bernie Babcock, Honoré Willsie Morrow, and Ann Colver—were rather sentimental, stereotypical portraits of Mary Lincoln, as were the early-twentieth-century novels about Abraham Lincoln, several of which were by the same authors. These works of fiction about Mary Lincoln were, by and large, unanalytical, admitting to her downside but stressing even more her positive contributions as wife, mother, social planner, and political advisor to her husband. The first novels about Mary were also quite limited and narrowly focused in their historical coverage.

Irving Stone's *Love Is Eternal* proved to be something of a turning point. Even though quite sympathetic in its portraits of Mary and Abraham, the novel avoided the cloying sentimentalism of the earlier fiction, replacing it with wide-angle contextual historical research. Zeroing in on the Lincolns, and seen through eyes of Mary, Stone's work broke new ground in the historical fiction about Mary Lincoln.

The civil rights movement and historical revisionism dealing with racial and ethnic matters in the 1960s and 1970s pushed aside positive writing about the Lincolns and brought in more negative interpretations of President Lincoln. When the path-breaking novels by William Safire and Gore Vidal appeared in the mid-1980s, they foreshadowed a new era of more analytical, complex, and full-bodied fiction about the sixteenth president. Similar kinds of probing fiction about his wife were coming—but a generation later.

The novels about Mary Lincoln by M. Kay duPont, Barbara Hambly, and Janis Cooke Newman presented a much more multifaceted female protagonist. These novelists drew straighter and stronger lines of experience and influence linking Mary's youth, her marriage, and her widowed years. The reasons for her erratic actions as adult became clearer in these novels; so did her personal reactions to these shaping events. These writers made more use of the "I" narrator, provided extensive first-person perspectives, and imagined more often what Mary thought about her surroundings and her own actions. At the same time previously untouched topics about Mary Lincoln emerged in full view. For these recent writers, Mary may have been sexually active before marriage, passionately so after marriage, and perhaps straying during her marriage. Under the pressures of mounting frustrations, disappointments, and tragedies, she relied too heavily—in fact, overindulged herself—on drugs. Depression and derangement lurked often at her doorstep and sometimes even overcame her. These three novels, through uses of first-person and multiple perspectives, stream of consciousness thinking, and a rather amoral approach to Mary's actions, illustrate postmodern tendencies fully at work in contemporary American fiction—and in recent novels about Mary Lincoln.

Similar parallels are clear in comparing biographies and novels of Mary. The first full-length biographies written about Mrs. Lincoln—namely those by Katherine Helm (*The True Story of Mary, Wife of Lincoln,*

1928), W. A. Evans (*Mrs. Abraham Lincoln*, 1932), and Ruth Painter Randall (*Mary Lincoln: Biography of a Marriage*, 1953)—were much like the initial novels about Mary.[19] They were sympathetic, rather unanalytical, and quite limited portraits of the First Lady. But the later biographies by Turner and Turner (*Mary Todd Lincoln*, 1972), Jean Baker (*Mary Todd Lincoln*, 1987), and Catherine Clinton (*Mrs. Lincoln*, 2009) were fuller, more evaluative, and contextually driven works than the first life stories of Mary Lincoln.[20]

Scholars making such comparisons as these among novelists, historians, and biographers must also keep in mind essential differences between fictional and historical writings. The best historical fiction is inductive, piling up scene after scene of dramatic action leading readers to conclusions about Mary Lincoln or any other heroine or hero. Many perceptive analytical historians and biographers take a different tack; they are more deductive, announcing early on what thesis is to be pursued and then stringing together incident after incident or quote upon quote illustrating the persuasiveness of the announced theme of emphasis. If historians and biographers tend to use stories that *tell*, most novelists prefer stories that *show*. Novelists who turn deductive are often accused of writing tracts rather than appealing works of art.

As important as these differences are, and as much as they should be remembered, similarities between historical novelists and historians are equally if not even more significant. These parallels, too, should be recalled and reiterated. The largest contribution of recent fiction writers about Mary Lincoln is their seeing her life more completely. Through context and complexity, novelists help us to see how Mary's girlhood and premarital years influenced—even shaped, or misshaped—her life with Abraham Lincoln and beyond. Like recent historians and biographers, writers such as Irving Stone, M. Kay duPont, Barbara Hambly, and Janis Cooke Freeman paint a more complex Mary Lincoln, demonstrating not only the ongoing themes of her life but also the shifting sociocultural contexts influencing her life. For these insightful contributions, historical novelists deserve more credit and attention as provocative interpreters of Mary Lincoln.[21]

## Notes

1. Don E. Fehrenbacher, "The Fictional Lincoln," *Lincoln in Text and Context: Collected Essays* (Stanford, CA: Stanford University Press, 1987), 245. For historical information on Mary Lincoln, I have relied primarily on Justin G. Turner and Linda Levitt Turner, *Mary Todd Lincoln: Her Life and Letters* (New York: Knopf, 1972), and Catherine Clinton, *Mrs. Lincoln: A Life* (New York: Harper/Collins, 2009). For a very useful listing of the major scholarship on Mary Todd Lincoln, see Jason Emerson, "Mary Lincoln: An Annotated Bibliography," *Journal of the Illinois State Historical Society* 101 (Fall/Winter 2008): 260–71.

2. Bernie Babcock, *Lincoln's Mary and the Babies* (Philadelphia: J. B. Lippincott, 1929), 288. Subsequent citations to the content of this and other works discussed in this essay will be within the text. Babcock was also the author of *The Soul of Ann Rutledge* (Philadelphia: J. B. Lippincott, 1919) and *The Soul of Abraham Lincoln* (Philadelphia: J. B. Lippincott, 1923).

3. Honoré Willsie Morrow, *Mary Todd Lincoln: An Appreciation of the Wife of Abraham Lincoln* (New York: William Morrow, 1928). Fehrenbacher describes this volume as "a rather curious mixture of literary invention and historical essay" ("The Fictional Lincoln," 335).

4. Honoré Willsie Morrow, *Forever Free: A Novel of Abraham Lincoln* (New York: William Morrow, 1927), *With Malice toward None* (New York: William Morrow, 1928), and *The Last Full Measure* (New York: William Morrow, 1930). These three works are gathered in Morrow, *Great Captain* (New York: William Morrow, 1930). Earlier, Morrow also published *Benefits Forgot: A Story of Lincoln and Mother Love* (New York: Frederick A. Stokes, 1917) and *The Lost Speech of Abraham Lincoln* (New York: F. A. Stokes, 1925).

5. Ernest D. Leisy, *The American Historical Novel* (Norman: University of Oklahoma Press, 1950), especially 3–20, 214–17. Provocative essays on historians and novels in dialogue—and conflict—are collected in Mark C. Carnes, ed., *Novel History: Historians and Novelists Confront America's Past (and Each Other)* (New York: Simon and Schuster, 2004).

6. Mrs. Morrow married her publisher, William Morrow, in 1923, after writing several books about the West but before most of her work on Abraham and Mary Lincoln appeared.

7. Anne Colver, *Mr. Lincoln's Wife* (New York: Holt, Rinehart, and Winston, 1943, 1965); Irving Stone, *Love Is Eternal: A Novel of Mary Todd and Abraham Lincoln* (Garden City, NY: Doubleday, 1954).

8. For helpful brief comments on Stone as a writer of biographical fiction, see Edwin McDowell, "Behind the Bestsellers," *New York Times Book Review*, September 14, 1980, 42.

9. Douglas L. Wilson, *Honor's Voice: The Transformation of Abraham Lincoln* (New York: Alfred A. Knopf, 1998), particularly chapters 7 and 8. By "Fatal First," most historians and biographers refer to a break in Abraham Lincoln and Mary Todd's engagement on or about January 1, 1841. But biographer Ronald C. White Jr. suggests "Fatal First" could also refer to challenges Lincoln's best friend, Joshua Speed, was facing in his stumbling steps toward matrimony. See White, *A. Lincoln: A Biography* (New York: Random House, 2009), 112.

10. See, for example, Michael Burlingame, *The Inner World of Abraham Lincoln* (Urbana: University of Illinois Press, 1994), 268–355, and Burlingame, *Abraham Lincoln: A Life.* 2 vols.(Baltimore: Johns Hopkins University Press, 2008).

11. The three references in this paragraph appear in Roy P. Basler, Marion Dolores Pratt, and Lloyd A. Dunlap, eds., *The Collected Works of Abraham Lincoln* (New Brunswick, NJ: Rutgers University Press, 1953–55): 3:511 (Lincoln's autobiography); 3:339 (the Lincoln-Douglas race of 1858); and 5:388 (the Greeley letter).

12. The two notable exceptions to this generalization are Gore Vidal, *Lincoln: A Novel* (New York: Random House, 1984), and William Safire, *Freedom: A Novel of Abraham Lincoln and the Civil War* (Garden City, NY: Doubleday, 1987). Historian James Tackach deals with these two novels and other recent works of Lincoln fiction in his helpful essay "Abraham Lincoln in Recent American Fiction," *Lincoln Herald* 110 (Winter 2008): 238–51.

13. M. Kay duPont, *Loving Mr. Lincoln: The Personal Diaries of Mary Todd Lincoln* (Atlanta: Jedco, 2003).

14. Barbara Hambly, *The Emancipator's Wife: A Novel of Mary Todd Lincoln* (New York: Random House, 2005).

15. Clinton, *Mrs. Lincoln*, 15.

16. Janis Cooke Newman, *Mary: Mrs. A. Lincoln* (2006; Orlando, FL: Harvest Books of Harcourt, 2007).

17. Ann Rinaldi, *An Unlikely Friendship: A Novel of Mary Todd Lincoln and Elizabeth Keckley* (Orlando, FL: Harcourt, 2007).

18. Elizabeth Keckley, *Behind the Scenes; or, Thirty Years a Slave, and Four Years in the White House* (New York: G. W. Carleton, 1868).

19. Katherine Helm, *The True Story of Mary, Wife of Lincoln* (New York: Harper, 1928); W. A. Evans, *Mrs. Abraham Lincoln: A Study of Her Personality and Her Influence on Lincoln* (New York: A. A. Knopf, 1932; reprinted Carbondale: Southern Illinois University Press, 2010); Ruth Painter Randall, *Mary Lincoln: Biography of a Marriage* (Boston: Little, Brown, 1953).

20. Turner and Turner, *Mary Todd Lincoln: Her Life and Letters*; Clinton, *Mrs. Lincoln: A Life*; Jean Baker, *Mary Todd Lincoln: A Biography* (New York: Norton, 1987).

21. The final two paragraphs draw on Richard W. Etulain, "Farmers in Southwestern Fiction," in Henry C. Dethloff and Irvin M. May Jr., eds., *Southwestern Agriculture: Pre-Columbian to Modern* (College Station: Texas A&M University Press, 1982), 28–46; and Etulain, "Telling Lewis and Clark Stories: Historical Novelists as Storytellers," in James P. Ronda and Nancy Tystad Koupal, eds., *Finding Lewis and Clark: Old Trails, New Directions* (Pierre: South Dakota State Historical Society Press, 2004), 114–33.

## "I Look Too Stern"
## Mary Lincoln and Her Image in the Graphic Arts

*Harold Holzer*

In mid-June 1864, less than a week after Abraham Lincoln won renomination for the presidency, and only a few days before he was scheduled to leave for Philadelphia to visit its Great Central Sanitary Fair, the White House received an intriguing letter from one of that city's most prominent pro-Republican newspaper editors. It offered the chief executive a valuable and unusual gift.

Feeling that he "owe[d] the President a debt of gratitude," publisher and philanthropist Thomas Fitzgerald generously proposed to commission a professional portrait likeness, not of the "wise and good President," but of his "good wife." For the beleaguered Lincoln, a perennially cooperative sitter for artists and sculptors, it must have been something of a relief to receive a request for sittings that did not require his personal participation.

What was more, this would be a painting by no ordinary artist. "We have living here" in Philadelphia, Fitzgerald boasted, "the greatest portrait painter in America—perhaps the greatest in the world—Mr. *Thomas Sully*—he, who was honored with the commission to paint that excellent woman, Queen Victoria." FitzGerald, one of his city's leading art patrons, had come to appreciate the artist from personal experience, for he had commissioned a treasured Sully portrait of his *own* wife. If Mary Lincoln could be persuaded to "sit to Mr. *Sully*," he vowed—noting that such sessions would require only six or eight hours altogether at her "convenience" during the upcoming Philadelphia visit—he would "present the portrait" to the Lincolns' "oldest son," Robert. "Mention the matter to the good woman," FitzGerald urged the president's private secretary, John G. Nicolay, "and, if she approves, I shall be delighted."[1]

If Nicolay or the president ever relayed this proposal to Mary, however, she apparently responded with less delight than the magnanimous Philadelphian anticipated. Nicolay, who hardly enjoyed the best of relationships with Mrs. Lincoln, may never even have mentioned it. All we know is that she never took FitzGerald up on his intriguing invitation. And never before or after did she have the opportunity to pose for such an accomplished painter. Nor, for that matter, did her husband, though he cheerfully sat for many far more pedestrian artists between 1860 and 1865.

The British-born, eighty-one-year-old Sully had been famous for so long—he had painted Victoria a full quarter of a century earlier—that the failure of the project to materialize was certainly more Mary Lincoln's loss than the artist's. As critic Henry T. Tuckerman observed just three years later, in one of the publishing world's first ever critical surveys of American art and artists: "If ever there was a man specially endowed to delineate our countrywomen . . . it is Thomas Sully. . . . Some of them float before the gaze like spirits of the air, or peer from a shadowy canvas like enchanted ladies. They are half-celestial, and we tremble, lest they should disappear as we gaze."[2] Mary Lincoln's image, made harsh in the 1860s by photographs that showed her aging and overdressed, would surely have benefited from one of Sully's ethereal portrayals. Yet it is not impossible to imagine that if Thomas FitzGerald's offer was placed before her, the obsessive and compulsive wife of the president threw up enough obstacles to doom the project before it even began.

On the other hand, it can be shown through a complete survey of Mary Lincoln iconography that she occasionally proved herself nearly as skillful a manipulator of her public image as her husband. Mary, who imagined herself both a glamorous hostess and a politically influential force within the Lincoln administration, contrived from time to time to circulate flattering, cosmeticized images of herself that she conceivably thought would soften her reputation even as she hungered for increased political influence behind the scenes. But what surprises the modern viewer is how seldom this supposedly vainglorious woman availed herself of opportunities to enhance her reputation through portraiture.

As with so many other noticeably diverging aspects of the Lincolns' public roles and private temperaments, Mary proved throughout her life as mercurial and unpredictable a subject for artists as her husband generally was easy to please. When it came to portraiture, while Lincoln called himself "a very indifferent judge"[3] of the varied results, Mary tended to be more opinionated, not only about pictures of herself, but also those of her husband.

Abraham Lincoln was renowned for mocking his own appearance, subjecting artists who sought sittings to a barrage of self-deprecating one-liners. "It is allowed to be ugly in this world," he told one, "but not as ugly as I am."[4] As he exclaimed when he first beheld one lifelike sculpture: "There is the animal himself!"[5] Yet even as he professed astonishment that anyone should want to own, much less create, a portrait of him, he also slyly managed to find time to pose for photographers more often than nearly all of his contemporaries. During his pressure-filled presidency, he also willingly endured prolonged sittings with painters and sculptors, one of whose projects (in that same year of 1864) required his presence at the White House for an astonishing six months.[6] Yet his diffidence always made it seem as if he were consenting to pose reluctantly, a perfect posture of modesty in the prevailing culture of Victorian restraint. Accordingly, Lincoln almost never made suggestions to artists on how they might improve their work—especially on the subject of how to smooth out the rough lines of his haggard face.[7]

Mary, who unlike her husband wore her opinions and emotions like badges of honor, left more specific commentary and opinions regarding those handful of pictorial projects in which we have documentary evidence of her participation. We typically see in these remarks the efforts of an image-conscious woman trying to make herself look younger, slimmer, and daintier, perhaps in the vain hope that ameliorating portraiture might counter the terrible press coverage she so routinely attracted during her White House years. Mary may not have been unique among First Ladies who cared about how they appeared to the public (Dolley Madison was famous for her colorful bonnets, for example). But she was the first president's wife (Lincoln's predecessor, Buchanan, was unmarried) to enter the White House in the new age of mass-produced photography, in which portraits could be widely and quickly distributed to a vast public. Such opportunities—and dangers—would have been very much on Mary's mind when she began shopping for a new wardrobe in New York following her husband's election.

We know, too, that painters who portrayed her husband occasionally asked for her opinions and endorsements. Of one such picture, an 1860 campaign portrait by Alban Jasper Conant, she commented approvingly: "That is the way he looks when he has his friends about him."[8] And that same summer, she remarked of a "perfect" and "excellent" miniature Lincoln portrait on ivory: "I see no fault or defect whatever."[9] The latter image inspired an engraving widely circulated in Pennsylvania before the presidential election. Mary must have known, as her husband did, that its sponsors considered its dissemination crucial to Republican hopes for victory in that state. As Mary thus came to learn, pictures not only illustrated; they influenced.

The first time that Mary—or, for that matter, Abraham—posed for an artist in any medium came when neither husband nor wife were famous: around 1846 in their Springfield, Illinois, hometown, when itinerant photographer Nicholas H. Shepherd took separate companion daguerreotypes of the couple (figures 1 and 2). Each dressed in handsome outfits for the occasion (and posing for a lengthy portrait in those early days of photography was an occasion indeed). The result shows Lincoln's hair slicked down for the sitting (perhaps even combed again at the gallery), making his ears appear to jut out from his head like pitcher handles. At best, he looks terribly ill-at-ease. Twenty-eight-year-old Mary, wearing her shoulder-length hair in ringlets, is clad in a fashionable belted dress of alternating vertical and horizontal stripes, accented by a vest or short coat gathered at the collar by a large cameo pin. The primitive camera cannot conceal her beauty. She looks simply lovely.

Figure 1. Nicholas H. Shepherd, [*Mary Lincoln*]. Daguerreotype, Springfield, Illinois, c. 1846. (Library of Congress)

Figure 2. Nicholas H. Shepherd, [*Abraham Lincoln*]. Daguerreotype, Springfield, Illinois, c. 1846. (Library of Congress)

Shepherd, an émigré to Springfield from New York, had first advertised his new "Daguerreotype Miniature Gallery" in the local paper, the *Sangamo Journal*, at the beginning of that year. His ad no doubt attracted the Lincolns' attention by quoting one of the couple's favorite poets, Robert Burns. "[B]y this process," the photographer claimed of his technique,

"'The giftie gie' us / To see oursel's as ithers see us.'" Shepherd's notice ended with the invitation, "The public are invited to call," and the Lincolns probably did so soon afterwards.[10] But this chronology is speculative and unavoidably imprecise; some experts (as well as the Lincolns' eldest son, Robert) subsequently attributed the picture to as late as 1849, and we will probably never be certain of when the couple actually posed for Shepherd.[11]

Actually, there was a time when the subjects' very identity was questioned, too. Although the oddly dandified Lincoln portrait once inspired no less an expert than biographer Albert Beveridge to insist, "it is the picture of some other man," Robert Lincoln always insisted it was genuine. He further reported that, together with the companion portrait of his mother, it hung on proud display "in my father's house as far back as I can remember anything there."[12] It came to light only in 1895, when Abraham Lincoln's sole surviving son showed the daguerreotype of the future president to journalist Ida Tarbell. She published it later that year in *McClure's Magazine*, prompting the late president's old legal colleague Henry Clay Whitney to agree: "It is without doubt authentic and accurate," adding irreverently: "I never saw him with his hair combed before."[13]

Yet while experts thus long ago resolved early doubts about their provenance and authenticity, most have missed a vital point about these pictures, one that can best be understood by again viewing them side-by-side. While Abraham Lincoln was of course by far the larger person physically—"the long and the short of it!" is how he described how he looked alongside his diminutive wife[14]—this early pair of portraits made Mary appear every bit as imposing as her husband, perhaps even more so. Technically, Shepherd accomplished this conceit simply by moving his camera closer to Mary than he had positioned it for Abraham. Was he trying to make them look equal in what were obviously designed as a matching pair of pictures? Or did Mary specifically ask Shepherd to make her look grander?

There is more to this conjecture than speculation about the techniques photographer Shepherd might have employed to make husband and wife appear of comparable stature. What should also intrigue the modern observer is what Shepherd did *not* produce that day: a portrait of the couple together. Other husbands and wives of the day, famous and ordinary alike, often posed side-by-side for photographers. Such pictures offered visual evidence of marital compatibility and permanence. The precious results—and it is important to keep in mind that these early-process daguerreotypes were one-print-per-exposure images that could not yet be mass-reproduced—became treasured keepsakes for married couples, their children, and their grandchildren. For those subjects without large incomes—like the Lincolns of this period—the option provided a bargain as well: a picture of two people for the price of one.

Then why did the Lincolns elect *not* to sit for Shepherd together? According to lore, Mary then and thereafter rejected the idea of posing with her husband because of their height disparity. This assertion is an oddity of sorts since she otherwise enjoyed reminding people that they were inseparable, even when the evidence, including later testimony by Mary herself, suggested otherwise. Surely visual evidence of their original closeness would have been welcome.

Legend persists that Mary disliked such pictures because Abraham was so much taller that they simply looked ridiculous standing side-by-side.[15] But this reasoning is unconvincing, since photographers of the day helped many similarly mismatched couples mask such height disparities by having the wife pose standing up alongside or behind her *seated* husband. Surely Nicholas Shepherd was fully capable of arranging such a composition for the "long and short of it" Lincolns. Though it is difficult to prove a negative—and inherently dangerous to draw a conclusion about the *absence* of evidence—we may well be justified in imagining that Mary *wanted* her own separate image, her own independent identity, consecrated in early photography. And as so often in their marriage, she got what she desired. As Lincoln once told a crowd of well-wishers, he "had always found it very difficult to make her do what she did not want to."[16] And for her first-known experience in a photographer's studio, and ever after, she simply did not want to pose with her husband.

For the next nineteen years of their marriage, much of it spent in the public eye, Mary Lincoln never again even accompanied him to a photographer's studio, although Lincoln posed on at least three occasions with one or more of their sons, and Mary herself once posed with both of the younger boys—but without their father. It would be left to artists and printmakers of the 1860s to invent for her, and for curious citizens, the domestic scenes that she so stubbornly and inexplicably eschewed. Unfortunately for Mary, these appeared much later, when whatever domestic bliss she enjoyed had been shattered by tragedy, and her dreams of making a reputation of her own had evaporated.

Although the increasingly famous Abraham Lincoln went on to pose for additional photographs in 1854, 1857, 1858, 1859, and again on several occasions during the year of his election to the presidency in 1860.[17] In an age in which women—even political spouses—were, with few exceptions (Jessie Benton Frèmont perhaps the most notable) never heard and seldom seen, Mary distanced herself from the scrutiny of visual reporters. For the next decade and a half, she grew older and stouter beyond the reach of the camera. If there are any identifiable exceptions to what may have been self-imposed seclusion, we have not yet discovered them. The closest she is said to have come to posing came in the summer of 1860, when she may have been lurking in the shadows behind an upper-story window of her Springfield home on the day her husband posed for a picture on their front step during a campaign rally. But it is impossible to pick her out with certainty among the crowd of ladies peering out to watch the event.

Otherwise, Mary remained out of sight, even when yet another photographer took a picture of candidate Lincoln and their two sons on the same front porch during that campaign summer.[18] Mary did not join them, even though by 1860 she surely knew that such photographs could be widely reproduced and sold to a public that increasingly regarded Lincoln as a national celebrity. Camera portraits and paintings of her husband were soon inspiring engraved and lithographed adaptations that were toted at political rallies, displayed at Republican clubs, or hung like icons above the family hearths in loyal homes. If Mary was ever as mania-cally ambitious for public favor as her critics have charged, the absence of any attempts to inspire her own public portraiture at this time testifies convincingly otherwise.

When Mary finally did pose again before the cameras, this time it was she who stood alongside her boys Willie and Tad. It was perhaps a sentimental keepsake of the small-town life she was about to leave behind, or a reaffirmation of what society considered her principal role, that of caregiver to her children.

The result showed all of them preening before a standard-issue but patently fake bucolic backdrop at the Springfield studio of photographer Preston Butler shortly after her husband's election to the presidency in November 1860[19] (figure 3). Wearing an ornate day dress, a shawl, and a flower-bedecked bonnet, she looks proud of her new station in life, but nonetheless rather grim, and it comes as no surprise that she intensely dis-liked the woodcut adaptation published in the popular periodical *Frank Leslie's Illustrated Newspaper* on December 15 (figure 4). Even though the newspaper proudly promoted its engraving as "splendid," the print was indeed crude and hardly introduced Mary to the American public as glamorously as she would have liked. Worse, perhaps, it identified her sons Willie and Thomas ("Tad") as "*Robert* and Thomas" (emphasis added), even though Robert was much older, and what was more, away at school. Nonetheless, as the original photo represented her very first portrait as wife of the new president-elect, Mary apparently overcame her disappointment and eventually shared copies with others. A year and a half later, probably referring to this very picture, the US minister to Russia, Cassius Clay, would write to President Lincoln to acknowledge "the photograph of Yourself, and her, and the children," adding: "They will be kept with pride, and handed down to our latest posterity."[20] More importantly, even if Mary did not yet recognize its impact, the *Leslie's* woodcut reproduction had finally made her own image public for a broad audience for the very first time.

Figure 3. Preston Butler, [*William Wallace Lincoln, Mary Lincoln, Thomas "Tad" Lincoln*]. Photograph, Springfield, Illinois, probably November 1860. Posed inside a studio before a piece of roll-down scenery suggesting the outdoors, this image was frequently mistaken for an authentic portrait of the mother and sons as they departed Springfield for Washington. (Library of Congress)

Figure 4. Printmaker unknown, after a photograph by Preston Butler, *Mary, William, and Thomas Lincoln*. Woodcut engraving, published in *Frank Leslie's Illustrated Newspaper*, New York, December 15, 1860. (Jack Smith Lincoln Graphics Collection, Indiana Historical Society, ID 8)

It would not be the last time, even though the next incarnation of the Mary Lincoln image must have displeased the subject even more, for it came in the form of caricature that mocked both husband and wife. Whether she liked it or not, Mary was now in the public spotlight, and that made her the object not only of inferior portraiture but also of objectionable lampoons—at time when caricature only portrayed females if they were suffragists or free-love advocates.

The first was inspired in February 1861, when Abraham Lincoln briefly left Mary and their boys behind in Springfield to commence the long journey to Washington for his inauguration (they were reunited the following morning in Indianapolis). His departure inspired an irreverent newspaper cartoon in a comic weekly called *Phunny Phellow*, showing their supposed farewell embrace (figure 5). The daub-like engraving made both of them look like country bumpkins. A second lampoon was inspired by Mary's visit to Barnum's Museum in New York, which at the time featured a sideshow attraction called "What Is It," featuring an underdeveloped black teenager cruelly advertised as half-man, half-beast. The "What Is It" display had only recently been inserted into an anti-Republican campaign print to suggest that the party's presidential candidate planned to make such backward people the equal of white citizens. The president-elect himself prudently avoided Barnum's sensational display during the family's New York stopover. But his absence did not prevent *Phunny Phellow*'s artist from portraying both Abraham *and* Mary Lincoln viewing the retrograde Barnum attraction at his vulgar museum.

Things got far worse for the Lincoln image when the president-elect separated from his family again in Harrisburg, Pennsylvania, to commence the final leg of his trip in secret to thwart an assassination plot allegedly awaiting him in Baltimore. Cartoonists had a field day lampooning the evasion. They typically exaggerated his attire into the disguise of a Scotch cap and a military cloak, implicitly charging him with cowardice. Mary, who had engendered criticism of her own for conducting a well-publicized preinaugural shopping spree to New York to purchase a new wardrobe for the White House, was thus spared from the harshest preinaugural pictorial assaults. It was perhaps not lost on readers of the day that one print published at the very same time by *Comic Monthly* ironically showed the president-elect, not his wife, wearing women's clothes—for any male, a most humiliating disguise. After enduring criticism for her lavish spending, it was Mary's husband who ended up in caricature garbed as a woman (years before cartoonists so depicted the captured

Figure 5. Printmaker unknown, *Progress of "Honest Old Abe" on His Way to the White House*, first page of a double-page woodcut engraving published in the *Phunny Fellow*, New York, April 1861. Mary was depicted in two of the eighteen panels: number 2, "Takes an affectionate farewell of his family," and number 14, "Goes to see What Is It? [at Barnum's Museum in New York]—has heard of him frequently." (Courtesy American Antiquarian Society)

Confederate leader Jefferson Davis after the Civil War).[21] At this early
stage of Lincoln image-making, the incoming chief executive appeared
ridiculous; Mary, shown in one cartoon wearing a stars-and-stripes dress,
briefly seemed more the patriot than her quaking husband.[22]

Although Mary returned to invisibility at the March 4, 1861, inaugural
ceremonies—segregated with other ladies at the US Capitol according to
the sexist traditions of the day—her patriotism would be usefully stressed
anew a few months later in an Alfred Waud *New-York Illustrated News*
illustration showing Lincoln, Mary, and one of their sons watching "The
New Jersey Brigade Passing in Review before the President" (figure 6).
The picture was clearly meant to signal to a nation in crisis that the new

Figure 6. Engraver unknown, after A[lfred]. Waud, *The New Jersey Brigade Passing
in Review before the President.* Woodcut engraving, published in the *New-York Illustrated News*, May 25, 1861. (Library of Congress)

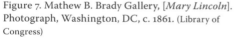

Figure 7. Mathew B. Brady Gallery, [*Mary Lincoln*]. Photograph, Washington, DC, c. 1861. (Library of Congress)

Figure 8. Kimmel and Fo[r]ster , after a photograph by Mathew B. Brady, *Mrs. President Lincoln*. Engraving, New York, c. 1861. (Library of Congress)

presidential family encouraged other American families to send recruits to confront secession and rebellion. Sadly, it was the last time that this woman who, in future years, spent much time comforting wounded soldiers at local hospitals, was so sympathetically or realistically portrayed. But in a sense, the fault was no one's but Mary's.

Printmakers relied on photographs to serve as models for the prints, and though Mary finally caught on to the medium's vast potential, she responded with the wrong kind of photographs. During that first presidential year of 1861, she regularly visited Washington's choicest photography

galleries, including Mathew Brady's, to pose for a series of ill-advised portraits that stressed not her commitment to the war effort but her love of
ostentatious clothes. In images published in *carte-de-visite* format editions ostensibly for loyal and celebrity-mad Americans to collect in their
family albums, Mary wore her best ball gowns, sometimes even bringing
a change of clothes and accessories so she could pose for additional and
varied pictures at the same sittings.[23] One particularly ornate ensemble,
featured in a full-length profile of Mary in an exquisite floor-length frock,
her hair bedecked in fresh flowers, came from the Mathew Brady studios in
late 1861 (figure 7). It was not only reproduced as a *carte* but also inspired
an extremely flattering lithographic adaptation by Kimmel and Fo[r]ster
of New York (figure 8) in which Mary was made to appear far younger and
better-situated than she was even the Executive Mansion. Adding to its
air of unreality, the print, titled *Mrs. President Lincoln*, showed Mary not
in a studio, not in a setting even vaguely resembling the White House,
but on what appeared to be the veranda of a splendid European villa. The
likeness later appeared in a vignetted, close-up edition no less retouched
but at least devoid of most of its absurdly ornate background and now
more modestly retitled *Mrs. Abraham Lincoln*. Yet the damage was done.

Perhaps her public, such as it was, rejected the idea of such a grandiose
image in the midst of a worsening war. Whatever may have motivated a
change of course, her later 1861 photographs showed a much more plainly
attired Mary Lincoln, inspiring a succession of popular prints over the
years that perhaps endeavored to reintroduce her as a more sensitive
figure for the age. A now-lost photographic pose from one such sitting—
marked by a simple hairstyle and plain dark dress with prim white collar—ultimately inspired a lithograph (figure 9) that attempted to present
Mary in this new dressed-down vein.

Philadelphia engraver Samuel Sartain used another lost photograph
(printmakers occasionally copied, and then disposed of, the photographic
models they adapted) for a well-made but rather unflattering engraving
(figure 10) copyrighted on November 15, 1864, and later photographed and

Figure 9. Printmaker unknown, *Mrs. Lincoln.* Lithograph, c. 1862. (Library of Congress)

sold as a keepsake for family albums. His equally successful printmaking brother William Sartain used yet another photographic original to produce a portrait of his own around this same time (figure 11), meant as one of a pair with a handsome—but separate—companion portrait of the President.

Not surprisingly, Mary was seldom fully satisfied with any of these results, particularly the unretouched photographs occasionally copied by printmakers. After reviewing "some of my photographs" from Brady's gallery in New York in 1861, for example, Mary sent an icy message to the studio urging the gallery "to have them destroyed." In a letter to Brady's

Figure 10. Samuel Sartain, *Mrs. Abra-ham Lincoln*. Philadelphia, engraving, copyright November 15, 1864. (Library of Congress)

Figure 11. William Sartain, *Mrs. Lincoln*. Philadelphia, engraving, c. 1864. (Library of Congress)

publishers, Edward and Henry Anthony, she added: "You will certainly oblige me, by doing so—The only one at all passable, is the one, standing, with the large figured dress—back almost turned—showing only side face—You will readily remark, which is the one—This you might retain—On Monday—I will sit for another, which we will send you, if you destroy the others."[24] From the surviving photographic archive, it is clear that the Brady operation did not heed her wishes, for the objectionable poses survive in copies published during this period. And they inspired print adaptations as well. Even if she was unsuccessful at halting their distribution, however, her pointed commentary marked Mary's first overt attempt to manage, and in this case censure, her image. But after her son Willie's death in February 1862, her visits to the photographers all but ceased. After seeing to a flood of gaudy new images that would remain in circulation for years, Mary again withdrew from the public gaze.

Much as she may have endeavored to transform herself from insensitive clotheshorse to sober wartime wife, however, Mary could not completely avoid portrayals that depicted her as a White House hostess. And until the loss of her son, Mary seemed intent on becoming the social leader of Washington despite fierce resistance from her many detractors. Though "Mrs. Lincoln was the peer of any woman in Washington in education and character," writer Leslie Perry later observed, "every ingenuity of malice was resorted to to discredit the new régime."[25] Fighting against the tide of public opinion, which questioned the propriety of her grandiose entertaining style and even hinted that the Southern-born First Lady was guilty of secret, secessionist leanings, Mary tried to maintain social leadership. Newspaper criticism only intensified. "No lady of the White House," charged the *Chicago Tribune*, under the headline "Press Hounding Mrs. Lincoln," had "ever been so maltreated."[26] As another sympathetic journalist, Noah Brooks, lamented in 1888: "Mrs. Lincoln could not enjoy that opportunity of vindicating, by her amiable and dignified life, her own much-misrepresented character. To this day, doubtless, the slanders of the gossips survive in some degree those evil times."[27]

Only Willie's tragic death—just days after the most ornate of all her White House soirees yet—inhibited social life in the president's mansion. For a time, the only widely circulated new photograph of Mary was an 1863 Brady Studio portrait showing her in a black dress, though extraordinarily accessorized with a suite of elaborate black mourning jewelry (figure 12). For many years it was the sole portrait image retained in the Lincoln family's photo album. And since Mary assembled the album's contents herself, the portrait certainly represents her own view of how she should be perceived and remembered.[28] Parlor prints of the period that continued to show her in formal attire, like Boston lithographer Louis Prang's glamorous portrait likeness (figure 13), must have seemed

MRS. LINCOLN.

L. Prang & C? Boston

Figure 12. Mathew B. Brady Gallery, [*Mary Lincoln*]. Photograph, probably Washington, published by E. and H. T. Anthony, New York, c. 1863. (From the Lincoln Financial Foundation Collection, courtesy of the Indiana State Museum; LM 0097)

Figure 13. L[ouis]. Prang and Co., *Mrs. Lincoln.* Lithographic carte-de-visite, Boston, c. 1861. (Jack Smith Lincoln Graphics Collection, Indiana Historical Society, ID 458)

discordant to period viewers aware of the family's loss. But since she made no efforts, as did her husband, to sit for paintings whose portrayals she might have been better able to control, Mary invariably remained the victim of her original poor judgment in posing at Brady's so often in her ostentatious gowns.

Print adaptations mass-produced for domestic display at least did succeed in somewhat softening her prevailing image. Before the unrelenting gaze of the camera, tightly pursing her lips for the long exposures that mid-nineteenth-century photographs required, Mary seemed chronically unable to look pleasant. Printmakers—even those who adapted these unflattering photographic originals—characteristically removed the lines in her face and reduced her stout figure, making her appear younger and slimmer. They served also to keep her in the public eye, even though she described herself as living in "the fiery furnace of affliction."[29]

Following the protracted seclusion she chose for herself following Willie's death, Mary eventually returned to entertaining, throwing a particularly memorable White House reception in March 1864 to welcome newly commissioned Lieutenant General Ulysses S. Grant to Washington. Artist Peter Rothermel almost certainly had this event in mind when he produced his bravura canvas, *Republican Court in the Days of Lincoln* (figure 14).[30] Later, inexplicably, an advertising brochure for the painting promoted it as a depiction of Lincoln's second inaugural ball, a party that in fact took place not at the White House but at the US Patent Office (now the National Portrait Gallery).

Whatever the occasion or setting that inspired it, there was no denying Rothermel's talent for portraiture. His painting depicted tiny but uncannily accurate likenesses of both active and former members of the military and political establishments, friends and foes alike, incongruously gathered together in an East Room that assumes the proportions of a European palace. A towering Lincoln stands on a receiving line alongside General Grant (who was certainly not present at the 1865 second inaugural), while Mary tenderly fusses over the elderly general Winfield Scott—"Mrs. Lincoln

Figure 14. Peter F. Rothermel, *"The Republican Court" in the Days of Lincoln.* Oil on canvas, c. 1867. (The White House Historical Association [White House Collection], 202)

addressing the late Gen'l Scott," the brochure boasted. In truth, by the time of either the 1864 Grant reception or the 1865 inaugural, Scott was very much alive but had been long retired to West Point, never again to return to Washington. His inclusion as a central character, however, offered advantages to both the artist and to Mary Lincoln. First, it allowed Rothermel to showcase yet another recognizable celebrity in his bustling scene. And second, it encouraged him to depict Mary in a low-cut gown, bending over the aging old war hero. It was often said by admirers that Mary had the best neck, shoulders, and bosom in Washington—and here the painter gave his audience the chance to glimpse her assets for themselves.

"This great historical work has engaged the attention of Mr. Rothermel for nearly two years," the period advertisement boasted, "and is intended to give to the present generation and to posterity, portraits of the prominent personages of the time, in the most pleasing manner possible."[31] That it included Chief Justice Roger B. Taney, a sworn enemy of the president who in fact died before the second inaugural, could not have pleased literal viewers. Far more ridiculous was the inclusion of former general

George B. McClellan, of all people, fired by Lincoln in 1862, and by 1864 the Democratic presidential candidate challenging Lincoln for reelection. Here, in the most bizarre incongruity of all, Rothermel depicted him not only back in uniform, but *dancing*. Still, the overall result must have thrilled Mary, who, shown attired in white, stands out in the sea of black-clad men like a glistening angel. Historical accuracy hardly mattered as much as flattering portraiture.

Rothermel's complex composition was never reproduced by printmakers; it probably posed too much of a challenge. But for mass audiences, the scene was quickly pirated by Frank Leslie's sprawling publishing empire and reimagined for a large lithograph copyrighted on April 8, 1865,

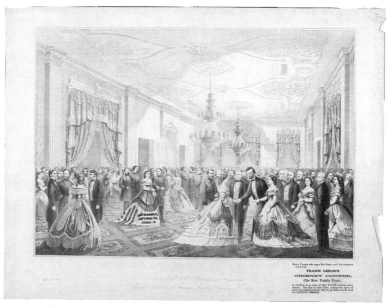

Figure 15. [Henry B.] Major and [Joseph] Knapp, *Grand Reception of the Notabilities of the Nation, at the White House 1865. Dedicated to Mrs. Abraham Lincoln by the Publishers of Frank Leslie's Chimney Corner.* Lithograph, published by Frank Leslie, New York, 1865. (Collection of the New-York Historical Society, gift of Henry O. Havemeyer, PR 052)

titled *Grand Reception of the Notabilities of the Nation* (figure 15)—and specifically "dedicated to Mrs. Abraham Lincoln." In this more modest but still sprawling scene, Lincoln and Mary, appearing in the right foreground alongside Vice President Andrew Johnson and General Grant, greet notables at a less palatial, more realistic-looking East Room reception. The print likely achieved wide circulation. Though it was priced at a hefty three dollars, a considerable sum, it was offered as a free premium to anyone who paid but ten cents for the first two editions of the firm's new "family paper," *Frank Leslie's Chimney Corner.* To help readers identify the bargain print's large cast of characters, the paper also published a key to all thirty-seven of the celebrities portrayed (cleverly withholding the key's publication until issue number 4, to sustain circulation), including military men, politicians, famous ladies, and even three New York newspaper publishers.[32] Within weeks of the print's appearance, however, it would be copied and reissued by another lithographer, now retitled *Lincoln's Last Reception*—for just days after Leslie issued the original, the president was dead by an assassin's hand.

Ironically, nothing the controversial First Lady ever did in her life benefited her image as much as did her husband's death on April 15, 1865. Mary's stormy reign as mistress of the country's largest residence ended in the tiny back room of a common boardinghouse, across the street from a setting many Americans thought indecent (especially on the day they attended, Good Friday): a theatre. Yet as it turned out, these unlikely settings launched Mary Lincoln's temporary visual salvation.

Within weeks of the tragedy, printmakers rushed out wholly imagined reverential prints of both Lincoln's murder (figures 16 and 17) and final moments (figures 18 and 19), in nearly all of which Mary had a prominent role as herself a victim of the heinous crime. These engravings and lithographs showed her seated alongside her beloved husband in the theater box as John Wilkes Booth crept behind them to take Lincoln's life; or lovingly attending him in the room where he died nine hours later, often clutching her hands in sorrow, a latter-day Mary at a modern Golgotha.

Figure 16. H. H. Lloyd, *Assassination of President Lincoln, at Ford's Theatre Apl. 14th 1865. "Treason and Murder Work Together."* Engraving, New York, 1865. (Library of Congress)

Figure 17. [Nathaniel] Currier and [James Merritt] Ives, *The Assassination of President Lincoln, at Ford's Theatre Washington, D.C. April 14th 1865.* Lithograph, New York, 1865. (Library of Congress)

Figure 18. Currier and Ives, *Death of President Lincoln, at Washington, D.C. April 15th 1865. The Nation's Martyr.* Lithograph, New York, 1865. (Collection of the New-York Historical Society, PR 052)

Figure 19. P[eter]. Kramer, *Death Bed of Lincoln.* Engraving, printed by A. Brett, published by Jones and Clark, New York, C. A. Asp, Washington, and W. M. Kohl, Cincinnati, 1865. (Library of Congress)

Technically, this Mary was not actually present at his bedside when her husband expired at the Petersen House. Reduced to hysteria by the horrific crime, she was unceremoniously banished to an adjacent parlor by Secretary of War Edwin M. Stanton after her outbursts and fainting spells unnerved the other witnesses to the president's final moments. There she remained, isolated and excluded, sobbing outside the crowded death chamber, when Stanton finally proclaimed to other eyewitnesses: "Now he belongs to the ages." Only then was Mary permitted back inside for one final glimpse at her husband's remains.

Most printmakers of the day ignored this inconvenient truth. Engravers and lithographers, who rushed deathbed scenes to the market to satisfy public hunger for visualizations of the worst crime in American history, judged that audiences expected to see the president's wife represented in their portrayals of Lincoln's final moments whether she was actually present or not. Tradition required nothing less, and only a handful of printmakers opted for reality and omitted the widow from the tragic scene. Most did not. And thus the long-maligned clotheshorse, pretentious hostess, and suspected traitor was transformed virtually overnight into a brave and aggrieved Civil War widow—winning empathy by sharing the same fate as the hundreds of thousands of women who had lost loved ones in America's bloodiest war. Prints showed her weeping at or sprawled over Lincoln's sanitized deathbed, or clinging to her little son Tad, who in fact was not brought to the scene at all that night.[33] Except for the occasional print that also included Clara Harris—the celebrated actress starring in the play the Lincolns were viewing when he was shot—Mary was the only woman in these historic scenes, a touch of deeply affecting private emotion at an otherwise glaringly public death. Lincoln's death thus breathed new life into her image.

The two extremes that wartime Mary Lincoln iconography emphasized—vainglorious or victimized—were of course oversimplified. Mary never behaved quite as badly as her critics charged or well as her admirers hoped. But for a nation caught up in mass mourning, such details now hardly seemed to matter. Mary may have lost her happiness and her husband on Good Friday, April 1865, but for a time she regained her place alongside the martyred national hero—at least in the assassination and deathbed pictures that Americans now clamored for and reverently displayed in their homes. In countless variations on this theme, published here and abroad, Mary became the unquestioned First Lady of the Union at last.

The assassination inspired yet another genre of image-making that likewise did immense, if temporary, good to Mary Lincoln's tarnished reputation. Long averse for whatever reason to posing with her husband, she now benefited from the publication of cleverly created composite photographs that showed her "alongside" the late president (figure 20). These concocted pictures invariably made her look taller than she really was and, more importantly, linked her formally and permanently to her husband. *Carte-de-visite* copies filled many Northern family albums.[34] Artist Pierre Morand's earlier life sketch of Abraham and Mary strolling outside the White House gates (figure 21) probably delineated when they were en route to their summer residence at the Soldiers' Home outside Washington, perhaps showed them more realistically, "the long and the short of it" again. But this drawing was neither reproduced nor even known at the time, and remains merely a historical curiosity, albeit a compelling one.

Even more ubiquitous were the elaborate group portraits bearing titles like "President Lincoln and Family Circle" or "Lincoln at Home," dozens of examples of which circulated widely throughout the North after the assassination. Long appreciated as images that gave Americans the comforting impression that the late president had enjoyed a nurturing domestic life during the Civil War, the pictures deserve to be seen, too, as image-softening breakthroughs for Mary. After all, they firmly and convincingly placed her within the most sacred of American spheres outside the church—the family parlor—implicitly nurturing her husband and sons even if she was seldom specifically identified in the titles to such pictures. She was simply there, part of America's most famous diminished family, and that was more than enough.

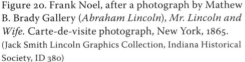

Figure 20. Frank Noel, after a photograph by Mathew B. Brady Gallery (*Abraham Lincoln*), *Mr. Lincoln and Wife*. Carte-de-visite photograph, New York, 1865. (Jack Smith Lincoln Graphics Collection, Indiana Historical Society, ID 380)

Figure 21. Pierre Morand, [*Abraham Lincoln and Mary Lincoln*]. Ink sketch, Washington, c. 1864 (National Portrait Gallery, NPG.75.28, Smithsonian Institution / Art Resource, NY)

Of course, such images of family togetherness were inaccurate, and not just because its members had never actually posed together. The fact is, they probably seldom even dined together during the Lincoln presidency. We have Mary's own testimony that she rarely enjoyed her husband's company once the Civil War started. "I consider myself fortunate," she confided to one of her old friends in the fall of 1864, "if at eleven o'clock, I once more find myself, in my pleasant room & very especially, if my tired & weary Husband, is *there*, resting in the lounge to receive me—to chat over the occurrences of the day."[35] But as early as 1860 Mary confessed that her husband no longer had time for "home affairs."[36] After that date, the entire family was rarely together as a unit. Robert spent much of the war years away at college and law school in Boston and then joined the army. And Willie died less than a year after the Lincolns moved into the White House, casting a permanent pall over the entire family. Nevertheless, postassassination domestic scenes, however contrived, established Mary as an important and continual presence alongside her beleaguered husband and three sons. Lincoln family pictures usually included Willie, his early death notwithstanding (figure 22). And they often portrayed Robert wearing the uniform of a Union army captain (figure 23), a post he held only for the last few months of the war and, as it happened, against the will of his mother, who feared for his life should he volunteer. (Lincoln saw to his appointment to Grant's staff to minimize risk.)

Surely more than a few sophisticated Americans must have suspected that these usually oversize display pieces (as well as the miniature photographic copies printed for family albums) hardly qualified as accurate depictions of the star-crossed Lincolns. But for the unschooled, they were surely convincing enough. In the absence of original photographs or paintings showing the Lincoln parents and children, they too were composites, pieced together awkwardly from existing individual poses, or wholly fabricated ("Tad" sometimes appeared as an anonymous, not to mention androgynous, drummer boy with uncharacteristically long, flowing hair). A photograph of Lincoln and Tad taken at Mathew Brady's Washington gallery under artist Francis B. Carpenter's personal supervision in February 1864 (figure 24) more often than not served as a central model for these scenes—around which other family members were added—though they sometimes transformed Tad into Willie and never acknowledged Carpenter with the credit he deserved for arranging the famous original pose. In a sense, the 1864 Brady sitting at which it was created also represented yet another missed opportunity for Mary to be captured for posterity with her family. Nevertheless she "joined" such scenes anyway (figure 25), the last missing piece in the puzzle that, as assembled

Figure 22. J[oseph]. Hoover, after a photograph of Lincoln and Tad by Anthony Berger, Brady's Gallery, *President Lincoln and Family Circle.* Lithograph, Philadelphia, 1864. (From the Lincoln Financial Foundation Collection, courtesy of the Indiana State Museum, LM 2248)

Figure 23. Anton Hohenstein, after a photograph of Lincoln and Tad by Alexander Gardner, *President Lincoln and His Family.* Lithograph, published by Joseph Hoover, 1865. (Library of Congress)

by ingenious printmakers, granted her after death had destroyed her family circle the motherly image she had done so little in life to promote.

One of the best of the family genre was William Sartain's adaptation (figure 26) of a now-lost painting by Samuel B. Waugh, but similarly based on existing photographs. The engraving showed the Lincolns gathered

Figure 24. Anthony Berger, Brady's Gallery, [*Abraham Lincoln and His Son, Thomas "Tad" Lincoln*]. Photograph, Washington, February 9, 1864. (Library of Congress)

Figure 25. Currier and Ives, *President Lincoln at Home, Reading Scripture to His Wife and Son.* Lithograph, New York, 1865. (Jack Smith Lincoln Graphics Collection, Indiana Historical Society, P0406_182, ID 182)

around a parlor table: a grown-up-looking Tad, a solemn Robert, and the late and lamented Willie represented by a painting in the background. Mary is shown resting her dainty feet on an embroidered pillow, tending dutifully to her sewing as the president tenderly reaches a hand in her direction. Its publishers boasted that "in accuracy of portraiture and artistic excellence of execution [the print] is acknowledged to be unsurpassed by any Engraving ever issued in America." Here, its creators may have been guilty of commercially motivated marketing hyperbole, but a circular published to promote the print was certainly accurate in noting: "The grouping is graceful and harmonious." Critics agreed. With enthusiasm, the *Boston Post* declared it "one of the best artistic productions of its kind," predicting it would become "a desirable picture for thousands of homes in the land." The prints were expensive: Copies sold for $7.25, with artist's proofs priced at $20.[37] But the large number of surviving copies indicates that they were popular in their day.

Ironically, by the time this outpouring of family images began flooding the market, the widow Lincoln had again completely isolated herself from

Figure 26. William Sartain, after photographs and a painting by Samuel B. Waugh, *Lincoln and His Family.* Mezzotint engraving, published by Bradley and Co., Philadelphia, 1866. (Library of Congress)

the public, the press, and the image-makers—with one notable exception. When Mary learned that artist Francis Carpenter was to undertake a Lincoln family painting of his own, one that would also be reproduced as a fine engraving "in superb style,"[38] Mary agreed to participate in the project personally. The artist had not only posed Lincoln and Tad at Brady's a year earlier; he had spent six months during the summer and fall of 1864 painting a huge canvas titled *The First Reading of the Emancipation Proclamation before the Cabinet,* an enormous popular and critical triumph that inspired one of the best-selling engravings of the entire nineteenth century. Showing her old wit, Mary had ruefully commented at its unveiling that it appeared to portray the president's "happy family"—that is, his official, rather than his personal, one.[39] If he conveyed such an impression in his masterwork, Carpenter labored to make up for it in private. While working at the White House in 1864, he also executed a handsome pair of paintings of Abraham and Mary Lincoln (figures 27 and 28), undoubtedly from life sittings but modeled at least in part on existing photographs. In a way, they provided updated "pendants" to the companion daguerreotypes made in Springfield only eighteen years—but a lifetime of experience—earlier. Carpenter also used his time in the White House to make a small painting of Lincoln with Tad, and, it was long believed, an additional canvas of Mary wearing a brooch adorned with a photograph of her husband—later proven to be a fake.[40]

Understandably, Mary came to regard the attentive painter highly. She even testified that Carpenter's 1864 study head of her husband, engraved by Frederick W. Halpin of New York, was "the most perfect likeness of my husband, that I have ever seen," adding in a unique letter of endorsement that Carpenter released to the press: "the resemblance is so accurate, that it will require far more calmness, than I can now command, to have it continually placed before me."[41]

Though no calmer, Mary offered if not her fullest possible cooperation, then at least her input, for Carpenter's Lincoln family project. In her

Figure 27. Francis B. Carpenter, [*Abraham Lincoln*]. Oil on canvas, Washington, c. 1864. (Lilly Library, Indiana University, Bloomington)

Figure 28. Francis B. Carpenter, [*Mary Lincoln*]. Oil on canvas, Washington, c. 1864. (Courtesy Lilly Library, Indiana University, Bloomington, Indiana)

agitated condition after the assassination, she could not bring herself to pose for a fresh photographic model herself, not even to accommodate Carpenter's quest for the perfect portrait. It would be "utterly impossible," she insisted, "in my present nervous state, to sit"[42]—besides which, as she well knew, she had aged markedly in recent years and certainly looked particularly worn and swollen after months of intense grieving for her late husband. Still, she managed to pull herself together enough by November 1865 to become an active participant in Carpenter's ambitious project.

When Carpenter obligingly proposed using an existing photographic portrait of her as a model, Mary weighed in with a litany of objections that suggested not only irritation over photographic techniques generally, but notwithstanding her distractions and distress, a frank and surprisingly detailed critique of her own imperfect appearance and unyielding standards. While the "attitude in the one, you sent me, of myself, is very good," she argued, "my hands are always *made* in *them*, very large and I look too stern. The drapery of the dress, was *not* sufficiently flowing—and my hair, should not be so low down, on the forehead & so much dressed." Instead she urged the artist to use what she called "an excellent painted likeness of me, at Brady's in N. Y. taken in 1861," adding: "I am sure you will like it & I believe, it was taken, in a black velvet."[43]

It comes as no surprise that Mary favored that particular photograph (figure 29)—or that she referred to it as a "painted likeness." Brady had generously retouched the original camera study, prettifying her typically sour facial expression and nipping and tucking at the waist and hips to make her appear much thinner than she was in life. Though Carpenter did not ultimately follow Mary's instructions to adapt this particular pose, preferring to depict her seated so she could be shown together with the president and their three sons at their dining table, the artist did follow the widow's implicit instructions to glamorize her. And he followed her advice to the letter when it came to selecting models for the portraits

Figure 29. Mathew B. Brady Gallery, [*Mary Lincoln*]. Photograph, Washington, c. 1861. (Library of Congress)

of Robert (the "best likeness," Mary advised, was a photograph taken by John Goldin in 1864) and of "my precious sainted Willie" (she personally sent Carpenter a favorite photograph, though she noted: "Even, in *that* likeness . . . justice, is not done him, he was a very beautiful boy, with a most *spiritual* expression of face." Mary assured Carpenter that these poses would "answer very well, for the picture, you propose painting."[44]

New York publisher J. C. Derby paid Carpenter a fee of $500 for the resulting chiaroscuro oil study (figure 30),[45] which John Chester Buttre then engraved in mezzotint (figure 31), faithfully reproducing the original canvas but generously eliminating the double chin afflicting Mary in Carpenter's original. Although it did not appear until 1867, a full two years after the market had been flooded with wholly invented, unauthorized, and occasionally grotesque Lincoln family images, the Carpenter-Buttre collaboration endures as the only officially sanctioned image of Mr. and Mrs. Lincoln and their three sons together, in a domestic setting adorned by books and food (physical and intellectual nourishment) that suggest a stability and happiness that in real life eluded them. It is the closest we have to the "official" Lincoln family portrait.

If Mary ever saw and admired Carpenter's handsome engraving, however, she never said so. By then she had characteristically broken with him. Although during its creation she thoughtfully presented the artist with one of her husband's precious canes in recognition of how "connected" Carpenter had been "for months, with the White House," within a year a livid Mary unconvincingly dismissed him as one of those "silly adventurers, with whom my husband had scarcely the least acquaintance."

Carpenter's sin was that he had begun not only painting but also writing. After he published memoirs of his six months' experience at the White House, and worse in Mary's eyes, retitled a second edition of his best seller *The Inner Life of Abraham Lincoln*, the president's protective widow proclaimed to the world that he was nothing but a "stranger" to the family after all.[46] The only part of the volume to which Mary might conceivably have objected was its use of a letter the widow had written to

Figure 30. Francis B. Carpenter, after photographs by Mathew B. Brady and John Goldin, *The Lincoln Family in 1861.* Oil on canvas, c. 1865–6. (Collection of the New-York Historical Society)

Figure 31. J[ohn]. C[hester]. Buttre, after Francis B. Carpenter, *The Lincoln Family in 1861.* Engraving, published by Derby and Miller, New York, 1867. (New-York Historical Society, PR 052)

the artist after the assassination—but it merely reported that the president had been "supremely happy" that fateful day.[47] Had Mary accepted the popular and highly flattering Carpenter book with more grace, the artist might have continued working to revive Mary's again-declining image. But they never reconciled, and as usual Mary suffered more from the rift than her perceived enemy. In the brief, turbulent history of Mary Lincoln iconography, it is clear, Mary's worst enemy was always herself.

Aside from sitting for one subsequent photograph enshrouded in widow's weeds around 1869,[48] Mary never again participated in a project aimed at reversing her public disfavor—a situation made worse when her later, ill-advised attempt to sell used gowns triggered a humiliating scandal covered in both words and pictures. In one sketch for a New

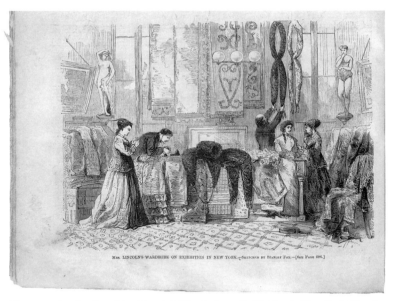

Figure 32. Stanley Fox, *Mrs. Lincoln's Wardrobe on Exhibition in New York*. Woodcut engraving, published in *Harper's Weekly*, October 26, 1867. (Collection of the New-York Historical Society, G71.H29)

York weekly (figure 32), artist Stanley Fox showed eager shoppers greedily rummaging through trunks of dresses, scarves, and muffs as classical statues of naked women (deprived of clothing, the joke suggests, like the late president's wife herself) look on with symbolic disapproval from pedestals in the background. The Mary Lincoln image, always a fragile thing, now descended into mockery. It would never recover.

In the years since the couple had sat for Nicholas H. Shepherd in Springfield, her husband's reputation had soared, taking him from obscurity to immortality: In print portraits, he had progressed from homespun prairie candidate to national saint, depicted in some postassassination images in the embrace not of Mary but of George Washington.[49] Mary, so intent on appearing as a separate personality from the moment she entered a Springfield daguerrian gallery in 1846, ended up enduring more loneliness than she could have imagined, losing her husband in 1865 and Tad to tuberculosis in 1871, and ultimately falling out painfully with her sole surviving son, Robert. Along the way, and in criticism that only increased after 1865, she was recalled as a selfish spendthrift whose husband perhaps loved another woman more than his wife. The family circle portrayed in the group portraits of 1865–1867 had irrevocably broken, and Mary was no longer sufficiently viable commercially as an individual subject to inspire prints that might have presented her in a more sympathetic light.

As it turned out, Mary Lincoln's very last image, much like her very first, was made not for public consumption, but for private contemplation. Just as the Shepherd daguerreotype a quarter of a century earlier had showcased her youthful vigor and self-control, her final portrait could not disguise her deterioration and desperation. Mary Lincoln's last portrait was a so-called "spirit image" made at her request by a Boston charlatan who preyed on bereft widows who, like Mary, believed in spiritualism. Photographer William Mumler posed his gullible subjects in his unadorned studio, then used crude trickery in the darkroom to craft composites that supposedly "revealed" the ghosts of dearly departed

Figure 33. William H. Mumler, [*Mary Lincoln, with the "Spirits" of Tad and Abraham Lincoln*]. Photograph, Boston, c. 1871–1875. (College of Psychic Studies, London, England)

relatives, returned to the earthly world to offer solace.[50] The Mary Lincoln pose that Mumler made sometime between 1871 and 1875 shows a small, pitifully bloated old lady, still dressed completely in black. But looming behind her is a ghostly Lincolnesque apparition, his spectral hands resting comfortingly on her shoulders (figure 33).

At long last, albeit in an obvious and pathetic fake, Mary and Abraham Lincoln had finally posed together.

## Notes

1. Thomas Fitzgerald to John G. Nicolay, June 13, 1860, John G. Nicolay Papers, Library of Congress. The eclectic Fitzgerald later founded the Philadelphia Athletics baseball team; Lincoln made his son Ritter Fitzgerald a member of the diplomatic corps. The Sully portraits of Mrs. FitzGerald are now in the Ogden Museum of Southern Art.

2. Henry T. Tuckerman, *Book of the Artists: American Artist Life* (1867; reprinted New York: James F. Carr, 1967), 158–59

3. Abraham Lincoln to Thomas Doney, July 30, 1860, in Roy P. Basler, Marion Dolores Pratt, and Lloyd A. Dunlap, eds., *The Collected Works of Abraham Lincoln* (New Brunswick, NJ: Rutgers University Press, 1953–1955; hereinafter cited as *Collected Works of Lincoln*), 4:89. For a discussion of the image-making project that inspired this comment from candidate Lincoln, see Harold Holzer, Mark E. Neely, and Gabor S. Boritt, *The Lincoln Image: Abraham Lincoln and the Popular Print* (New York: Charles Scribner's Sons, 1984), 22–23.

4. Marie de Mare, *G. P. A. Healy, American Artist: An Intimate Chronicle of the Nineteenth Century* (New York: David McKay, 1954), 191.

5. Leonard W. Volk, "The Lincoln Life-Mask and How It Was Made," *Century Illustrated Monthly Magazine* 23 (December 1881): 223.

6. See Harold Holzer, Gabor S. Boritt, and Mark E. Neely Jr., "Francis Bicknell Carpenter (1830–1900): Painter of Abraham Lincoln and His Circle," *American Art Journal* 16 (Spring 1984): 66–89.

7. For examples, see Holzer, Boritt, and Neely, *The Lincoln Image*; also Harold Holzer, "Some Contemporary Paintings of Abraham Lincoln," *Magazine Antiques* 107 (February 1975): 314–22; Harold Holzer and Lloyd Ostendorf, "Sculptures of Abraham Lincoln from Life," *Magazine Antiques* 123 (February 1978): 382–93. An exception to Lincoln's reluctance to advise artists came in an 1864 letter to lithographer E. C. Middleton, in which he criticized a print portrait and advised the artist "to carefully study a photograph." See Lincoln to Middleton, December 30, 1864, Basler et al., *Collected Works of Lincoln*, 8:191–92.

8. Mary Lincoln quoted in R. Gerald McMurtry, *Beardless Portraits of Abraham Lincoln* (Fort Wayne, IN: Lincoln National Life Foundation, 1962), 39.

9. Mary Lincoln to John Meredith Read, August 25, 1860, in Justin G. Turner and Linda Levitt Turner, *Mary Todd Lincoln: Her Life and Letters*, hereinafter cited as *MTL Letters* (New York: Alfred A. Knopf, 1972), 65. This comment was made about a miniature on ivory by Philadelphia artist John Henry Brown.

10. *Sangamo Journal*, January 15, 1846, reproduced in Lloyd Ostendorf, *Lincoln's Photographs: A Complete Album* (Dayton, OH: Rockywood, 1998), 5.

11. Robert Lincoln to the editors of *McClure's Magazine*, November 21, 1896, in Louis A. Warren, "Portraits of Congressman Lincoln," *Lincoln Lore*, no. 1382 (October 3, 1955).

12. Ibid.

13. Philip B. Kunhardt III, Peter W. Kunhardt, and Peter W. Kunhardt Jr., *Lincoln, Life-Size* (New York: Alfred A. Knopf, 2009), 2.

14. See, for example, remarks at Leaman Place, Pennsylvania, February 22, 1861, in *Collected Works of Lincoln*, 4:242. The remark "produced a loud burst of laughter," noted the *Lancaster Evening Express.*

15. Pioneer Lincoln photograph expert Stefan Lorant speculated that her sensitivity about their height difference accounts for why "they were never photographed together." See Lorant, *Lincoln: A Picture Story of His Life*, rev. ed. (New York: W. W. Norton, 1969), 303.

16. Remarks at Ashtabula, OH, February 16, 1861, Basler, et al., *Collected Works of Lincoln*, 4:218.

17. See Ostendorf, *Lincoln's Photographs*, 381–91.

18. Ibid., 390, 392. William A. Shaw took the picture of the campaign rally on August 8; J. A. Whipple made the image of Abraham, Willie, and Tad sometime that summer.

19. Lloyd Ostendorf, *The Photographs of Mary Todd Lincoln* (Springfield: Illinois State Historical Society, 1969), 10–11.

20. Cassius Clay to Abraham Lincoln, August 13, 1862, Abraham Lincoln Papers, Library of Congress.

21. See Mark E. Neely Jr., Harold Holzer, and Gabor S. Boritt, *The Confederate Image: Prints of the Lost Cause* (Chapel Hill: University of North Carolina Press, 1987), 79–96.

22. The images were rediscovered by historian Gary L. Bunker and published in his *From Rail-Splitter to Icon: Lincoln's Image in Illustrated Periodicals* (Kent, OH: Kent State University Press, 2001), 86–89.

23. Ostendorf, *The Photographs of Mary Todd Lincoln*, 43–49.

24. Mary Lincoln to "Mr. Anthony," November 1861, *MTL Letters*, 116.

25. Quoted in Katherine Helm, *The True Story of Mary, Wife of Lincoln* (New York: Harper and Brothers, 1928), 173

26. *Chicago Tribune*, August 13, 1861, quoted in Catherine Clinton, *Mrs. Lincoln: A Life* (New York: HarperCollins, 2009), 151.

27. Noah Brooks, *Abraham Lincoln and the Downfall of American Slavery* (New York: G. P. Putnam's Sons, 1888), 422.

28. Mark E. Neely Jr. and Harold Holzer, *The Lincoln Family Album* (1990; rev. ed. Carbondale: Southern Illinois University Press, 2006), 62. Robert marked the back of the family copy, "Return to the Hon. R. T. Lincoln," suggesting that he often lent the pose to publishers who wished to reproduce it.

29. Mary described herself after Willie's death as in "*deep waters*" that seemed to "overwhelm her." See *MTL Letters*, 116, 189, 285.

30. "The Republican Court in the Days of Lincoln, by P. F. Rothermel" (New York: Russell's American Steam Printing House, c. 1869), Broadside, Ephemera Collection, Library of Congress.

31. Ibid.

32. "Key to This Plate," in Holzer, Boritt, and Neely, *The Lincoln Image*, 145. The key did not appear until the fourth issue of *Chimney Corner*, encouraging subscribers to sign on long-term. The three publishers appearing in the print were Horace Greeley, Henry Raymond, and James Gordon Bennett.

33. For a full range of examples, see Harold Holzer and Frank J. Williams, "Lincoln's Deathbed in Art and Memory: The 'Rubber Room' Phenomenon," in Holzer, Craig L. Symonds, and Williams, eds., *The Lincoln Assassination: Crime and Punishment, Myth and Memory* (New York: Fordham University Press, 2010), 9–53.

34. For examples, see Lorant, *Lincoln: A Picture Story of His Life*, 303.

35. Mary Lincoln to Mercy Conkling, November 19, 1864, *MTL Letters*, 187.

36. Mary Lincoln to Hannah Shearer, October 20, 1860, *MTL Letters*, 66.

37. *Lincoln and His Family*, no date. Advertising brochure in the former Lincoln Museum collection, photocopy in the author's collection.

38. Quoted in Holzer, Boritt, and Neely, *The Lincoln Image*, 177.

39. Quoted in Francis B. Carpenter, "Anecdotes and Reminiscences of President Lincoln," in Henry R. Raymond, *Life, Public Services, and State Papers of Abraham Lincoln* (New York: Derby and Miller, 1865), 763.

40. The discredited painting long hung in the governor's mansion in Springfield, Illinois. Though Carpenter dated all later works "1864," there is no proof that he really painted them from life during his White House period, since he continued using that date on the pictures he produced into the 1890s. See Holzer, Neely, and Boritt, "Francis Bicknell Carpenter," 82; *New York Times*, February 12, 2012.

41. Mary Lincoln to Francis B. Carpenter, December 25, 1866, *MTL Letters*, 403. The endorsement was excerpted and published in the advertising sheet *Abraham Lincoln. The Standard Portrait—Now Ready*, c. 1866, copy in Harold Holzer collection.

42. Mary Lincoln to Francis B. Carpenter, November 15, 1865, *MTL Letters*, 283.

43. Mary Lincoln to Carpenter, November 15, 1865, *MTL Letters*, 283–285.

44. Ibid.

45. The original is in the New-York Historical Society.

46. Mary Lincoln to Francis B. Carpenter, December 25, 1866, and to Henry Deming, December 16, 1867, *MTL Letters*, 404, 463–64.

47. Francis B. Carpenter, *Six Months at the White House with President Lincoln: The Story of a Picture* (New York: Hurd and Houghton, 1867), 301. For a reprint of the original letter, see Mary Lincoln to Carpenter, November 15, 1865, *MTL Letters*, 284.

48. Ostendorf, *The Photographs of Mary Todd Lincoln*, 56–57.

49. Harold Holzer, *Washington and Lincoln Portrayed: National Icons in Popular Prints* (Jefferson, NC: McFarland., 1993), 218–36).

50. *Personal Reminiscences of William H. Mumler in Spirit-Photography. Written by Himself* (Boston: Colby and Rich, 1875), 29–31; Neely and Holzer, *Lincoln Family Album*, xvi–xviii.

## Epilogue
## THE COMPELLING MRS. LINCOLN

*Catherine Clinton*

The many Marys to emerge from this rich and varied collection of essays provide quite a complex cast of characters. I have spent much of the last decade with the turbulent life and times of this woman—born Mary Todd in Kentucky in 1818 and died Mary Lincoln in Springfield, Illinois, in 1882.[1] She has fascinated and frustrated rising generations of historians for well over a century. This particular examination appears within a very specific and specialized context—a volume examining the woman the Abraham Lincoln Presidential Library in 2007 dubbed "First Lady of Controversy."[2] With the escalating allure of all things Lincoln during the 2008 presidential election, followed on by the 2009 bicentennial of the sixteenth president's birth, Mary Lincoln became even more of a historical cause célèbre—and her ability to generate debate seems a renewable energy source.

Perhaps many still yearn for the definitive insight, for the final word, for the shadows and doubts to fade with the bright light of irrefutable evidence. Reconciliation is a difficult trick for scholars, as the academically trained are taught to revise, to remedy—but rarely to reconcile. Further, the group who prefers to denounce Mary Lincoln (as if to enhance her husband's status?) thrives. The distance between these two camps appears to have widened rather than reduced within recent memory, and there seems very little can be done to bridge the gap. At the same time, there will always be gaps—in the literature, between academic fiefdoms, in our understanding of the past. And we must continue our quest to add as much new and fascinating material as possible and to refine sources already uncovered. It remains our mission to explore what has come before, which several of the essays within this collection do beautifully.

Lincoln studies abound with seekers of holy grails, including a handful so eager for the "Aha!" factor that they might even invent one.[3] This is the natural outcome of a century and a half of relentless and robust curiosity. It is the wishful thinking of a Lincoln cottage industry that has spawned roughly sixteen thousand volumes and promises more with each passing year. In a parallel universe, Mary Lincoln continues a neglected vein of premium ore—well worth mining. She is capable of creating a media stir when a trunkful of her lost letters (transcriptions rather than the originals!) were uncovered in an attic.[4] And even more when scholars clash over the significance or interpretation of the contents. Regardless, scholars will continue to exploit the popular interest in Lincoln's wife, as well as the fascination with a separate cult of Mary.

I found investigating Mrs. Lincoln led me into another kind of minefield. Her enigmatic quality has spawned investigations that track not just the integrity of her own experience, but, quite understandably, address anything relating to her relationship with her husband. Mary's role during and after the deification of her assassinated spouse sparks lively debate. No one was more vigilant in preserving Abraham Lincoln's reputation for virtue and greatness than his widow.

Mary Lincoln provokes extreme opinions, alluded to in several of the essays within—most explicitly in the pieces by Douglas L. Wilson on Mary and William Herndon, by Michael Burkhimer on the Lincolns' political partnership, and by Dr. James Brust on "diagnosing" Mrs. Lincoln. But these dozen essays do much more than outline the current status of the scholarship and rehash old debates. Because, as Frank Williams at the outset reminds us, Mary Todd Lincoln enjoys her own dynamic following.

Our collection takes us from the wartime White House to Niagara Falls, from the pastoral setting of a Batavia, Illinois, sanatorium to European capitals, from fleeing the coop in France to confinement in her sister's Springfield home, where she had married her young Mr. Lincoln. The elusive Mrs. Lincoln might not be pinned down, but she does come into sharper focus. Whether her halo is tilted or even if devil horns are scribbled onto her forehead, Mary Lincoln still attracts attention, something she so craved in her own lifetime. She would have detested the vulgarity and invective that taints some contemporary discussions. But what hypercritical modern detractors seem to forget is that campaigns to discredit Mrs. Lincoln undermine shrill insistence that we pay her too much attention.

This volume's scholarly slideshow affords readers a kaleidoscopic appreciation of Mary Lincoln's extraordinary life and times, and of the historical debates her name conjures. The sum of her parts may seem difficult to add up, as history is not an exact science. Therefore, varied and intense points of view make for fluid, colorful portraits, rather than the static black-and-white snapshots to which she has been consigned.

Most twenty-first-century Lincoln scholars move beyond hagiography, even as they come to grips with the cult of Lincoln. How and why Lincoln generates so much interest has been joined by the question, how and why does Mary Lincoln stir up so much debate? Voila, this book takes us back to the very beginning. Stephen Berry's aptly titled opening chapter, "There's Something about Mary," focuses on the Todd siblings, but anyone interested in the period will find his essay engaging. While sketching the most basic outlines of her early life, Berry fleshes out gnawing questions: What elements of her childhood created such a legendary character? How did she survive the death of her mother and endure the competitive marathon unleashed by her gaggle of stepbrothers and stepsisters?

The rattle and snap of Berry's prose allow us to peer through a window onto her world, noses firmly pressed to appreciate the cramped dimensions of Mary Todd's youthful dramas and domesticity. Berry does not just dwell on the cozy hearthside; he confronts some uncomfortable truths, taking us to the auction block and beyond. By telling us a local paper advised against holding more than ten slaves, in case "slavery lost its personal touch," we perceive the flavor of life within this self-styled "Athens of the West." Violins and pistols were sold on the same shelf at the local store and suggests that Lexington's veneer of respectability was "as thin as muslin."[5]

Mary Todd grew up dependent on black servants, worshipping Henry Clay, and she drank deeply from the springs of self-deception that pleasantly burbled near her "old Kentucky home." Mary was raised to be a Southern belle, yet she emerged as the number one symbol of Confederate treachery—a woman who deserted kith and kin, turning her back on her homeland.

The complex dance of regional rivalries emerges with explorations of Mary Todd's early years. In Lexington during the 1830s, the Yankee wife of a Southern judge bursts into the headlines when she throws a young household slave out a second story window. Mary's father is ensnared by the investigation, but the town averts its eyes—and the cruel mistress continues her reign of terror. The contradictions and requisite whitewashing were part and parcel of Mary's education in her earliest years.

Further, Berry delves into what he has christened her "financial bulimia," a topic of dramatic interest and violent disagreement amongst scholars of the Lincoln presidency and Mary Lincoln's later years. But from the roots of her shopping mania, to the delicate imbalance of Todd sibling rivalries, Berry sets the scene for much of the drama to come.

I was grateful to have both Brian Dirck and Richard Lawrence Miller track Mary's development from her Kentucky days until she left Springfield for the White House. Elements of Mary Todd's background are repeatedly retrofitted to blend with whatever new history comes along, as Mike Burkhimer details in his essay, "The Reports of the Lincolns' Political Partnership Have Been Greatly Exaggerated." These debates show scholars not just grasping at straws, but tugging on loose threads that allow such "seamless" theories to unravel. Again, history is not an exact art form, and such surgical excavations show that neat and tidy is not always possible, particularly true on matters involving race.

Within current historiography, Mary might be portrayed as a belle of the Bluegrass—a wee bonnie lass from a slaveholding family (indeed the record is replete with lawsuits involving disputed slave property). She might seamlessly morph into an underground abolitionist who either loved, honored, and obeyed her husband's antislavery views or, conversely, who prodded him into his precocious emancipationist stance. Scholars suggest she was a helpmeet or a hurdle, a faithful partner or a bloody nuisance. It seems impossible to reconcile the feud. And scholars perform intellectual contortions to fit evidence and theories into a neat package, but this appears an impossible task.

Evidence is selectively plucked from the records to bolster competing views. Brian Dirck does a good job of teasing out the major elements of this historiographical puzzle in "Mary Lincoln, Race, and Slavery." As he rightly complains, "Lincoln and slavery" has been an intersection ripe for scholarly exploration—with the Library of Congress listing 175 volumes on this topic. Eric Foner's magisterial *The Fiery Trial: Abraham Lincoln and American Slavery* (2010) tops this long list of impressive volumes. Especially since the 2000 publication of Lerone Bennett Jr.'s *Forced into Glory: Abraham Lincoln's White Dream,* the subject of "Lincoln and race" has generated more confrontational than civil debates. Increasingly scholars seem at an impasse when trying to deconstruct their diametrically opposed interpretations.

Too few contemporary readers grasp so many of the nuances of historical debates over slavery; crucial contextualization goes missing if experts simply give the number of times Abraham Lincoln can be found to have used the word *nigger* as some calculation of his racial politics. It is crucial to disentangle issues relating to slavery as a system of forced labor, from the persons who survived the system. Enslaved persons were labeled as a race and subsequently deemed biologically inferior. Racial differentiation—and its not so silent partner, white supremacy—underpinned American slavery, but it persisted well past slavery's overdue demise.

Solid and imaginative discussions of these topics are riddled with flaws—particularly sins of omission. Too few blacks as well as whites of the nineteenth century left behind any fully articulated records of the known world of racial etiquette and racist violence that permeated nearly all aspects of antebellum society. Dirck points out that there is "no reliable record of any conversations [between Abraham and Mary Lincoln] concerning the peculiar institution" but builds a case that Mary followed her husband's lead, transforming her views to keep pace with Lincoln's gradual evolution.

Mary's personal opinions on race are more challenging to track. I agree that Mrs. Lincoln held views typical for her class, race, and region: asserting repeatedly in her writings that African Americans were a "far inferior" race. Yet as First Lady, she exhibited atypical behavior upon occasion. Her warm regard for Elizabeth Keckly, the African American dressmaker who became a confidante during her White House years, might be interpreted as some measure of rejection of her slaveholding past. Mary turned her back on family members who allied themselves and even died in the service of the Confederate cause.[6] Her devotion to her husband grew exponentially following his tragic death, and Mary Lincoln made a brilliant gesture by presenting Frederick Douglass with one of her husband's canes—aligning the cause of the African American leader to the late martyr president. Mary Lincoln was keen to elevate her husband's status, perhaps even more so following his death.

Lincoln had been murdered by John Wilkes Booth, a twenty-six-year-old actor with Confederate sympathies who had even more of a flair for the dramatic than did the First Lady. Booth was outraged by Lincoln's speech on April 11, 1865, when the president tipped his hand by suggesting that he favored extending voting rights to black men, "I would myself prefer that it were now conferred on the very intelligent, and on those who serve our cause as soldiers."[7] Within three days of this speech, he was shot and died. These last public pronouncements on race demonstrate the arc of Lincoln's intellectual evolution regarding the color line, the distance he had travelled from his own old Kentucky home.

In the wake of her husband's traumatizing death, Mary Lincoln might have been in a sleepwalking state barely able to function, but as she slowly emerged from her paralysis, she reached out to reward those she saw as solidifying her husband's place in history—and sent Frederick Douglass her husband's walking stick and a letter to make the point of Douglass's crucial connection to the sixteenth president. Nearly a century later, Jacqueline Kennedy met with T. H. White in Hyannisport on November 29, 1963, a week after her husband's assassination, to tell him the story of JFK's favorite lyrics from a Broadway musical,

> Don't let it be forgot
> That once there was a spot
> For one brief, shining moment that
> was known as Camelot.

This planted a seed, which blossomed into a cult; the Kennedy presidency remains a fabled era that historians struggle to demystify in the wake of such effective campaigning.

Mrs. Lincoln might not have imagined all the import historians would attach to this simple gesture of writing to Frederick Douglass when donating such a memento.[8] But at the same time, it would underestimate Mary Lincoln to imagine she did not intend to offer proof of her husband's key role in the emancipation of slaves. And it is perhaps a tribute to her savvy and sentimentality that "the Great Emancipator" became a role by which Lincoln is remembered, especially on the global scale, which she perhaps intended.[9]

Mary Lincoln was someone who dreamed big, and it was that quality (and perhaps living beyond her means) that was nurtured during her marital perch. Richard Lawrence Miller's "Life at Eighth and Jackson" offers intriguing perspective on the "chaos" of the Lincoln household, a portrait framed tightly by recent assessments of the couple, for example, Daniel Mark Epstein's 2008 *The Lincolns: Portrait of a Marriage*.

Historical judgment is constrained by peering backward from the vantage point of the gossip and judgment that dogged the Lincoln marriage during their lifetime. We are all affected by the historical scales upon which they have been weighed since. For any biographer, myself included, we cannot pretend we are writing without a very specific context—when we are writing is part of the formula of understanding our subject. I knew that in some ways my own interpretation could not be read without some consideration of the oceans of ink spilled to delineate Lincoln's marital miseries, from William Herndon to Michael Burlingame.

At the same time, interpretations in the manner of an inquest can puzzle even the most sophisticated readers. We know our subject is innocent until proven guilty—but to begin with a trial, presenting evidence and arguing pro and con, irritates most readers. We cannot write in a vacuum, but we also do not need to celebrate contradiction. A seesaw approach can give some readers motion sickness, as we try to cite evidence, cite other scholars, discredit evidence, refute other theories—losing them in the maze of historiographical minutiae. Yet we can get caught up in the richness afforded by a wealth of evidence.

I read with great delight the essays by Wayne C. Temple and Donna McCreary. By looking so intently at travel and fashion, two controversial aspects of Mary's image, the writers present the president's wife as both backlit and highlighted. Seeing her hopping aboard the *Great Eastern* or posed on a wooden walkway at Franconia Range Notch in the White Mountains, we are pulled along in her wake. Some readers may not want to plunge headlong into the sumptuous descriptions of billowing lace and feathered headdresses, to wallow amongst gems of information studding McCreary's portrait. But peeling back, layer by layer, touches the core of female sensibilities within Victorian America, a key illumination of Mary's world. When we are inundated with elements of couture, consumerism,

and status anxiety, Mary Lincoln's woes—real or imagined—come into
sharper perspective. Why did Mrs. Lincoln decide to redecorate the White
House when her husband was forced to declare war and expand the army
to prepare for battle? Why would the First Lady be ordering three hundred pairs of gloves in the wake of her husband's reelection in 1864? (On
this explosive point within the scholarly debates, McCreary and I are
in agreement that there is a reasonable explanation, not just insanity or
conspiracy at work.) Mary justified her own lavish adornment, believing
that the wardrobe of a First Lady reflected "patriotic duty."

Was Mrs. Lincoln just a figure of fun? Consigned to suffer obsessive
organza disorder in advance of her husband's death and a bombazine addiction afterwards? Can we really dismiss her so easily as fashion victim?
How dare she elevate shopping into an art form in the middle of a Civil
War? The view of Mrs. Lincoln too many know and hate, captured with a
Brady studio photograph, deserves a more nuanced context. But how and
why Mary Lincoln became a lightning rod for vitriolic attacks remains
as much of an enigma as the woman herself. (Although, again, many
historians, and even her own sister suggested within the pop vernacular:
"she brought it on herself.")

Mary Lincoln's political role—on her own and within her husband's
life—has undergone a scholarly makeover. Some may dwell on interpretive debates advanced by previous biographers such as Ruth Painter
Randall and Jean Harvey Baker (and their critics), but we can just cata-
pult into the present to reassess Mary Lincoln's neglected roles as public
intellectual and political wife.

How much did Lincoln provide a cocoon for Mary Todd's chrysalis?
Several historians have commented on her autonomous political interests,
especially during the Log Cabin Campaign of 1840 when her relationship
with Lincoln was at a crossroads. I was convinced that Lincoln was ini-
tially smitten by Mary—seeing her as an intellectual equal, a woman with
whom he could discuss his lyceum debates or papers from the Hickory
Club. It was not just the house on Aristocracy Hill or the creamy shoulders

she loved to display at cotillions that drew Lincoln to Mary Todd: What she had upstairs, conveyed within sparkling conversation, bewitched suitors. Whatever the source or dimensions of their falling out in 1841, the coupler kindled their romance within the context of a political imbroglio during the summer of 1842 when they were involved with the Rebecca, or "Lost Township" letters.[10]

It has become fashionable to place Mary at center stage, reprising her role as "political wife." Kenneth J. Winkle places her within the context of Whig womanhood, and readers discover Mary described her own role as hostess (to advance her husband's career) as her *work*. Many scholars may wish to minimize Mrs. Lincoln's contribution to her husband's career, and Michael Burkhimer goes so far as to claim she hindered his political success. Again and again, Mary is placed on the scales and found wanting. Even within Douglas L. Wilson's judicious piece, "William H. Herndon and Mary Todd Lincoln," harsh presumptions sting: Did they "hate" one another? Who was nasty first? And why did exaggerations and denials seem to flow like lava once Abraham was removed from the equation? Herndon and Mary needled one another and both resorted to name-calling, fighting like "cats and dogs." But the lingering image of Mary as a "hellcat," a crazed feline, rises up like some ghostly hologram. I can believe that Herndon felt he was being restrained rather than rough on Mrs. Lincoln. But again and again, from the vantage point of this Mrs. Lincoln biographer, Mary ends up getting roughed up.

I am dubious concerning many of the displays of empathy that have gushed within the past decade. A "poor Mrs. Lincoln" school portrays Mary as someone who was severely handicapped by her illness: withhold scorn, heap on the pity. Thus a new generation of doctors—of medicine and history—rally to the cause: Mary is ready for her rescue.

My skepticism for those who would diagnose the dead remains. My judgment is tempered by the imprecision that current experts encounter as they struggle to treat even the living. Further, how can one be so sure when the dead cannot speak for themselves? Scholars remain advocates and adversaries, and in light of these extremely personal as well as political matters, readers must judge the evidence put forward by authors and experts for him or herself.

My credo when completing *Mrs. Lincoln: A Life* continues—we all put forward our theories and evidence, trying to follow best practices. I can only put forward an educated guess. There certainly is no definitive answer to the perennial query, "Was she crazy?" My refusal to offer a definitive answer at times confounds, especially those who sally forth so assuredly with "right" answers. I found on my 2009 book tour for *Mrs. Lincoln: A Life*, some members of the audience were quick to identify with Mary Lincoln—either as a sufferer of a mental disorder, as a victim of a legal ambush, as a woman mistreated by her family, as a female caught in the tangled web of medical practitioners, as a protofeminist persecuted for being ahead of her time—and the list goes on and on. Just as likely, audience members might identify for me *exactly* what Mary Lincoln's problems were—and how they knew with such conviction her particular disorder.[11]

Jason Emerson, among others, hints that Mrs. Lincoln has been misdiagnosed and repeatedly suggests that Mary Todd suffered from mental illness from early adolescence. It was quite striking to me that after Emerson discovered copies of letters written by Mrs. Lincoln in 1875 (while confined at Bellevue in Batavia, Illinois), he and I came to different conclusions when presented with this new evidence. He casts his eye on Mrs. Lincoln as it relates to her oldest son, Robert, and this may color most of his assessments. Mary cannot fend for herself, and James S. Brust, MD, suggests in his piece, "A Psychiatrist Looks at Mary Lincoln," that Mary was a sufferer of bipolar disorder.[12]

During his assessment, Dr. Brust lays out the major aspects of the historiography on Mrs. Lincoln's "insanity episode." He asks and answers a series of questions involving Mary Lincoln's mental state, closing with clinical overviews of cultural attitudes toward mental illness including a quote from Carrie Fisher—whom he identifies as "Princess Leia in the *Star Wars* movies." Brust warns Mary's biographers may "so fear the stigma that they deny the illness." Scholars will have to agree to disagree, preferably with decorum and civility. Publishers and authors alike may want to proclaim they are serving up the last word, with "hot-off–the-press" evidence. But sadly, this concept is as quaint as such outmoded phrasing.

Mary Lincoln is undoubtedly a very modern figure, easily sculpted into a postmodern icon. It is perhaps a traditional concept to view our historical vocations as seeking answers to unanswerable questions. We pose our queries within complex frameworks, where shifting definitions dictate differing outcomes. Again, our instruments and circumstances are rarely exact. Historians must not pretend our job is a simple matter of extracting truth. We puzzle the how, where, and who, fascinated by the matters of when and why that continue to haunt us. Few figures within nineteenth-century America have been so haunting as the enigmatic Mary Lincoln.

Why Robert Todd Lincoln placed his mother in Bellevue, the Batavia asylum, remains one of most embittering of historical debates, but also a topic that has been at the center of several musical versions of Mrs. Lincoln's life, most recently the 2006 off-Broadway musical, "Asylum: The Strange Case of Mary Lincoln" (with book by June Bingham and score by Carmel Owen).

Yes, Robert might have needed to become his mother's legal conservator, but did he need to break her spirit as well? The humiliation of a public hearing and the sham of her legal representation were devastating. Then Mary Lincoln was confined to a sanatorium *against her will*. Robert's concern for his mother may be unassailable, but the interpretation of his actions remain a subject of controversy. She left for Europe after her 1876 release from legal custody (ostensibly to avoid any further institutionalization). Mother and son lost touch for years—although both could have been in contact with one another. They were reconciled, although the dimensions of this reunion and its results remain unclear. Maybe evidence was preserved in the trunks she carted around.

Following Mary Lincoln's death, Robert's 1882 message to the Lincoln Honor Guard, quoted by Emerson, shows that Robert wanted to protect his mother's body "so that there can be no danger of a spoliation." While her remains might have stayed undisturbed in her coffin, her reputation was picked apart by worms and buzzards.

This result needs to be placed alongside any measure of devotion. It may well be that Robert withheld his mother's will—perhaps not with any venal motives in mind, but just to advance his Victorian sensibilities of the less said the better. Robert inherited his mother's fifty trunks, crammed with mementos and goods of which we can say little, because Mary Harlan Lincoln, Robert's wife, disposed of the contents. So Mary's remnants and letters were too often consigned to the trash heap or the flames. We know for a fact that Robert's wife went to a great deal of trouble to obtain her mother-in-law's letters to Myra Bradwell, and can presume she destroyed the originals.

Is it any wonder that Mrs. Lincoln may be the most famous First Lady in modern political cartooning? She made striking appearances during the 2008 election campaign. And with the outpouring of new novels, and the promise of new screen portraits, Mary Lincoln may even be just hitting her stride in this new century.

Near the end of the twentieth century, I was hoping to contribute my own fictional study of Mary Todd Lincoln. Since the early 1990s, I had been writing for different audiences, and trying my hand at other mediums. Why not a novel? What a capital idea. When I began to research her life and times—I discovered both that the scholarship had not been particularly abundant, especially in proportion to the literature on her husband, and even more disappointing, so much was dismissive and distorted.

I was struck at the outset that even her name was a matter of myth and misunderstanding. Mary Lincoln was known throughout much of the twentieth century by both her maiden and married names, as if Todd and Lincoln were conjoined or hyphenated. Imagine my surprise to discover that no known autograph or signature used this form—that she had always preferred Mary Lincoln or Mrs. Lincoln (unless employing a pseudonym as she often did—a favorite from her White House days: "Mrs. Clarke"). As with another First Lady, Dolley Todd Madison, the "Todd" seems to have been artificially inserted. The Todd family commissioned and donated a portrait of their famous ancestor for display in the White House.[13] And in 1928, a Todd descendant penned *The True Story of Mary, wife of Lincoln*. This Todd campaign shaped her modern image and stimulated the biographer in me to set aside my "novel" idea, and concentrate on how and why Mary Lincoln remains such a compelling figure.

Mary was at the center of Irving Stone's 1954 fictional blockbuster, *Love Is Eternal*, which appeared one year after Ruth Painter Randall's sympathetic biography, *Mary Lincoln: Portrait of a Marriage*. Richard W. Etulain, in his survey of fictional treatments, suggests these two volumes, instead of launching a new era of fascination with Mary Lincoln, ushered in a literary drought. The second half of the twentieth century witnessed Jean Baker's prize-winning and pioneering 1987 reappraisal, *Mary Todd Lincoln: A Biography*, but it wasn't until the first decade of the twenty-first century that Mary reemerged more strongly than ever with a quartet of novels, with new screen portraits set to follow—most notably Sally Field in Steven Spielberg's filming of Tony Kushner's script, based on Doris Kearns Goodwin's *Team of Rivals*.

Harold Holzer's "'I Look Too Stern': Mary Lincoln and Her Image in the Graphic Arts" is a fascinating look at nineteenth-century images and modern imagination. He identifies a Nicholas H. Shepherd daguerreotype (c. 1846) made in Springfield, Illinois, and pinpoints when this image of Mary was rediscovered and its family provenance: Robert Lincoln described it as part of a pair he remembered on the family mantel. Photographed separately yet joined on display: Holzer's analysis shows the value of having his practiced eye trained on this evidence.

He addresses the larger question of why the Lincolns were never photographed together—deriding the old chestnut that their difference in height prevented a simultaneous sitting. He speculates with a cautious yet convincing argument: "Though it is difficult to prove a negative—and inherently dangerous to draw a conclusion about the *absence* of evidence— we may well be justified in imagining that Mary *wanted* her own separate image, her own independent identity, consecrated in early photography." He goes on to add: "And as so often in their marriage, she got what she desired." Mary's desires and images are vibrantly reflected in this survey, as are also Lincoln's keen appreciation of his role as a photographic subject. Between the beard and the stovepipe hat: Abraham Lincoln fired up our historical imaginations. Holzer grapples with fascinating conundrums, the dimensions of this visual medium within historical legacy and, in particular, the image of the Lincoln family as well as Mary.

Mrs. Lincoln's last known image—where the spiritualist photographer reunited the sad former First Lady with her lost husband in a Boston darkroom—was intended for private consumption only. But like many matters Lincoln, things did not always turn out as Mary intended. And this portrait of the couple has become such a strangely popular image—a favorite on display in 2005 at the Metropolitan Museum of Art exhibit of spirit photography entitled *The Perfect Medium: Photography and the Occult*. Mary Lincoln may have imagined she was reunited with her husband, if only for a fleeting fake photograph.

Mary Lincoln continues to fascinate those interested in nineteenth-century America. She remains one of the most complex women ever to inhabit the White House. Again, there are too many Marys to capture them all between two covers, but this collection goes a long way toward advancing our appreciation of the many facets of Mrs. Lincoln's legacy. These authors all contribute to the ways in which her controversial legacy will continue to encourage us to recast and revisit this beguiling figure.

## Notes

The author would like to thank her Queen's University student Jonathan Lande for his assistance with citations. She would also like to acknowledge helpful suggestions from Frank Williams and Michael Burkhimer.

1. Catherine Clinton, "Wife versus Widow: Clashing Perspectives on Mary Lincoln's Legacy," *Journal of the Abraham Lincoln Association* 28, no. 1 (Winter 2007): 1–19. See also *Mrs. Lincoln: A Life* (New York: Harper Collins, 2009).

2. http://www.alplm.org/events/Mary_Todd_Lincoln.html>, accessed November 2009.

3. A notable outsider who tried this was Larry Kramer, who proclaimed the discovery of a "secret diary" located in the vicinity of the Speed "love loft," as he would style the sleeping quarters over a Springfield store, that Lincoln shared with Joshua Speed, among others. Later Kramer confessed that this diary had been his invention. Conversations with Harold Holzer, November 2009.

4. Jason Emerson, "The Madness of Mary Lincoln," *American Heritage Magazine* 57, no. 3 (June/July 2006): 56–65.

5. Berry does not shy away from the particulars of family quarrels—the nursed grudges and imagined grievances—within the feuding offspring of Robert Todd, whetting readers' appetites for the fuller story revealed in his *House of Abraham: Lincoln and the Todds; A Family Divided by War* (2007).

6. Dirck sidesteps the issue of Mrs. Lincoln's embrace of her half sister Emilie, widow of Confederate general Ben Helm, who visited the White House in December 1863, which pertains more to issues of Confederate loyalism than antislavery or racial attitudes.

7. Abraham Lincoln online: April 11, 1865 <http://showcase.netins.net/web/creative /lincoln/speeches/last.htm>, accessed November 2009.

8. Exemplified by James Horton's remarks at a symposium sponsored by the Virginia Sesquicentennial of the American Civil War Commission: "Race, Slavery, and the Civil War: The Tough Stuff of American History and Memory" at Norfolk State University, September 24, 2010. <http://www.virginiacivilwar.org /2010conference.php>, accessed December 30, 2010.

9. See, for example, Harold Holzer, Edna G. Medford, and Frank J. Williams, *The Emancipation Proclamation: Three Views* (Baton Rouge: Louisiana State University Press, 2006).

10. David Herbert Donald, *Lincoln* (New York: Simon and Shuster, 1996), 90–93.

11. From Todd descendants, to lawyers and doctors, audience members have often lectured me during the Q and A following my *Mrs. Lincoln* talks. No other biography or project I have done has elicited such ferocity of opinion.

12. A view reflected in a 2010 episode of the popular television series *Glee*, "The Substitute," when Gwyneth Paltrow portrays a substitute history teacher who dresses up and impersonates Mary Lincoln: "Mary Todd Lincoln in the house," then behaves erratically and proclaims she is bipolar.

13. This portrait was by Katherine Helm, a niece, completed in 1925.

# CONTRIBUTORS
## INDEX

# Contributors

**Stephen Berry.** Associate professor of history at the University of Georgia. Author or editor of four books, including *House of Abraham: Lincoln and the Todds, A Family Divided by War.* Currently writing *Jingle-Man: The Death and Times of Edgar Allan Poe* for Houghton Mifflin Harcourt.

**James S. Brust, MD.** Assistant clinical professor of psychiatry at the David Geffen School of Medicine at UCLA. Chairman of the Department of Psychiatry and medical director of the psychiatric unit at Providence, Little Company of Mary Medical Center in San Pedro, California. Coauthor of *Where Custer Fell: Photographs of the Little Bighorn Battlefield Then and Now* and contributor of an essay titled "The Psychiatric Illness of Mary Lincoln" to *The Madness of Mary Lincoln* by Jason Emerson.

**Michael Burkhimer.** Review editor for the *Lincoln Herald.* American history teacher for Haverford Township School District. Author of two books on Abraham Lincoln: *One Hundred Essential Lincoln Books* and *Lincoln's Christianity.*

**Catherine Clinton.** Chair in American history at Queen's University Belfast. Author of a number of books on nineteenth-century America and women's history, including a biography of Harriet Tubman and the authoritative *Mrs. Lincoln: A Life.*

**Brian Dirck.** Professor of history at Anderson University in Anderson, Indiana. Author of numerous books and articles on Abraham Lincoln and the Civil War era, including *Lincoln and Davis: Imagining America, 1809–1865*; *Lincoln Emancipated: The President and the Politics of Race*; and *Lincoln the Lawyer.* Currently writing a book on Abraham Lincoln and race, forthcoming from the University Press of Kansas.

**Jason Emerson.** Independent historian and freelance writer. Former National Park Service historical interpreter at Lincoln Home National Historic Site and Gettysburg National Military Park. Author of *Giant in the Shadows: The Life of Robert T. Lincoln*; *The Madness of Mary Lincoln*; and *Lincoln the Inventor.* Editor of *The Dark Days of Abraham Lincoln's Widow, As Revealed by Her Own Letters* and the upcoming, *Mary Lincoln's Insanity Case: A Documentary History.*

**Richard W. Etulain.** Professor emeritus of history and former director of the Center for the American West at the University of New Mexico. Author of numerous articles and reviews on Abraham Lincoln. Editor of *Lincoln Looks West: From the Mississippi to the Pacific* and coeditor of the Concise Lincoln Library series for Southern Illinois University Press.

**Harold Holzer.** Chairman of the Abraham Lincoln Bicentennial Foundation. Author, coauthor, or editor of forty-one books on Lincoln and the Civil War era. These include *The Lincoln Image*; *The Confederate Image*; *The Lincoln-Douglas Debates*; *Lincoln as I Knew Him*; *Dear Mr. Lincoln: Letters to the President*; *Mine Eyes Have Seen the Glory: The Civil War in Art*; *The Lincoln Family Album*; *Lincoln on Democracy* (coedited with Mario Cuomo and published in four languages); and *Lincoln at Cooper Union: The Speech That Made Abraham Lincoln President*, which won a second-place Lincoln Prize. Winner of the National Humanities Medal.

**Donna McCreary.** Freelance author, actress, and historian. Recipient of the Outstanding MTL Award, the Glenn Schnizlein Memorial Award, and the Lincoln Legend Award. President and cofounder of Mary Lincoln's Coterie. Author of *Fashionable First Lady: The Victorian Wardrobe of Mary Lincoln*.

**Richard Lawrence Miller.** Independent scholar and author of nine books, including *Truman: The Rise to Power*. Author of multivolume account of Lincoln's life in Illinois entitled *Lincoln and His World*, published by Stackpole Books and McFarland and Company.

**Wayne C. Temple.** Former John Wingate Weeks Professor of History at Lincoln Memorial University. Chief deputy director of the Illinois State Archives. Author of eight volumes on Abraham Lincoln, including *Abraham Lincoln: From Skeptic to Prophet*.

**Frank J. Williams.** Former chief justice of the Rhode Island Supreme Court. Chair and cofounder of The Lincoln Forum and member of the U.S. Lincoln Bicentennial Commission. Author and editor of a number of books on Abraham Lincoln, including *Judging Lincoln* and *Lincoln Lessons*. Currently compiling an exhaustive and annotated bibliography on all books written on Abraham Lincoln, forthcoming from Fordham Press.

**Douglas L. Wilson.** George A. Lawrence Distinguished Service Professor Emeritus at Knox College, codirector of the Lincoln Studies Center. Author or editor of six books on Lincoln, including *Honor's Voice: The Transformation of Abraham Lincoln* and *Lincoln's Sword: The Presidency and the Power of Words*, both of which were awarded the Lincoln Prize.

**Kenneth J. Winkle.** Sorenson Professor of American History at the University of Nebraska–Lincoln. Author of numerous books on nineteenth-century America, including *The Young Eagle: The Rise of Abraham Lincoln*, which won the Abraham Lincoln Institute Book Award, and *Abraham and Mary Lincoln* for the Concise Lincoln Library series, Southern Illinois University Press.

# Index